Candela Isler Müther

Positions on Shell Construction

Candela
Isler
Müther
Positions on Shell Construction

Edited by Matthias Beckh, Juan Ignacio del Cueto Ruiz-Funes,
Matthias Ludwig, Andreas Schätzke and Rainer Schützeichel

Birkhäuser
Basel

Contents

Introduction

In architecture, the heyday of concrete shell construction began in the years after World War II. Already during the first decades of the twentieth century, engineers such as Robert Maillart (1872–1940), Eugène Freyssinet (1879–1962), Franz Dischinger (1887–1953), Ulrich Finsterwalder (1897–1988), Eduardo Torroja (1899–1961), and Giorgio Baroni (1907–1968) had contributed significantly to its development by enhancing knowledge on the efficient usage of reinforced concrete as well as on the structural behavior of thin concrete shells. The full structural and artistic capacity of these structures, however, only unfolded from the late 1940s onward, made possible inter alia by the breakthrough of new methods and developments such as, and certainly not least, prestressed concrete. During the following roughly three decades, technically advanced structures of sensational expressiveness were created worldwide. The design and space-shaping possibilities that shell buildings offered met the demands and the spirit of the time. Not only did a large number of civil engineers and architects contribute to this, but also an array of clients from industry as well as from the public sector, not forgetting publicists, curators, and architecture critics all around the globe.

In this book, three protagonists of shell construction are treated as examples for the respective building production of this time: the architect Félix Candela (1910–1997) and two engineers, Heinz Isler (1926–2009) and Ulrich Müther (1934–2007). Their work unfolded against the background of different political, socioeconomic, and cultural conditions. Nevertheless, they were engaged in a lively professional exchange across the boundaries of political systems, which on the one hand took place via personal networks. On the other hand, organizations such as the International Association for Shell Structures (IASS, now International Association for Shell and Spatial Structures), founded in 1959 by Eduardo Torroja, triggered an international exchange of knowledge. Regardless of their mutual influences and their common field of activity in general, though, the professional work of Candela, Isler, and Müther is also characterized by remarkable differences: while Candela, in Mexico and beyond, became the undisputed master of elegant shells, which he mostly realized as hyperbolic paraboloids (hypars) in public and industrial buildings, Isler, in Switzerland, positioned himself successfully as an entrepreneurial engineer, particularly with his standardized system of industrial shells that was optimized in both planning and construction, although he also gained a significant reputation as an expert for the design of free-form shells. Müther, for his part, in East Germany, was able to achieve a monopoly position under the conditions of the socialist planned economy, both in the design, as well as in the construction and execution, of shell buildings by the company he managed, which for a large part of the time existed as a publicly owned enterprise.

In the past decades, significant historiographical contributions have already been made regarding Félix Candela, Heinz Isler, and Ulrich Müther. Numerous books have been published, essays have been written, and exhibitions have introduced their works to a broader public—sometimes in a critical scientific, sometimes in an affirmative manner. This book is, therefore, not intended to be another (three-part) monograph. Instead, it grew out of current research and is primarily based on archival sources that to a considerable extent were accessed for the very first time. The contributions in this volume, therefore, shed new light on commonly known themes in the works of Candela, Isler, and Müther, and they also bring to the fore overlooked or—up to now—only superficially addressed topics. They analyze buildings and projects of the three protagonists against the background of the developments in architecture and engineering of their time, and they deal with mutual influences, similarities, and differences in their form-finding and design processes as well as in construction and execution. Furthermore, questions of reception are addressed alongside the problem of preservation and an adequate current use of the now historic shell structures.

The book is the result of a collaboration between three scientific institutions: the Facultad de Arquitectura de la Universidad Nacional Autónoma de México (FA-UNAM, Faculty of Architecture at the National Autonomous University of Mexico), the Institute for the History and Theory of Architecture (gta) and the Chair of Structural Design at the Swiss Federal Institute of Technology (ETH) Zurich, and the Hochschule Wismar – University of Applied Sciences, Technology, Business and Design. In particular, it brings together the results of a series of international symposia that we have jointly organized, beginning with the first *Candela Isler Müther International Symposium: Concrete Shells in Mexico, Switzerland and Germany* (CIMIS), which took place in Mexico City in November 2018.

All three universities house archives without which our research would not have been possible: the Archivo de Arquitectos Mexicanos (AAM, Archive of Mexican Architects) at FA-UNAM holds a part of the estate of Félix Candela as well as bequests of important architects with whom he cooperated, such as Enrique de la Mora, Juan Antonio Tonda, and Alberto González Pozo; the posthumous papers of Heinz Isler are kept in the gta Archives at ETH Zurich; the estate of Ulrich Müther is accessible in the Müther Archive at Hochschule Wismar, where it laid the foundation stone for the Baukunstarchiv Mecklenburg-Vorpommern (Architecture Archives of Mecklenburg-Western Pomerania). The bequests of Isler and Müther have both only recently been catalogued and are now open for scientific use. This material contributes decisively to this critical comparative study on the works of Candela, Isler, and Müther. The editors hope that these fresh findings, which are presented here for the first time, will provide new insights and trigger further research.

Matthias Beckh
Juan Ignacio del Cueto Ruiz-Funes
Matthias Ludwig
Andreas Schätzke
Rainer Schützeichel

Three Cultures and Ways of Making Reinforced Concrete Shells

JUAN GERARDO OLIVA SALINAS

The latter period of a century of great transformations and contributions in the art of designing and building reinforced concrete shells is covered, between 1949 and 2009. Félix Candela (Madrid, Spain, 1910–Durham, USA, 1997), Heinz Isler (Zollikon, Switzerland, 1926–Bern, Switzerland, 2009), and Ulrich Müther (Binz, Germany, 1934–Binz, Germany, 2007) are three protagonists of this interesting era.

An enthusiastic research group on the study and development of reinforced concrete shells focuses on the projects and constructions realized by these three outstanding builders. By meeting and exchanging the information and knowledge they have on the subject, they combined their efforts to collect and disseminate the legacy of reinforced concrete shells that these three important characters bequeathed us. The reader should consider that during this period, other important builders also designed and constructed reinforced concrete shells, among whom the following stand out: Pier Luigi Nervi (1891–1979), Ove Arup (1895–1988), Eduardo Torroja (1899–1961), and Nicolas Esquillan (1902–1989). This essay is focused exclusively on how concrete shells by Candela, Isler, and Müther were made and on discussing the form-finding and construction procedures followed by each one of them.

SHELLS AND INFLUENCES LINKING CANDELA, ISLER, AND MÜTHER

Through the design and construction of novel reinforced concrete shells, Félix Candela, Heinz Isler, and Ulrich Müther made important contributions to architecture and engineering. The main works of these three shell pioneers were realized in different countries: Mexico, Switzerland, and East Germany, respectively. However, the three builders made significant works in other countries as well. Candela, in addition to demonstrating his creative capacity as an architect, made important contributions to the engineering, geometry, and structural calculation of shells. He designed many outstanding and unique surfaces with double inverse curvature through the development of his admirable hyperbolic paraboloid surfaces. For their parts, Müther and Isler, in addition to demonstrating the masterful handling of mechanical calculations as civil engineers, made important contributions to the conception, design, and control of the architectural form. The three shell builders applied different procedures to determine the shapes of their structures and to construct them, but with common objectives: they all looked for structures of high efficiency with the

1 Enrique de la Mora and Félix Candela, San José Obrero church, Monterrey, 1959: view of the construction site

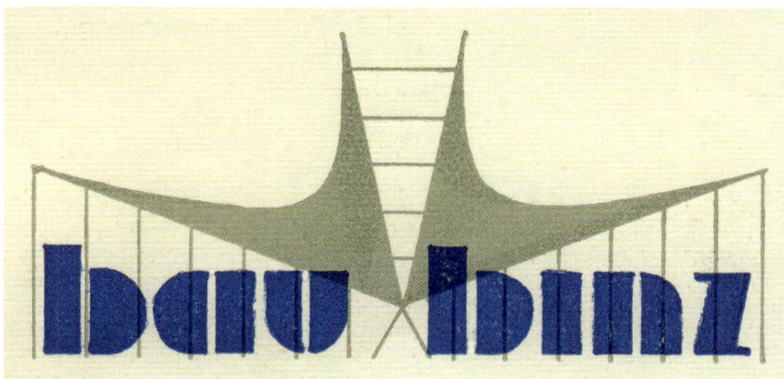

2 Logo of the PGH Bau Binz, the specialist building cooperative run by Ulrich Müther, ca. 1968

lowest environmental impact and where strength is achieved through form.

Candela's reinforced concrete shells were one of the sources of inspiration and motivation for both Isler and Müther to become interested in the design and construction of these unique structures. The cover of a book showing the restaurant Los Manantiales in Xochimilco, Mexico City, which Isler saw in the early 1960s, led to his great interest in thin concrete shells that were only 4 centimeters thick.[1] It was probably the book *Schalenbau* by the theoretical architect Jürgen Joedicke, published in 1962 in Stuttgart, the cover of which shows a color photograph of that restaurant.[2] Regarding the previously mentioned shell, "Isler considers that not only the minimal thickness of this shell but also its unmistakable wave form, with its perfect curves gives the structure its unique thrill."[3]

In 1963 Müther also ended up being influenced by the shells of Candela when he developed his diploma thesis at the Technische Universität Dresden. As part of his work, Müther had originally considered developing a cover for the Haus der Stahlwerker (Steelworkers' Home) in Binz based on barrel vaults. This deck would serve to cover a terrace that would function as a meeting room, as part of the extension to the vacation center of the steel and rolling mill VEB Rohrkombinat Stahl- und Walzwerk Riesa. However, the architect Ingo Schönrock, former fellow student and good friend of Müther, suggested that the roof deserved the design of a shell in the manner of Candela.[4] The above indicates that Candela's shells had already crossed the borders of many countries in the world. Subsequently, Müther designed a roof to cover an area of 200 square meters consisting of four hypars. This work constitutes his first reinforced concrete shell.

One more influence of Candela on Müther was the logo he used for his construction company PGH Bau Binz, which is based on the form of the San José Obrero church built in 1959 by Candela and Enrique de la Mora in Monterrey.[5] Undoubtedly, Müther recognized and admired the fascinating forms of Candela's shells. The silhouette of this shell was also engraved on the tombstone of Müther's grave.

The author of this article had the opportunity to meet and talk with Candela and Isler and to attend presentations by both builders in Europe and in Mexico. With this background, he was able to verify that both characters shared common characteristics of simplicity, humility, and enthusiasm for innovating in the design and structural calculation of shells. Isler also enjoyed a very good sense of humor that characterized him and his wife, Maria. For both, a permanent smile was a typical feature that will always be associated with them. In 2003 Margarete Fuchs produced the documentary film *Für den Schwung sind Sie zuständig* (You are responsible for the Momentum) which she presented a couple of years later at the Faculty of Architecture of the Universidad Nacional Autónoma de México. The life and work of Ulrich Müther is described concisely in this film, in which he is portrayed as a simple, humble, and affable person.

FÉLIX CANDELA'S SHELLS

Félix Candela was not the first to build reinforced concrete shells shaped like a hyperbolic paraboloid (HP), but he knew how to handle and control the shape of these surfaces in a masterly manner. By varying the proportions, adding, duplicating, or sectioning HP surfaces, Candela adapted the shape to the spatial architectural requirements, thus generating structures with maximum mechanical efficiency and with a minimum of material. Beauty was an aspect that Candela emphasized in an impromptu presentation given during the closing ceremony of the international symposium *Weitgespannte Flächentragwerke* (Wide-span Surface Structures) held from May 14 to 18, 1979, at the Universität Stuttgart: "Let me finish by talking of one thing that always strikes me in this kind of meetings. Nobody speaks of beauty, perhaps because it cannot be measured and engineers have a professional deformation to deal only with the so-called facts. Therefore, there are a lot of serious talks about stresses in all

3 Jorge González Reyna and Félix Candela, Cosmic Rays Pavillion, Ciudad Universitaria, Mexico City, 1951

4 Joaquín Álvarez Ordóñez and Félix Candela, Los Manantiales restaurant, Xochimilco, Mexico City, 1958; photograph by Juan Guzmán

directions, concentrations of them and subsequent deformations, but poor beauty is always forgotten. We should remember, however, that a great part of the success of these structures is due to the fact that they are usually very beautiful [...]."[6]

Candela experienced two anecdotal events at the initiation of his interest in thin reinforced concrete shells: first, the rejection he suffered in his approach to Eduardo Torroja; and second, the rejection of the first article he sent for publication to the *Journal of the American Concrete Institute* in 1951. As a student, and when he was in the sixth year of his career as an architect at the Universidad Politécnica de Madrid, Candela visited the construction site of the Frontón Recoletos, a Basque pelota indoor court. There he found Eduardo Torroja and asked him to explain in general terms the mechanical behavior of the large vaults of his roof. His response was unkind, and Candela felt rejected and his feelings were hurt.[7] Subsequently, in 1951 he sent the *Journal of the American Concrete Institute* a manuscript entitled "Considerations Concerning the Design of Reinforced Concrete Structures." It was rejected, indicating that it was inappropriate for publication in the journal: "The principal reason was that it is argumentative and reveals no new data on which the reader might base or review his opinions of design methods."[8] Nevertheless, that same year Candela sent a new article to the same journal that was accepted and published.

Candela knew how to understand the socioeconomic context of Mexican society in the 1950s. Labor was extremely cheap, and this context allowed him to carry out constructive procedures that required many workers, whose low salaries did not impact on the final cost of the work previously agreed with the client. With an army of workers, he assembled the impressive wooden formwork, which ultimately turned out to be sculptural works that would be destroyed once the thin reinforced concrete membrane had been cast. The cost of wood was not excessive at the time, but certainly the amount of wood required had a negative impact on the care of natural resources that Candela and his two colleagues Müther and Isler sought to achieve with the execution of their shells.

The workers paraded in long lines, transporting the concrete mixture to pour it over the wooden formwork and the reinforcing steel, which typically consisted of 3/8-inch (10-millimeter) steel bars spaced at 20 centimeters on center. Most of Candela's shells were only 4 centimeters thick. At the top half of the shells for the Cosmic Rays Pavilion designed by the architect Jorge González Reyna in the Ciudad Universitaria in Mexico City in 1951, Candela successfully achieved a minimum thickness of 1.5 centimeters.

The geometric and mechanical calculations of Candela started from the simple equation for a hyperbolic paraboloid surface in relation to a Cartesian coordinate system with three dimensions: $z = kxy$. As an architecture student, the author of this article recalls comments from professors working with Candela who affirmed the disbelief of many structural engineers in the face of the simplicity of Candela's equations. Furthermore, during his studies at the Universität Stuttgart in the late 1970s, the author was a student of Jürgen Joedicke. In his class on architecture theory, Joedicke described Candela's shell for the Los Manantiales restaurant, highlighting its perfect integration into the amazing urban landscape in Xochimilco, right next to one of the beautiful canals that make up the rainforest network of this unique and fascinating place. Years later, during a conference in Mexico City, Candela explained to the audience in a very colloquial way that in his Xochimilco shell, he had had the challenge to build a new cover as quickly and cheaply as possible to replace the former one, which had burned down. The owner of the restaurant was an acquaintance of his. Candela's beautiful combination of eight HP surfaces was the right solution in this particular case. His modesty was frequently manifested in his person and manner of behavior. This Candela project is one of the most beautiful examples of his shells, and its shape was repeated, built with fiberglass-reinforced concrete in West Germany by Jörg Schlaich and with reinforced concrete by Ulrich Müther in East Germany. This form would also be repeated in South America, in other countries of the world, and in the Ciutat de les Arts i les Ciències (City of Arts and Sciences) in Valencia by Candela himself shortly before his death.

Félix Candela did not have the support of a university as a framework to carry out experimental tests of his shells. However, in 1949 he built an experimental shell with a catenary directrix. Candela would go on to realize more than 1,400 projects over the next two decades and build about 900 shells. However, when he built the large metal roof of the Palacio de los Deportes (Sports Palace) for the 1968 Olympic Games in Mexico City, a scale model was constructed to analyze the mechanical behavior of the shell. This amazing roof is the last shell built by Candela in Mexico, in collaboration with Antonio Peyrí Maciá and Enrique Castañeda. The shell for the Palacio de los Deportes is the only one built with metal instead of reinforced concrete.

HEINZ ISLER'S SHELLS

Heinz Isler designed shells with shapes that were determined through physical models, unlike Candela and Müther, whose shells adhered to precise mathematical formulas. Isler claimed that the mechanical calculations necessary to determine the forces and the forces acting on their shells were relatively simple and feasible to be done with simple manual calculations. In the 1970s a

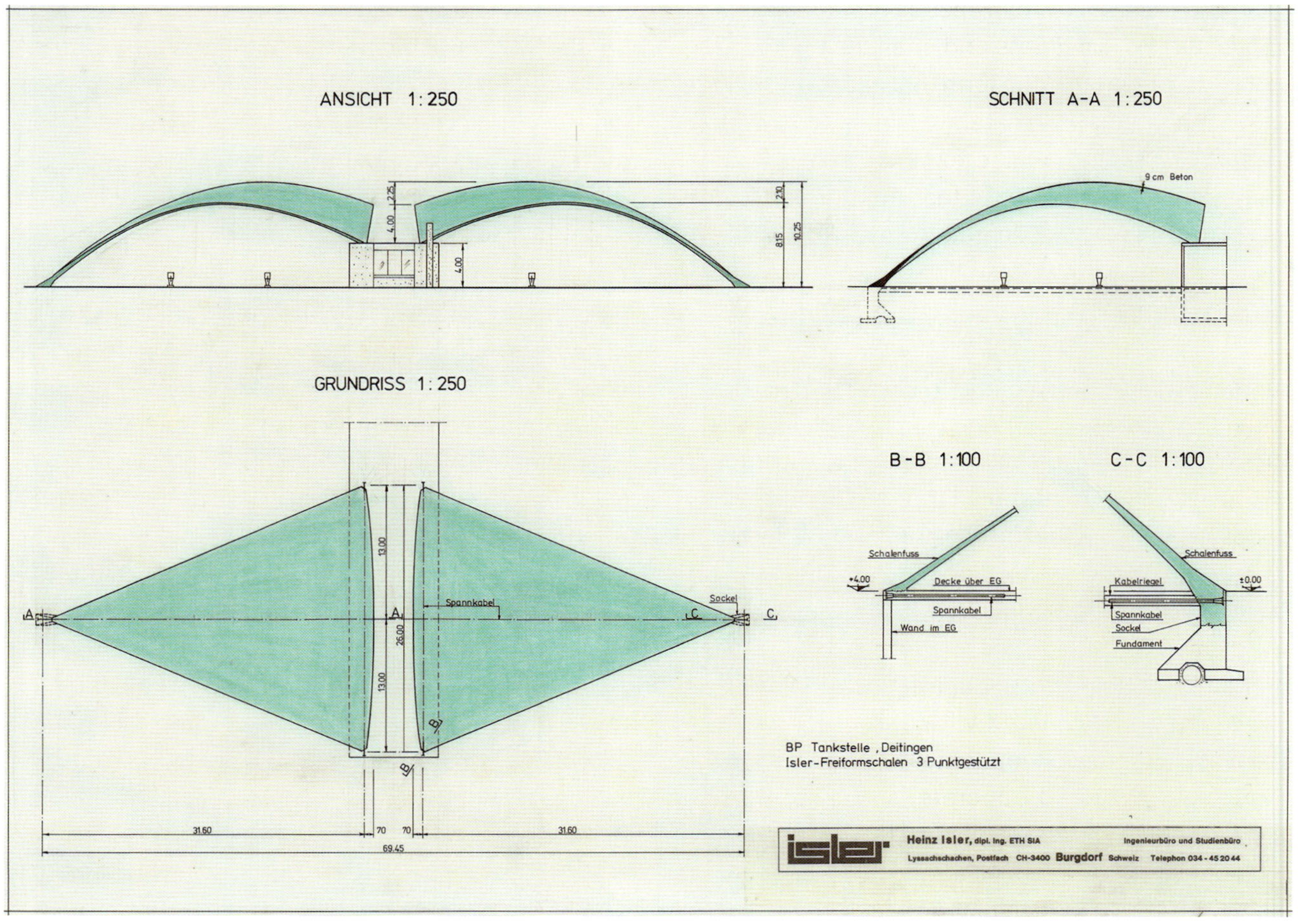

5 Heinz Isler, motorway station Deitingen Süd, 1968, undated colored plan

boom in the use of computers began; however, Isler dispensed with them since he did not consider them necessary. "Isler considers that even the best computer calculation is no better than his formula by hand."[9]

In addition to defining the shape, Isler's physical models were also used to examine the mechanical behavior of his shells. Despite applying different design methods, Candela, Müther, and Isler sought to generate shells to resist the loads to which they would be subjected with a minimum of material, but with a maximum of mechanical efficiency, generating a minimum of stresses and deformations—what we now call sustainability, a term not used at that time.

Isler generated the surface of his thin shells, ensuring that the loads produced by their own weight were transmitted exclusively by compression. Analogous to the form-finding methods applied by Antoni Gaudí (1852–1926) and Frei Otto (1925–2015), Isler started from the principle of the hanging model that works exclusively in tension because of its own weight and which, once inverted, works exclusively in compression. The design of Isler's first bubble shells was inspired by the shape of the pillow on his bed. To determine the geometry, he built physical models in which he inflated a rubber membrane attached to a rectangular wooden edge. Isler rounded the shape of the four corners to avoid generating undesirable negative curvature. Now the entire surface was positively curved and worked exclusively in tension; therefore, the said geometry was suitable for a concrete shell working only under compression. The original models used by Isler to determine the shape of his bubble shells remained preserved for many years in the basement of his office.[10]

Isler carried out tests to measure the distribution of stresses in his models, and after many tests and geometric and mechanical reflections he came to verify that 90 percent of the weight of the roof arrived directly at the four corners of the bubble shells. Based on the foregoing, Isler concluded that he could build stable and safe shells by ensuring adequate support at the corners and using slender edge beams. With these experiments Isler opened great possibilities for architects and structural engineers to design shells with a great freedom in their facades, free of any unnecessary support elements. "Isler has never been formally trained as an architect, yet he has an eye for beauty and elegant form, which stems from his appreciation of nature and love of painting and sketching."[11]

Isler also experimented with free-form shells based on shapes determined by hanging membranes. He hung a membrane at points of support that simulated the position of the supports that the structure would have and allowed that membrane to deform naturally due to its own weight. In a public demonstration of this principle, in Stuttgart, in 1994, Isler hung a four-point membrane located in the same plane and carefully dipped it in a vessel containing polyester resin. The weight of the resin as well as that of the membrane itself created a shape that again opened new possibilities of application to architects and shell designers. Other variants to determine the form that Isler experimented with were membranes saturated with resin that hung from a fixed point located toward the center of the membrane or membranes that hung in the garden during the winter and generated colorful and attractive natural shapes when frozen.[12]

ULRICH MÜTHER'S SHELLS

Ulrich Müther's shells were not recognized for many years. In 2000 the Ahornblatt (Maple Leaf) restaurant, one of his most significant shells, located in Berlin, was destroyed. Despite what happened, the destruction of these shells led to Müther's work being recognized both in Germany and worldwide.

Most of Ulrich Müther's and several of Heinz Isler's shells were constructed with a concrete spraying process. Sometimes they combined this process with conventional tipped concrete, similar to the construction procedures applied by Candela. However, in the project that Müther developed in his diploma thesis to cover a terrace of the Haus der Stahlwerker, which became his first hypar shell, the constructive procedures applied were analogous to those used by Candela. The roof measures 14.20 × 14.20 meters and is 7 centimeters thick. It was built in 1964 and demolished in 2001.[13] To perform the mechanical calculations and so that they could be supervised as part of his thesis, Müther had to resort to the new Department of Theory and Construction of Surface Structures directed by Professor Reinhold Rabich at the Technische Universität Dresden. Rabich was a renowned theoretician who had already worked as an assistant to the engineer Franz Dischinger (1887–1953), who was also a renowned German shell builder. Once Müther finished the mechanical calculations, Rabich performed mechanical tests on a physical model at the Technische Universität Dresden, necessary to ensure the stability of the shell. Müther would devote another 30 years to the construction of shells after his first hypar in 1964.

Other significant works by Müther are the Seerose café in Potsdam (1980–1983, in collaboration with the architect Dieter Ahting) and the Teepott restaurant in Rostock-Warnemünde (1967/1968, in collaboration with the architects Erich Kaufmann, Carl-Heinz Pastor and Hans Fleischhauer), the forms of which were inspired by Candela's shells for Los Manantiales (1958, in collaboration with the architect Joaquín Álvarez Ordóñez) and the La Jacaranda nightclub in Acapulco (1956/1957, in collaboration with the architect Juan Sordo Madaleno), respectively.[14] In 1984 the Teepott was declared a protected monument. It remained empty for a long time and in 2002 it was restored and significantly modified. Müther presented the Teepott in 1969 in Madrid during the annual symposium of the International Association for Shell Structures.[15]

6 Dieter Ahting and Ulrich Müther, Seerose café, Potsdam, 1983

7 Erich Kaufmann, Carl-Heinz Pastor, Hans Fleischhauer, and Ulrich Müther, Teepott restaurant, Rostock-Warnemünde, 1968

8 Juan Sordo Madaleno and Félix Candela, La Jacaranda nightclub, Acapulco, 1957

CONCLUSION

The vast majority of Félix Candela's and Ulrich Müther's shells were designed in collaboration with other architects who conceived the shells that these two builders would help to develop successfully. The only shell design that is attributed solely to Candela is the La Medalla Milagrosa church, built in 1954/1955 in Mexico City. Heinz Isler also built several shells in collaboration with other architects or construction companies. Candela's shells were on average 4 centimeters thick; Isler's shells, 8 to 10 centimeters; and Müther's shells, 7 centimeters. Laborers hand-pouring the concrete on the formwork of the shell was the procedure commonly used by Candela, while Isler and Müther used to apply the concrete mainly by pouring or through sprayed concrete procedures. Candela and Müther built mainly with masterly combinations of hyperbolic paraboloid surfaces, while Isler, although he occasionally utilized hypar surfaces, conceived and designed many of his shells with surfaces of positive curvature.

The differences in the design and construction among the three great builders of reinforced concrete shells previously described are not the whole story: there are exceptions that the reader should take into consideration. Despite these aforementioned differences, through the realization of their reinforced concrete shells, Félix Candela, Heinz Isler, and Ulrich Müther sought the conception, design, and construction of sustainable lightweight structures: high efficiency with the lowest environmental impact, care of natural resources, minimum quantity of building materials, strength achieved through the form, and low stresses that lead to low maintenance and long life.

References

2. Internationales Symposium. Weitgespannte Flächentragwerke. 14. bis 18. Mai 1979, Stuttgart, vol. 2, *Berichtsheft/Proceedings.* Stuttgart, 1979.

Cassinello, Pepa, ed. *Félix Candela: Centenario 2010, La conquista de la esbeltez / Centenary 2010, The Achievement of Slenderness.* Madrid, 2010.

Chilton, John. *Heinz Isler: The Engineer's Contribution to Contemporary Architecture.* London, 2000.

Del Cueto Ruiz-Funes, Juan Ignacio, ed. *Aquella primavera creadora ... cascarones de concreto armado en México / That Creative Spring ... Reinforced Concrete Shells in Mexico.* Mexico City, 2008.

Del Cueto Ruiz-Funes, Juan Ignacio, and Monique Lambie, eds. *Félix Candela, 1910–2010.* Madrid, 2010.

Faber, Colin. *Candela: The Shell Builder.* New York, 1963.

Fuchs, Margarete. *Für den Schwung sind Sie zuständig.* Documentary film, Germany, 2003.

Isler, Heinz. "Aplicaciones recientes de cascarones representativos," *Revista IMCYC* 5, no. 30 (1968): 41–68.

Joedicke, Jürgen. *Schalenbau: Konstruktion und Gestaltung,* with contributions by Walter Bauersfeld and Herbert Kupfer. Stuttgart, 1962.

Ludwig, Matthias, Johannes Liess, Asko Fromm, Andreas Schätzke, and Antje Diebermann. *Der Teepott in Rostock-Warnemünde,* edited by the Bundesingenieurkammer. Historische Wahrzeichen der Ingenieurbaukunst in Deutschland 23. Berlin, 2018.

Moreyra Garlock, Maria E., and David P. Billington. *Félix Candela: Engineer, Builder, Structural Artist.* New Haven/London, 2008.

Oliva Salinas, Juan Gerardo. "Ulrich Müther (1934–2007): El maestro constructor de la provincia de Rügen," *Anales del Instituto de Investigaciones Estéticas* 29, no. 90 (2007): 273–84.

Seeböck, Tanja. *Schwünge in Beton: Die Schalenbauten von Ulrich Müther.* Schwerin, 2016.

The author wishes to thank his colleagues Maria Garlock, David Billington, Pepa Cassinello, José Antonio Torroja, Tanja Seeböck, Matthias Ludwig, and John Chilton, who kindly presented him with five excellent books that compile the life and work of Félix Candela, Ulrich Müther, and Heinz Isler and whose content made it possible to compile the information contained in this essay. This study is partially sponsored by the General Issues Department for Academic Personnel DGAPA-UNAM, Program PAPIIT IG 400517.

1 See John Chilton, *Heinz Isler: The Engineer's Contribution to Contemporary Architecture* (London, 2000), 20.

2 Jürgen Joedicke, *Schalenbau: Konstruktion und Gestaltung,* with contributions by Walter Bauersfeld and Herbert Kupfer (Stuttgart, 1962). English edition: *Shell Architecture* (New York, 1963).

3 See Chilton, *Heinz Isler,* 20 (see note 1).

4 See Tanja Seeböck, *Schwünge in Beton: Die Schalenbauten von Ulrich Müther* (Schwerin, 2016), 77–78.

5 See Matthias Ludwig, Johannes Liess, Asko Fromm, Andreas Schätzke, and Antje Diebermann, *Der Teepott in Rostock-Warnemünde,* ed. Bundesingenieurkammer (Berlin, 2018), 42–43.

6 Félix Candela, "Remarks on the Stage of Development," in *2. Internationales Symposium. Weitgespannte Flächentragwerke, 14. bis 18. Mai 1979, Stuttgart,* vol. 2, *Berichtsheft / Proceedings* (Stuttgart, 1979), 14.

7 See Maria E. Moreyra Garlock and David P. Billington, *Félix Candela: Engineer, Builder, Structural Artist* (New Haven/London, 2008), 56.

8 Letter from Willam A. Maples, American Concrete Institute, to Félix Candela, April 13, 1951, in ibid., 70.

9 Chilton, *Heinz Isler,* 23 (see note 1).

10 See ibid., 33. The models are still preserved in the gta Archives at ETH Zurich.

11 Ibid., 156.

12 See ibid., 36–38.

13 See Seeböck, *Schwünge in Beton,* 312 (see note 4).

14 See Ludwig, Liess, Fromm, Schätzke, and Diebermann, *Der Teepott,* 13–14 and 48 (see note 5).

15 See ibid., 10.

Relations between Félix Candela, Heinz Isler, and Ulrich Müther

MATTHIAS LUDWIG

In January 2001 I was appointed as a professor for design at the Hochschule Wismar – University of Applied Sciences, Technology, Business and Design in the course of architectural studies. At that time, as a southern German, I did not know much about this region on the Baltic Sea except that there are beautiful beaches, numerous large brick churches enthroned above medieval Hanseatic cities, and that Caspar David Friedrich captured the wonderful atmosphere of the local landscape in his paintings. But there was something else that I remembered: in Mecklenburg–Western Pomerania there are shell structures made of thin reinforced concrete, which were planned and built by the East German civil engineer Ulrich Müther.

At the time of the Cold War, the public in West Germany knew hardly anything about these structures; only a few interested architects and engineers were aware of them. As a scientific staff member at the Institute for Building Construction, Chair 1, at Universität Stuttgart, I came across a volume of the Arcus: Architektur und Wissenschaft series on the work of Félix Candela.[1] Herrmann Rühle reports in it about the shell constructions of Ulrich Müther. A few years later, after the political change in Germany, this interest was stimulated again by Wilfried Dechau, who was editor-in-chief of *db: Deutsche Bauzeitung* at that time. Dechau was one of the first journalists to rediscover Müther and make him accessible to a wider public in the West German regions.[2] Especially his book *Kühne Solitäre*[3] and an exhibition catalogue on Heinz Isler's shell structures[4] inspired me to deal with the subject. Like Müther, Heinz Isler was at that time completely outside the focus of architecture enthusiasts, because the time of the great shell builders such as Eduardo Torroja or Félix Candela was long gone.[5]

In East Germany, Ulrich Müther's buildings eked out a miserable existence after the fall of the Berlin Wall and the insolvency of his construction company, with most buildings standing empty and quickly falling into disrepair. One did not see any engineering or architectural masterpieces in these structures, but only built gloomy memories of a Socialist Germany that nobody wanted to have anymore. The low point of this development can perhaps be seen in the demolition of the Ahornblatt restaurant in Berlin in 2000. It was precisely at this time that Müther founded his private company archive in the former KdF seaside resort of Prora.[6] In 2006 this situation took on a new dynamic: one of our students was working as a trainee in the planning office Müther Ingenieure in Binz at the time and arranged for the Müther archive to be transferred to the Hochschule Wismar. Ulrich Müther found that his office estate was in good

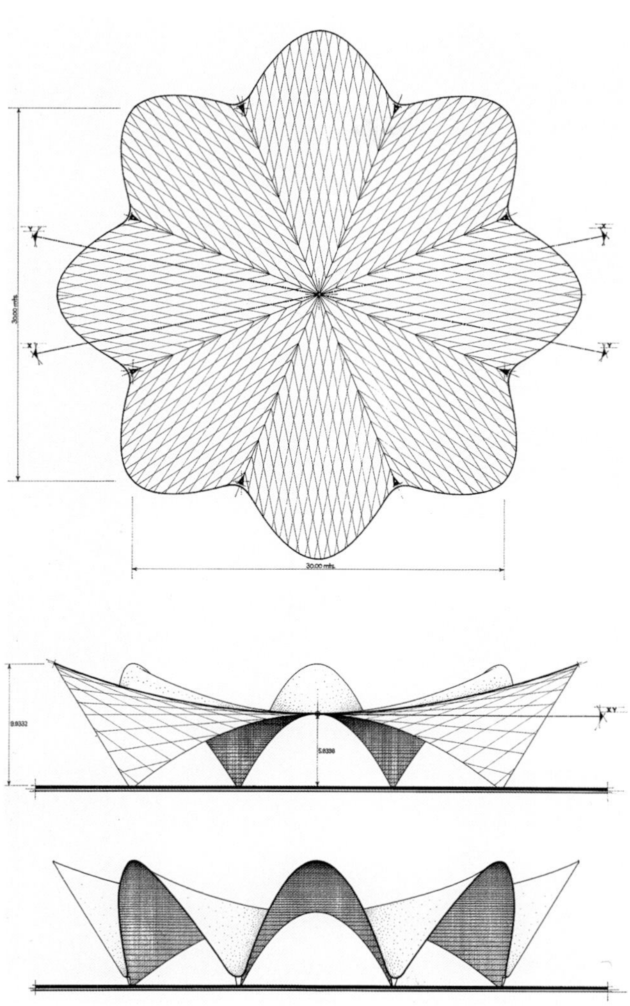

1 Joaquín Álvarez Ordóñez and Félix Candela, Los Manantiales restaurant, Xochimilco, Mexico City, 1958; from Colin Faber's book *Candela: The Shell Builder*, 1963

hands at the only architectural school in Mecklenburg–Western Pomerania. He died soon afterward in 2007. In the meantime, there have been quite a few searches in the archive for information on Müther's shell constructions. Publications about Ulrich Müther are accumulating, and buildings of the so-called Ostmoderne (Eastern modernism) are again in vogue.

FÉLIX CANDELA: HYPERBOLIC PARABOLOID SHELLS

Félix Candela (1910–1997)
Location: Spain, Mexico, USA | Architect (company: Cubiertas Ala S.A.) | ***Education:*** Escuela Técnica Superior de Arquitectura de Madrid, Real Academia de Bellas Artes de San Fernando | ***Shell type:*** hyperbolic paraboloid (barrel vault, spherical shell), some folded plate and conoid shells | ***Formwork:*** timber | ***Number of shells built:*** approximately 900, in Mexico, Guatemala, Venezuela, Colombia, and Cuba

For his first shell constructions Ulrich Müther strongly referred to the Spanish-Mexican shell builder Félix Candela, although he probably never met him personally, even though both had attended conferences of the International Association for Shell and Spatial Structures (IASS). However, we know from interviews with contemporary witnesses that Müther had a book about Félix Candela on his bookshelf—in the GDR it was not easily available in bookstores.[7] In addition, his architect colleague Ingo Schönrock had enthusiastically reported to Müther a lecture given by Candela in July 1961 to a Bund Deutscher Architekten (Association of German Architects) group in the GDR and had published an essay on Candela's umbrella shells in the journal *Deutsche Architektur* in 1962.[8] Inspired by Candela's architecture, Müther realized his first hyperbolic paraboloid, the Haus der Stahlwerker (Steelworkers' Home) in Binz on Rügen island (1963/1964), while still a student at the Technische Universität Dresden (see the contribution by Andreas Schätzke in the present volume, fig. 8). The model for this was the Herdez warehouse roof in Mexico City (1957).

As a civil engineer, Müther was, against the background of his parents' construction company, very fond of the geometry of the hyperbolic paraboloid, since the formwork can be constructed comparatively easily by simple manual methods using straight shuttering boards. In addition, these thin concrete shells were a good answer to the GDR's economy of scarcity, because they saved on expensive cement and there was enough cheap labor, a situation very similar to that of Mexico. At a later date, Müther even visually documented his veneration of the Mexican master builder: the company logo of PGH Bau Binz (later VEB Spezialbetonbau Binz/Spezialbetonbau Rügen), used from the late 1960s onward, depicts the San José Obrero church in Monterrey (1959) and not, as one might assume, a ship's anchor or even an *M* for Müther.

ULRICH MÜTHER: HYPERBOLIC PARABOLOID AND FREE-FORM SHELLS

Ulrich Müther (1934–2007)
Location: Binz, GDR (until 1990)/Germany (since 1990) Civil engineer and builder (company: PGH Bau Binz/VEB Spezialbetonbau Binz/VEB Spezialbetonbau Rügen/Müther Spezialbetonbau GmbH) | ***Education:*** Fachschule für Bauwesen Neustrelitz, Technische Universität Dresden | ***Shell type:*** hyperbolic paraboloid and free-form | ***Formwork:*** timber, shaped hill, without | ***Number of shells built:*** 75 (including monuments, folded plates, cable net structures, and projects where he only did the concrete work), in Germany, Finland, Libya, Kuwait, and Cuba[9]

The connections between Müther and Candela are most obvious in two projects: the Los Manantiales restaurant in Xochimilco, Mexico City (1958), and the

2 Dieter Ahting and Ulrich Müther, Seerose café, Potsdam, 1983

riverside pavilion Seerose (Water Lily) in Potsdam (1982/1983), both consisting of eight hyperbolic paraboloid segments, so their formal similarity cannot be overlooked. Los Manantiales is 32.40 meters in diameter and 5.84 meters in height, with a shell thickness of 4 centimeters. The Seerose is much smaller: 23 meters in diameter, with a shell thickness of 6 centimeters. Of course, Müther's riverside pavilion is a reworking of Candela's design. Müther also made nearby water surfaces his own, as a reflecting pool typical of the modern age, and his Seerose also became, like Los Manantiales, a popular restaurant for city dwellers.

Other architects have also recognized the attractiveness of Candela's building: Jörg Schlaich experimented with this form at the Bundesgartenschau (Federal Garden Show) in Stuttgart in 1977. Candela's building, designed in collaboration with the architect Joaquín Álvarez Ordóñez, was one of the most published buildings at the time of its construction. Of course, despite the formal similarity of these buildings, there are many differences in the construction and manufacturing processes.

After all, almost 25 years lie between Los Manantiales and the Seerose. The form and geometry of Candela's building is undoubtedly more elegant than that of Müther's. And of course, the mild climate of Mexico City's plateau allows for more beautiful details on the shell and facade. But the Müther building, which was built in collaboration with the architect Dieter Ahting, has adopted the technological advances of its time: with just a few specialists, Müther was able to project the concrete onto the formwork using the so-called Torkret (shotcrete) method, while Candela had to do this laboriously with small buckets and a hundred workers.

HEINZ ISLER: FREE-FORM SHELLS

Heinz Isler (1926–2009)
Location: Burgdorf, Switzerland | Civil engineer and painter | ***Education:*** Eidgenössische Technische Hochschule (ETH) Zurich | ***Shell type:*** Free-form, partially hyperbolic paraboloid | ***Formwork:*** timber, inflated, shaped hills, without | ***Number of shells built:*** approximately 1,400, including projects in Switzerland, Germany, France, Austria, Saudi Arabia, and the United Kingdom

At the founding congress of the IASS in Madrid in 1959, the young Heinz Isler gave a groundbreaking lecture on the diversity of shell shapes.[10] He reported to the experts, among them Eduardo Torroja and Ove Arup, that mathematically or geometrically defined shells—

3 Dietrich Otto and Ulrich Müther, observation tower of the water rescue service, Binz, 1981

such as those designed by Félix Candela and also later by Ulrich Müther with their hyperbolic paraboloids—were neither statically favorable nor aesthetically satisfactory. Heinz Isler learned in just a few years (from 1953 to 1959), through observations of nature, how physical laws determine the natural form. During this time, he developed all the essential form-finding methods for so-called free-form shells: the membrane under pressure, for bubble shells; and the hanging cloth and so-called flow form, which was derived from the principles of the freely shaped hill.

His colleagues were skeptical at first, but Heinz Isler had a very intensive phase of building from 1960 to 1969. Hundreds of bubble shells—and parallel to them, edge-beamless free-form concrete shells—were built. The success of this serial production would prove him right. Later, in the 1970s, he also created a few prototypes, spherical houses, and, in collaboration with artists, sculptures and monuments. For the smaller shells, Isler tried out materials such as glass fiber reinforced plastics (GRP), and for modeling or for experimental temporary forms, plaster and ice in addition to concrete.

Ulrich Müther and Heinz Isler first met in 1966 at a building exhibition in Budapest.[11] The connection between the two shell makers lasted for quite a long time: they later met in Burgdorf at Isler's office and in Binz to hold technical discussions, but they also got along very well privately. This can be seen from the fact that Heinz Isler was among the guests at the opening of the company archives in Prora on June 24, 2000, while Jörg Schlaich, among others, gave a lecture.

A closer look at the two lifeguard rescue towers in Binz from 1975 and 1981 suggests that Ulrich Müther was inspired by Isler's "freely formed hill" principle. This becomes clear when examining the manufacturing process of the two towers. The concrete negative mold of the two geometrically exactly identical halves of the shell was molded on a sand mound. The production of this free-form with a wooden formwork would have been very costly, especially at the strongly curved corners, where one would not have been able to cope with a straight plank formwork as used for hypar shells.

When the two beach towers were built in Binz, the young architect Dietrich Otto was working in Müther's company and took on the role of architect or form-finder for some rather futuristic-looking projects. Space design was in the air in the 1960s and 1970s; many designs, such as Buckminster Fuller's Dymaxion House (the prototype for which he had already designed in 1927) or Matti Suuronen's Futuro House (1968), were more reminiscent of cars or airplanes than of down-to-earth architecture. Stanley Kubrick's film *2001: A Space Odyssey* (1968) was a style-influencing work. Perhaps Otto had also seen Angelo Mangiarotti's Cnosso lamp

4 Kurt Tauscher and Ulrich Müther, swimming pool in the Baabe leisure spa, Sellin, 1977: formwork for the roof

5 Harry Neumann and Ulrich Müther, sports hall, Gingst, 1985

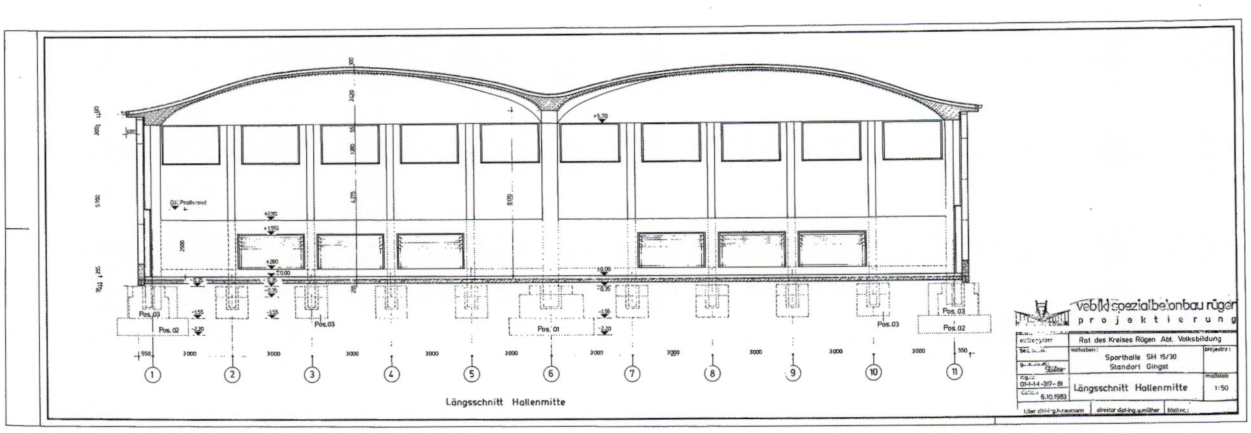

6 Harry Neumann and Ulrich Müther, sports hall, Gingst: longitudinal section; drawing by VEB Spezialbetonbau Rügen, 1983

manufactured by Artemide, which was produced from 1968 onward. If you put two of these lights together into a compact volume, you get a model of the beach towers, so to speak.

A few years earlier, in 1973, Dietrich Otto had designed a bus shelter in Buschvitz on the island of Rügen. This free-form shell, created as an MMM project, is very reminiscent of the so-called Kugelhäuser (spherical buildings) by Heinz Isler.[12] In the bequest of Heinz Isler in the gta Archives at ETH Zurich there are drawings of a similar bus shelter from 1977, a preliminary product of the concrete spherical shelters that was never realized.

Müther's bus-shelter project was produced with a so-called formless process. A kind of wire basket made of reinforcing steel was formed in the workshop of Spezialbetonbau Binz and covered with fine-mesh wire mesh. The concrete was then applied on site, using the Torkret shotcrete method, and finally smoothed by hand. Both Müther and Isler used porthole-shaped windows on the spherical houses. Isler further developed this type several times in 1977. For example, balloon houses built in Iran were designed with the architect Justus Dahinden. The special feature of these is the use of an inflated balloon as formwork. Three layers were applied to the balloon: first plaster with wire mesh inlay, then polyurethane (PU) foam, and finally concrete on the outside. The PU-foam was to provide thermal insulation for the building.

In this context, a building with spherical geometry by Félix Candela is also worth mentioning: La Jacaranda cabaret in Juárez, Mexico City, built in 1954 in collaboration with the architect Max Borges, Jr. This spherical segment shell with a diameter of 22.50 meters is one of the few that does not use the hypar geometry that distinguishes almost all of Candela's work. The spherical shape desired by the architect is at the expense of a formwork that is easy to make, as all the boards have to be bent into shape.

Ulrich Müther once said of himself that he did not like to experiment, but rather wanted to build solidly calculable projects, as he usually had the responsibility for the whole project in almost turnkey construction. An exception is the swimming pool roofing in the Erholungsheim (leisure spa) Baabe in Sellin (1977). Müther and his employees experimented with a rubber membrane clamped in a frame. This was loaded with small tile pieces and thus brought into a hanging form. As a process of finding the shape, this is not dissimilar to Isler's membrane under pressure or hanging fabric, in principle a combination of both: Isler's membrane under pressure was pressed upward in a frame with air pressure, while the hanging fabric is suspended, attached at three or four points.

Müther's shell shape for the swimming pool roof was thus developed by a membrane clamped in a frame and hanging downward. In order to be able to drain rainwa-

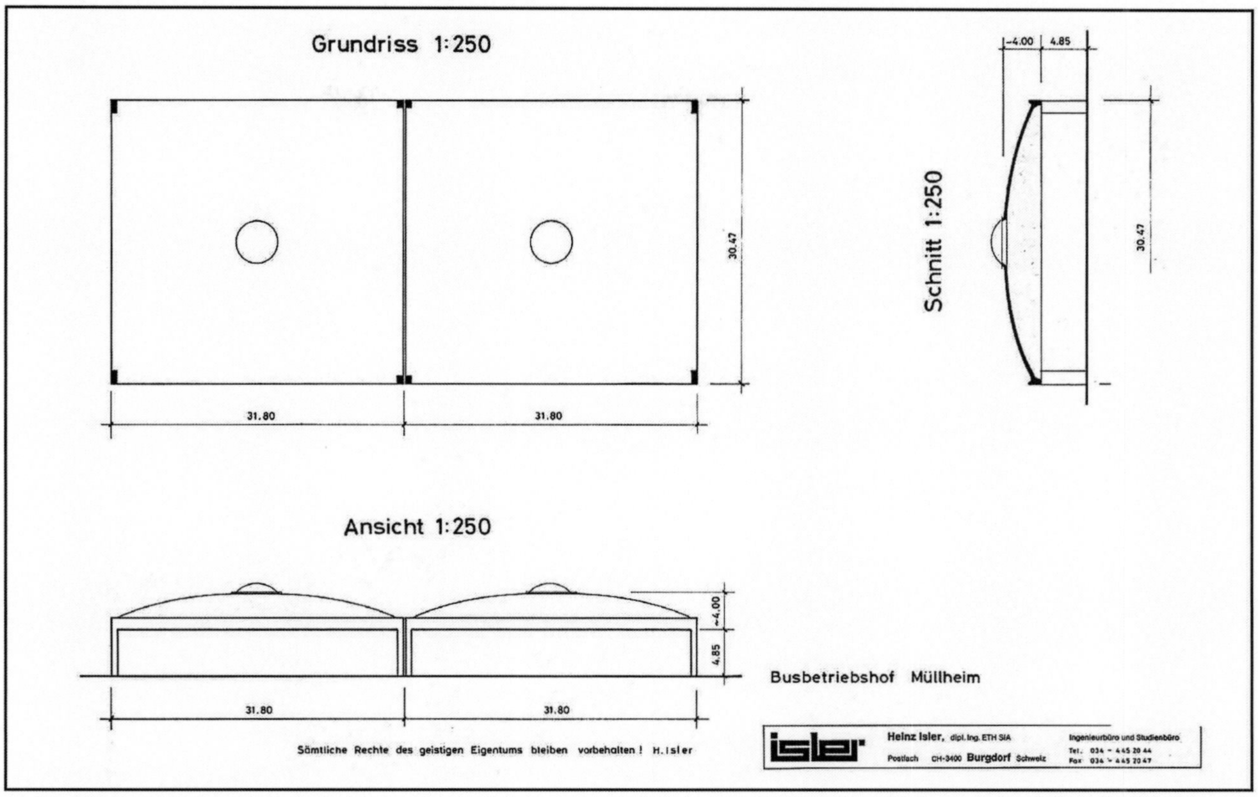

7 Heinz Isler, bus depot, Müllheim; drawing by Heinz Isler's engineering office, 1996

ter off the shell roof, a funnel shape was added to the bottom of the membrane. All in all, this creates a very impressive interior, which Müther developed together with his staff, so it cannot be attributed to the architect Kurt Tauscher, who also participated in the project. The resulting form had to be shuttered in a very complex way: the funnel was especially difficult to produce with curved wooden boards. Isler's bubble shells, the shape of which was created under pressure via the membrane, also had to be laboriously formed with curved wooden beams. In contrast to most of Müther's free-form shells, which were always unique, Isler built countless bubble shells and was therefore able to reuse the complex formwork several times.

Müther had probably observed the development of Isler's bubble shells closely over many years. However, it was not until 1984 that he approached a similar concept for a sports hall prototype. In this case, a series of inexpensive sports halls were to be built for the department of public education of the council of the district of Rügen. Two identical, 15 × 15-meter and 8-centimeter-thick bubble shells are supported on a total of six corner supports. Bent wooden beams, in combination with a lost formwork made of wood-wool lightweight panels, enabled the simple production of the two shells with one scaffolding and one set of wooden beams.

Heinz Isler used a very similar procedure for the production of his bubble shells. Here, too, wooden beams and wood fiber building boards were used, which adhered to the concrete interior as lost formwork after the scaffolding was removed. This resulted in good acoustics and, at the same time, interior thermal insulation that is useful for halls. However, Isler offered his shells in different sizes or dimensions: there was a 225-square-meter, a 300-square-meter, a 400-square-meter, and a 900-square-meter version; theoretically, dimensions of up to 100 × 100-meters are possible. The 225-square-meter version corresponded to the size of Müther's shells in Gingst, and the bearing on four corner supports is identical. However, differences can be found in the reinforcement of the shells. Isler included prestressing in the edge beams of the shell, while Müther used trajectory reinforcement in the edge areas of the formwork instead of prestressing. Due to the prestressing, Isler achieved smaller-dimensioned edge beams and slightly thinner shell thicknesses. Prestressing also controlled deflections in the shell and edge beams.[13] Another advantage of Isler's shells are the GRP skylights, which are designed as small shells and allow for better exposure to daylight.

8 Heinz Isler, bus depot, Müllheim, 1997: view from above

SHELLS AND MONUMENTS

Due to their expressive form and the possibilities inherent in the special malleability of the material, most shell constructions made of concrete come close to sculpture, as they are also created as free-form art. Especially in the 1960s and 1970s, there was an interest in large, expansive monuments, which also led to cooperation between artists and civil engineers or architects. This applied to Félix Candela as well as to Ulrich Müther and Heinz Isler: all three of them built large sculptures or monuments in cooperation with architects or artists. The supporting structure and construction of these sculptures played a more or less important role.

In order to realize the so-called flag monument in Magdeburg on the occasion of the 25th anniversary of the founding of the GDR, by the artist Joachim Sendler, Ulrich Müther's company in Binz was contacted. The form of the monument was developed purely artistically as an image of a Socialist workers' flag, initially as a plaster model. In order to geometrize this free form, a draftswoman made regular horizontal sections through the plaster model, from which Müther's company derived the construction and reinforcement plans. In terms of construction, the flag monument is not purely a surface-active structure, but is simply built up like a tower: inside, the remaining reinforcement is attached to a steel pipe clamped in the ground. Finally, a Torkret method was used, with shotcrete applied without formwork. The concrete thickness varies between 10 and 30 centimeters.

Heinz Isler worked out various sculptural designs for the Spanish artist Ángel Duarte, which varied in construction, material, and manufacturing methods. In size and shape similar to Müther's sculpture in Magdeburg on the Elbe, the "double sail" in Pully on Lake Geneva (1978) is about 9 meters tall and geometrically designed as a hyperbolic paraboloid, which is set up on three points. This geometrically determined shape was obviously not determined by Isler, but by Duarte. This becomes particularly clear when one looks at Duarte's art. He built numerous hyperbolic structures from soldered stainless-steel rods. One example is the sculpture *E 42 A.I.* (1974), which measures 62 × 63 × 47.50 centimeters. Isler's or Duarte's sculptures are much more delicate than the Magdeburg flag monument. This was made possible by using special mortar and ferro-cement on a pipe grid as reinforcement. The consequent interpretation of the sculpture as a hyperbolic structure favors the delicate appearance of its monumental form.

Félix Candela's monumental objects were already created in the 1950s, mostly in collaboration with the architects Guillermo Rossell and Manuel Larrosa. They are often much larger, expansive structures that were intended to accentuate special urban situations, similar to Müther and Isler. The Plaza de los Abanicos (Square of the fans) at the entrance to a residential estate in Cuernavaca (1958) and the sculpture at the entrance to the town in Tequesquitengo Lomas Tropicales (1957) are worthy of mention. Candela's monuments are defined mainly by hyperbolic paraboloids, but also by ad-

9 Joachim Sendler with Ulrich Müther, monument on the banks of the river Elbe, Magdeburg, 1974

10 Ángel Duarte with Heinz Isler, monument at the harbor, Pully, 1978

11 Félix Candela, sculpture on the Plaza de los Abanicos (Square of the fans), Cuernavaca, 1958

ditional tension and compression bars, some of which are made of steel. These reinforcements of the sculptures became necessary because the geometry was not consistently based on a surface-active structure; instead, a certain formally desired gesture was the main focus.

CONCLUSION

On closer examination, it can be seen that there are certain aspects that connect the work of Candela, Isler, and Müther but which also distinguish them from one another.

- The aspect of personal references: the three maintained collegial but also friendly relationships.
- The aspect of material: usually all three used only reinforced concrete, with the following exceptions: GRP (glass fiber reinforced plastic), plaster, and ice are used to a small extent by Isler; by Müther there is even a single wooden structure.
- The aspect of construction: all three mainly used formwork made of wood. Formwork with inflated membranes or with shaped natural hills was only applied by Isler and Müther, as well as concrete structures manufactured without formwork.
- The aspect of geometry: geometrically defined shells (hyperbolic paraboloids, spherical shells, or barrels) were mainly realized by Müther and Candela, while free-form shells were mainly realized by Isler, and to a lesser extent also by Müther.
- The aspect of building types: all shell makers mainly realized industrial buildings, public buildings, and sculptures—all structures that either needed a lot of free space or were meant to become icons in context.

If one wants to take quantitative and geographical aspects into account, Ulrich Müther realized 75 shell constructions, which is the lowest number, in Europe, North Africa, Cuba, and Kuwait. Félix Candela comes up with about 900 buildings, most of them realized with branches of Cubiertas Ala in Central and South America. Heinz Isler built by far the most shell constructions: his serial production brought him to almost 1,400, which he realized in Switzerland, Germany, France, Austria, Saudi Arabia, and the United Kingdom.

1 *Zum Werk von Félix Candela: Die Kunst der leichten Schalen,* Arcus 18 (Cologne, 1992).
2 See Wilfried Dechau, "Ulrich Müther: Landbaumeister aus Binz," in Bundesingenieurkammer, ed., *Ingenieurbaukunst in Deutschland: Jahrbuch 2001* (Hamburg, 2001), 134–141.
3 Wilfried Dechau, ed., *Kühne Solitäre: Ulrich Müther, Schalenbaumeister der DDR* (Stuttgart, 2000).
4 Ekkehard Ramm and Eberhard Schunck, eds., *Heinz Isler: Schalen* (Stuttgart, 1986).
5 See Jürgen Joedicke, *Schalenbau: Konstruktion und Gestaltung,* with contributions by Walter Bauersfeld and Herbert Kupfer (Stuttgart, 1962).
6 KdF, or Kraft durch Freude (Strength through joy), was a state-operated leisure organization in National Socialist Germany.
7 Probably Colin Faber, *Candela und seine Schalen* (Munich, 1965).
8 I[ngo] Schönrock, "Pilzförmige Schalenelemente," *Deutsche Architektur* 11 (1962): 420.
9 See Georg Giebeler, *Müther-Archiv: Systematische und kommentierte Bestandsaufnahme des Nachlasses von Ulrich Müther* (Cologne, 2016, self-published). See also Tanja Seeböck, *Schwünge in Beton: Die Schalenbauten von Ulrich Müther* (Schwerin, 2016), 311–389.
10 Heinz Isler, "New Shapes for Shells," *Bulletin of the International Association for Shell Structures* 8 (1961): paper C-3 (n.p.).
11 See Katinka Corts, "Müthers Freilichtmuseum," *tec21* 132, no. 22 (2006): 5–11, here 7.
12 MMM, Messe der Meister von Morgen (Fair for the masters of tomorrow) was a youth competition in the GDR.
13 See Peter Eigenraam, Andrew Borgart, John Chilton, and Qiang Li, "Structural Analysis of Heinz Isler's Bubble Shell," *Engineering Structures* 210 (2020).

Spaces for Industry
A Comparison of Modular Shell Systems by Félix Candela and Heinz Isler

MATTHIAS BECKH

This essay aims to shed light on the relationship between structure and architecture through the example of shell structures by Félix Candela (1910–1997) and Heinz Isler (1926–2009). Focusing on the standard products that both developed for industrial architecture, it will discuss the distinctive philosophies they pursued in negotiating shell design while balancing aspects of economy, efficiency, and architectural concerns.

After an introduction to common shell types and their structural behavior, the modular shell systems of Candela and Isler will be examined. Both designed specific systems for industrial architecture, which constitute by far the largest part of their built oeuvre. A comparison of their approaches shows the enormous variability within the field of shell structures, in one case allowing for a large number of variations, in the other for larger spaces. It showcases how the designers start out with the same set of technical requirements but arrive at very distinct structural languages.

A BRIEF INTRODUCTION TO THE STRUCTURAL BEHAVIOR OF COMMON SHELL TYPES

Shells are defined as single- or double-curved surface structures that are predominantly subject to internal compression and tension forces. The shape of a shell determines its structural performance and the behavior of the forces within the shell. If their form is structurally informed, their thickness can be extremely thin as compared to their span. This structural efficiency can lead to very lightweight and slender structures of great elegance. In general, we can differentiate between mathematically described forms, such as spherical segments, surfaces of revolution, or hyperbolic paraboloids; surfaces derived with specific form-finding techniques; and arbitrarily defined free-forms.

One important prerequisite for using the material in the best way is to have the internal forces follow the center line of the structure as closely as possible. This behavior, called *membrane action* in the case of surface structures, describes how the internal stresses are distributed evenly over the cross-section of the shell, thus ensuring the best utilization of the employed material. This is typically the case for doubly curved surfaces subjected to uniform loads: the two principal curvatures

1 Félix Candela, Rio Warehouse, Lindavista, Mexico City, 1954

allow a bidirectional flow of forces that helps to equalize the stresses within the shell. The advantages of doubly curved structures become clear when they are compared to single-curved constructions like arches.

The ideal form for an arch under a specific load combination will be the mirrored form of an identical rope or cable subjected to the same loads. The loads on the hanging cable will influence its form in such a way that all parts are in equilibrium, thereby causing tension forces within the cable. If the resulting form is mirrored along a horizontal line, one receives the thrust line of an arch under the corresponding load combination. This means that an arch designed in this way will carry that specific load solely with a compression force following its center line. As a consequence, the resulting internal stresses are evenly distributed over the cross-section of the arch, making the best use of the material employed. Being subjected to a uniformly distributed load, the resulting thrust line follows the curve of a parabola. Subjected only to its self-weight, the resulting thrust line of the arch follows the curve of a catenary. This curve is similar to the parabola but differs slightly due to the different distribution of the loads, mainly toward the supports. Barrel vaults can be understood as a series of arches; their form can thus be described by the translation of an arch along a straight generator line. If the generator line itself is curved as well, the resulting form becomes doubly curved: with two sets of internal arches it can now support the external load in two directions, which enhances the structural performance of the shell.

The phenomenon that the mirrored hanging cable provides the ideal arch geometry for a specific load case was first expressed by the English scientist Robert Hooke (1635–1703). It is not only valid for two-dimensional systems but also for spatial structures. The Catalan architect Antoni Gaudí (1852–1926) famously designed many of his structures with three-dimensional hanging models. For the predominant load combinations, the resulting vaults and domes are hence under compression. This is particularly important in the case of brittle masonry structures, where inner tension forces can easily result in cracks and fissures. In the twentieth century, Heinz Isler experimented with hanging models—ranging from nets to membranes—and explored the endless possibilities of organic shapes that can be derived with this method. By carefully varying the boundary conditions of the hanging membrane, a shell shape can be derived that aligns structural, spatial, and functional requirements.

Dome-shaped structures like a hemisphere and similar surfaces of revolution display a two-directional load-bearing behavior. A hemisphere under uniform loading will develop an arch-like load-bearing behavior along the meridians, with the compression forces accumulating from the apex downward to the supports. At the same time, hoop forces occur in the latitudinal direction, which discharge the forces in the meridian direction. The type of hoop forces depends on their location across the shell. In the upper region of the shell, where the gradient of the surface is shallow, the ring forces are in compression. If an opening is inserted at the apex of the dome, the adjacent ring elements will carry the thrust of the interrupted meridians. The hoop forces can also turn to tension, which is the case in the lower part of a hemispherical shell. Here, the hoop forces divert the meridian forces to stay within the shape of the shell and prevent the form from bulging outward.

A geometry commonly used for shells is the hyperbolic paraboloid, the hypar for short. Its distinct saddle surface—being concave in one direction and convex in the other—can easily be achieved by ruling a

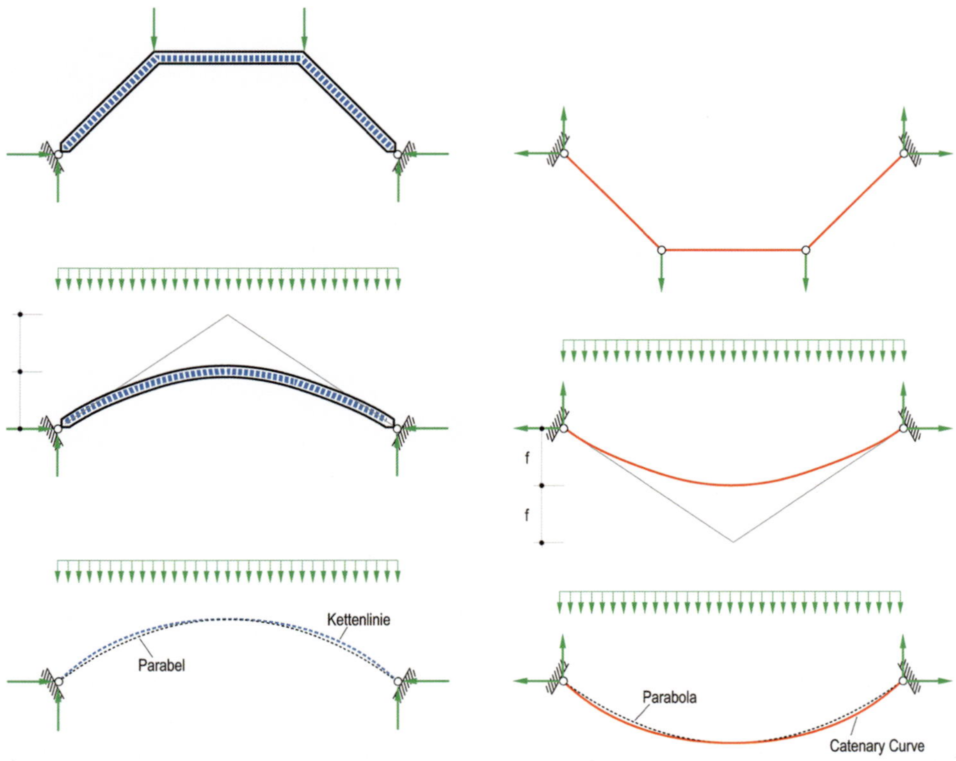

2 The form of a hanging cable subjected to: (a) two point loads; (b) a uniformly distributed load (parabola); and (c) uniformly distributed load versus self-weight

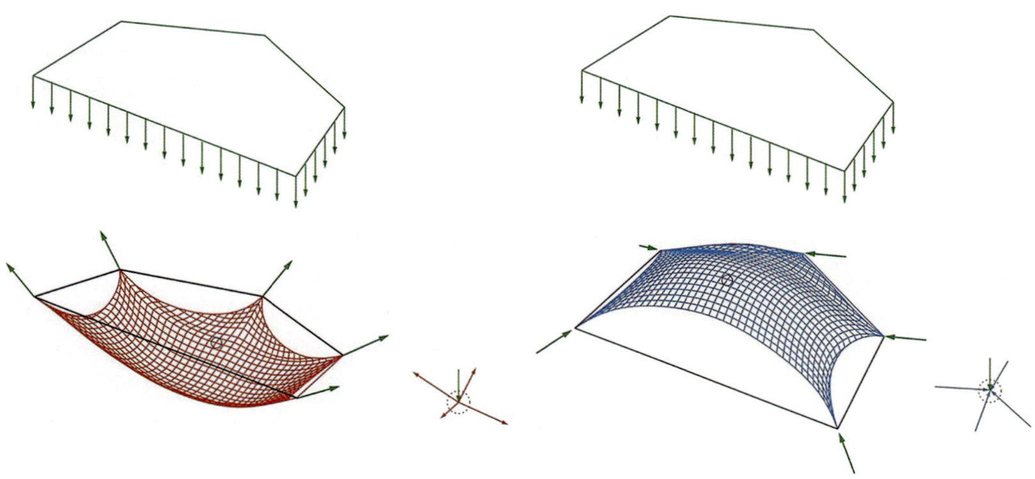

3 Hanging model and corresponding form of a funicular shell: tension forces are shown in red, compression forces are shown in blue

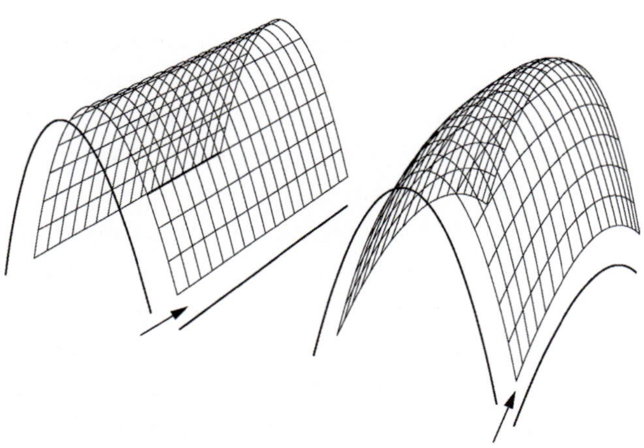

4 Creation of a barrel vault and a doubly curved shell by the translation of an arch (or arbitrary curve) along a generator line

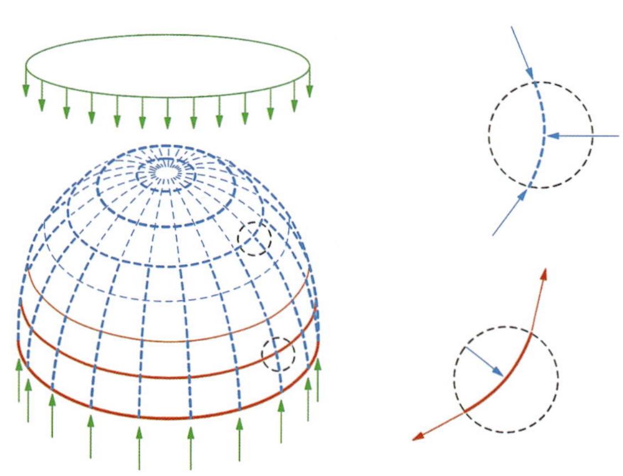

5 Hemisphere under uniformly distributed load and resulting meridian and hoop forces

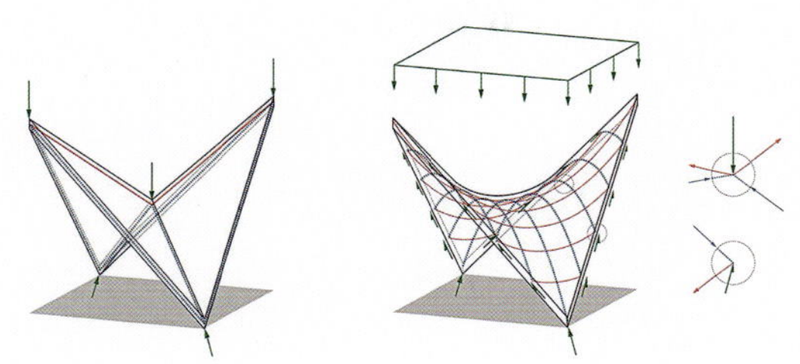

6 Force flow within a hyperbolic paraboloid under uniformly distributed load

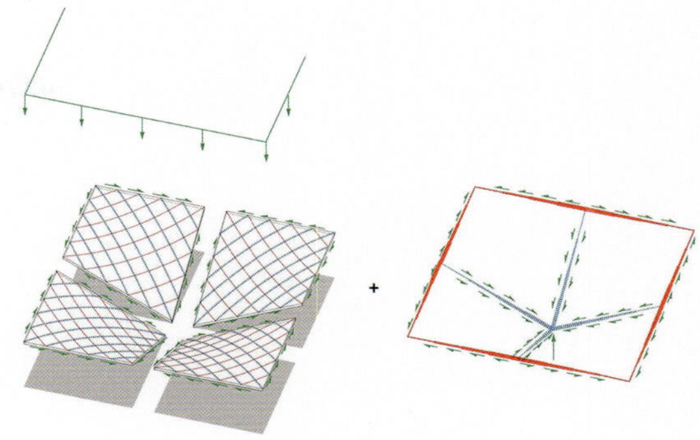

7 Force flow within an umbrella-like structure made of four hypar elements

straight element between two skew generator lines. Hence, it is a ruled surface with a double curvature made up of two families of straight lines. The sections in the principal directions of curvature are parabolas. The structural behavior of hypar shells under uniformly distributed loads can be understood as a combination of standing arches and hanging cables in the two main directions. A load acting on the surface of the hypar is thus carried in equal parts by a tension element and a compression element. At the edges, the support forces of the arches and the cables acting perpendicular to the edge cancel one another out. Hence, in the case of a single hypar, the edges are subject to compression forces that accumulate from the corner to the support.

Hyperbolic paraboloids can be easily combined into larger configurations. One arrangement consists in the joining of four identical elements placed on a central column to form an umbrella-like structure. In this case, all edges will be subjected to tension forces, which allows the realization of very thin rims. Compression forces build up in the valleys of the umbrella and accumulate toward the center, which can make it necessary to increase the thickness of the shell or to place a rib in this region. The fact that hyperbolic paraboloids can be composed out of straight elements makes them ideal for concrete shells, as the formwork can be constructed of slender timber battens. This is a considerable advantage over other doubly curved surfaces, for which the falsework is usually quite intricate and consequently very costly.[1]

BUILDINGS FOR INDUSTRY

The individual approaches of the two designers become most evident while analyzing and juxtaposing the bread-and-butter products of Félix Candela and Heinz Isler. Both designed a large number of projects for industry, such as warehouses and factory buildings. Candela mostly used a modular system of hypar shells with straight edges for this task, with a high level of differentiation to improve indoor lighting and structural expression. Isler instead built numerous projects with his standardized bubble shell system, varying the units in size and arranging them into large clusters. Despite the obvious differences in design between Candela's and Isler's shells, the concurrence of their developments from the early 1950s onward is striking.

THE UMBRELLA SYSTEM

Félix Candela had built his very first shell—a funicular barrel vault of modest span—in 1949. In the following years he would construct a multitude of different shell systems with his newly founded company Cubiertas Ala. In 1952, inspired by a famous paper[2] by the French engineer Fernand Aimond (1902–1984), Candela realized the first experimental hypar with straight edges. The square umbrella, with a side length of 10 meters and a rise of 1 meter, had a thickness of a mere 4 centimeters. Just one year later he would build a similar experimental umbrella in the Vallejo neighborhood of Mexico City.[3] This time, the square structure with a side length of 8 meters and a rise of 70 centimeters had a thickness of 8 centimeters. A photograph of Candela standing with 24 workers on the top of this shell to perform a load test soon became iconic and demonstrated convincingly the structural potential of this typology. Both experimental structures, however, suffered from significant deflections at the corners and prompted Candela to study the best ratio of rise to span. Later, he would state that the rise should equal approximately 0.015 times the area of the shell and that the area covered by one umbrella should be limited to approximately 200 square meters.[4]

8 Félix Candela, High Life textile factory, Coyoacán, Mexico City, 1955: the inserted glass bricks were later sealed from the top; photograph 2018

The first real project where this system was applied became the Rio Warehouse in Lindavista, Mexico City, built in 1954. The 36 umbrellas, each measuring 15.25 × 10 meters, were arranged on a triangular site and tilted 50 centimeters upward from the central columns to the edge to produce a saw-tooth roof. This tilt allowed the insertion of a 1-meter-tall ribbon window exposed to the north that provided generous natural lighting conditions inside. At the foundation level, the umbrella motif was repeated in the reverse direction to create a stiff single footing with little material. The columns were equipped with pipes to provide drainage for the roof planes. A moveable falsework system, which was subdivided into four sections, eased the construction process. With the use of fast-setting concrete that allowed one pour per week and four falsework systems in place, all 36 umbrellas were constructed within a mere three months.[5] The fine imprint of the formwork—typically 2 × 5-centimeter wooden battens were used to construct the top of the falsework—provides the underside of the hypars with a vivid and elegant texture that narrates the construction process.[6]

The umbrella shell system, with a rise of 2 meters and a thickness of only 4 centimeters, was not only an elegant and light design, but also rendered an extremely economical roofing system: the cost was roughly half that of the competing conventional systems then on the market.[7] The design of the Rio Warehouse thus became the starting point and blueprint for numerous industrial projects in the following years. Areas totaling more than 500,000 square meters were covered by Cubiertas Ala, the firm that Candela had cofounded, between 1955 and 1970.[8] At that time Candela said, "Nowadays, we have trouble persuading people to accept anything else."[9]

Besides this astounding extent of covered area, Candela varied the design, geometry, and arrangements of his umbrella system in many different ways. One of the architecturally most compelling indoor spaces was built just one year later in Coyoacán, Mexico City. The roof of the High Life textile company followed the saw-tooth design of the Rio Warehouse project. But in this case, the shells were pierced by glass bricks that flooded the indoor space with a mosaic of natural light. Unfortunately, this stunning design led to an overdose of light and unbearable indoor temperatures and thus was never replicated. Another strategy to improve the natural lighting conditions was pursued for the cover of the grocery markets in Acapulco and Arriaga (1970). Here the individual umbrellas are staggered in elevation following a chessboard pattern. The variation in ceiling heights and the ribbon windows create an intriguing and pleasant environment in the market.

Other variations concern the chosen geometries of the umbrella structures in plan. The geometries vary from square or almost square configurations to quite elongated shapes, as can be seen in the case of the storage facilities Candela built for Bacardi in Tultitlán in 1964. In order to allow for the best possible storage layout, the quite elongated umbrellas used here were not only eccentrically supported but also warped upward at their short ends. In this manner, the adjoining

9 Octavio Barreda Marín and Félix Candela, Mercado Municipal Belisario Domínguez (Belisario Domínguez municipal market), Arriaga, 1970

10 Félix Candela, Bacardi warehouse, Tultitlán, 1964

umbrella units create a ridge, which provides the necessary stiffness to bridge the 27.35 meters between the supports.[10] In a similar fashion, Candela also tweaked the geometry of the umbrella system for the Jamaica wholesale market in Mexico City, built in 1957. Two rows of twelve square umbrellas were placed to provide shelter for the vendors. With a side length of 18 meters, they were among the largest of their kind. In order to limit deflections of the large cantilevers, Candela subdivided the roofs into eight rather than the regular four segments to increase the stiffness of the umbrella.

Besides these projects for industrial purposes, Candela further exploited the formal potential of hypars with straight edges for public buildings. His virtuosity and ingenuity in dealing with these structural elements is nowhere better expressed than in the church Medalla de la Virgen Milagrosa (1953–1955) or the exuberant roof structure of the Candelaria metro station (1967), both in Mexico City.

THE BUBBLE SHELL SYSTEM

In the very same time frame, the Swiss engineer Heinz Isler set out to contrive a modular shell system on the other side of the globe. At the age of 28, Isler had built his first shell in 1954 to cover a small multipurpose hall in Langenthal. Dissatisfied with the geometrically defined shape of that shell, he had started to use pneumatic models to find a static form that would span a rectangular area in a smooth and natural way. In an elaborated process, he would inflate a rubber membrane confined by a wooden frame and transfer the resulting topography to representational models and testing models made of Plexiglas. Since the generated form could not be described mathematically and thus precluded exact calculations, Isler had to refer to testing models to accurately ascertain the structural behavior of the shell. This method was used for the first time to construct a factory building for Glas Trösch in

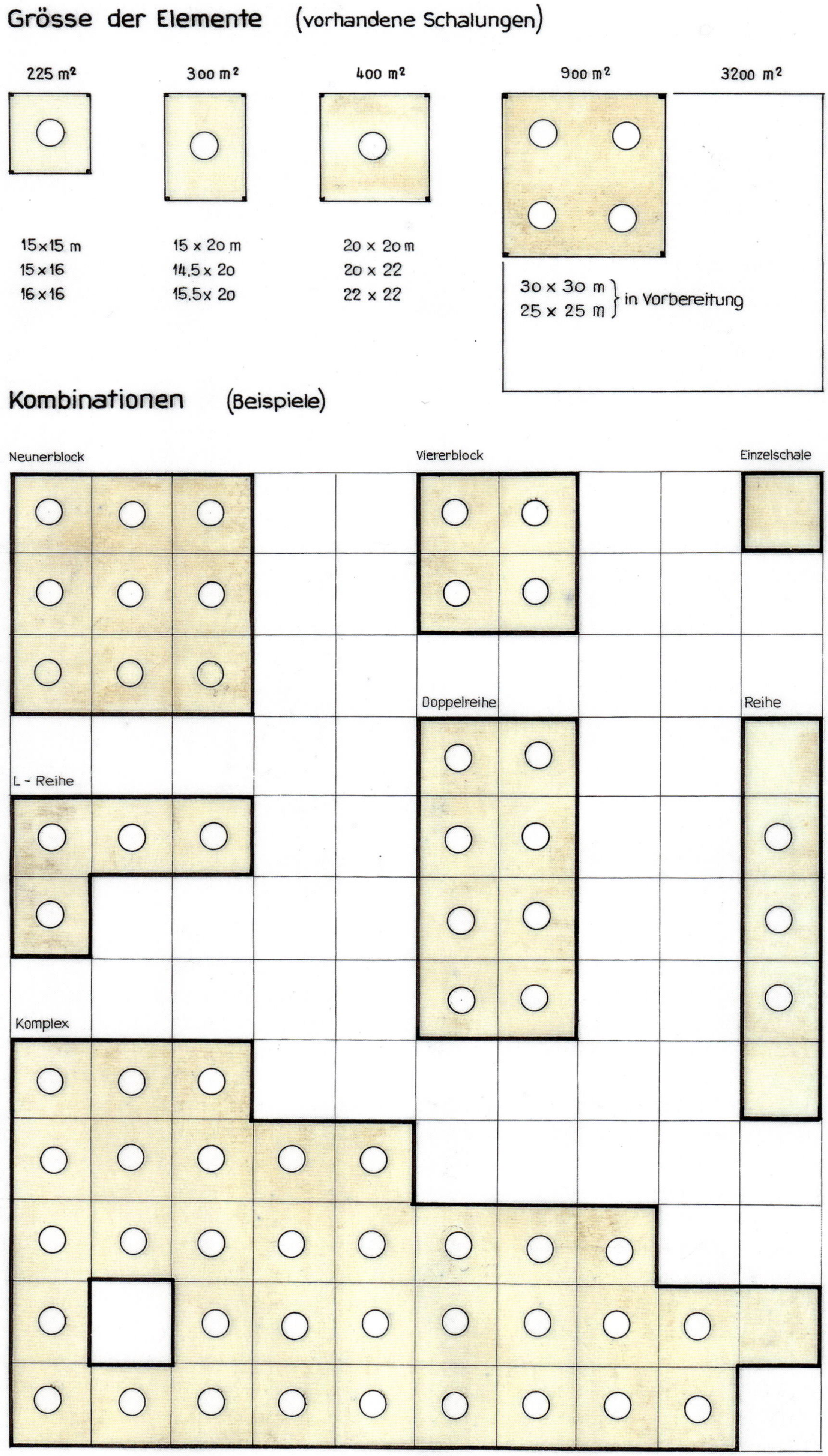

11 Overview of possible sizes and combinations of bubble shells from Heinz Isler's engineering office, undated

Thunstetten in 1955. Three "bubble shells," measuring 14 × 23 meters each, were confined by post-tensioned perimeter beams, which themselves were supported by a column at each corner.

Just one year later, in 1956, the same method was employed again to build a storage hall for the firm Blaser Swisslube. The four identical bubble shells of 14 × 20 meters were placed above a clear indoor height of 5 meters. The shells have a regular thickness of 8 centimeters, which increases slightly toward the edges. At the edge, the shells are supported by prestressed spandrel beams with an integrated drainage system. The spandrel beams, together with the columns, form a portal frame that provides lateral stability for each module. For the falsework, glulam beams were installed, on which were placed small wooden battens that described the curvature of the shell. Finally, mineral bonded wood-wool boards were mounted on top of the battens. These boards remained as lost formwork on the underside of the shell and served as thermal insulation and noise protection.

As compared to the previous example of Glas Trösch, the Blaser Swisslube shells display a novelty: a 5-meter-wide domed skylight is set on a small support at the top of the shell. As no commercial product was available on the market, Isler designed and engineered the polyester skylights as well. With this addition, the bubble shell system had now become technically mature and fully developed and would start its immense success story in Switzerland and beyond. In the following years, a multitude of bubble shells were realized, with a focus on the central plateau region of Switzerland. According to the reference list of Heinz Isler's office, between 1955 and 1970 a total floor area of nearly 200,000 square meters was roofed with the new system, covering factories, warehouses, and other industrial purposes in the booming postwar era.[11] With its shell being uniformly under compression, no cracks could develop on the surface and hence no further waterproofing had to be added on the roof. This feature and the consequent lack of maintenance work made the bubble shell system extremely cost-effective. Furthermore, its modular character—with unit sizes ranging from about 15 meters square up to almost 60 meters—allowed for all sorts of orthogonal arrangements and later extensions. In 1960 the largest bubble shell was realized for a Coop distribution center in Olten over a rectangular space of 54 × 58 meters. Seventeen circular openings pierced the 15-centimeter-thick shell, providing natural light inside.

The early industrial shells of Isler show a clear articulation of the individual structural components, expressed for instance in the shaping of portal frames according to their demands or the widened beam ends that would accommodate the anchor heads of the prestressing cables. This more sculpted approach would give way to more standardized system with little modulation in the design of the main structural elements and details. Besides the obvious savings in times of rising labor costs, the simplified geometries of beams and columns also facilitated the interfaces of construction in cases where frame and shell structure were not installed by the same contractor. The increase in labor costs demanded also the reuse of formwork systems from early on, resulting in tables of standard shell sizes that were offered to potential clients.

Within the bubble shell system, the organically vaulted ceilings result in a calm and more subdued atmosphere inside, which is further intensified by the translucent (but not transparent) skylights made of polyester. As the skylights are framed by a curb at the apex of the shell, its thinness—measuring in general just about eight centimeters—cannot be perceived by the visitor. Furthermore, the ceilings made of wood-wool boards prevent the spectator from visually experiencing the materiality and immediacy of the structural concrete. Unlike the spectacular forms that Isler conceived by using hanging models, like the building for Sicli in Geneva, which would display the ingenuity and lightness of its design, bubble shells remain discreet about their structural prowess. It is noteworthy in this context that this shell type has been very rarely used for representational or public buildings. One of these rare exceptions is the swimming center in Böblingen, where a bubble shell covering an indoor pool was built in 1973.

ON VARIETY AND SCALE

When directly comparing the modular shell systems of Candela and Isler, one difference is striking: Candela varied the geometry of the individual umbrellas and their arrangement with great virtuosity in many different ways. The overall sizes of the built modules, in contrast, do not alter that much. The inherent softness of the cantilevering umbrella systems and the resulting danger of deflections along the edges simply limited the achievable sizes of the modules and prevented them from becoming overly large. This structural limitation, however, was turned by Candela into an architectural advantage: by adjusting the comparatively small umbrella units to suit the specific requirements of the individual projects, the resulting structural compositions are often a unique response to the design brief. With the manifold variations in the arrangements of units, the buildings almost disguise the modular character of their origin.

In Isler's case, in contrast, the adaptability of the bubble shell system to respond to a wide range of different sizes is remarkable. By amalgamating his past experiences in shell design, model testing, and prestressing technology into a new shell system, he developed a unique product for industrial architecture. With possible unit sizes of more than 3,200 square meters of covered floor area for a shell only 15 centimeters thick, Isler's shell system proved also to be stunningly efficient. But the specifics of its form also implied certain restrictions. The design of the bubble shell system changed only a little over the more than four decades of its application. As the very specific forms of the modules demanded an intricate and costly falsework system, a competitive edge could only be kept with an increasing standardization of the product.

It is obvious that both designers worked on the same common ground set by physical laws and the technical requirements inherent to the specific shell types. Nevertheless, they both developed on the spectrum of physical and technical specifics a distinct design approach that would synthesize structural, functional, and architectural aspects into an individual structural language.

1 See Jürgen Joedicke, *Schalenbau: Konstruktion und Gestaltung* (Stuttgart, 1962); and Aurelio Muttoni, *The Art of Structures: Introduction to the Functioning of Structures in Architecture* (Lausanne, 2011).
2 Fernand Aimond, "Étude statique des voiles minces en paraboloïde hyperbolique travaillant sans flexion," *IABSE Proceedings,* vol. 4 (Zurich, 1936), 1–112.
3 See Enrique X. de Anda Alanís, *Félix Candela, 1910–1997* (Cologne, 2008), 9.
4 See Maria E. Moreyra Garlock and David P. Billington, *Félix Candela: Engineer, Builder, Structural Artist* (New Haven/London, 2008), 98 and 100.
5 See Colin Faber, *Candela: The Shell Builder* (New York, 1963), 89.
6 See ibid., 126.
7 See ibid., 89.
8 See Juan Ignacio del Cueto Ruiz-Funes, "Gestación y propagación de los paraguas de concreto armado, ¿especie en extinción?" in Catherine Rose Ettinger McEnulty, Louise Noelle Gras, and Alejandro Ochoa Vega, eds., *Segunda Modernidad urbano arquitectónica: Lecciones significativas de la Segunda Modernidad en México,* (Mexico City, 2014), 319–334.
9 Quoted after Faber, *Candela,* 89 (see note 5).
10 See Del Cueto, "Gestación," 328 (see note 8).
11 See Heinz Isler, Referenzliste Industrieschalen Schweiz (undated), and Heinz Isler, Referenzliste Ausland A. Bauten mit Isler-Industrieschalen (undated), gta Archives, ETH Zurich, bequest of Heinz Isler.

12 Heinz Isler, wool spinning mill, Huttwil, 1958; photograph 2018

13 Heinz Isler, Coop distribution center, Wangen near Olten, 1960; photograph 2016

Candela Isler Müther
A Photographic Essay

WILFRIED DECHAU

Moles Reina

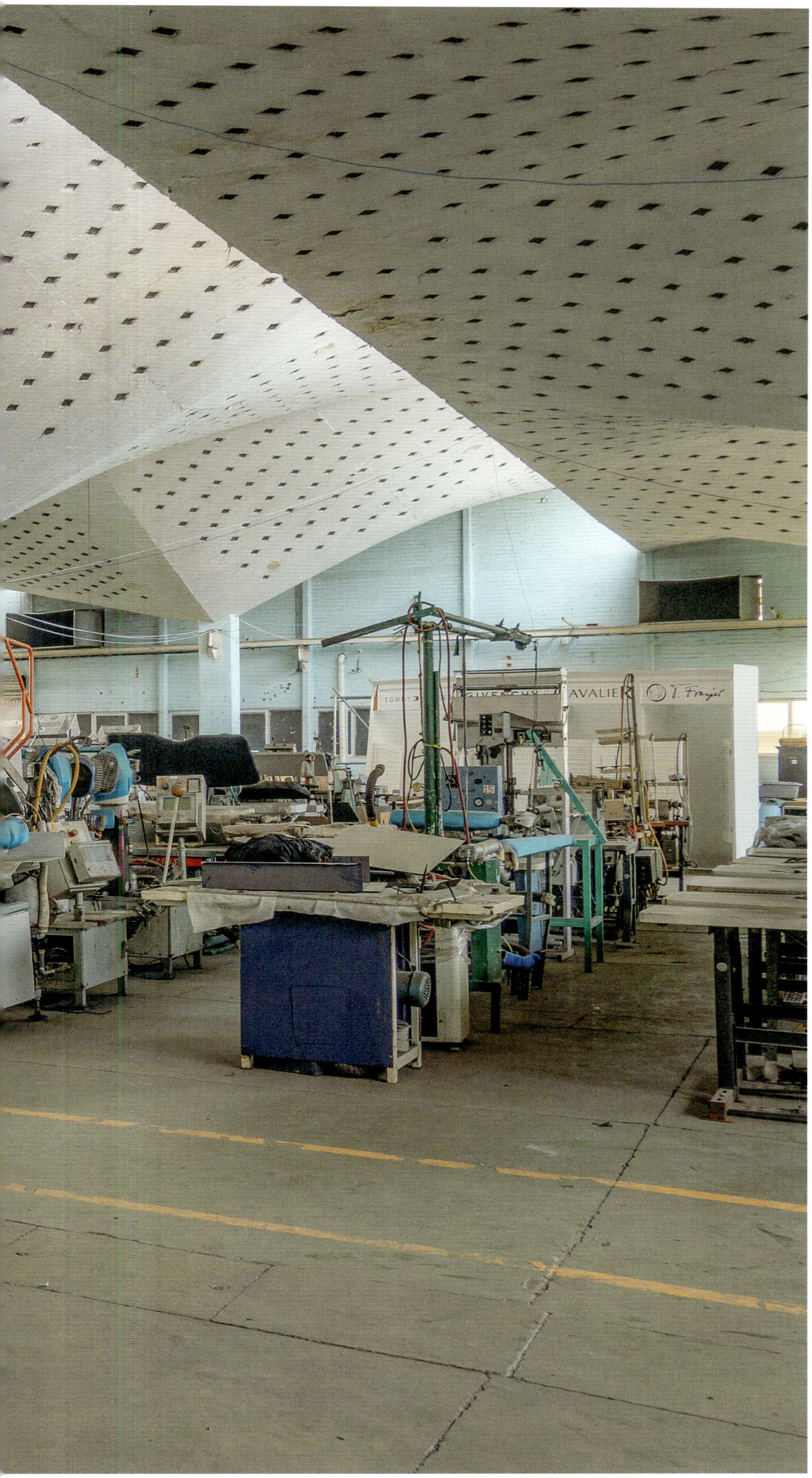

Félix Candela's Hypar Groined Vaults

Mexican Contribution to the Development of Concrete Shells

JUAN IGNACIO DEL CUETO RUIZ-FUNES

One can say that Félix Candela (1910–1997) lived three lives, and each one lasted for three decades: the first took place in Spain (1910–1939), the second in Mexico (1939–1971), and the last in the United States (1971–1997). His Spanish period was one of personal and academic training. He was born on January 27, 1910, in Madrid, where he did all his studies. He graduated as an architect in 1935 and a year later joined the Republican Army as a volunteer to fight in the Spanish Civil War (1936–1939). He arrived as a political refugee in Mexico, where he began the professional activity that would lead him to fame. In 1971 he accepted an invitation to join the University of Illinois at Chicago as full professor. This was the beginning of his "third life," mainly dedicated to academic work. In 1978 he retired and moved to New York City. After a few years in the Big Apple he settled in Raleigh, North Carolina, where he died on December 7, 1997.[1]

1 Advertisement of the company Cubiertas Ala in the journal *Arquitectura México*, 1952

On June 13, 1939, when he set foot on Mexican soil in the port of Veracruz along with 1,600 other exiled Spanish Republicans, at the age of 29 with no previous professional experience, Félix Candela could not have imagined that he would achieve worldwide fame with the laminated reinforced concrete structures (better known as concrete shells) that he would build in his adopted homeland in the 1950s and 1960s. Ten years after his arrival, he built his first experimental shell and founded his construction company Cubiertas Ala. This was encouraged by the promising career prospects that this technology opened up in the field of industrial architecture. He completed his first projects with cylindrical vaults, conical covers, or folded plates. However, in 1951 he used the geometry of the hyperbolic paraboloid (or hypar) for the first time to solve the challenge of building a roof not more than 15 millimeters (5/8 inch) thick. Thus were born the two extremely thin "saddles" that cover the Cosmic Rays Pavilion in Mexico City by architect Jorge González Reyna. This was the work that catapulted Candela to fame as a brilliant structural designer, and from then on, the number of commissions that reached Cubiertas Ala grew exponentially.

Due to the use of the hypar as the basic geometry, the construction technology of the laminar concrete structures that originated in interwar Europe (Eugène Freyssinet in France, Franz Dischinger and Ulrich Finsterwalder in Germany, Robert Maillart in Switzerland, and Eduardo Torroja in Spain) reached its maximum levels of inspiration, lightness, and elegance in Mexico at the hand of Candela. He applied in his designs three premises that he considered fundamental: common sense, structural efficiency, and economy. His restless spirit led him to continually experiment with the shells that he had the opportunity to design. For the most part, they were made for Mexican colleagues who came to his company in search of structural solutions for their projects that were attractive, innovative, and affordable.

When the hypar is applied with talent in the field of architectural design, it creates roofs of soft, wrapped, and expressive forms that generate fluid and unique spaces. Among Candela's great works, there are several projects resolved with hypar groined vaults, in which all the forces of the structure are transmitted to the supports through the groins that generate the intersections of the hypars, forming parabolic arches for reinforcement.

A FRUITFUL PROFESSIONAL RELATIONSHIP IS BORN

In mid-1953 the talented architect Enrique de la Mora y Palomar (Guadalajara 1907–Mexico City 1978) and his young collaborator Fernando López Carmona (Mexico City 1921–Querétaro 2018) were developing the project for the Mexican Stock Exchange building in Mexico City's historic center. They proposed an ingenious geometric solution to cover the rectangular space (26 × 15 meters) of the trading floor. It consisted of two saddle-type hypars that intersected perpendicularly. As their calculating engineers told them that it was very difficult to calculate and build, De la Mora decided to consult Félix Candela, who stated: "Their design seemed beautiful to me, and superbly logical."[2] Thus, he calculated it and looked for the constructive solution that could make it a reality. He did what logic demanded: he took advantage of the two diagonal parabolic arches that draw the groins at the intersection of the hypars to incorporate some stiffening ribs with a V-section that were hidden above the vertex of each groin to transmit the forces produced by the concrete laminas to the supports located at the corners of the room.

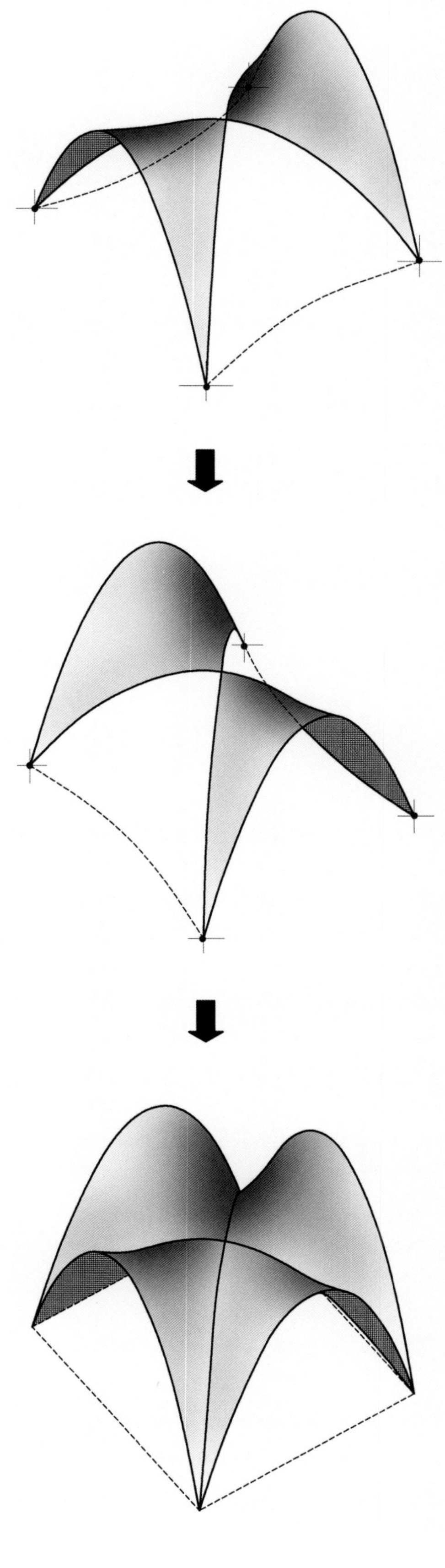

2 Sequence of the geometric solution of the hypar groined vault, raised by Fernando López Carmona from the intersection of two saddles

3 Enrique de la Mora and Félix Candela, trading floor of the Mexican Stock Exchange, Mexico City, 1955

This shell, the first of its kind in the world, was built between December 20, 1954, and July 21, 1955.[3] Its four perimeter arches were reinforced externally with edge beams. One of the great merits of the final design of the shell was to slightly incline the cutting plane of these arches toward the interior. This was done to make room for ventilation and allow natural light to "slide" down the vertical walls that close off the space, generating an optical effect that gives the shell a sensation of great lightness and the room a surprising luminosity.

The structural design of this shell initiated a fruitful professional collaboration between Enrique de la Mora, Fernando López Carmona, and Félix Candela. This would bring some of their emblematic works to twentieth-century Mexican architecture, particularly in the field of ecclesiastical buildings. Examples of this are the churches of El Altillo and San Vicente de Paul in Coyoacán (Mexico City, 1957 and 1959), San José Obrero (Monterrey, 1960), Santa Cruz (San Luis Potosí, 1965), and Divina Providencia (Mexico City, 1965). All of them are roofed with different solutions using straight-edged shells. The churches of San Antonio de las Huertas and Perpetuo Socorro (1956 and 1966) are roofed with hypar groined vaults.

A QUALITATIVE LEAP: THE FREE EDGE

Candela was not satisfied with the stiffening ribs he had had to apply to the perimeter arches of the Mexican Stock Exchange. It bothered him that in his best works, like the church of Medalla de la Virgen Milagrosa in Mexico City (1953–1955), the lightness of the shell was not perceived because of the unappealing reinforcements that were required to stabilize the edge elements. He was convinced that these could be eliminated by analytically determining a state of stress that did not produce normal forces along the perimeter arches, which would allow him to leave the four- or five-centimeter thickness of the lamina visible: the desired "free edge." In the Stock Exchange it had not been achieved because the rectangular plan broke the biaxial symmetry that was required to achieve it. "If the vault had had a square plan, its edges could also have been free of tangential stresses, and there would have been no need for stiffening ribs [...]."[4]

Candela was finally able to prove his theory about the free edge in a new commission from Enrique de la Mora: "But by June 1956, when the architects were sketching the roofs of San Antonio de las Huertas, Candela knew the fundamentals and the tricks of the calculations [...]. He was confident enough to suggest at once, given the symmetry of the vaults, that their edges be left free of arches."[5] In 1956 the first shells of this type were built: three hypar groined vaults that are aligned and separated from each other and form the main nave of the church of San Antonio de las Huertas.[6] Each vault is almost square (14 × 16 meters) and the height varies from 7.50 meters at the intersection of the vaults at the center to 10 meters at the crown of the perimeter arches, where the free edge gives a sensation of lightness. The vaults are separated by 2 meters from the enclosure walls and between vaults. These separations are covered with thin parabolic arches at a higher level, which are delicately attached to the perimeter arches of each vault by means of a light triangulated metal structure that, placed vertically, supports some amber-colored stained-glass windows. A sifted light filters through them, creating a mystical atmosphere inside the sanctuary.

With this new variant, Candela achieved one of the greatest aesthetic achievements in the field of laminar structures: the free-edge shell. "Everything is so simple," he said, "when you know it that you are really angry for not having seen it all at first glance, instead of having to go through the painful process of thinking. I knew the free edge was a practical idea a long time before I understood how it worked and dared to build it."[7]

4 Enrique de la Mora and Félix Candela, San Antonio de las Huertas church, Mexico City, 1956

SHIFTING THE PACE: THREE, EIGHT, FIVE ...

With the free edge dominating, Candela gave free rein to his creativity, rehearsing "rhythmic variations" that moved away from the traditional solution of shell vaults with four segments to experiment with bolder ones formed by three, eight, or five segments (in exactly that chronological order). With those variations he covered the cabaret La Jacaranda at the Hotel Presidente in Acapulco, the restaurant Los Manantiales in Xochimilco, and the restaurant at the Hotel Casino de la Selva in Cuernavaca, respectively.

5 Juan Sordo Madaleno and Félix Candela, La Jacaranda cabaret, Acapulco, 1957

In 1957 architect Juan Sordo Madaleno approached Cubiertas Ala looking for a solution to protect the sea-view terrace of the Hotel Presidente in Acapulco. Candela proposed a roof derived from the intersection of three hypars in which the resulting edges transmit the forces to the three supports. Each hypar is cut with a plane inclined toward the perimeter, generating a graceful curved visor that protects the users from solar radiation.[8] Unlike the roofs of Xochimilco and Cuernavaca, the "concrete *palapa*" of Acapulco did not require external enclosures, which gives it a surprising lightness. This shell was demolished when the hotel was expanded. With this, one of Candela's masterpieces disappeared.

While the Acapulco Jacaranda was being planned, a fire destroyed the wooden structure of the traditional restaurant Los Manantiales in Xochimilco, a beautiful lake area located in the south of Mexico City. The reconstruction project was entrusted to the young architect

6 Joaquín Álvarez Ordóñez and Félix Candela, Los Manantiales restaurant, Xochimilco, Mexico City: view of the construction site with the finished roof, 1958

7 Félix Candela with Juan Antonio Tonda, restaurant at the Hotel Casino de la Selva, Cuernavaca, 1960

Joaquín Álvarez Ordóñez,[9] who also decided to commission the structural design from Cubiertas Ala. Candela then raised a "concrete eight-petal flower" over the canals in the lake area, formed by the intersection of four hypars that revolve around an axis and generate groined vaults that cover an octagonal area of 750 square meters.

The profile of the shell follows a sinuous and rhythmic line that rises and falls without any kind of interruption due to the solution of the eight supports that are skillfully tucked behind the lower inflection curves to allow the delicate 5-centimeter-thick edge to flow freely, creating the illusion that the building is levitating. As in Acapulco, each lamina is cut with a plane inclined toward the perimeter, achieving a dynamic shape that seems to extend its wings to lift into flight. "This is the structure which Candela considers to be his most significant work. I think it is unsurpassed, and all that a shell should be: simple, graceful, and light. Almost certainly, it is the most delicate concrete membrane ever to bridge such a span."[10]

The earthquake that rattled Mexico City on September 19, 2017, had terrible repercussions in Xochimilco. Due to this, the structure of Los Manantiales was severely damaged. A team of volunteers from the Faculty of Architecture and the Engineering Institute of the Universidad Nacional Autónoma de México have been working on the current building survey, the damage report, and the restructuring project of that building. In the analyses carried out, we have been able to confirm that much of the damage suffered by the emblematic shell comes from years ago and is not a direct result of the earthquake.

As for the restaurant at the famous Hotel Casino de la Selva in Cuernavaca, it was inspired by Los Manantiales but was solved with another variant: a five-segment vault that generates a pentagonal floor plan. The distance between the supports (17 meters) was considerably larger than that in Xochimilco (12.50 meters). Therefore, the perimeter arches had a greater span than those in their predecessor, although their proportionally smaller height generated more reduced parabolas. The roof worked in conjunction with two other laminar structures: an attractive canopy marking the entrance to the building; and the hypar of the adjacent auditorium. Juan Antonio Tonda (Madrid 1931–Mexico City 2016), a close collaborator of Candela in Cubiertas Ala, took an active part in the design of this system of interlocking shells, as in that of other constructions in the complex. Unfortunately, the entire Casino de la Selva holiday complex disappeared at the beginning of this century during the peak of real estate speculation.

REACHING THE LIMIT

The Bacardi-Mexico bottling plant, located in Tultitlán, State of Mexico, at the northern exit from Mexico City, was designed in 1957 in Havana, Cuba. The industrial complex was in charge of the group of Cuban engineers and architects SACMAG (Sáenz-Cancio-Martín-Álvarez-Gutiérrez), who entrusted the structural design and construction of most of their buildings to Cubiertas Ala. Therefore, the complex ended up becoming a showcase for Candela's different variations: folded plates, cylindrical vaults, umbrellas, and groined vaults. With the latter, he worked out the surprising shells that house the bottling area, where he introduced a new variation by using inclined supports to separate the vaults from the ground, instead of displacing them from ground level as he had been doing since he built the Mexican Stock Exchange. In Bacardi, the hypars begin to unfold at a height of three meters, forming a continuity with the inclined columns that follow the parabolic curve of the groins, thus creating the rigidizing V-shaped arches that transmit the loads of the structure to the foundations. Each vault has a square floor plan of 30 meters per side, making them the largest clear-span shells built by Cubiertas Ala.

The bottling building was built in two phases.[11] In the first phase (1958–1960), three shells were made in a row, forming a 2,700-square-meter bay without interior supports. In the 1971 expansion, the original solution was "mirrored" to give the building the appearance it has today: six groin vaults with hypars that, grouped into two bays, enclose a space of 5,400 square meters with only two support areas inside. At each of these, the inclined columns of four vaults converge. The glazed perimeter enclosure and the triangular skylights, skillfully resolved at the joints of the shells to capture zenithal light, give great luminosity to a dynamic and diaphanous interior space that forms one of the most surprising architectural spaces of the twentieth century.

REPETITIONS OR VARIATIONS?

Having mastered the know-how for the design of these types of shells, Candela continued to make interesting variations, as shown by some works built later: the sales booth in the Fraccionamiento Verde Valle, Guadalajara (with Alfredo Terrazas de la Peña, 1961, now demolished), and the churches of La Florida (with Juan Antonio Tonda, Naucalpan, State of Mexico, 1964) and Nuestra Señora del Perpetuo Socorro (with Enrique de la Mora, Mexico City, 1966). The first of these churches introduces a new variant, since it is composed of two eight-segment vaults superimposed. The lower one forms the octagonal nave of the church, while the

8 Engineers and architects Sáenz-Cancio-Martín-Álvarez-Gutiérrez and Félix Candela, Bacardi bottling plant, Tultitlán: interior view of the second construction period, early 1970s

9 Félix Candela, La Florida church, Ciudad Satélite, Naucalpan: view of the construction site, 1964

10 Félix Candela, La Merced market, Mexico City, competition entry: bird's eye view, 1956

upper one is smaller and works as a curious little lantern reminiscent of Los Manantiales. As for the parish church of El Perpetuo Socorro, it is covered by the highest vault built by Cubiertas Ala. It rises over a rectangle of 20 × 22 meters (almost a square). The height of the shell varies from 21 meters at its lowest point, where the parabolas that form the groins intersect, to 25.40 meters at the crown of the perimeter arches. Its interior is surprising because of the high proportion between the space covered and the atmosphere generated by the light that enters through the large, colorful stained-glass windows that close three of its four sides.

Although the shells of the Bacardi-Mexico bottling plant were the largest hypar groined vaults ever built by Cubiertas Ala, there was a project that would have surpassed them if it had been built. For the competition for the new La Merced market (1956, won by Enrique del Moral), Candela proposed a complex system of hypar groined vaults with staggered heights that were grouped together to form an enormous Latin cross shape. The vault of the crossing was raised above the others and measured a whopping 52 meters per side.

The hypar groined vault emerged from the fruitful professional relationship that united the design talent of Enrique de la Mora and the analytical capacity of Fernando López Carmona with the pragmatism and audacity of Félix Candela, who was able to calculate and construct a conceptual idea that no engineer would

11 Félix Candela with Alberto Domingo and Carlos Lázaro, restaurant in the Oceanographic Park, Valencia, 2003

have dared to pursue. The family of concrete shells that emerged from that discovery was spectacular. This type of solution constitutes a contribution of Mexican architecture to the evolution of laminated reinforced concrete structures in the world.

In different countries you can identify the wake of Candela in buildings inspired by his structural solutions with different typologies such as umbrellas, straight-edge shells, and hypar groined vaults. The local interpretations of his masterpiece, such as the restaurant Los Manantiales in Xochimilco, stand out in such distant latitudes as Azerbaijan, Ecuador, and Germany. It is in this country that Dieter Ahting's and Ulrich Müther's Seerose café stands, built in Potsdam in 1983.

Candela's last professional work is also an eight-segment hypar groined vault. In 1994, when he was 84 years old, he was invited to develop two projects in the Oceanographic Park in Valencia, Spain. He was asked to take inspiration from two of his emblematic creations: San José Obrero church for the access to the underground aquarium (the final project was entrusted to another office) and Los Manantiales for the restaurant. He worked enthusiastically on the design of a clone of the shell he had built in Xochimilco 40 years earlier. However, he died in 1997, leaving the project unfinished. The structural calculation and construction were then left in the hands of the young Valencian engineers Alberto Domingo and Carlos Lázaro, who raised a worthy posthumous tribute to this genius of structural design.

In a lecture given in 1954, precisely when he was designing the cover for the Mexican Stock Exchange, Candela argued that "the originality of a correct structure is always ephemeral. Once a structural type is successful, its repetition is inevitable, since among the conditions of that success must be economy, efficiency, and ease of execution."[12] However, we can affirm that Candela never repeated himself, but rather developed inspired variations on a single theme in the manner of a musical composer.

References

Alarcón Azuela, Eduardo. "Aquella primavera perdida ... La historia del hotel Casino de la Selva en Cuernavaca," *Bitácora,* no. 23 (2011): 68–73.

Basterra Otero, Alfonso. "Félix Candela y el borde libre: El caso de la capilla de Palmira en Cuernavaca," *Bitácora,* no. 5 (2001): 38–47.

Del Cueto, Juan Ignacio. *Guía Candela.* Mexico City, 2013.

Del Cueto Ruiz-Funes, Juan Ignacio. "Candela in Xochimilco: The Construction and Evolution of the Restaurant 'Los Manantiales': A Masterpiece by Félix Candela in Mexico." In *Pioneros de la arquitectura moderna española: Aprender de una obra,* 72–87. Madrid, 2015.

Del Cueto Ruiz-Funes, Juan Ignacio. "Las bóvedas por arista de Félix Candela: variaciones sobre un mismo tema," *Bitácora,* no. 23 (2011): 38–47.

Del Cueto Ruiz-Funes, Juan Ignacio, and Monique Lambie, eds. *Félix Candela, 1910–2010.* Madrid, 2010.

Faber, Colin. *Candela: The Shell Builder.* New York, 1963. Translated into Spanish as *Las estructuras de Candela.* Mexico City, 1970.

Moreyra Garlock, Maria E., and David P. Billington. *Félix Candela: Engineer, Builder, Structural Artist.* New Haven/London, 2008.

The research for this essay was supported within the project DGAPA-UNAM PAPIIT IN-405218 "Cascarones de concreto armado en México y el mundo: pasado, presente, futuro."

1 For more information regarding the life and work of Candela, see Juan Ignacio del Cueto Ruiz-Funes and Monique Lambie, eds., *Félix Candela, 1910–2010* (Madrid, 2010); and Juan Ignacio del Cueto, *Guía Candela* (Mexico City, 2013).

2 Colin Faber, *Candela: The Shell Builder* (New York, 1963), 128.

3 See Archivo de Arquitectos Mexicanos, Facultad de Arquitectura, Universidad Nacional Autónoma de México (in the following: AAM FA-UNAM), Fondo Candela, Catalogue of Projects and Works of Cubiertas Ala S.A., 53/32.

4 Faber, *Candela,* 133 (see note 2).

5 Ibid., 177.

6 The shells were built between June 26 and November 22, 1956. See AAM FA-UNAM, Fondo Candela, Catalogue of Projects and Works of Cubiertas Ala S.A., 56-36.

7 Faber, *Candela,* 183 (see note 2).

8 The construction was carried out in a record time of six weeks, from October 5 to November 16, 1957. See AAM FA-UNAM, Fondo Candela, Catalogue of Projects and Works of Cubiertas Ala S.A., 57-91.

9 Álvarez Ordóñez was born in 1932. Thus, he was only 25 years old when he received this commission. Recently, he was awarded the National Architecture Prize 2018 in Mexico.

10 Faber, *Candela,* 194 (see note 2).

11 The construction of the first phase lasted two years, from August 2, 1958, to August 20, 1960. Eleven years later, in 1971, Juan Antonio Tonda developed the second phase. This was due to the fact that Candela was already living in the United States. See AAM FA-UNAM, Fondo Candela, Catalogue of Projects and Works of Cubiertas Ala S.A., 58-27 and 71-5.

12 Félix Candela, "Structural Form at the Service of an Eloquent Religious Architecture," lecture read before the Twenty-fifth National Conference in Church Architecture in Dallas, Texas, April 7, 1954. Unpublished manuscript, Félix and Dorothy Candela Archive, Department of Civil and Environmental Engineering, Princeton University, Princeton, USA.

Beautifully Shaped Forms
The Shells of Enrique de la Mora and Félix Candela

ELISA MARÍA TERESA DRAGO QUAGLIA

This study is a selection of some projects and buildings designed by Enrique de la Mora y Palomar architects' studio and calculated and built by Félix Candela's construction company, Cubiertas Ala. The objective is to show how the collaboration between both firms realized some of the most representative shell examples designed and built in Mexico. Also, from a personal point of view and interpretation, as inferred while analyzing the historical trends of their projects, it would seem that the teamwork between them was a kind of turning point for the two firms in their own future independent activities. This essay has a historical bias and is based on primary research sources, contrasting and assimilating the information between De la Mora's and Candela's documentary records, both preserved at the Archivo de Arquitectos Mexicanos (Archive of Mexican Architects) at the Faculty of Architecture of the Universidad Nacional Autónoma de México. As a starting point, the research is supported, mostly, from De la Mora's archive. The complement is the catalogue of Cubiertas Ala and, finally, research online at Félix Candela's free catalogue at Columbia University for cross-referencing information.[1] Through this, some questions started to emerge, as simple as trying to determine what their first collaboration was, if it was built or not, and where they met and how they started to collaborate.

At this point, it is essential to say that, although the projects that will be shown subsequently were conceived at De la Mora's office, all designs were resolved—although not necessarily built—thanks to the team that he led. De la Mora's creativity might not have been as good as it was without the structural geometric conceptualization of Fernando López Carmona and the collaboration with Alberto González Pozo. Those ideas were possible thanks to correction, calculation, and building by Félix Candela's company Cubiertas Ala and his close collaborator, Juan Antonio Tonda. All of them were essential. This demonstrates that good architecture is a product of collective capacities.

SEARCHES AND ENCOUNTERS

This chapter focuses on showing a kind of timeline about the projects and works, not necessarily built, where it is possible to reveal the collaboration between De la Mora and Candela. As a hypothesis, it could be established that the collaboration between both was fruitful because, on the one hand, Candela was able to build De la Mora's ideas. On the other hand, De la Mora was able to stimulate Candela, as a researcher, to open up the diversity of shapes, behavior, and geometry of

1 Félix Candela, San Cayetano church, Mexico City: sketch with floor plan and views for a competition entry, 1950

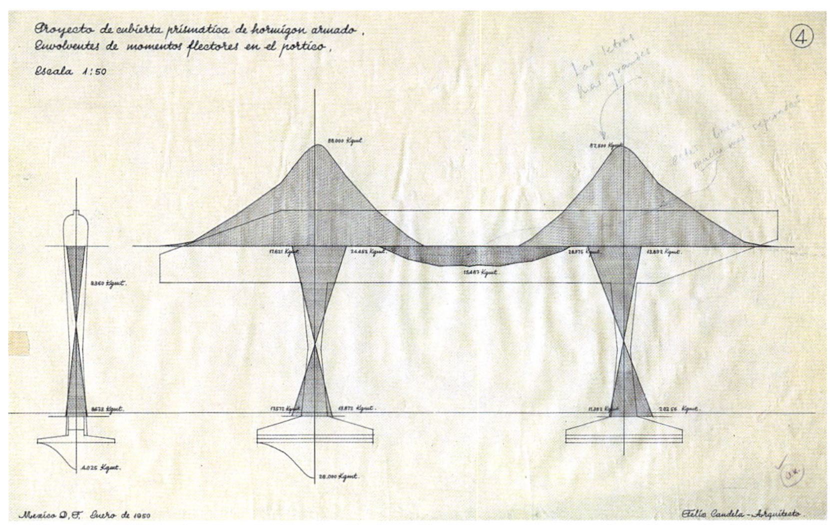

2 Félix Candela, project for a prismatic covering of reinforced concrete, 1950

shell structures. At this point, it is important to say that the first works registered in Félix Candela's papers at the Archivo de Arquitectos Mexicanos start from 1939: they consist of some drawings of a group of houses in Chihuahua and two commercial buildings, the first in Acapulco, in 1941, and another, dated 1949, in Mexico City. None of those projects reflects any special qualities of a great designer.

As the first documented works supporting this research show, the beginnings of his exploration of long-span spaces can be found for a winery in Xochimilco, Mexico City, in 1948, and for the project for a demountable president's tribune, in 1949, even though the solutions were not innovative and not different from standard solutions for these kinds of buildings. It was just a large space to be covered with a roof, with no other intentional design content. In 1950—before Cubiertas Ala, with its proposed thin lamina system, was officially established—Candela started to understand and solve geometric vaults with a project for a competition for the San Cayetano church in Mexico City.[2] This project was a clue, with a significant number of drawings and sketches that demonstrate the evolution of an idea. These are based on a neogothic style church and how the vault ribbed structures and the geometry of the materials work and are stressed in compression. The drawings also contemplate another idea that was not developed further for the competition: a parabolic thin vault that covers a classical Latin cross church floor plan. This design looks similar to the La Purisima Concepción church, built in the early 1940s by Enrique de la Mora in Monterrey.[3] After that project, Candela began to develop and study concrete structures with special attention, finding a flexible solution linked to structural behavior, as is shown in the study named "cubierta prismática" that does not belong to any particular project but is just research for a slim roof.[4]

3 Enrique de la Mora and Félix Candela, trading floor of the Mexican Stock Exchange, Mexico City, 1955: view from above

The possibility that Candela knew of De la Mora's project is based on the knowledge that it was published in Mexico and all around the world, in newspapers and magazines, as an example of what the modern ecclesiastical architectural language of the future should be. The very next project in Candela's documents that follows this timeline is a study of the behavior of thin prismatic concrete plate structures.[5]

After that, the skittle bowling alley Boliches Marsella, the Pisa Warehouse, and the Junior Club were the first projects assigned to and built under the Cubiertas Ala company signature, all of them in Mexico City, in 1950.[6] In the Boliches Marsella roof, the intention of a thin, corrugated vault is evident, but it was not yet a shell. External tensors spanning between columns that extend above the roof resist the outward thrust of the cylindrical/catenary vaults, which spring from the columns and are in compression.[7] This solution would be used some years later to solve other shells inserted between preexisting buildings, and, with it, it is possible to find a starting point that led to other pursuits too: covering large areas with thin structures that work by supporting themselves with geometry. This solution of a free floor with a good-looking roof came to popularize Candela's work as a great shell builder. Architects from all over Mexico started to call on him to solve, calculate, and build their projects. This same year, 1950, seems to be when Candela and De la Mora met and started their fruitful working relationship.

As a young architect, De la Mora's career started in 1934 with his first important project and building, the El Puerto de Liverpool department store in Mexico City. Between then and 1950 he designed and built more than 100 projects. Following a development parallel to Candela's, the documents that illustrate De la Mora's design research started some years before, showing a young architect with a special interest in solving modern structures. At the same time his projects show some consistent features: architectural program, use, purpose, and beauty were ruled by structural proposals. In his own words, modernity in architecture, in contrast to the main zeitgeist "form follows function," must be the result of concrete elastic attractive shapes: "[...] as I see it, because modern forms are used decoratively without having any vital or social content, it is the specification, the cladding materials (glass, mosaics, stone, etc.) that is asked to provide the originality that the creative impetus does not give. To overcome this dilemma we have to go deeper, to use agile, free, wide-span structures (lamellas, shells, etc.) that allow on the one hand the creation of new, as yet unimaginable, beautiful architectural forms, and on the other hand, the flexibility and capacity necessary in these structures, which responds to the social variability in which we live and which demands constant changes in needs and programs."[8]

As a way to understand this relationship between form and structure beyond function, it is possible to determine that De la Mora worked with three different kinds of structural category: first, predominantly pneumatic structures that work in tension as self-supporting skeletons; second, structures that work mainly in compression, such as the use of parabolic arches and; finally, tension-compression structures, with a structural bucket and tree system and bending structures with simple curvature and double curvature shells. The pneumatic structures were the main kind of self-supporting skeleton exploration. In his use of parabolic arches, Enrique de la Mora had developed two variants: translation parabolic arches and rotation parabolic arches. Finally, the proposals for flexion structures were solved with conoids, hyperbolic paraboloids, and reticulated nodal and branching structures.[9] Most of his mature projects, in the 1960s and 1970s, presented mixed solutions. But those are outside the scope of this essay.

All these structural models come together within a great denominator that was intended to release architectural plans, regardless of use, function, and architectural program, from intermediate vertical elements that impeded spatial fluidity and total spatial freedom—that is, a continuous search for the open plan in the broad meaning of the term. According to published analysis of historical documentation until now, Candela and De la Mora's first work together was the Bolsa Mexicana de Valores (Mexican Stock Exchange) trading floor.[10] However, in documents relating to three of De la Mora's other projects, it is apparent that Candela started to collaborate with him, as a construction consultant and structural designer, some years before their first famous shell together. Two of the projects, however, were unbuilt: the first, a civic center and a social project in Monterrey (1950–1952);[11] the second, a structural solution and budget for a building project for the Secretaría de Comunicaciones y Obras Públicas (SCOP,

Secretariat of Communications and Public Works) Center in Mexico City.[12] The third, the canopy construction for the shopping center El Puerto de Liverpool,[13] seems to be their first main work together. However, it is true that what started the most productive shell era for both was the trading floor (1953–1955).

STRUCTURES IN COMPRESSIVE STRESS: THE PARABOLIC ARCH

In 1939 De la Mora was assigned the first work that would become not only iconic, but an example of what a modern Catholic place of worship could be: the Purísima Concepción de María church in Monterrey.[14] Its importance lies in the formal exploration of shape and the use of the parabolic arches running through a Latin cross floor plan. This church has the peculiarity that the parabola starts from the ground, merging visually as a wall and becoming the roof in a continuous movement generated by two parabolic translation vaults. The crossing, instead of being resolved in a classic way with a domed drum, is intersected. As a structural exploratory device, and because of the heavy weight of the reinforced concrete, the solution was to propose a linking brace at the mid-height of the vault. It is important to highlight how, from the first inception of the project, a shell-like building envelope was introduced, and to consider that the scientific and technical elements were still being developed for its calculation. The detail of the cantilever at the facades, which seem to be thinner on the edge than they are, is a trompe-l'oeil. The resulting profile is the beginning of the idea of the shells: thin concrete slabs. From the inside, it is important to note the visual aspect that is produced by the intersection of the parabolic vaults. This was the main initiation of the modern groin vault, masterfully developed by Enrique de la Mora's study and Fernando López Carmona's knowledge of Euclidean geometry, structural behavior, and limits of material strength.[15] The roof-based parabola of translation, with a solid slab, would be abandoned by De la Mora almost immediately after finishing it. As stated earlier, Candela sketched this same idea for a church design competition ten years later.[16]

At the same time, the idea of solving spaces with huge parabolic vaults was a constant of De la Mora's design proposals. Instead of the barrel vault, the exploration of the parabolic arch shape evolved into a rotation around the center, as a vault. The unbuilt library for the Instituto Tecnológico de Estudios Superiores de Monterrey,[17] the San Luis Gonzaga church,[18] a first version for the Church of Nuestra Señora de Guadalupe in Madrid,[19] and an alternative design for the Church of Divina Providencia in Mexico City[20] show the design of a double-curvature solution with thin shells. However, it is important to emphasize that the acceptance of losing the shape and the structural solution with shells was not completely done. That is why, within the pilgrims' refuge in San Juan de los Lagos,[21] in order to obtain the parabolic shape in a less distorted way, it was reinforced laterally with four substantial lateral buttresses. This structure was solved with a mixed technique: reinforced concrete structure and ashlars. To get the shape of the arch that works in compression, a traditional material was used: stone. The proposed form, with simple and thin shells, would not withstand the structural load. This building was proof of it, and this structural exploration ended for De la Mora. Candela did not even try it. He knew that that solution would not be possible with thin concrete slabs or shells.

BENDING STRUCTURES: GROIN VAULT

From the transept of the La Purísima church, formed by the translation of the parabolic arches of the church, the next solution departed from the geometry but not from the material. At this point, Fernando López Carmona's expertise was crucial. This would be the beginning of the modern groin vault. Geometrically, it was possible to calculate and propose slim covering shells. However, the structural limits of the construction were still unknown. This was the starting point for the adventure undertaken by Félix Candela's newly created company.

Re-created in the trading floor for the Bolsa Mexicana de Valores, their first groin vault was geometrically solved in 1953 by Fernando López Carmona. It was structurally solved and built by Candela between December 1954 and July 1957.[22] In it, it is possible to discover that the result is a combination of two different explorations: to cover a large area without retaining the columns of the buildings built before. It had to be a slim, independent and free height structure. The idea of the shell surface being suspended at the border is close to the solution used for the Boliches Marsella roof, but instead of a slab spanning between concrete columns, thickened groin vaults were introduced.[23] This solution solved the need for natural illumination too, creating one of the most interesting, attention-grabbing perception spaces of modern architecture that shows the beauty of the shell shapes.

In 1954, and with that experience, Enrique de la Mora and Fernando López Carmona proposed a building for the reading room in the competition for the Jalisco State Library.[24] A rectangular prism with a proportion of 1:3 was planned with three groin vaults per long edge, but it was not built. However, the same solution would be adapted for San Antonio de las Huertas church[25] and, 20 years later, the same proposal was used again in the

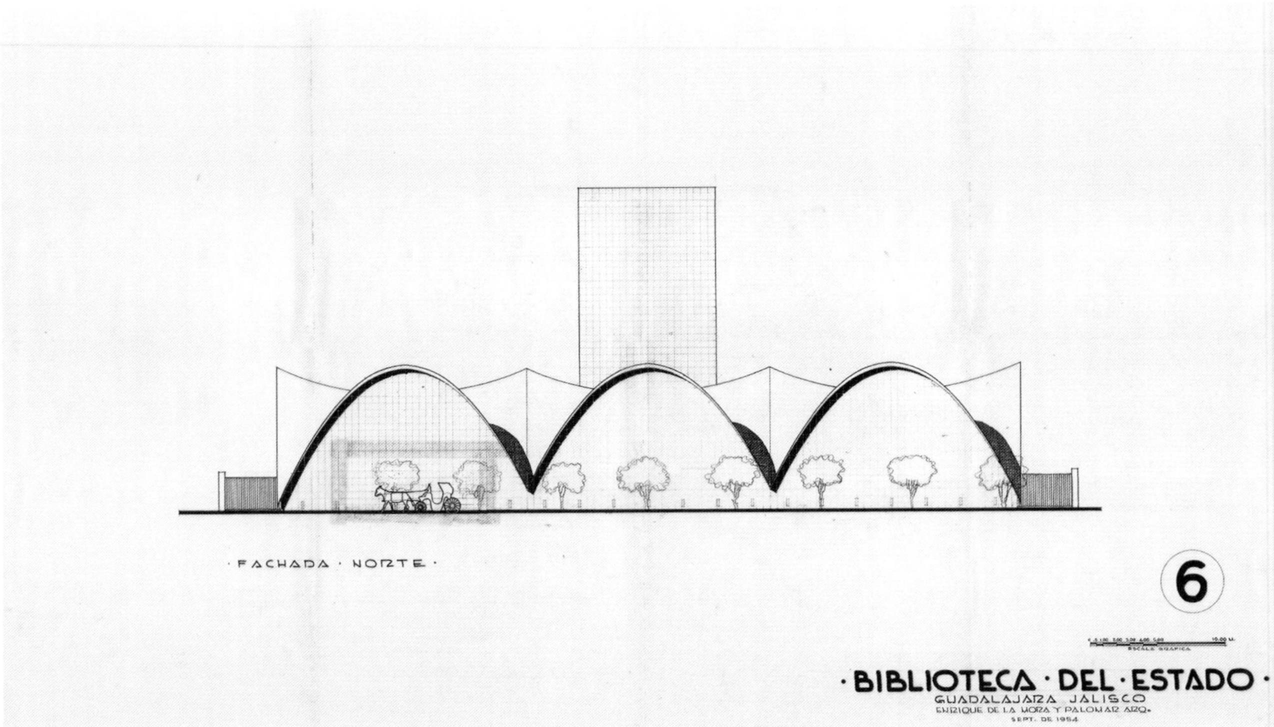

4 Enrique de la Mora, Jalisco State Library, Guadalajara, competition entry: view from the north, 1954

5 Enrique de la Mora and Félix Candela, San Antonio de las Huertas church, Mexico City, 1956: view of the construction site

Bacardi bottling plant in Tultitlán,[26] begun by Félix Candela in 1959/1960 and finished by Enrique de la Mora and Juan Antonio Tonda in 1972.[27]

HYPERBOLIC PARABOLOID (HYPAR)

Within the records for the civic center planned for the Colonia Cuauhtémoc neighborhood in Mexico City in early 1950, there is an undated document found in De la Mora's archive signed with the logo of Cubiertas Ala del Norte in the first stages of the project.[28] This development is probably from 1953. This urban project is the direct antecedent of San José Obrero church, which was built in the same neighborhood six years later. It is likely it was the only building of the project that was planned to sit in a new popular area surrounded by industries and which, at first, was thought of as a satellite of the nearby capital.

Nevertheless, the widely publicized chapel Nuestra Señora de la Soledad de San José el Altillo in Mexico City[29] was the first church with a hyperbolic parabolic shell composed of a single mantle, totally designed by Enrique de la Mora's team and structurally solved and built by Cubiertas Ala. This chapel was erected a decade ahead of the new provisions of the Second Vatican Council, and it became an exemplar of how a modern

6 Enrique de la Mora and Félix Candela, San José Obrero church, Monterrey, 1959: aerial view of the construction site

Catholic church should be planned. Apart from De la Mora, López Carmona, and Candela's working together, it is important to emphasize that this is one of the first Catholic churches in the world that not only broke with the customary shape in three dimensions but also changed the way the communal ritual was disposed around the priest. The original and unprecedented distribution of space was the transformation and modernity that had been sought for years for a new kind of open Catholic community in accordance with the times. At this point, designers of hypar shells started an exploration of solutions, possibilities, and positions, creating multiple spaces that were enclosed with different kinds of structures. And those were, with the new space distribution, the perfect spirit for new Catholic churches and chapels. The main idea was to make slender shells supported by thinner columns. The beautiful shape seemed to flow.

Some examples that followed, for almost a decade, using and exploring these hypar shell possibilities, designed and built together, were the cathedral in Tapachula[30] and the San José Obrero church,[31] both solved with two exterior linked mantles; the chapel San Vicente de Paul in Mexico City, solved with three hypar mantles;[32] the project for the main church for the Benedictine convent competition, an alternative proposal for Nuestra Señora de Guadalupe church in Monterrey and the Santuario de Guadalupe in Madrid were solved with eight mantles;[33] the chapel for the Minor Seminary solved with eight mantles of straight angular ruled surfaces; and the Church of Divina Providencia with three mantles linked together with a pinnacle.[34] An identical solution to this was proposed for three more churches: Nuestra Señora de los Remedios in San Luis Potosí,[35] Santa María Corredentora chapel in 1965,[36] and the chapel of the Colegio de México in San Luis Potosí.[37] This cycle of exploration closed with the Santa Cruz church in San Luis Potosí (1966–1974),[38] which was built with two mantles and looks like San José Obrero church, and is even closer to the original proposal for the first idea for the civic center in Monterrey.

A BRIEF CONCLUSION

As shown, the collaboration between the two firms started through their exploration and research into solving vaults and then hypar roofs in multiple situations, once the minimum thinness of the shell had been achieved. But this esthetic solution shows that, as we can determine from their later works together, after 14 creations they started to repeat themselves. It seems that they arrived at the climax of shape possibilities. It is interesting to note that the relationship started and ended with the same idea drawn in a sketch 16 years earlier. Enrique de la Mora abandoned the exploration of shell shapes and moved on to other structures that offered new and experimental possibilities, with one exception: he finished the last shell vaults for the Bacardi Company, in 1972, following the same module that Candela had used years before. The separation between their mutual interest and works came also because Candela moved to the United States at the end of the 1960s.

It is important to say that everyday use and living was not as perfect as the shape design and the beauty of the interior. Some of these buildings have been modified because they have several problems in common: they are not good at withstanding extreme weather; they do not work very well in terms of acoustic performance; and, if they are not well-maintained, they suffer from humidity problems due to moisture penetration through the roof. This are the reasons, apart from their high cost, why shells were not built anymore.

Even though this work has focused on shells that are mostly used to cover Catholic churches, it has shown that the same shapes could provide space for multiple uses and functions: church, library, factory, or auditorium. Also, even if those examples are the most beautiful and important architectural proposals, it does not mean that De la Mora and Candela only worked together on this kind of structural solution. To date, more than 20 collaborations have been found registered in both archives, and those deserve a special study, too.

1 Columbia University Libraries, New York, Archival Collections, Félix Candela architectural records and papers, 1950–1984, https://findingaids.library.columbia.edu/ead/nnc-a/ldpd_3464748/dsc/3.
2 See Iglesia de San Cayetano (concurso). Expedient 007, 1950, Archivo de Arquitectos Mexicanos, Facultad de Arquitectura, Universidad Nacional Autónoma de México, Mexico City (in the following AAM/FA/UNAM), Fondo Félix Candela. Francisco J. Serrano won the competition and built the church close to Parque España in Mexico City.
3 See Parroquia de la Purísima. Expedient 20, 1940–1943, AAM/FA/UNAM, Fondo Enrique de la Mora.
4 See Proyecto de Cubierta Prismática de concreto armado. Expedient 008, 1950, AAM/FA/UNAM, Fondo Félix Candela.
5 See Proyecto de Cubierta Prismática. Planos Barra 1, Separador 8, 1950, AAM/FA/UNAM, Fondo Félix Candela.
6 See Catálogo Cubiertas Ala (1950–1976). Register 50/1-9; 50/5; 50/6, AAM/FA/UNAM, Fondo Félix Candela.
7 See Colin Faber, *Candela: The Shell Builder* (London, 1963), 23.
8 Expedient 21, 1955, AAM/FA/UNAM, Fondo Enrique de la Mora, EDLM21, 1955. "[...] y se debe a mi modo de ver que las formas modernas son usadas decorativamente sin tener ya ningún contenido vital ni social, se le pide a la especificación, a los materiales de recubrimiento (vidrios, mosaicos, piedras, etc.) la originalidad que no da el ímpetu creador. Para superar esta crisis hay que ir a fondo, emplear estructuras ágiles, libres, amplias (lamelas, cascarones, etc.) que permitan por un lado la creación de nuevas formas arquitectónicas de belleza aún no imaginable y por el otro la elasticidad y capacidad necesarias en estas estructuras, que responde a la variabilidad social en la que vivimos y que demanda cambios constantes en las necesidades y programas." English translation by the author.
9 See Luis Fernando Solís, *Principios estructurales en la arquitectura mexicana* (Mexico City, 2010).
10 See Juan Ignacio del Cueto Ruiz-Funes, "Las bóvedas por arista de Félix Candela: variaciones sobre un mismo tema," *Bitácora,* no. 23 (2011): 38–47.
11 See Centro Cívico, Expedient 210, 1950, AAM/FA/UNAM, Fondo Enrique de la Mora; Cubiertas Ala catalogue (1950–1976). Register 50/17, AAM/FA/UNAM, Fondo Félix Candela.
12 See Centro SCOP, Expedient 123, 1950–1954, AAM/FA/UNAM, Fondo Enrique de la Mora.
13 See Almacenes Puerto de Liverpool, Expedient 03, 1936, AAM/FA/UNAM, Fondo Enrique de la Mora.
14 Also known as La Purísima. See Parroquia de la Purísima, Expedient 20, 1940–1943, AAM/FA/UNAM, Fondo Enrique de la Mora.
15 See Del Cueto Ruiz-Funes, "Las bóvedas por arista" (see note 10).
16 This solution was taken and used for many modern churches built in Mexico since then. As a point of fact, the Altillo chapel also became as famous as this, and was used as a model as well. This is a different kind of research, but it is important to mention it.
17 See Instituto de Estudios Superiores del Tecnológico de Monterrey, Expedient 52, 1945–1950, AAM/FA/UNAM, Fondo Enrique de la Mora.
18 See Templo San Luis Gonzaga, Expedient 213, 1956–1957, AAM/FA/UNAM, Fondo Enrique de la Mora.
19 See Santuario de Guadalupe, Expedient 276, 1958–1962, AAM/FA/UNAM, Fondo Enrique de la Mora.
20 See Iglesia Divina Providencia, Expedient 294, 1964–1970, AAM/FA/UNAM, Fondo Enrique de la Mora.
21 See Santuario para Peregrinos, Expedient 259, 1959–1965, AAM/FA/UNAM, Fondo Enrique de la Mora.
22 See Cubiertas Ala Catalogue, Register 53/32-3, AAM/FA/UNAM, Fondo Félix Candela.
23 See Faber, *Candela,* 128–133 (see note 7).
24 See Concurso para biblioteca pública del Estado de Jalisco, Expedient 179, 1954, AAM/FA/UNAM, Fondo Enrique de la Mora.
25 See Cubiertas Ala, Register 56/36-3 and 59/61-3, AAM/FA/UNAM, Fondo Félix Candela; and San Antonio de las Huertas, Expedient 178, 1957–1964, AAM/FA/UNAM, Fondo Enrique de la Mora.
26 See Cubiertas Ala, Register 54/42 and 59/61-3; 62-57; 62-68; 63-17; 63-43; 64-15; 64-19; and 65-19, AAM/FA/UNAM, Fondo Félix Candela.
27 See San Antonio de las Huertas, Expedient 351, 1970–1972, AAM/FA/UNAM, Fondo Enrique de la Mora.
28 The same place, Colonia Cuauhtémoc, where low-cost houses were built in 1953–1957 with umbrellas, Cubiertas Ala del Norte was directed by Fernando and Javier García Narro with Candela as consultant. See Centro Cívico, Expedient 210, 1950, AAM/FA/UNAM, Fondo Enrique de la Mora; and Columbia University Libraries, New York, Archival Collections, Félix Candela architectural records and papers, 1950–1984, box 38: folder 08-14, Paraguas Variables/Casas Cimientos, Cimientos, 1953.
29 See Capilla de Nuestra Señora de la Soledad, San José el Altillo, Expedient 193, 1955–1977, AAM/FA/UNAM, Fondo Enrique de la Mora; Columbia University Libraries, New York, Archival Collections, Félix Candela architectural records and papers, 1950–1984, drawer 72: folder 7, box 34: folder 24, box 34: folder 25, box 35: folder 14, box 40: folder 24–28, Our Lady of Soledad chapel, a.k.a. Chapel of St. Joseph of the Altillo (Mexico City), 1955; and Cubiertas Ala, Register 55/31-4, AAM/FA/UNAM, Fondo Félix Candela.
30 See Catedral de San Agustín, Expedient 206, 1958, AAM/FA/UNAM, Fondo Enrique de la Mora.
31 See San José Obrero, Expedient 233, 1957–1967, AAM/FA/UNAM, Fondo Enrique de la Mora; Columbia University Libraries, New York, Archival Collections, Félix Candela architectural records and papers, 1950–1984, box 35: folder 21, box 40: folder 66, box 40: folder 67, Iglesias, San José Obrero, 1959.
32 See Capilla de San Vicente de Paul, Expedient 253, 1959–1963, AAM/FA/UNAM, Fondo Enrique de la Mora; Columbia University Libraries, New York, Archival Collections, Félix Candela architectural records and papers, 1950–1984, box 35: folder 22, box 40: folder 72, Iglesias, San Vicente de Paul Coyoacán D.F., 1957–1960; and Cubiertas Ala catalogue, Register 58-86-38, AAM/FA/UNAM, Fondo Félix Candela.
33 See Santuario de Nuestra Señora de Guadalupe en Madrid, Expedient 278, 1960–1977, AAM/FA/UNAM, Fondo Enrique de la Mora; Columbia University Libraries, New York, Archival Collections, Félix Candela architectural records and papers, 1950–1984, box 35: folder 25, drawer 113: folder 20, Iglesias, Santuario de Nuestra Señora de Guadalupe, Madrid, 1962; and Cubiertas Ala catalogue, Register 61-64, AAM/FA/UNAM, Fondo Félix Candela.
34 See Iglesia de la Divina Providencia, Expedient 294, 1964–1970, AAM/FA/UNAM, Fondo Enrique de la Mora; Columbia University Libraries, New York, Archival Collections, Félix Candela architectural records and papers, 1950–1984, drawer 72: folder 7, Divine Providence church, 1966; and Cubiertas Ala catalogue, Register 65-76, AAM/FA/UNAM, Fondo Félix Candela.
35 See Nuestra Señora de los Remedios, Expedient 301, 1965, AAM/FA/UNAM, Fondo Enrique de la Mora; and Cubiertas Ala catalogue, Register 66-1, AAM/FA/UNAM, Fondo Félix Candela.
36 See Capilla de Santa María Corredentora, Expedient 303, 1965, AAM/FA/UNAM, Fondo Enrique de la Mora; and Cubiertas Ala catalogue, Register 66-27, AAM/FA/UNAM, Fondo Félix Candela.
37 See Iglesia de la Escuela Apostólica, Expedient 301, 1965, AAM/FA/UNAM, Fondo Enrique de la Mora; Columbia University Libraries, New York, Archival Collections, Félix Candela architectural records and papers, 1950–1984, drawer 72: folder 4, Chapel and crypt (San Luis Potosí, Mexico), undated, and drawer 113: folder 21, Mexico College, chapel (San Luis Potosí, Mexico), 1966; and Cubiertas Ala catalogue, Register 66-13, AAM/FA/UNAM, Fondo Félix Candela.
38 See Iglesia de la Santa Cruz, Expedient 310, 1966, AAM/FA/UNAM, Fondo Enrique de la Mora; and Columbia University Libraries, New York, Archival Collections, Félix Candela architectural records and papers, 1950–1984, drawer 72: folder 5, Holy Cross church (San Luis Potosí, Mexico) 1965.

7 Enrique de la Mora and Félix Candela, San Vicente de Paul chapel, Mexico City, 1960

8 Enrique de la Mora and Félix Candela, Nuestra Señora de los Remedios church, San Luis Potosí, 1967

9 Enrique de la Mora and Félix Candela, Santa Cruz church, San Luis Potosí, 1974

The Bodily Economies of Concrete Technologies

MARÍA GONZÁLEZ PENDÁS

Halfway through a working day in November 1966, Joaquín Adam Barrales, a 26-year-old *peón* employed by the Mexican construction company Cubiertas Ala, was in the midst of decentering one of the company's thin-concrete shells, structures designed by its founder and architect, Félix Candela. Barrales balanced over the twisted planes and wooden formwork that held the hardened concrete when, as he would later recall it, "a wood beam of a weight of over 110 pounds" fell over, crushing his left wrist. His hand incapacitated, Barrales left the site. It was his second accident in the five months he had been with the company.[1]

Designers and scholars have thoroughly studied the structural, aesthetic, and economic virtues of the thin-concrete shells built by Cubiertas Ala in the roughly two decades that it stayed in business under the engineering shrewdness of Candela and the managerial work of his siblings Antonio and Julia. In the mid-twentieth century, shell technology was widely embraced and critical to the landscape of development across Latin America, from Mexico to Uruguay, a phenomenon in which Cubiertas Ala played a leading role. As other chapters in this publication remind us, scholars have long taken note, eagerly celebrating Candela's work. This has ranged from detailed surveys and biographies—Candela's trajectory from precarious political exile of fascism to the higher echelons of Latin American modernization and North American academia deserves as much—to thorough reconstructions and calculations of the structural system he developed with dedication, innovation, and unquestionable success. By the time of Barrales's mishap, Cubiertas Ala had designed or built more than 500 concrete shells in a variety of geometries for everything from churches and markets to factory plants, across Mexico and beyond. With Candela deemed a "magician of concrete," his shells were already the subject of countless articles, a monograph, and a handful of prestigious international prizes.[2]

Absent from the ongoing recognition of the shells, both at the time of their construction and in the scholarship that followed, were stories like that of Barrales and the accident that incapacitated him, precluding him from working, at least temporarily, in mid-November 1966. Certainly neither the episode nor its protagonist seemed particularly noteworthy. Barrales, likely an indigenous migrant from Puebla, was one of hundreds of *peones*, the least skilled and lowest-ranking construction workers employed by Cubiertas Ala at any given time; his accident, similarly one of many that characterized work on site. Only three days after Barrales's misfortune, for instance, Victor Rivero

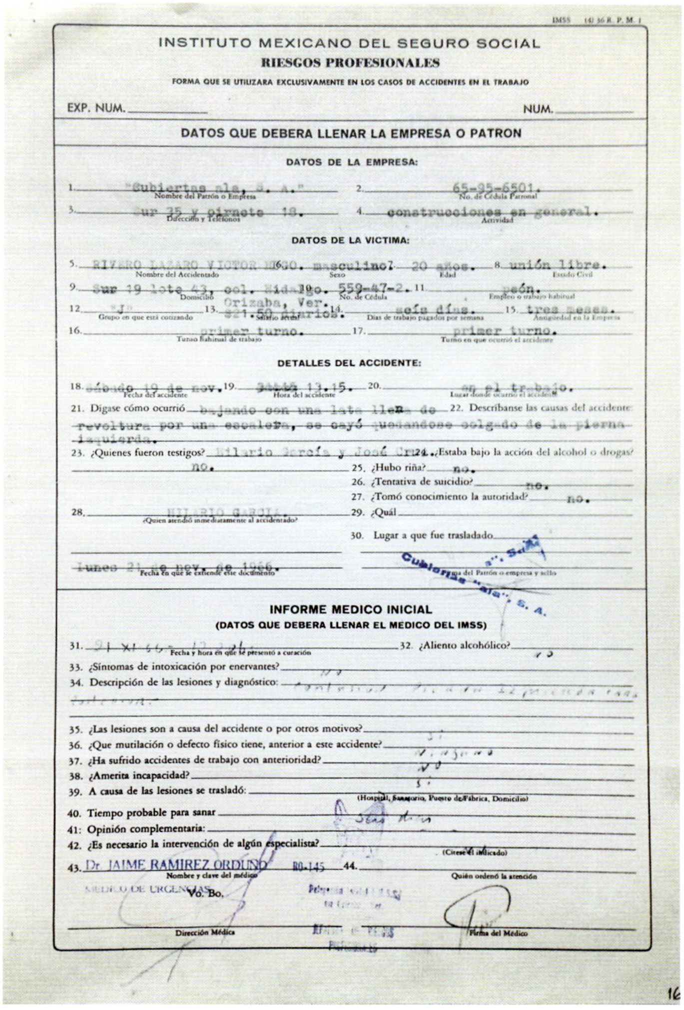

IMSS 14 36 R. P. M. 1

INSTITUTO MEXICANO DEL SEGURO SOCIAL
RIESGOS PROFESIONALES
FORMA QUE SE UTILIZARA EXCLUSIVAMENTE EN LOS CASOS DE ACCIDENTES EN EL TRABAJO

EXP. NUM. ____ NUM. ____

DATOS QUE DEBERA LLENAR LA EMPRESA O PATRON

DATOS DE LA EMPRESA:

1. "Cubiertas ala, S. A." (Nombre del Patrón o Empresa) 2. 65-95-6501. (No. de Cédula Patronal)
3. Sur 35 y pirnete 18. (Dirección y Teléfonos) 4. construcciones en general. (Actividad)

DATOS DE LA VICTIMA:

5. RIVERO LAZARO VICTOR HUGO. (Nombre del Accidentado) 6. masculino (Sexo) 7. 20 años. (Edad) 8. unión libre. (Estado Civil)
9. Sur 19 lote 43, col. Hidalgo. Orizaba, Ver. (Domicilio) 10. 559-47-2. (No. de Cédula) 11. peón. (Empleo o trabajo habitual)
12. "J" (Grupo en que está cotizando) 13. $21.50 diarios. (Salario actual) 14. seis días. (Días de trabajo pagados por semana) 15. tres meses. (Antigüedad en la Empresa)
16. primer turno. (Turno habitual de trabajo) 17. primer turno. (Turno en que ocurrió el accidente)

DETALLES DEL ACCIDENTE:

18. sábado 19 de nov. (Fecha del accidente) 19. 13.15. (Hora del accidente) 20. en el trabajo. (Lugar donde ocurrió el accidente)
21. Dígase cómo ocurrió bajando con una lata llena de 22. Descríbanse las causas del accidente revoltura por una escalera, se cayó quedandose colgado de la pierna izquierda.
23. ¿Quienes fueron testigos? Hilario García y José Cruz. 24. ¿Estaba bajo la acción del alcohol o drogas? no.
25. ¿Hubo riña? no.
26. ¿Tentativa de suicidio? no.
27. ¿Tomó conocimiento la autoridad? no.
28. HILARIO GARCIA. (¿Quien atendió inmediatamente al accidentado?) 29. ¿Quál
30. Lugar a que fue trasladado

lunes 21 de nov. de 1966. (Fecha en que se extiende este documento) Cubiertas "ala", S. A. (Firma del Patrón o empresa y sello)

INFORME MEDICO INICIAL
(DATOS QUE DEBERA LLENAR EL MEDICO DEL IMSS)

31. (Fecha y hora en que se presentó a curación) 32. ¿Aliento alcohólico?
33. ¿Síntomas de intoxicación por enervantes?
34. Descripción de las lesiones y diagnóstico:
35. ¿Las lesiones son a causa del accidente o por otros motivos?
36. ¿Que mutilación o defecto físico tiene, anterior a este accidente?
37. ¿Ha sufrido accidentes de trabajo con anterioridad?
38. ¿Amerita incapacidad?
39. A causa de las lesiones se trasladó: (Hospital, Sanatorio, Puesto de Fábrica, Domicilio)
40. Tiempo probable para sanar
41: Opinión complementaria:
42. ¿Es necesario la intervención de algún especialista? (Cítese el indicado)
43. Dr. JAIME RAMIREZ ORDUÑO RO-145 (Nombre y clave del médico) 44. (Quién ordenó la atención)
MEDICO DE URGENCIAS
Vo. Bo.
Dirección Médica Firma del Médico

16

1 Labor Risk form of the Mexican Social Security Institute for an employee of Cubiertas Ala, 1966

Lázaro, 20 years old and also a *peón*, was "walking down a stair with a bucket full of *revoltura* [liquid concrete]" when he tripped and was left "hanging from the left leg," as he would describe it. Later in the month, José Bautista Romero, a higher ranking *albañil* (bricklayer), squashed a finger of his left hand while mounting formwork. José Cardenas Contreras, another *peón*, slipped while carrying a bucket "of about 34 kg of *revoltura*" and lost a toenail. Avelino Carrera Trujillo stepped on a 4-inch (10-centimeter) nail that pierced through his left foot.[3]

These are just a few of the many episodes of this kind recorded in the Riesgos Profesionales (Labor Risks) forms that began to track on-site accidents for the Instituto Mexicano del Seguro Social (IMSS, Mexican Social Security Institute) in the 1960s. Part of an archive of shell history heretofore untapped—the administrative trail of shell construction neglected even by Félix Candela—these documents capture everyday life on-site.[4] And as they tell it, on the crowded and informal sites of Cubiertas Ala, accidents like Barrales's were certainly commonplace.

In their ordinariness, these stories remain unremarked in our consideration of thin-shell architecture, their implications largely unquestioned. Much in the vein of the dominant discourse deployed both in modern architecture historiography and architects' positivist uses of history and technology, evaluations of shell architecture doggedly focus on the exceptional: the formal breadth of the structures, the genius of the author, the numerical virtues of the geometries. Amid accounts of innovation and invention, Barrales's ordinary mishap seems to have held little value for the shells and for our understanding of their conditions of production.

Yet upon close inspection, Barrales's misfortune proves not only telling but also significantly valuable to the shells' history. As this chapter will sketch, and as I have argued elsewhere in more detail, the value of these "normal accidents" was as technological as it was indeed economic.[5] For Barrales's accident and those of his coworkers not only shed light on the manual, labor-intensive technologies that sustained shell building. They also, and most critically, help us unwrap the cost of the shells well beyond their financial valuation, explicating the bankruptcy of Cubiertas Ala, the obsolescence of shell technology that ensued, and the social and economic relations that the shells effectively produced. In all of their ordinariness and anonymity, workers like Barrales and their routine accidents offer an archive with which to craft a more critical, less colonial approach to the history of some of modern architecture's most alluring objects.

That Barrales's injury was to the hand, as others' were to hands and feet, was in fact not accidental, as shell technology relied chiefly on the bodily work deployed during construction. This point has not gone unnoticed. Following Candela's own descriptions of the design process, many have explained the ways in which his engineering know-how developed through the testing of materials and geometries on-site as opposed to modeling the shells mathematically in the studio.[6] This amounted to a collective, progressive, and primarily empirical process of architectural innovation, what I have described elsewhere in terms of an "artisanal epistemology" that relied heavily on the workers and their craft.[7]

Félix Candela was always quick to praise his *maestro de obras* (site foreman) and, in numerous lectures and publications, advanced a theory of technology that cast the shells as leading a craft-based model of modernization alternative to, and redemptive of, the alienating forces of industrial mechanization. For Candela, shell building retained manual labor at the center of modern production to advance an ethics of progress that "does not exclude man but instead facilitates simple instruments to lighten his labor, without eliminating him."[8] As Candela envisioned them, the shells were not only part of Mexico's growing infrastructure in the age of development. While under construction, they were also disciplining instruments for the *peón* as he entered a new technical workforce, a process of self-modernization

2 Joaquín Álvarez Ordóñez and Félix Candela, Los Manantiales restaurant, Xochimilco, Mexico City, 1958: view of the construction site; photograph by Juan Guzmán

3 Enrique de la Mora and Félix Candela, trading floor of the Mexican Stock Exchange, Mexico City, 1955: view of the construction site

performed through the body, as "the command of a technique," he wrote, "grows out of a training period of muscular and mental habits."[9]

Candela's idealization of the shells, their construction site, and the bodies that inhabited them found visual counterpart in photographs by the likes of Armando Salas Portugal and Juan Guzmán.[10] Widely published at the time, these snapshots of life on site exposed how great a value shell technology placed in manual labor. Barely protected by straw hats and espadrilles, workers appear in the photographs stirring the aggregate with wooden poles and laying steel rods by hand; troweling the concrete and nailing wood planks while balancing on their feet; shouldering full buckets up the shells and the empty buckets down. Perhaps most tellingly, workers appear atop the shell right after completion, attesting to its structural viability with the weight of their bodies. The worker's body was in fact the main technical device in shell technology.[11]

Yet neither these alluring images nor Candela's words dwelt much on the specificity of the worker or zoomed into the economic relations that were at stake. As heroic representations of the worker and his labor, both accounts in fact hid the subjects that were at the center of the narrative: in the pictures, their faces behind their hats, and in Candela's statements, their embodied risk obscured by a rhetoric of efficiency and "humanism." Cubiertas Ala employed hundreds on any given day—between 300 and 600 as officially recorded once the Mexican legislature mandated social security registration in late 1959.[12] However, in his many lectures and publications Candela seemed oblivious to these numbers. As insistent as he was on the improbable numbers of the shells' structural and financial systems—the 2-inch (5-centimeter) thickness, the 50 cents cost per square foot—he rarely quantified the sheer excess of bodies that inhabited the shells, the high risks that they incurred, or the amount of labor that went into shell building—the thousands of nails nailed and buckets of *revoltura* mixed, shouldered, and troweled.[13]

Félix Candela's neglect towards this other form of calculating the shells was in many ways a necessary one. For these excessive numbers, what I refer to as the shells' corporal economy, radically undermined the "mantra of efficiency" he so proudly mobilized to justify the financial and aesthetic virtues of the system.[14] Indeed, shell architecture was appealing to his clientele and financially viable, at all, mainly on the basis of efficiency, an argument only sustainable under the precarious labor conditions that predated policy reforms throughout the 1960s. In addition to establishing a stronger social security apparatus through the IMSS, President Adolfo López Mateos set minimum daily wages for government employees in 1960, which Gustavo Díaz Ordaz extended to all nongovernmental workers in 1964.[15] Cubiertas Ala contracted some pub-

4 Jorge González Reyna and Félix Candela, Cosmic Rays Pavilion, Ciudad Universitaria, Mexico City, 1951: view of the construction site

lic projects and regularly adjusted to these numbers. From 1954 to 1964 the *peón*'s daily wage rose from 9.60 to 21.50 pesos; by 1973, this number had doubled to 41.43 pesos.[16] Ten times higher than when the company started up, minimum wages threw the shell's alleged efficiency out of balance. In addition, the company faced its share of social security payment, the so-called Cuotas de Obreros Patronales, which at the time was primarily dedicated to cover sick leave and medical costs.

These new policies gave Candela's heroic-yet-abstract "man" specificity and a quantifiable form through documents that named the bodies populating the sites and numbered their attendant economies: long handwritten lists of workers with their full names, days worked, skill groups, and pesos earned; social security identification cards; weekly summaries of number of workers employed.[17] From then on, no matter how thin the shells rose, there was no hiding their excesses. These documents follow the ubiquitous but invisible *peón* as he turned into an actor of modernity (something Candela had hoped for), specifically as a worker with legal rights (something he had not, as he condemned unions and other workers' rights).[18] Critically, this paper trail helps us to understand how the risks that afforded the speculative drive behind the invention of shell technology transferred to, or at least became shared by, the worker's body, the contractor, and the state.

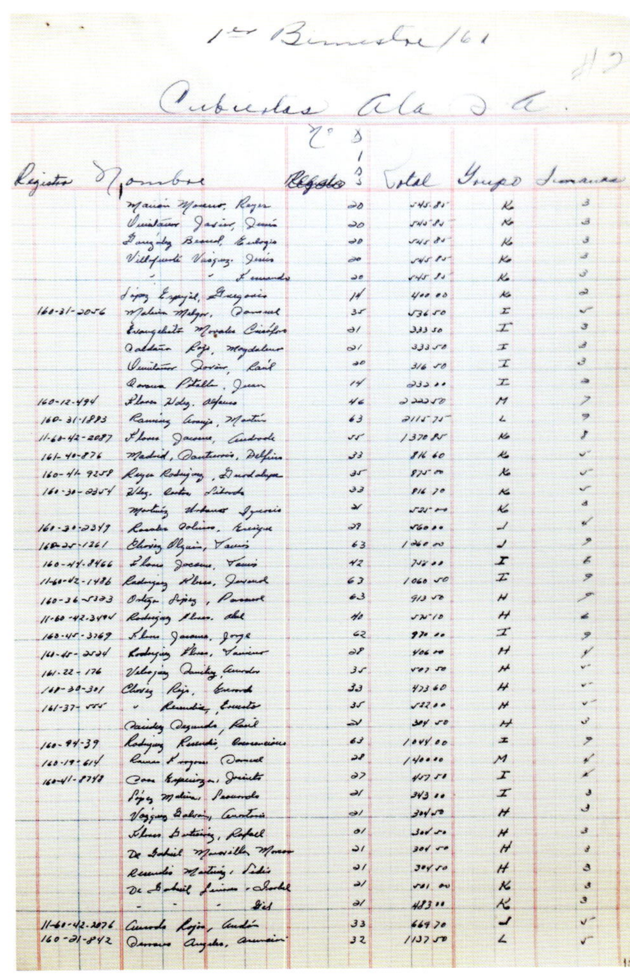

1er Bimestre / 61

Cubiertas Ala S.A.

Registro	Nombre	Días	Total	Grupo	Semana

5 Bimonthly workers' list of Cubiertas Ala, 1961

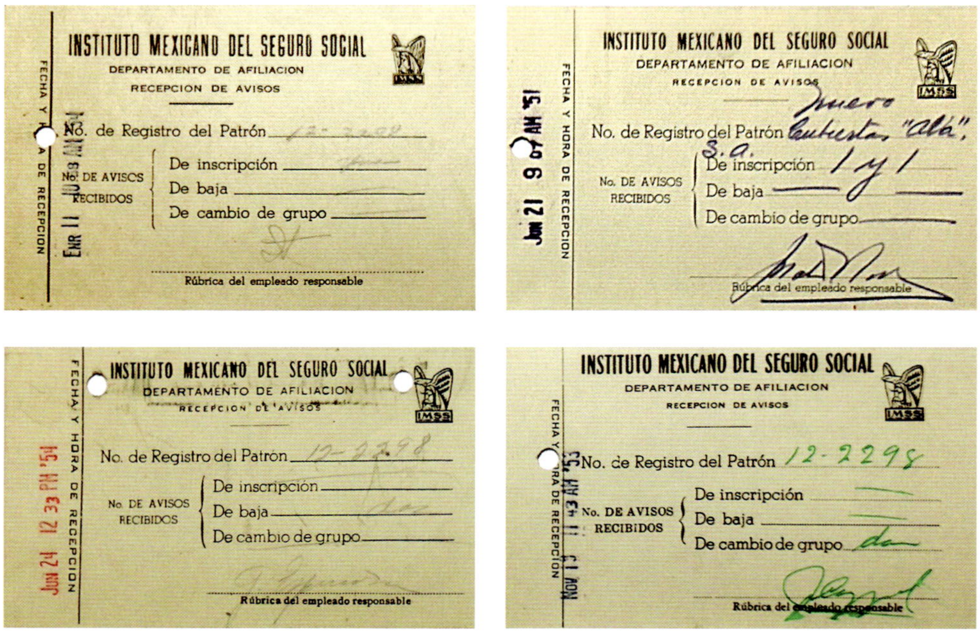

INSTITUTO MEXICANO DEL SEGURO SOCIAL
DEPARTAMENTO DE AFILIACION
RECEPCION DE AVISOS
FECHA Y HORA DE RECEPCION
No. de Registro del Patrón
No. DE AVISOS RECIBIDOS
De inscripción
De baja
De cambio de grupo
Rúbrica del empleado responsable

6 Social security cards for employees of Cubiertas Ala, 1951–1954

The Riesgos Profesionales forms dutifully performed this transvaluation of risk—in the document that introduced us to our protagonist Barrales, for instance, who would have otherwise fallen into the oblivion of normalcy. The form records how, following the mishap, Barrales received first aid on-site, after which he reported to Cubiertas Ala and then visited an IMSS-approved physician, who granted him a seven-day leave from work. His coworkers followed protocol to similar outcomes. Collectively, the documents capture the mounting costs as workers' absences piled up. In addition, the IMSS filed debt claims against the company to cover expenses from accidents that "proved to have been produced intentionally by the patron." Critically, these claims were retroactive. On May 4, 1967, for instance, Cubiertas Ala was debited 295.20 pesos to reimburse for an injury that Juan Cervantes Martínez had suffered five years earlier.[19]

The overall cost of these many accidents and these many workers once they took on legal form is unknown, but it was significant enough to seal the fate of the shells. On July 4, 1973, as the administrative archive continues to tell, an official of the Secretaria de Hacienda y Crédito Público (SHCP), the Mexican internal revenue service, walked into the company's offices in the center of Mexico City and executed a seizure order for the company's furniture, typewriters, and electric adding machines. Three remaining calculating machines were seized on October 22. They were all in impeccable condition. With an estimated value of just over 24,000 pesos, the goods were meant to settle overdue "Cuotas de Obreros Patronales."[20] The episode was the endpoint of a financial fall long in the making. Having filed a petition to cease operations with the SHCP in November 1970, and with very few projects from then on, Cubiertas Ala was virtually out of business after the 1973 foreclosure. At the top of the bankruptcy list were overdue social security and labor payments. The experience of workers on site had played a crucial role in inventing shell technology throughout the 1950s—and it was likewise central to the obsolescence of shell technology by the 1970s.[21]

As we revisit Félix Candela's work through a global narrative of crossings and exchanges with his European peers, we might do well to also craft a less technodeterministic, more critical and postcolonial approach. To this end, I have here called attention to what were considered normal stories of construction labor and to the technologies, bodies, economies, and social relations that they help illuminate in Mexico and beyond. Labor remains a glaring absence in most architectural histories, its actors notoriously invisible. However, as with Barrales's accident, ghostly traces of labor are there for us to reconstruct, hidden in alternative archives and latent in the materiality of the buildings themselves. However, these traces, and the histories of the often subaltern subjects of architecture, will only gain legibility through an analytical shift, one that moves away from the history of innovation and invention and toward the history of technology in use and maintenance;[22] away from hagiographies and authorship and toward the politics of architectural production; away from reconstructions of forms and toward critical deconstructions of form-making.

Approaching shell technology in these terms, as a social history of construction labor, retains numbers and calculations as a method of architectural research. But they are not the well-known numbers of the shells' structural rationalism or material economy, and they certainly will not help mimic or repeat this architecture across time and space. Quite the contrary, the other set of numbers sustaining thin-concrete shells was radical in its historicity and pertained to the immeasurable numbers of *peones* and buckets, and the enormous risk.

These excessive numbers undermine the touted "efficiency" and "rationalism" of the system to reveal the bodily economy shaping the shells as aesthetic objects, as a technological system and, perhaps most critically, as a site of social and political change—that is to say, as a site of history.

My argument is, however, far from being historiographical alone. Today, as labor conditions and the human costs of construction remain largely neglected by architects and historians, workers and their bodies continue to serve architecture as resources for exploitative extraction.[23] Underpinning the invention of shell architecture in midcentury Mexico was the mining of value from craft practices and indigenous bodies by the white technical elites. This dynamic is indeed normal and, sadly, far from exceptional; the shells but a sliver of a longer history in which spectacular architecture continues to give form to the uneven economies and labor exploitation that define developmentalism at its core. It is well past time that we more candidly unpack the normal conditions of production of our most beautiful architecture, ugly as these histories might be. For neglect only further normalizes the social, economic, and racial relations that were at stake.

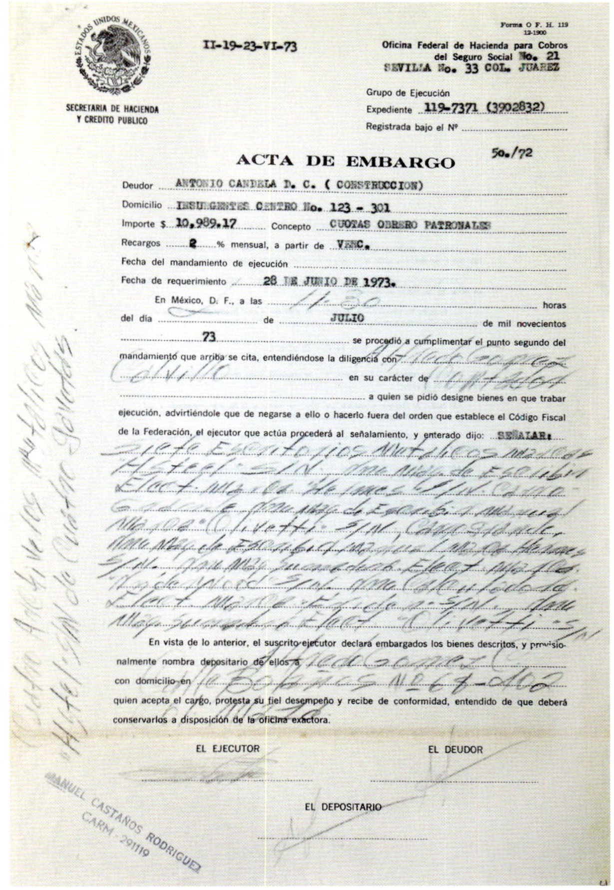

ESTADOS UNIDOS MEXICANOS

SECRETARIA DE HACIENDA Y CREDITO PUBLICO

II-19-23-VI-73

Forma O F. H. 119 12-1900

Oficina Federal de Hacienda para Cobros del Seguro Social No. 21
SEVILLA No. 33 COL. JUAREZ

Grupo de Ejecución
Expediente 119-7371 (3902832)
Registrada bajo el Nº

50./72

ACTA DE EMBARGO

Deudor ANTONIO CANDELA D. C. (CONSTRUCCION)
Domicilio INSURGENTES CENTRO No. 123 - 301
Importe $ 10,989.17 Concepto CUOTAS OBRERO PATRONALES
Recargos 2 % mensual, a partir de VENC.
Fecha del mandamiento de ejecución
Fecha de requerimiento 28 DE JUNIO DE 1973.

En México, D. F., a las 11.30 horas del día de JULIO de mil novecientos 73 se procedió a cumplimentar el punto segundo del mandamiento que arriba se cita, entendiéndose la diligencia con en su carácter de a quien se pidió designe bienes en que trabar ejecución, advirtiéndole que de negarse a ello o hacerlo fuera del orden que establece el Código Fiscal de la Federación, el ejecutor que actúa procederá al señalamiento, y enterado dijo: SEÑALAR:

En vista de lo anterior, el suscrito ejecutor declara embargados los bienes descritos, y provisionalmente nombra depositario de ellos a con domicilio en quien acepta el cargo, protesta su fiel desempeño y recibe de conformidad, entendido de que deberá conservarlos a disposición de la oficina exactora.

EL EJECUTOR EL DEUDOR

EL DEPOSITARIO

MANUEL CASTAÑOS RODRIGUEZ CARM - 291119

7 Certificate of the Mexican internal revenue service on the seizure of Cubiertas Ala's office equipment, 1973

1 See Riesgos Profesionales, Archivo de Arquitectos Mexicanos, Facultad de Arquitectura, Universidad Nacional Autónoma de México (in the following: AAM FA-UNAM), Archivos Cubiertas Ala, Folder 8.7. My research within this archive would not have been possible without the wonderful support of Dino del Cueto, Lourdes Cruz, Cristina Uribe, and Hugo Hernández Quezada. All translations by the author unless otherwise noted.

2 "Wizard of the Shells," *The Architectural Forum* 111 (1959): 154–159. The literature on Candela's shells is vast. See Juan Ignacio del Cueto Ruiz-Funes and Monique Lambie, ed., *Félix Candela, 1910–2010* (Madrid, 2010); Pepa Cassinello, ed., *Félix Candela: Centenario 2010: La conquista de la esbeltez/Centenary 2010: The Achievement of Slenderness* (Madrid, 2010); and Enrique X. de Anda Alanís, *Félix Candela, 1910–1997: The Mastering of Boundaries* (Cologne, 2008). Since the seminal monograph by Colin Faber, *Candela: The Shell Builder* (New York, 1963), the most common interpretation of Candela pertains to a technical description of the shells. See Maria E. Moreyra Garlock and David P. Billington, *Félix Candela: Engineer, Builder, Structural Artist* (New Haven/London, 2008). I have offered an alternative approach by unpacking the political ideology underpinning Candela's theory of technology in "Technics and Civilization: Félix Candela's Geopolitical Imaginary," in Patricio del Real and Helen Gyger, ed., *Latin American Modern Architecture: Ambiguous Territories* (New York/London, 2013), 270–290, here 271. A critical revision of Candela's work in the political context of midcentury Mexico is in Luis M. Castañeda, *Spectacular Mexico: Design, Propaganda, and the 1968 Olympics* (Minneapolis, 2014).

3 See Riesgos Profesionales (see note 1).

4 Candela did not include them in the voluminous archive he brought with him when he left Mexico. For an account of Candela's relationship with the USA see Angela Giral, "Félix Candela en los Estados Unidos," *Bitácora*, no. 23 (2011): 48–57.

5 See María González Pendás, "50 Cents a Foot, 14,500 Buckets: Concrete Numbers and the Illusory Shells of Mexican Economy," *Grey Room*, no. 71 (2018): 14–39; and eadem, "Errores concretos, o la magia de los cascarones," *Bitácora*, no. 37 (2018): 32–43. For a social history of so-called normal accidents in technological or financial systems, see Charles Perrow, *Normal Accidents: Living with High-Risk Technologies* (Princeton, 2011).

6 Most thoroughly in Moreyra Garlock and Billington, *Félix Candela*, 170–173 (see note 2). A firsthand account of the workings of Cubiertas Ala is in Juan Antonio Tonda, "Experiencias y vivencias: Aprendiendo con Candela," in Del Cueto Ruiz-Funes and Lambie, ed., *Félix Candela*, 241–262, here 245–250 (see note 2).

7 González Pendás, "50 Cents a Foot," 22 (see note 5).

8 Félix Candela, "Influencia de la tecnología en la creatividad arquitectónica [1975]," *Arquitectura*, no. 303 (1995): 60–66, here 66.

9 Ibid., 67.

10 See Elisa Lozano, "Fragmentos: Candela: Arquitectura, fotografía y cine," in Del Cueto Ruiz-Fues, ed., *Félix Candela*, 211–240 (see note 2).

11 The body as a technology crucial to architecture has a long history. For a classic articulation, see John Ruskin, *The Seven Lamps of Architecture* (London, 1849). Historians of early modernity have called attention to the hand as both a technology and a means of knowledge; see Lissa Roberts, Simon Schaffer and Peter Dear, eds., *The Mindful Hand: Inquiry and Invention from the Late Renaissance to Early Industrialisation* (Amsterdam, 2007).

12 Article 123-B, December 30, 1959

13 Following from Dino del Cueto's suggestions in his unrelenting dissemination of Candela's work atop many shells, I have unpacked these numbers—most notably the number of buckets Dino often refers to—and their cost. See González Pendás, "50 Cents a Foot" (see note 5).

14 See Jennifer Karns Alexander, *The Mantra of Efficiency: From Waterwheel to Social Control* (Baltimore, 2008). For Candela's argument on efficiency see note 2 in this essay.

15 See Nora Hamilton, *The Limits of State Autonomy: Post-Revolutionary Mexico* (Princeton, 1982); and Dan La Botz, *The Crisis of Mexican Labor* (New York, 1988).

16 See Lista bimestral de trabajadores, AAM FA-UNAM, Archivos Cubiertas Ala, Folder 8.7. This argument was advanced by Juan Ignacio del Cueto, "El ocaso de los cascarones," in Del Cueto Ruiz-Funes and Lambie, ed., *Félix Candela*, 103–106, here 106 (see note 2); and Castañeda, *Spectacular Mexico*, 279 (see note 2).

17 See AAM FA-UNAM. Archivos Cubiertas Ala, Folders 8.3–8.14.

18 See Félix Candela, "Reflexiones de un tripulante sobrecogido [1969]," in *En defensa del formalismo y otros escritos* (Bilbao, 1985), 129–132, here 131.

19 Ley de Seguro Social, Article 48, as stipulated by the Debt Services of the IMSS in a "Notificación" to Cubiertas Ala, 4 May 1967, AAM FA-UNAM, Archivos Cubiertas Ala, Folder 8.10.

20 Actas de Embargo, 1973, AAM FA-UNAM, Archivos Cubiertas Ala, Folder 8.10.

21 A new episode to Daniel M. Abramson, *Obsolescence: An Architectural History* (Chicago, 2016).

22 I here draw on current debates in the history of technology; see, for instance, David Edgerton, *The Shock of the Old: Technology and Global History since 1900* (London, 2006); and Andrew L. Russell and Lee Vinsel, "After Innovation, Turn to Maintenance," *Technology and Culture* 59 (2018): 1–25.

23 Notable exceptions are in Adrian Forty, *Concrete and Culture: A Material History* (London, 2016), 225–252; and Peggy Deamer, ed., *The Architect as Worker: Immaterial Labour, the Creative Class, and the Politics of Design* (London/New Delhi/New York/Sydney, 2015). A contemporary call to arms in these issues and much an incentive for my questioning of Candela's shells along these lines is the US-based web platform *Who Builds Your Architecture?* (WBYA?) (whobuilds.org).

Félix Candela's Last Shells in Mexico
The Roof Structures for Mexico City's Underground Stations

EDUARDO ALARCÓN AZUELA

The end of the 1950s in Mexico City brought forth the need to build an underground transportation system like those of the great metropolises such as London, New York, and Paris. Back then buses and trams were starting to lack the efficiency needed to transport a considerable number of passengers who commuted daily from the outskirts of the city towards its center. The project, which involved great technical difficulties due to the characteristics of the lacustrine subsoil of the city, gathered the country's best engineers and a group of renowned architects, who proposed modern structures that expressed the latest local contemporary architectural trends. One of the architects was Félix Candela, who was selected to design the roofing of four metro stations. This work focuses on those four constructions.[1]

GENERAL VIEW OF MODERN MEXICAN ARCHITECTURE

The appropriation of ideas regarding modern architecture in Mexico has been directly linked to the country's postrevolution situation: the need to encourage public education, working-class housing, and public sanitation toward the end of the 1920s. The achievement of these great projects represented a huge challenge for the renowned architects, all of whom were aware of the premises of functionalism in architecture, which had been introduced some years earlier by Le Corbusier in France and by the Bauhaus design school in Germany. One of the best examples of functionalism at the time was architect José Villagrán García's project for the Tuberculosis Hospital in Huipulco, which resided far from the preceding academic architectural tendencies. On the other hand, Juan O'Gorman, a young architect at that time, built the first functionalist house in México in the San Ángel district, in 1929, a building in which he literally adapted the principles of Le Corbusier to the environment of a traditional Mexican neighborhood. The following years brought a great deal of success to modern Mexican architecture. It was specifically in Mexico City where works of urban infrastructure yielded the so-called *milagro mexicano* (Mexican miracle).[2]

1 Félix Candela, San Lázaro metro station, Mexico City, 1969; view of the construction site

The project that best demonstrated the great talent of the architects of the time was, without a doubt, the making of the Ciudad Universitaria, the place of the Universidad Nacional Autónoma de México, located to the south of the city and inaugurated in 1952. The master plan was overseen by the architects Mario Pani and Enrique del Moral. Each school or institute within the project was assigned to a group of three architects: one who was an experienced architect; another, a recent graduate; and the third, someone with an intermediate level of expertise. It is, therefore, easy to identify each one of the buildings of the Ciudad Universitaria with the renowned modern architects of the time: the Rectory Tower with Enrique del Moral and Mario Pani, the Central Library with Juan O'Gorman, the Olympic Stadium with Augusto Pérez Palacios, and the National School of Architecture with José Villagrán, just to mention a few. In addition, the main campus would hold artistic works by the great muralists, which remain today: the stadium's mural by Diego Rivera, the Rectory Tower's mural by David Alfaro Siqueiros, the four walls of the Central Library covered by a stone mural by Juan O'Gorman, who was also a painter, the Faculty of Science's artwork by José Chávez Morado, and the Faculty of Medicine's murals by Francisco Eppens.

In time, the urban centers in the country grew exponentially, thus increasing their social demands. Mexico City observed the biggest population explosion between the 1940s and 1970s. Massive apartment units were the solution to the housing needs of an overpopulated city. Mario Pani and his team developed some of those projects: the Centro Urbano Presidente Alemán, the Centro Urbano Presidente Juárez, the Unidad Habitacional Santa Fe, and the Conjunto Nonoalco Tlatelolco. These new housing ideas led the fundamentals of modern architecture, as they promised a better lifestyle, one that eradicated poverty once and for all—an idea which was evidently promoted by the government.

Mexico City became the place where most of the achievements of modern Mexico were best conveyed. Consequently, the country was made host for the 1968 Olympic Games, gaining an opportunity to show the world its economic and cultural development. Once again, the projects for the new Olympic buildings would become a challenge for both architects and the construction industry. The Olympic Village was built to the south of the city, along with the Palacio de los Deportes (Sports Palace) in the Ciudad Deportiva Magdalena Mixihuca, the Olympic swimming pool, the rowing tracks, and many other Olympic facilities.

UNDERGROUND TRANSIT IN MEXICO CITY: BACKGROUND AND DEVELOPMENT

As mentioned above, accelerated demographic growth in Mexico City demanded a more efficient system for public transportation, one that would facilitate mobility in such a dynamic city. One of the main advocates of the underground project was the engineer Bernardo Quintana, a high-ranking representative of the Ingenieros Civiles Asociados (ICA) construction company.[3] Ernesto Uruchurtu, the city's mayor, opposed the idea of implementing this means of transportation, as he did not see the project as viable. This opposition was obvious, as during his term he strongly encouraged the use of automobiles, thus promoting the construction of highways. When Uruchurtu left his post and was replaced by Alfonso Corona del Rosal, this policy was rectified, since the latter's main goal was to promote ICA's project: the construction of an underground system in Mexico City.

Following approval, ICA was in charge of implementing the construction work for the underground project, starting in 1967. After several studies of the citizens' commuting habits, ICA suggested the first stage for the system's construction, consisting of three lines that would surround Mexico City's central area: the first would run across the city from east to west, the second from the northwest to the south, and the third would run from north to south. The construction of Line 1 started in June 1967. The original plan was due for completion by October the following year, so as to be ready for the Olympic Games, for which Mexico was to host athletes from more than 100 countries. However, the inauguration of Line 1 had to be postponed until 1969, due to the many technical difficulties that arose during construction.[4]

The construction was coordinated by the architect Ángel Borja Navarrete, one of ICA's partners, along with a group of young architects and engineers. Among those professionals was the architect Julio Michel, who designed San Lázaro station with Félix Candela. It was because of the speed at which the construction of the underground station was running that ICA decided not to hire any independent architecture firms for its design. The lines would run underground and a genuine unity in terms of style was required; these needs did not allow for celebrity architectural authorship.[5] Nevertheless, there were some exceptions: the project for Insurgentes station was awarded to architect Salvador Ortega. This is one of the few stations that ended up marking its presence and giving a new face to one of the most important avenues in the city: la Glorieta del Metro Insurgentes (Metro Insurgentes Roundabout). Likewise, Candela applied his singular way for solving the roofing of four different metro stations by using his well-known *cubiertas* (roof shells), which are described in more detail below. For Line 2, Enrique del Moral designed the external part of the stations running along Calzada de Tlalpan. And lastly, Luis Barragán participated as a consultant regarding the colors and materials for the stations.[6]

It is pertinent to also mention the participation of the American designer Lance Wyman, who created the metro's graphic image, and who was actively collaborating with the architect Pedro Ramírez Vázquez in the graphic design for the 1968 Olympic Games. For the metro, Wyman came up with a series of symbols associated with the urban landscape of each station, so that foreigners and illiterate people would be able to identify the stations by their logos.

THE ARCHITECTURE OF THE METRO STATIONS

The underground metro stations in Mexico City were an unprecedented project in terms of Mexicans' idiosyncrasy and culture, since they were used to traveling in the open air and could be prone to suffering claustrophobia when in enclosed spaces beneath the ground. Thus, ICA's architects needed to design harmonious spaces with appropriate materials and lighting, capable of generating a peaceful sensation for the users while allowing 60,000 people to move through the stations every hour.[7]

The architectural plan for the stations included the following spaces:

Accesses: These would be located on pavements or plazas, in buildings or covered entrance spaces, and would include stairways that ended in an open space, and have doors to allow the stations to be closed during emergencies or closing hours.

Vestibules: Indoor and outdoor, depending on the stations' entrance locations; its function would be to take the user from the street to the platform while avoiding crossing circulation routes.

Ticket booths: There would have to be at least two per station located outside, and they must be isolated from one another, each equipped with a ticket machine, a safe, and a cash box for the cashier.

Controls (turnstiles): One-directional; only those at the entrance would have a ticket counter.

Circulation (horizontal and vertical): Horizontal circulation to allow users to go from the platforms to the vestibules and vice versa: the capacity would depend on the flow of people, as they should be able to evacuate in less than three minutes in the case of an emergency. The vertical circulation would have the same function as the horizontal, and only if the stations had more than one level. Escalators with the capacity to carry 5,000 to 10,000 people per hour were also

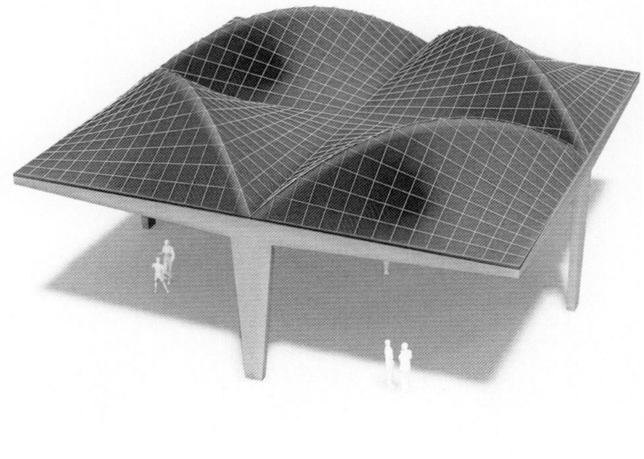

2 Félix Candela, Balderas metro station, Mexico City, 1969: construction principle of the roof shell, perspective view; rendering by Eduardo Alarcón Azuela with Moisés Escárcega Olivares

3 Félix Candela, Merced and Candelaria metro stations, Mexico City, 1969: construction principle of the roof shells, perspective view; rendering by Eduardo Alarcón Azuela with Moisés Escárcega Olivares

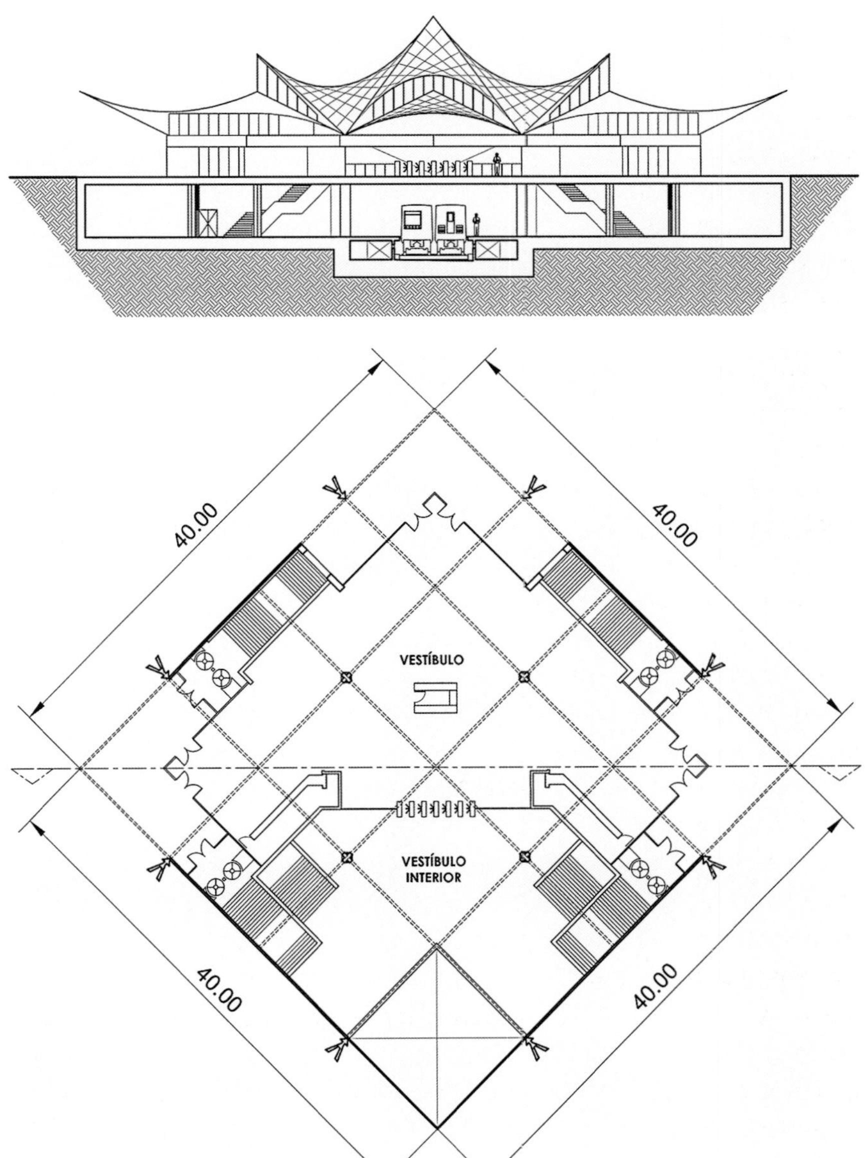

4 Félix Candela, San Lázaro metro station, Mexico City, 1969: floor plan and cross-section; drawing by Eduardo Alarcón Azuela

5 Félix Candela, Balderas metro station, Mexico City, 1969; photograph 2012

6 Félix Candela, Candelaria metro station, Mexico City, 1969; photograph 2012

7 Félix Candela, San Lázaro metro station, Mexico City, 1969; photograph 2013

needed, as well as footbridges to change platforms.

Platforms: The main element of the station. Platforms would enable users to enter and exit the trains. They would be 150 meters long, in accordance with the length of the nine-car trains. For security reasons there would be a 40-centimeter strip on the floor along the platform marked with a different material, in order to separate users from the train cars.

Each station was designed to include space for control machinery and operation rooms, such as ventilation rooms, machinery rooms, electrical substations, and services for the underground operators.[8] As for materials and finishing, marble from Santo Tomás was used for most of the floors, a material that withstands erosion, although some of the stations' floors were made with ceramic slabs. Some walls were also covered with marble, and others with stone or limestone.

FÉLIX CANDELA'S COLLABORATION IN THE METRO PROJECT

By the end of the 1960s, the name Félix Candela was already well-known internationally due to the construction of architectural structures such as the Cosmic Rays Pavilion in the Ciudad Universitaria (with Jorge González Reyna), the chapels El Altillo and San Vicente de Paul (with Enrique de la Mora and Fernando López Carmona), the main markets in Coyoacán, Azcapotzalco, and Anáhuac (with Pedro Ramírez Vázquez), the Concha Acústica (Acoustic Bandstand Shell) at Unidad Habitacional Santa Fe (with Mario Pani), and the chapel of Palmira in Cuernavaca (with Guillermo Rossell de la Lama and Manuel Larrosa), just to mention a few.

It was through Manuel Larrosa, who had previously collaborated with the architect Ángel Borja in ICA, that the idea of inviting Félix Candela to design some of the roofs for the metro's first line was brought forward.[9] By that time, Candela had already left his family business, Cubiertas Ala, and was working for the Palacio de los Deportes project, which was supposed to be completed for the 1968 Olympic Games, along with the architects Antonio Peyrí and Enrique Castañeda. Candela designed the roof shells for the stations Merced, Candelaria, and San Lázaro, as well as a small part of the roof for Balderas station.

The entrance roof shell of Balderas station might go unnoticed from the street. It is only from the inside that the virtues of the hyperbolic paraboloids can be better appreciated. The roof shells, as seen in the floor plan, are composed by a square of 18 × 18 meters, at the middle of which a very low groin vault rises. This vault is enclosed by four hypar segments with mixed edges (two straight edges and a curved one) standing on T-shaped supports (tapering cantilevered beams integral with central columns) on each side of the square, which joined at the end of each beam, making for an interesting solution. This geometric and structural solution had already been used by Candela in a roof shell for the Instituto Anglo Mexicano de Cultura, a project by Enrique de la Mora.

An alternative structural system was used for the roofs of both the Merced and Candelaria metro stations: a series of umbrellas supported by columns with a hexagonal cross-section, which make a six-pointed star shape above the middle of the shaft. This way, twelve hypar covers are formed from each column (two from each star point); each cover is formed by four straight edges sitting on two different planes. Each of the umbrellas makes up a rectangular cover, forming two hallways. There are eleven pairs in Candelaria station and eight in Merced station. The hallway roofs do not meet in the middle; thus, a skylight illuminates the station with natural light during daytime. Candelaria station might seem more striking, as one of its vestibules allows the users to observe the beauty of the roof shells from under a double height, right in the middle of the station. Merced station is probably less distinctive, as it does not have a huge vestibule due to the limitations imposed by the surrounding streets.[10]

Lastly, a 40-meter-sided square, under which the platforms run diagonally, composes the roof shells of San Lázaro station. On the floor plan the square is subdivided into sixteen 10-meter-sided squares, twelve of which are placed on the perimeter and form hypars, which are supported on edge beams to the exterior; these are in turn resisted by buttresses. Inside, the hypars sit on cross-shaped columns. This composition of what seem like broken lines, along with the golden limestone covering the intermediate walls, results in very interesting facades. Inside the station, the other four squares form taller hypars, also resting on cross-shaped columns. The change in height forms skylights that bathe the vestibule with compelling natural illumination. At the top of the stairs that lead to the platforms, a very large window is used to illuminate the whole station with natural light.

CURRENT STATE OF THE METRO STATIONS DESIGNED BY FÉLIX CANDELA

Nowadays, the stations made by the team of architects from ICA, along with Félix Candela, at the end of the 1960s are in poor condition. The context has not been favorable, as the access spaces have been crowded by informal commerce. The least alarming case is the roof shells of Balderas station, which at first sight show no visible damage.

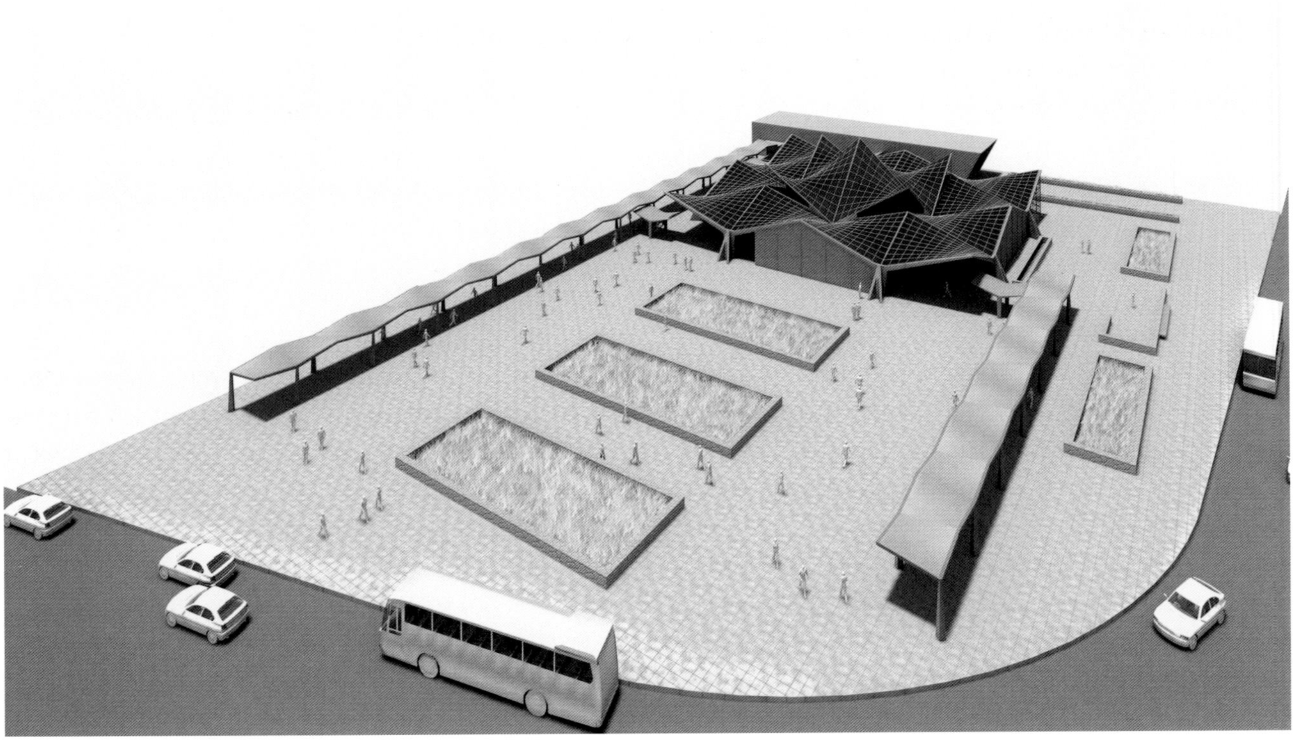

8 Félix Candela, San Lázaro metro station, Mexico City, 1969: aerial view, author's proposal for the square in front of the station. The building for the connecting walkway is omitted; instead the design of the new covered corridors creates a space of lesser importance compared to the architecture of the station; rendering by Eduardo Alarcón Azuela with Moisés Escárcega Olivares

9 Félix Candela, San Lázaro metro station, Mexico City, 1969: cross-section with perspective interior view, author's proposal showing elevators for disabled people connecting the vestibules to the platforms; rendering by Eduardo Alarcón Azuela with Moisés Escárcega Olivares

The Merced and Candelaria stations are located in the Barrio de la Merced,[11] where street sellers have invaded the immediate surroundings. These spaces deserve an urban plan project, since La Merced quarter has been overpopulated during recent years. However, such a proposal would exceed the scope of this research, which is limited to the analysis of roof shells. The lack of maintenance of these two singular shells can be seen from the inside, where humidity has taken a toll on the concrete; therefore, delamination and exposed oxidized steel reinforcement rods can be seen. This damage, if it remains untended, could result in irreversible harm. Thus, there is a pressing need for a restoration project.

San Lázaro station has lost all the virtues of its original conception, as the adjacent buildings have transformed its image: firstly, in the original project there were walkways covered by roof shells which connected the station's entrance to the streets via an access plaza. Nowadays, the plaza remains underused and the roof shells have been demolished. In addition, the Terminal de Autobuses de Pasajeros de Oriente (Eastern Passengers Bus Terminal), inaugurated in 1978, sits behind the metro station; consequently, a path linking the main street to the station was improvised without adding any architectural design value. Finally, a roofed transfer path was placed around the roof shells when Line B of the metro San Lázaro was built at the end of the 1990s. This last space caused the inside of the roof shells lose the original natural lighting that Félix Candela and Julio Michel had accomplished with the original design.

SALVAGE PROPOSAL FOR SAN LÁZARO STATION

Part of the deterioration of San Lázaro station is due to the state of the immediate contexts. The following statements are intended to lead the salvage design project for the metro station:

- It is necessary to refurbish the plaza that links the station to the main streets; thus, the proposal is to redesign and rebuild new walkways covered by roof shells.
- The circular structure transfer pathway must be demolished because it diminishes the roof shell's aspect, and the space design does not respond to universal accessibility principles.
- The interior of the station must be designed according to universal accessibility principles; therefore, two elevators must be installed to connect the two platforms to the vestibule.
- The design of a smaller transfer pathway that does not compete with Candela's original design is needed.
- In order to ensure an efficient mass transit, the station's vestibules must not have any obstacles; therefore, the commercial stands must be relocated.

FINAL WORDS

The legacy of Félix Candela and his collaborators, all of whom provided innovation and a field of possibilities for the reinforced concrete roof shells, belongs to an admirable construction period in Mexican architectural history. The metro stations' roof shells are proof of that.

Nevertheless, the utilitarian status of these metro stations has led to their deterioration—all of the stations' transformations are intended to achieve more efficient mobility and not to preserve their original aspect. On the other hand, and maybe due to a lack of budget, the stations have not been given adequate maintenance; at the same time, new spaces have been improvised. These circumstances have negatively affected the stations, as has been analyzed in this text. In 50 years of existence, both the context and the original design of the metro stations have suffered radical modifications. These additions have not always efficiently provided the mobility required by the public transportation system.

The metro stations built by Félix Candela at the end of the 1960s are examples of a design guided by originality that reflects the constructive and structural innovations of the time. Today they are important icons for the thousands of users who transit these sites every day. Hopefully, in the near future the conservation proposal for San Lázaro station's spaces and roof shells, mentioned above, will be taken into account so as to recover the station's spatial dignity. All for the recuperation of modern architecture in our country, which is characterized by its unmatched making.

I dedicate this work to Dino del Cueto for introducing me to the research of reinforced concrete shells, a work that we have shared for the last decade.

1 A more detailed version of this text appeared in the author's master's degree thesis "Conservación de cascarones de concreto armado como parte del patrimonio arquitectónico moderno en México: Propuesta de rescate para la estación del metro San Lázaro" [Conservation of reinforced concrete shells as part of Mexico's modern architectural heritage: A proposal for the salvage of the San Lázaro underground station] (master's thesis, Universidad Autónoma Metropolitana, Unidad Azcapotzalco, 2018).

2 The period between 1940 and 1970 is known as *milagro mexicano,* a time frame during which the big urban infrastructure works were fostered and constructed by the country's government.

3 ICA was the most important construction company in the country toward the mid-twentieth century. The engineer Bernardo Quintana was one of the founding partners.

4 See E. Alcantar, "La estación del Metro Insurgentes: El discurso urbano de la modernidad en la Ciudad de México" (graduate thesis, Universidad Nacional Autónoma de México, 2014), 21–58.

5 See Manuel Larrosa Irigoyen, *Ángel Borja Navarrete: Vida y obra* (Mexico City, 2005), 25.

6 See ibid.

7 See *Treinta años de hacer el Metro: Ciudad de México* (Mexico City, 1997), 177–187.

8 See ibid.

9 Author's interview with the architect Julio Michel Sinner (ICA collaborator for the Metro de la Ciudad de México project) at San Lázaro and Candelaria metro stations, Mexico City, July 28, 2015.

10 See Fernando López Carmona and Xavier Guzmán Urbiola, "Evolución de los cascarones de concreto armado en México," in Juan Ignacio del Cueto Ruiz-Funes, ed., *Aquella primavera creadora ... cascarones de concreto armado en México. That Creative Spring ... Reinforced Concrete Shells in Mexico* (Mexico City, 2008), 34–36.

11 The Barrio de la Merced is located east of the historic center of Mexico City. In addition to its history and tradition, the area is characterized by intense commercial activity. During the last decade it has become overpopulated by street vendors, which has led to severe social conflicts.

Félix Candela's Legacy in the United Kingdom

MARISELA MENDOZA

In 1959, invited by the British Council and the Cement and Concrete Association, Félix Candela traveled to the United Kingdom to give a series of lectures at several cities, including London, Cardiff, Leeds, Edinburgh, and Belfast.[1] This was Candela's second trip to the UK, the first having been in 1948 to attend a soil mechanics conference in London, using some of the money he had won in a lottery. Before his visit to the UK in 1959, Candela's work was already well known outside Mexico, particularly through the publications of the American Concrete Institute, as well as the various conference papers he had presented in the USA. During visits to conferences in the USA, Candela became a close friend of the Texan architect O'Neil Ford, who, after collaborating with Candela in the construction of inverted hypar shells in Texas (1958), was commissioned to design and build the Texas Instruments (TI) factory in Bedford, UK, (1959), the first TI factory outside the USA. Candela's vast knowledge and experience in the potential of reinforced concrete shell structures for industrial buildings found a strong voice during his lectures in the UK and was summarized in *Concrete Quarterly* in 1959.[2] The article highlighted Candela's experience and confidence in using this innovative roofing method outside Mexico. Without doubt Candela's lectures inspired British architects and engineers to further explore the potential of inverted hypar shells in the UK.

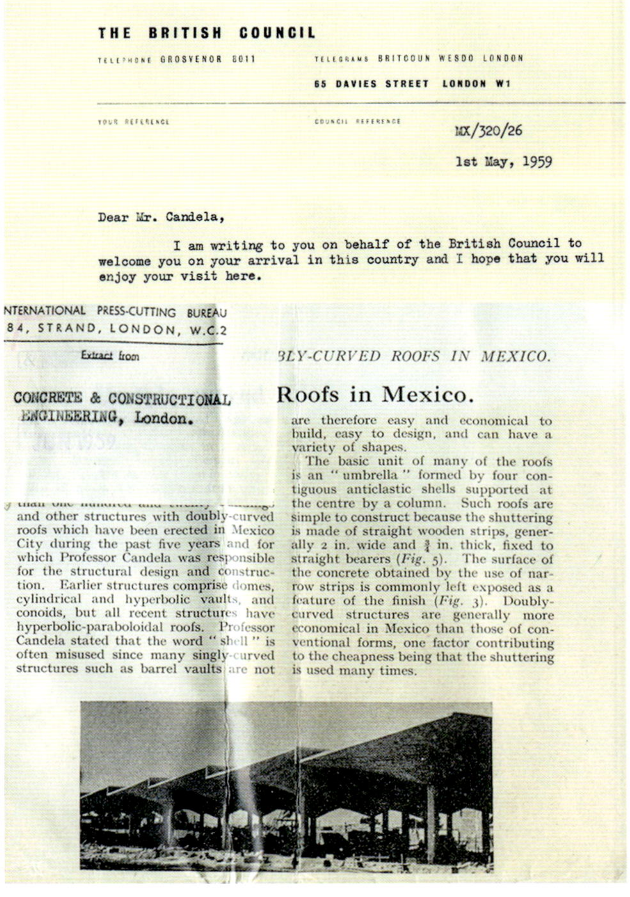

THE BRITISH COUNCIL
TELEPHONE GROSVENOR 8011 TELEGRAMS BRITCOUN WESDO LONDON
65 DAVIES STREET LONDON W1
YOUR REFERENCE COUNCIL REFERENCE MX/320/26
1st May, 1959

Dear Mr. Candela,

I am writing to you on behalf of the British Council to welcome you on your arrival in this country and I hope that you will enjoy your visit here.

NTERNATIONAL PRESS-CUTTING BUREAU
84, STRAND, LONDON, W.C.2
Extract from
CONCRETE & CONSTRUCTIONAL ENGINEERING, London.

3LY-CURVED ROOFS IN MEXICO.

Roofs in Mexico.

and other structures with doubly-curved roofs which have been erected in Mexico City during the past five years and for which Professor Candela was responsible for the structural design and construction. Earlier structures comprise domes, cylindrical and hyperbolic vaults, and conoids, but all recent structures have hyperbolic-paraboloidal roofs. Professor Candela stated that the word "shell" is often misused since many singly-curved structures such as barrel vaults are not

are therefore easy and economical to build, easy to design, and can have a variety of shapes.

The basic unit of many of the roofs is an "umbrella" formed by four contiguous anticlastic shells supported at the centre by a column. Such roofs are simple to construct because the shuttering is made of straight wooden strips, generally 2 in. wide and ¾ in. thick, fixed to straight bearers (*Fig.* 5). The surface of the concrete obtained by the use of narrow strips is commonly left exposed as a feature of the finish (*Fig.* 3). Doubly-curved structures are generally more economical in Mexico than those of conventional forms, one factor contributing to the cheapness being that the shuttering is used many times.

1 Letter from the British Council welcoming Félix Candela to Britain and magazine clipping, 1959

FELIX CANDELA

by Betty Campbell

FELIX CANDELA, whose series of lectures in five British cities last May caused such a stir, is a remarkable man in every way. Certainly he is one of the leading structural designers in the world today. And has become so, it would appear, almost by chance. The chance being that he has applied his naturally brilliant brain to the solution of this particular problem—he might as well, one feels, have applied it to some quite other problem, with equally remarkable results—and may yet do so.

Felix Candela was born, forty-nine years ago, in Spain. He looks less than his age, a man with a spring in him, slim, and very alive. Once a rugger player of national standing as well as Spain's champion skier, he plays squash regularly and has all the alertness, both physical and mental, that one might expect—even when relaxed he seems on his toes. Nor are his resilience and vitality merely physical, or mental. Life treated him, at one stage, pretty harshly, but he could still say "I have always been very lucky indeed". Luck, to Candela, has meant the opportunity to develop his personality, a process which he has observed with a conscious interest.

He came of a home where money was not too plentiful and he helped to pay for his training as an architect in the Escuela Española de Arquitectura in Madrid by coaching his fellow students in the complications of statics, which were to him no complication at all, because he happened to find them interesting.

And so, a young man still mainly interested in sport, he became an architect—as he might, he felt, have become anything else, simply at the suggestion of a friend—and found himself, in 1936, the holder of a

2

2 First page of the article on Félix Candela by Betty Campbell in the journal *Concrete Quarterly*, 1959

3 Thomas H. B. Burrough and Derek Bond of Clarke Nicholls & Marcel, Mound Stand of the Gloucestershire County Cricket Club, Bristol, 1959

Candela's second trip to the UK became a remarkable event in both his personal and his professional life. London became his favorite city, where he used to meet his beloved and much-admired friend Ove Arup, and Stevenage, the first UK New Town, became the host of his first European project.[3] Candela's 1959 lectures in the UK were attended by notable architects and engineers interested in the innovative construction methods and architectural qualities of concrete shells. Candela's encounters with the engineer Oliver Marcel and the architect Francis Reginald Stevens Yorke[4] were instrumental, as they would lead to, in 1963, Candela's first European project: the John Lewis Warehouse, in collaboration with one of the most representative postwar architecture partnerships in the United Kingdom: Yorke, Rosenberg and Mardall (YRM).[5]

CONCRETE SHELL STRUCTURES IN THE UK

By the time Candela visited the UK in 1959, there were some 500 concrete shell roofs in the country.[6] However, the prewar development of concrete shells in Europe did not resonate strongly in the UK until the 1950s. When an interest in the immediate postwar period resumed at the 1952 *Symposium on Concrete Shell Roof Construction* organized by the Cement and Concrete Association no hypar concrete shells were presented. "However, architects were finding the cylinder restrictive and their interest was turning towards a number of double curved surfaces."[7]

Although Candela arrived in Mexico in 1939, the outset of his most relevant architectural work did not occur until the beginning of the 1950s. In 1951 Candela designed and built his first inverted hypar prototype for industrial buildings and, in 1952, he designed and built his first commissioned hypar structure: the Cosmic Rays Pavilion in Mexico City, a small concrete shell with a thickness of only 5/8 inch (15 millimeters)—the thinnest reinforced-concrete shell ever built at that time, and with which Candela gained authority in the realm of structural art. Candela's presentations at important conferences, such as the Cement and Concrete Association conference in Denver and the Massachusetts Institute of Technology *World Conference on Thin Concrete Shells* in 1954, became instrumental in disseminating his work to an international audience.[8] Furthermore, and prior to Candela's visit to the UK in 1959, an article dedicated to Mexican architecture in *Concrete Quarterly* in 1957 was also important in introducing Candela's work to a British audience of expert engineers, architects, and builders concerned with reinforced-concrete shells.[9]

4 Yorke, Rosenberg and Mardall with Félix Candela, John Lewis Warehouse, Stevenage, 1963: aerial view

INVERTED HYPARS IN THE UK

The first inverted hypar shells constructed in the UK were those to roof the Mound Stand of the Gloucestershire County Cricket Club ground at Bristol (1959, demolished in 2013). The project was developed by the architect Thomas H. B. Burrough and the engineer Derek Bond of Clarke Nicholls & Marcel. Another early example of inverted hypars in the UK was the Five Ways Garage at Wolverhampton (1961), designed by Mason Richards Partnership in collaboration with GKN Reinforcements Ltd.[10] The roof consisted of four 40-foot (12.19-meter) square inverted hypars to shelter a filling station.

THE TEXAS INSTRUMENTS FACTORY, BEDFORD

By the end of the 1950s, the construction sector showed an initial mobilization, supported by the abolition of rationing of construction materials in 1949 and solid economic growth during the 1950s and 1960s, when the era of the "affluent society" as described by John Kenneth Galbraith emerged.[11] This new period of prosperity encouraged production and consumerism, which in turn boosted the industrial and retail sectors. Thus Candela's and Ford's innovative inverted hypar shells for industrial buildings found fertile ground during the second phase of postwar reconstruction in Britain. From 1953 to 1965, O'Neil Ford and Associates were commissioned for various projects for the American company Texas Instruments. Architecturally, the most representative buildings for TI were those roofed with concrete shells: the Semiconductor Building in Dallas, Texas, USA (1958), and the factory in Bedford, UK (1959). These two buildings were highly inspired and influenced by the hypars that O'Neil Ford had developed in collaboration with Félix Candela for an industrial community in Arlington and for the Great Southwest Corporation in Texas in 1958.

Bedford's industrial and urban developments during the post-austerity period provided the perfect opportunity to host the first Texas Instruments factory outside the USA. The chosen site was well connected with key roads, such as the A6 trunk road and the newly built M1 motorway. The design and construction methods applied in the TI factory were pioneering, and the experience that Ford and Candela had acquired in erecting the inverted hypars constructed in Texas was instrumental to Ford's venture in Bedford. The shells to be erected in Bedford presented both a great challenge and an opportunity to innovate in a different context with different construction skills and methods. This in turn gave rise to more innovative collaboration from the British construction industry.[12] Furthermore, the Bedford TI shells exemplified the British intention to showcase and promote technical and scientific progress through innovative industrial architecture.[13]

5 O'Neil Ford, Texas Instruments factory, Bedford, 1959

6 Yorke, Rosenberg and Mardall with Félix Candela, John Lewis Warehouse, Stevenage, 1963: partial view with inverted hypar shells

THE JOHN LEWIS WAREHOUSE, STEVENAGE: FÉLIX CANDELA'S FIRST EUROPEAN PROJECT

The John Lewis Warehouse (JLW) represents an important milestone in the timeline of Candela's practice as a shell-builder, as it constitutes his first architectural collaboration in Europe, showcasing his trademark inverted hypar shells to roof industrial buildings.[14] The John Lewis Partnership (JLP), based in London, had already experienced the fast growth of the city after the war and was finding it difficult to maintain its distribution center in London. In 1961 the JLP started planing to relocate their central London stockrooms and the selected site was a green field in the industrial area of Stevenage New Town. The architectural project was commissioned to the architectural firm Yorke, Rosenberg and Mardall, which had previously completed the John Lewis Cole Brothers Shop in Sheffield in 1962.[15] YRM's architectural proposal for the warehouse consisted of a rectangular plan, 465 feet (141.73 meters) long by 330 feet (100.57 meters) wide, to accommodate five bays transversely and fifteen longitudinally for the warehouse, and next to it an administration and services building. The bays were roofed with rectangular inverted hypar shells, 60 feet (18.29 meters) long and 31 feet (9.45 meters) wide, tilted to allow diffuse north light and supported by 13-foot (3.96-meter) tall, 2-foot (610-millimeter) square section columns. Furthermore, the timber planks of the formwork used to cast the shells for the JLW were similar to those used in the warehouses and markets built in Mexico to achieve a richer texture on the exposed concrete, as Candela was dissatisfied with the result of using wider boards for hypars constructed in Texas.[16]

The timber formwork used to cast all 75 shells (five bays transversely and fifteen longitudinally) was made up of half-shells. Furthermore, the formwork design included an ingenious and detail unprecedented in Candela's previous shells. Considering that the design included a 5-foot (1.52-meter) variation in level between the east and west edges of adjacent shells, it would have been necessary to lower the south edge by 5 feet (1.52 meters) for the formwork to pass clear under the cast shell. Therefore, a hinge included in the formwork along the east–west axis allowed the inside of the formwork to drop flat, and it was only necessary to lower it far enough to detach it from the concrete before transferring it to cast the next shell.[17] The JLW is an important piece in Candela's repertoire of inverted hypar shells to roof industrial buildings, not only because it was his first European project but also because of the collaboration with YRM, one of the most prestigious postwar British architectural firms. Furthermore, the JLW possesses a prominent architectural character which "relates to a structural beauty through which the ephemeral became monumental, where spatial character and expressive materiality provided a sense of place and mnemonic identification for the people inhabiting them."[18] For its architectural merits, the JLW was awarded Grade II listed building status in November 1995 by English Heritage (Historic England since 2015).[19]

THE QUEENSGATE MARKET HALL, HUDDERSFIELD

The Queensgate Market Hall (QMH) in Huddersfield (1969/1970) is considered an architectural landmark (Grade II listed) in the UK due to its iconic reinforced concrete inverted hypar shells and the integration of public art. The QMH is also a totemic figure of the rich and long-standing history of trade in Huddersfield.[20] The inverted-hypar shells designed to roof the market were inspired by the markets built by Candela in the 1950s—mainly through the publications of Candela's work in *Concrete Quarterly* and in Colin Faber's book *Candela: The Shell Builder*.[21] Furthermore, the design, construction, and integration of services was directly informed by the John Lewis Warehouse.[22]

The same postwar urban planning policies that saw the development of the first New Towns and the

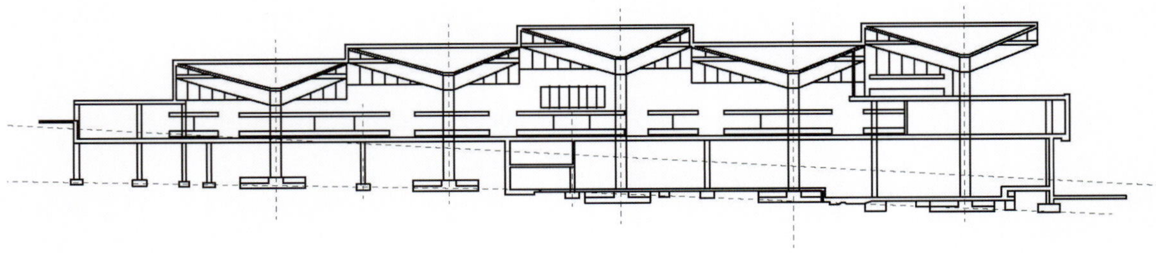

7 Seymour Harris Partnership with Leonard and Partners, Queensgate Market Hall, Huddersfield, 1970: longitudinal section; drawing by Esther Cheng, based on a plan by Seymour Harris Partnership

8 Seymour Harris Partnership with Leonard and Partners, Queensgate Market Hall, Huddersfield, 1970: partial view of the facade with inverted hypar shells and with ceramic tiles by Fritz Steller

decentralization of London would also seek to address the industrial development in the depressed northeast and south Wales areas.[23] In accordance with the 1947 Act, local authorities were invited to submit planning proposals to the Ministry of Local Government and Planning by 1951. In the early 1960s, Huddersfield's Council opened an exhibition to the public to display the proposed regeneration plan, giving priority to the Southgate area in the first five years of the development.[24] The regeneration plan area, known as the Comprehensive Redevelopment Area, was divided in two, one of which was commissioned to the Murrayfield Real Estate Company, including the New Market Hall.[25] The demolition of the existing market hall (built 1878–1880) was rather contentious but necessary to meet the requirements of the town center regeneration plan to build a larger new market and on a different site.[26] The Murrayfield Real Estate Company commissioned Seymour Harris Partnership to develop the architectural scheme of the new market with Kenneth Wood as the project's manager, and the young architect Gwynfor Edwards Roberts was a collaborator in his team. Roberts, who was assigned to explore the most economical proposal for an enclosed market hall,[27] was well acquainted with concrete shells and was interested in exploring the potential of inverted-hypar shells to roof the proposed market. After a series of speculative and unviable proposals, both Roberts and Alan Vaughan (Seymour Harris's quantity surveyor) decided to visit the JLW in Stevenage.

Roberts's final proposal, strategically informed by this visit, consisted of 21 isolated asymmetrical inverted umbrellas of 17 × 9.50 meters, each supported on a single column of 1 × 0.70 meters, and aligned in four rows of four and one row of five columns. The structural design was developed by Nicholls of Leonard Partners, based on previous research and calculations done by Eliah Traum on asymmetrical inverted hypar shells.[28] Unlike the JLW inverted hypar shells, those used to roof the QMH were neither tilted nor connected, but they were asymmetrical. Openings between the edges of the shells, to provide natural light, were created by gradually increasing the column heights from the north to south of the site. The innovative structure was also accompanied with customized architectural and construction details, such as the neoprene-like concertina joint for the sophisticated glazing, used to allow the free movement of each independent shell.[29] Furthermore, the concrete mixture was carefully considered to achieve a whiter color appearance to resemble the white cloth canopies used in open markets.[30] In addition, the structural beauty of the market provided a canvas to host the ceramic expression of the artist Fritz Steller.[31] However, and despite having been granted Grade II listing status in August 2005 by English Heritage,[32] the market has been at risk of partial or total demolition.[33] Fortunately, the market's administration and Huddersfield's town center community have succeeded in conserving and preserving the building.

CONCLUSION

Félix Candela's international reputation was mainly built on the magnificent sacred spaces he crafted with hypar concrete shells in Mexico. However, the works he developed for more profane buildings, such as industrial warehouses and markets, were in fact more numerous, and gave him the opportunity to work with internationally acclaimed architects and engineers such as O'Neil Ford and YRM. This paper has presented the early developments and most representative inverted hypar shells in Britain inspired or executed by the master shell builder Candela. These structures bear witness to the urban and regional planning considerations as well as the economic, political, and technological factors, that promoted the industrial and retail market architecture of the postausterity period in Britain. Out of the five inverted hypar concrete shells discussed in this paper, three (TI factory, JLW, and QGM) have been preserved as listed buildings due to their perceived architectural merit. However, the TI factory's function changed in the 1990s following the departure of Texas Instruments from Bedford. In 2014 the building was bought by Verve Developments, which refurbished the building to convert it into a business center, thus securing its preservation. Furthermore, the excellent condition of the inverted hypar shells roofing the John Lewis Warehouse (Costco Wholesale Corporation Warehouse since 2018) and the Queensgate Market Hall can be attributed to the fact that they have maintained their original function as well as to the community's recognition of their architectural and historical value.

1 See Félix Candela, Itinerary of the visit to the UK in 1959, Princeton University Library, Special Collections, Princeton, USA, Félix Candela Papers, C1455, Box 25, Folder 11.
2 Betty Campbell, "Félix Candela," *Concrete Quarterly,* no. 42 (1959): 2–13, here 4.
3 See Félix Candela, Unpublished autobiography, Princeton University Library, Special Collections, Princeton, USA, Félix Candela Papers, C1455, Box 25, Folder 11.
4 See Félix Candela's personal documents from the visit to the UK in 1959 (see note 1).
5 See Marisela Mendoza, "Félix Candela's First European Project: The John Lewis Warehouse Stevenage New Town," *Architectural Research Quarterly* 19 (2015): 149–160.
6 See L. G. Booth, "The Design and Construction of Timber Hyperbolic Paraboloid Shell Roofs in Britain: 1957–1975," *Construction History* 13 (1997): 67–90.
7 Ibid., 67.
8 See Félix Candela, Unpublished autobiography, Princeton University Library, Special Collections, Princeton, USA, Félix Candela Papers, C1455, Box 25, Folder 11.
9 Betty Campbell, "Mexico: Building Today," *Concrete Quarterly* no. 33 (1957): 2–29.
10 See J. D. Bennett, "The Structural Possibilities of Hyperbolic Paraboloids," *Reinforced Concrete Review* (December 1961): 733–757.
11 See Nigel Taylor, *Urban Theory Planning since 1945* (London, 1998), 38.
12 See "Factory under Concrete Umbrellas," *The New Scientist* 7, no. 187 (1960): 1535.
13 See ibid.
14 See Mendoza, "Félix Candela's First European Project" (see note 5).
15 See ibid.
16 See Colin Faber, *Candela: The Shell Builder* (London, 1963), 126.
17 See "New Warehouse at Stevenage," *The Builder* 206 (1964): 459–460.
18 Mendoza, "Félix Candela's First European Project," 157 (see note 5).
19 See "John Lewis Warehouse," *Historic England,* https://historicengland.org.uk/listing/the-list/list-entry/1117372.
20 See Marisela Mendoza, "Construction of the 21 Inverted Hyperbolic Paraboloid Concrete Shells to Roof the Queensgate Market Hall, Huddersfield," in James W. P. Campbell et. al., ed., *Building Histories: The Proceedings of the Fourth Annual Construction History Society Conference* (Cambridge, 2017), 447–456.
21 Author's interview with Colin Prior, resident engineer of the Queensgate Market Hall, September 22, 2015.
22 See Christopher Rolfe Marsden, "The Engineering and Construction of 21 Asymmetric Freestanding Hyperbolic Paraboloid Umbrella Concrete Shells," in Juan Gerardo Oliva Salinas, ed., *Proceedings of the Symposium of the International Association for Shell and Spatial Structures, Acapulco 2008,* (Madrid, 2008), 169.
23 See Alan Booth, "The Second World War and the Origins of Modern Regional Policy," *Economy and Society* 11 (1982): 1–21.
24 See "The Shape of Huddersfield in Years to Come," *Huddersfield Post,* 1960.
25 See Mendoza, "Construction of the 21 Inverted Hyperbolic Paraboloid Concrete Shells" (see note 20).
26 See "Revolution in Shopping Habits Calls for Greatest Care in Planning," *Daily Examiner,* November 12, 1965.
27 Author's interview with Christopher Marsden, coordinator of Huddersfield Gem, a community group formed to study and promote interest in the market hall, and to safeguard its future, July 2011.
28 Author's interview with Colin Prior (see note 21).
29 Author's interview with the Queensgate Market Hall administration, July 2014.
30 See Colin Prior, "Account of the Construction of Twenty-one Concrete Umbrella Shells for a Market Roof," unpublished paper submitted to the Institution of Civil Engineers for the Institution Medal and Premium (Local Association, Yorkshire), 1969, Colin Prior personal archive.
31 See Marsden, "The Engineering and Construction" (see note 22).
32 See "Queensgate Market," *Historic England,* https://historicengland.org.uk/listing/the-list/list-entry/1391505.
33 See Mendoza, "Construction of the 21 Inverted Hyperbolic Paraboloid Concrete Shells" (see note 20).

The Formative Years of Heinz Isler

MATTHIAS BECKH AND RAINER SCHÜTZEICHEL

Heinz Isler (1926–2009) is one of the outstanding figures in shell design in the second half of the twentieth century. His voluminous oeuvre and his specific approach to experimental form-finding secure him a place in the history of this building typology. But where did his design method stem from? What was the background that he could rely on? In order to throw light on these questions, this essay turns to the early years of Isler's career, from his graduation in 1950 to his seminal contribution "New Shapes for Shells" at the first IASS congress in 1959. It reveals the extent to which the way of thinking of Isler's professor Pierre Lardy (1903–1958) provided the cornerstone and guiding ideas for the work of his disciple.[1]

THE LASTING INFLUENCE OF ISLER'S TEACHER PIERRE LARDY

Lardy had been appointed professor for statics, structural and civil engineering in stone, concrete and reinforced concrete (Baustatik, Hoch- und Brückenbau in Stein, Beton und Eisenbeton) at ETH Zurich after the death of professor Max Ritter (1884–1946). Lardy was at the forefront of the development of prestressed concrete in Switzerland and beyond,[2] and he had worked closely with his predecessor on the development of this new technology: in the year of Ritter's demise, they had published a book on the theory and design of prestressed concrete structures.[3]

Heinz Isler started to study structural engineering at ETH Zurich in 1945 and gained his diploma in 1950. During his studies, he attended at least five of Lardy's courses between 1947 and the year of his graduation.[4] In his diploma thesis, he had to design and engineer a factory building for a textile company. The brief required a well-lit floor area of 32 × 124 meters, with a minimum column spacing of 15 meters in either direction and a clear height of 4.20 meters. In the introductory chapter of his explanatory report, Isler discussed four different options. He finally adopted a saw-tooth shell structure, since this had the advantage of requiring a minimum amount of material and of providing better indoor lighting quality than the other options. In the following chapters, Isler designed and calculated a shell roof with a thickness of 6 centimeters, as well as all other structural elements, and he prepared detailed plans and steel bar reinforcement drawings.

The thesis was submitted in December 1950. Isler's advisor, Pierre Lardy, graded it as "excellent"; hence it is no surprise that soon after his graduation, in 1951, Isler became an assistant at his former professor's chair.

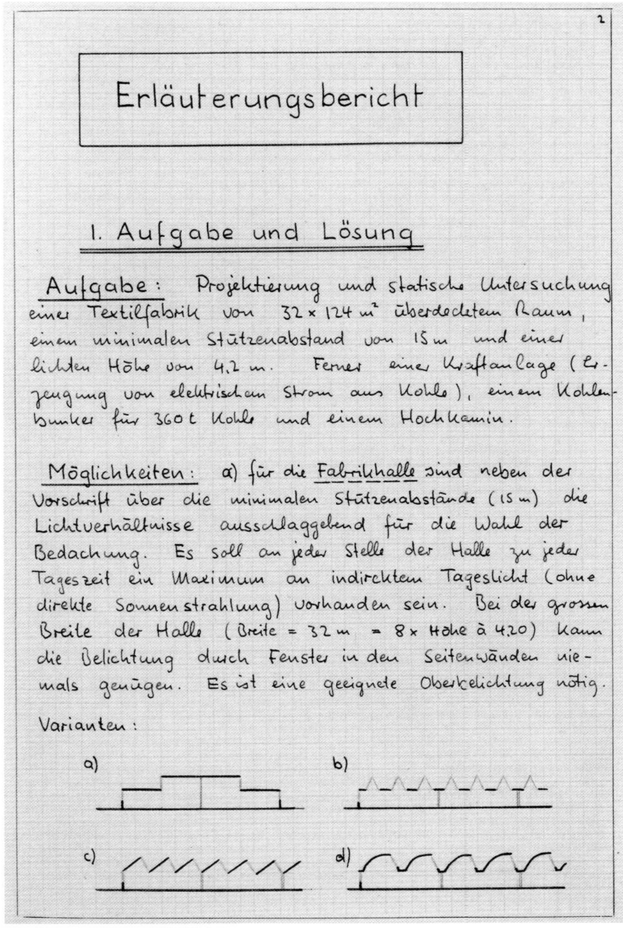

2

Erläuterungsbericht

1. Aufgabe und Lösung

Aufgabe: Projektierung und statische Untersuchung einer Textilfabrik von 32 × 124 m² überdecktem Raum, einem minimalen Stützenabstand von 15 m und einer lichten Höhe von 4.2 m. Ferner einer Kraftanlage (Erzeugung von elektrischem Strom aus Kohle), einem Kohlenbunker für 360 t Kohle und einem Hochkamin.

Möglichkeiten: a) für die Fabrikhalle sind neben der Vorschrift über die minimalen Stützenabstände (15 m) die Lichtverhältnisse ausschlaggebend für die Wahl der Bedachung. Es soll an jeder Stelle der Halle zu jeder Tageszeit ein Maximum an indirecktem Tageslicht (ohne direkte Sonnenstrahlung) vorhanden sein. Bei der grossen Breite der Halle (Breite = 32 m = 8 × Höhe à 4.20) kann die Belichtung durch Fenster in den Seitenwänden niemals genügen. Es ist eine geeignete Oberbelichtung nötig.

Varianten:

1 Heinz Isler, diploma thesis at ETH Zürich, 1959: page of the explanatory report showing four options for the roof structure of a textile factory

There, the graduate gained firsthand insight into Lardy's model testing workshop, as well as into his key themes in teaching; both fields would decisively influence the professional development of Isler's own practice.

Lardy's Model Testing Laboratory

In March 1948, three years before Isler joined Lardy's chair, the eminent Spanish shell designer Eduardo Torroja (1899–1961) lectured at ETH about his progressive concrete structures.[5] In his presentation, Torroja stressed the important role of physical models in the process of structural design, and he described the testing procedures used with small-scale models in his laboratory. This incident led Lardy to establish a model testing laboratory at his chair, which was built up in the following years by his assistant Hans Hauri (1924–2018). Lardy included the new insights gained in his model laboratory in his teaching: in his course "Experimental Methods," he stressed the necessity to explore the structural behavior of complex structures with physical models and to measure the short- and long-term behavior of built structures in order to gain comprehensive information about the aging characteristics of concrete.[6] He highlighted the reciprocity of theory and thorough calculation on the one hand, and observation and monitoring on the other, as insights in one area would foster better understanding of the other.

The course comprised all state-of-the-art measurement methods for model testing of the time, which were based on mechanical, optical, and electrical techniques as well as geodetic methods for the measurement of large built structures such as bridges or dams. Lardy's model testing laboratory was often hired to analyze the stress distribution or deformations of complex structures like saw-tooth shell structures,[7] combined mushroom flat slab systems,[8] and dams.[9] It is not coincidental that the structural testing models that Isler used early in his career would later follow exactly the same principles as those employed at Lardy's testing laboratory.

Lectures on Reinforced Concrete

Although Lardy, who had studied mathematics before turning to engineering, had been appointed professor due to his outstanding achievements in the theoretical development of prestressed concrete and had little experience as a practitioner, he became highly influential on an entire generation of ETH-trained structural engineers.[10] One of the reasons for that may be found in the fact that his lectures were often accompanied

2 Plexiglas testing model of a saw-tooth shell for the Langendorf watch company, scale 1:30, study carried out in Pierre Lardy's model testing laboratory in 1953

by critical discussions of built examples, in which Lardy would also talk about the aesthetic qualities of the structures in question and would not shy away from showing negative examples as a kind of "Horrorkabinett."[11] As David P. Billington has shown, this influence was due to his holistic approach to engineering and his emphasis on material-appropriate structural design, as well as the importance he placed on the aspect of aesthetics in structural and civil engineering.[12]

In this regard, the course "Die Formgestaltung in Eisenbeton" (Form and Shape of Reinforced Concrete) epitomized Lardy's way of thinking and was most likely the most influential on his students. Within the course, he stressed the necessity of contemporary, material-appropriate design of reinforced concrete structures based on material characteristics and the latest research. Lardy connected the characteristics of different building materials with the appropriate design of structural elements—hence the best utilization of the respective material. Stone and masonry, characterized by their negligible tensile capacity—and the consequent requirement to keep the resultant design force within the cross-section of the structure—led to a massive, bulky appearance and character for these structures; Lardy referred to this as "compression monolithism." Concrete, by comparison, with the advantage that it could be cast into any shape, would a priori allow any structural form. This feature should be fully utilized in order to create monolithic two- or three-dimensional structures.

Lardy advocated a design concept that considered the global behavior of the overall structure, thereby embracing the monolithic character of concrete structures and the resulting joint behavior of all components, instead of the hitherto commonly employed concept of analyzing only individual components, which often disregarded the positive effects of spatial load-bearing behavior. It is precisely this new idea of structural integration that would later be employed by Isler in the conception of his shells.

Another significant impact on the formation of Isler's structural thinking stemmed without a doubt from two courses on special topics in reinforced concrete design. In the first, a course on shell structures, Lardy mainly focused on simple geometries like domes, barrel vaults, cylinders, or cooling towers. Apart from the mostly analytical content of the lectures, which mainly focused on membrane theory, Lardy also presented and discussed recent shell structures designed by Franz Dischinger (1887–1953), Eugène Freyssinet (1879–1962), or Torroja. Lardy emphasized that shell design opened up one of the most interesting areas of application for reinforced concrete and that the abundance of possible forms and architectural possibilities was virtually untapped.

In the other course he focused on prestressed concrete and thereby familiarized his students with an, at that time, still very young technology. When Lardy took over Ritter's chair in 1946—that is, while Isler was still one of his students—he established a relevant course that became part of the curriculum.[13] The development of Isler's pneumatic-form shells is not conceivable without the skilled integration of prestressing tendons and, therefore, again strongly relies on Lardy's example.

LEARNING TO WALK: HEINZ ISLER'S EARLY REALIZED PROJECTS

After leaving Lardy's chair, Isler joined the engineering firm of Weder & Prim in Burgdorf for a few years, where he would later establish his own office. From this early period, three projects will be examined here. The first two, dating from 1954 and 1955, will be discussed with regard to the involvement of small-scale models during the design process, while the later project from 1956 will build a bridge to Isler's earliest application of reinforced polyester as a building component. Furthermore, two presentations of these projects that predate the legendary founding conference of the International Association for Shell Structures (IASS) in Madrid in 1959 will be presented, shedding light on Isler's first steps in the academic field.

An Awkward Start: The Shell Roof for Hotel Kreuz in Langenthal, 1954

One of the earliest projects that Isler realized for Weder & Prim was the roof of a multipurpose hall at the Hotel Kreuz in Langenthal. According to John Chilton, this was "the venture that was to launch him on his lifelong exploration of the fascinating world of thin shells."[14] However, it was not love at first sight: Starting from a design by the local architect Hans Sohm (1906–1994), which with its geometrically defined cylindrical vault did not meet with Isler's approval, he elaborated the

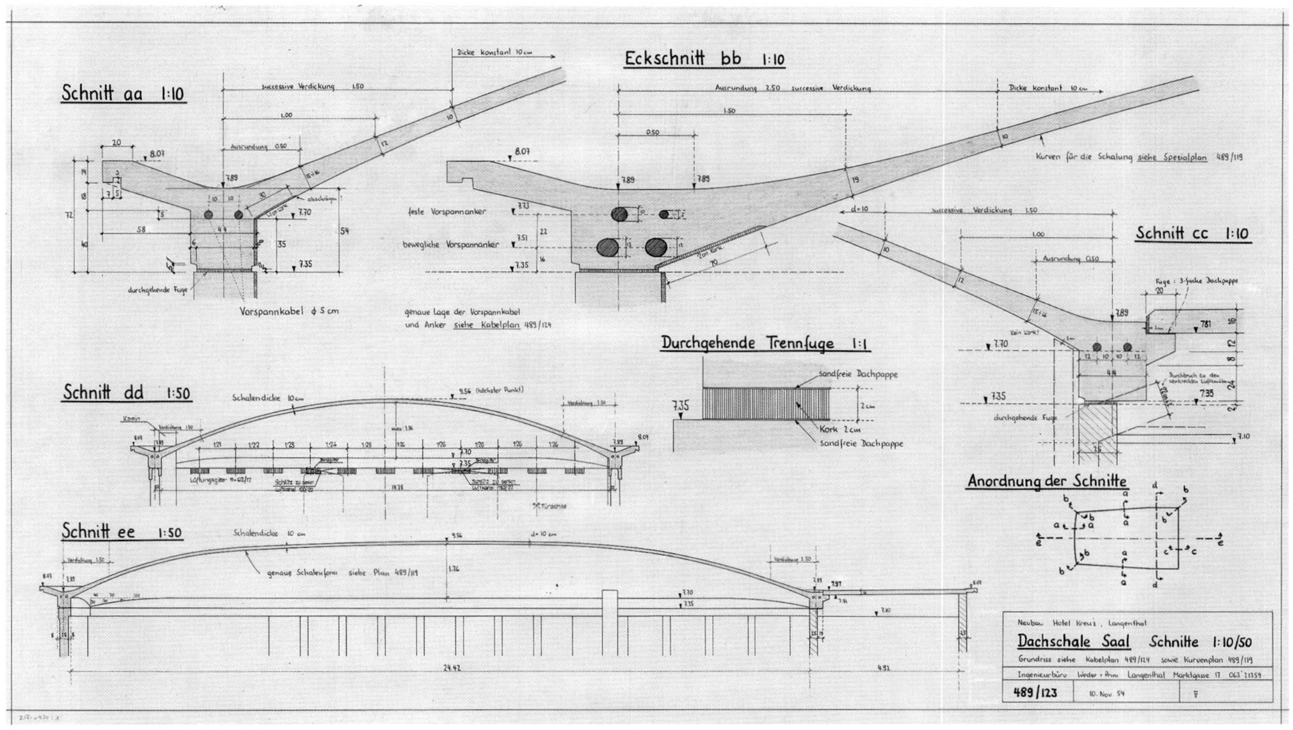

3 Weder & Prim, Hotel Kreuz, Langenthal: sections of the shell covering the multipurpose hall; drawing by Heinz Isler, 1954

form of the shell on the drawing board for a long time, and in the end still was unsatisfied, especially with its shape in the corners. It was this project that made him realize that designing an appropriate and aesthetically pleasing shape solely using the means of drawing "is a task which cannot be solved."[15] As a consequence, in the future he would primarily consult scale models for form-finding processes. It is remarkable, however, that also at the Hotel Kreuz project Isler had already made use of models—but in contrast to later experiments, it has to be emphasized that at this early stage of his career, the model was nothing more than a three-dimensional representation of a form that had already been developed at the drawing board.

Isler presented the scale model he had used for testing the Hotel Kreuz shell only a year after the completion of this project in 1955. At the second congress of the Fédération International de la Précontrainte in Amsterdam, he made public his arduous examination of the most suitable, yet still awkward, form by showing four pictures of the model as well as the testing device to which it was connected.[16] This testing device represented the state of the art in model testing. Isler had encountered such an experimental approach while at Lardy's chair, and he even made use of the same scale (1:30) as his former professor. Furthermore, the model was molded from Plexiglas and attached to weights and gauges in order to measure its deflection under load, just as had been customary at Lardy's laboratory. In this respect, Isler had not yet left familiar ground: neither the form-finding process nor the testing device were innovative.

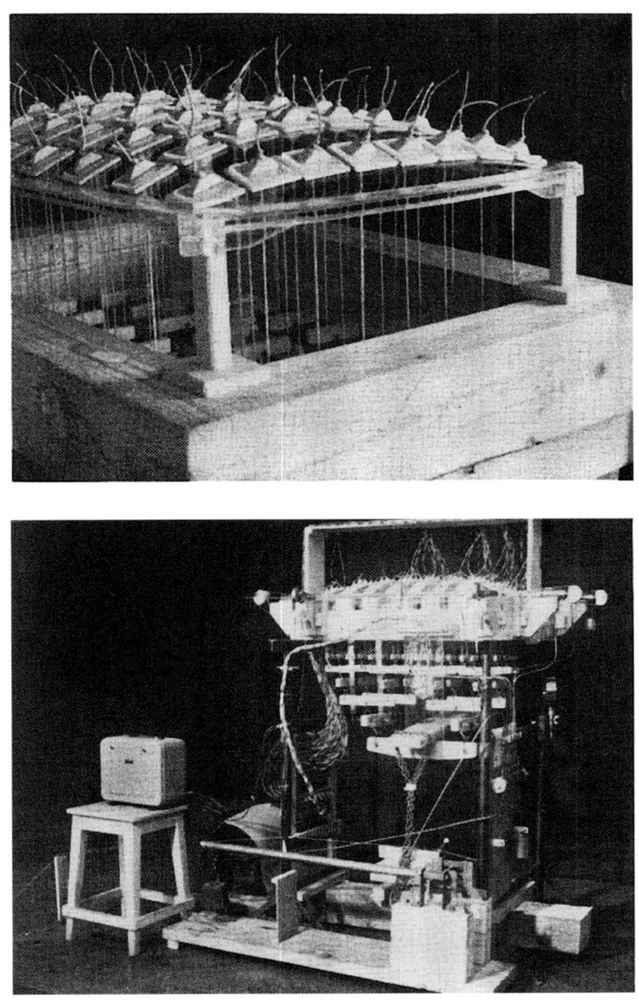

4 Scale model and testing device of the Hotel Kreuz, Langenthal, as presented by Heinz Isler at the second congress of the Fédération Internationale de la Précontrainte in Amsterdam, 1955

5 Heinz Isler, Glas Trösch factory, Thunstetten, 1955: view from the south; photograph ca. 1956

Interestingly enough, in 1957 at the *Second Symposium on Concrete Shell Roof Construction*, which was held in Oslo, Isler came up with almost the same set of pictures taken from the Plexiglas model. Unlike in Amsterdam, however, he now made an explicit reference to his former employer and his colleague Hauri. With regard to the process of designing the roof for the Hotel Kreuz hall, he stated: "Because a theoretical calculation of a freely shaped, i.e. nonmathematical, shell was not possible at that time, I made a model test, following methods developed by Prof. Lardy and dipl. Ing. Hans Hauri, Zürich."[17]

Innovative Form-Finding: A "Rubber Model" for Glas Trösch in Thunstetten, 1955

Comparing the congress contribution of 1955 with that of 1957—and contrasting both with Isler's presentation at the first IASS conference in 1959, where he would create "a minor sensation"[18]—his remarkably limited and conservative choice of models is quite a surprise. The reason for that lies in another project that Isler had already presented in Amsterdam and that he again touched on in Oslo: the Glas Trösch factory building in Thunstetten, built in 1955. During the design of this project, Isler had already arrived at a far more elaborate usage of models for form-finding purposes than the state-of-the-art testing device extensively presented to the audience might suggest. Here, he had used a model with an inflated membrane in order to define the shape of the three identical shells. But it was not until the founding conference of IASS four years later that he would present this method to the public by showing a picture of a "rubber model for shaping."[19] Although in 1957 Isler explicitly mentioned that "there is a wide range of possibilities [doing a model test] from most primitive analogies up to perfect and complete testing-machineries,"[20] he spoke of the Glas Trösch project only in a subordinate clause.[21]

There might be two reasons that could explain this reserve: Firstly, he might not have gained enough self-confidence in order to replace the reference to his well-established teacher Lardy with his own innovative approach to form-finding. Secondly, at the time of the two conferences, Isler was still in the phase of testing his new model-based form-finding method at real scale, and because of that it would not have been prudent for him to share his insights publicly at such an early stage.

The design for the Glas Trösch roof, undertaken four years after graduating from ETH, refers back to Isler's diploma project: the idea of a shed roof still survived in the preliminary designs for Glas Trösch and sketches in the archival documents reveal that he worked out four preliminary designs altogether. In all of these variants, the roof comprises three similar shells that differ by the arrangement of the shells, and in one case also by the shell's form. The first variant stands out due to relatively large central skylights. The second shows two roof

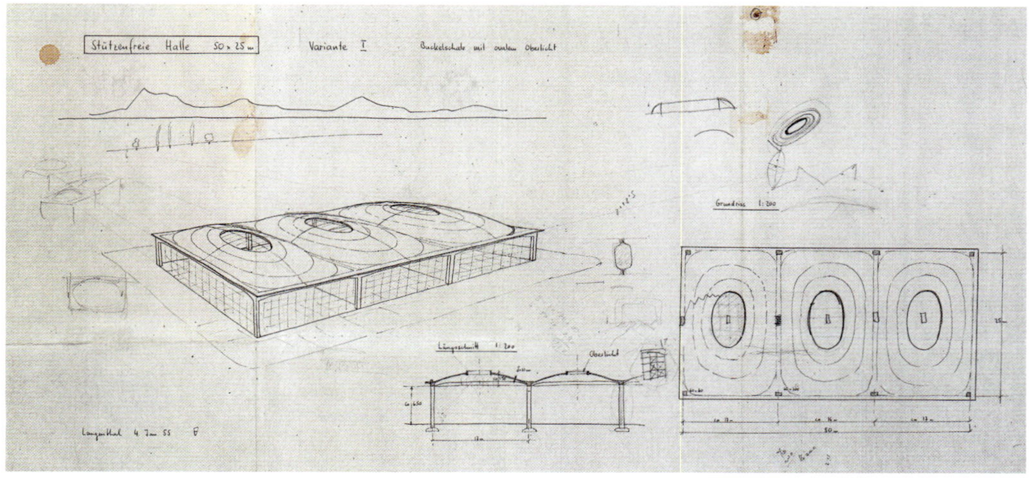

6 Heinz Isler, Glas Trösch factory, Thunstetten, 1955: variant I

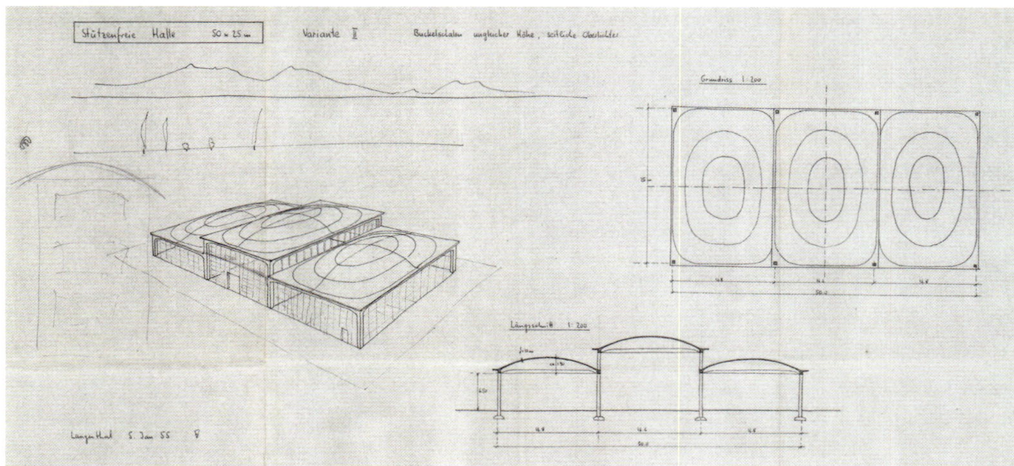

7 Heinz Isler, Glas Trösch factory, Thunstetten, 1955: variant II

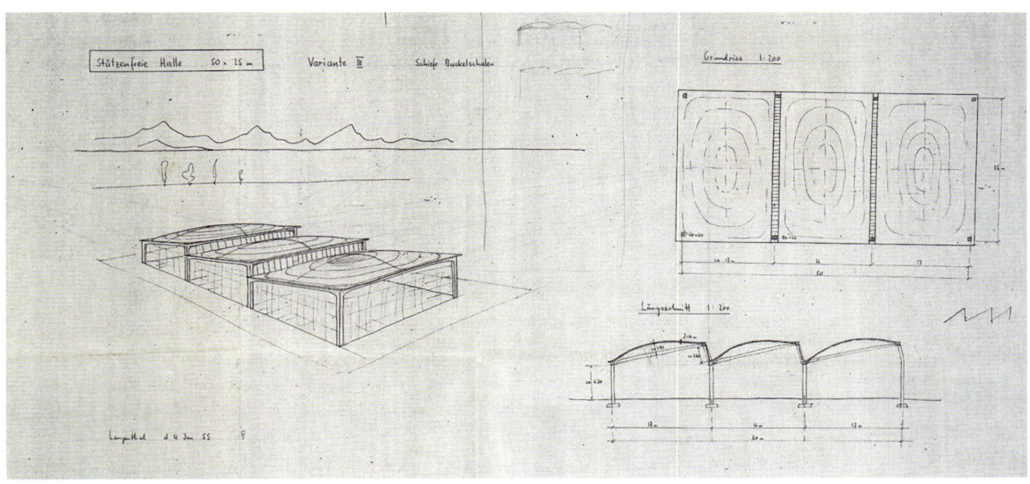

8 Heinz Isler, Glas Trösch factory, Thunstetten, 1955: variant III

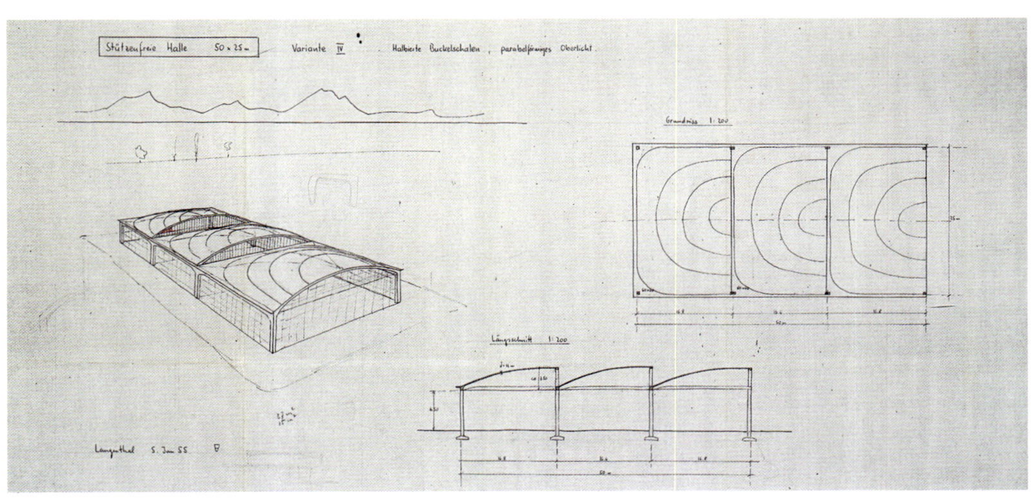

9 Heinz Isler, Glas Trösch factory, Thunstetten, 1955: variant IV

10 Inflated membrane model for the Glas Trösch factory shell, 1955

levels, the shell in the middle being lifted in comparison to the two outer shells. In the other two variants, Isler dealt with the natural light problem by going back to the shed design of his diploma and translating it into a solution that, instead of classical shedroofs, made use of shells. The third variant shows the three pneumatic-form shells being lifted at one side, with this making possible the illumination of the interior by longitudinal windows under each elevation. Finally, the roof in the fourth variant consists of three conoid shells, each cut in half, allowing light to fall into the building through parabolic curved windows.

As mentioned above, the form-finding model for the Glas Trösch shells was comparatively innovative. It consists of a wooden frame, measuring 84.10 × 65.50 centimeters, held together by eight screw clamps; between the upper and lower parts of the two-part frame, a rectangular rubber membrane is attached. Originally, a small tube was passed through the lower frame in order to inflate the membrane by air pressure—by this means the shape of the pneumatically generated form that had fallen into its shape naturally could be taken and measured at the top. The resulting shape resembles that of a plumped-up pillow, and the story of Isler's inspiration for developing that method after having seen exactly such a pillow has often been told.[22] However, what has not been elaborated in research is the way he presented his model-based method in the professional field, starting with a conventional Plexiglas model—a method common at Lardy's chair—and moving forward to his own independent and creative methods of form-finding.[23] He did not undertake this before having verified his newly found methods through various realized buildings; so building practice appeared to be necessary for him to confirm his theoretically grounded method before it could become the subject of discourse.

Development out of Necessity: Isler's First Large Domed Polyester Skylights for Blaser, 1956

Another anecdote that is often told is connected to the development of Isler's first polyester skylights. After completing at least two warehouses consisting of four shells each for the Blaser chemical factory in Rüegsau with "holes of 5 m diameter in the roof,"[24] Isler realized that no manufacturer was able to produce Plexiglas skylights of such a size; he was told that a maximum of 1.60 meters was conceivable. As a consequence, the roofs had to be covered provisionally for the time being. At that point, a trusting relationship with his client Willy Blaser (1916–2008) turned out to be fertile ground for innovative approaches in the development of building components, since Isler decided to manufacture the missing skylights himself. After he had completed prototypes in reinforced polyester, Blaser supported the engineer by letting him build the skylights with "active support by the personnel in the large spaces of the firm."[25]

For the prototype of the skylight, Isler produced and assembled eight triangular-shaped segments, most probably in autumn or winter 1956/1957 (see the contribution by Elke Genzel and Pamela Voigt in the present volume, figs. 1 and 2). This prototype, which had the disadvantage of gaps between the segments, was mounted as a trial over one of the holes and obviously fulfilled the client's as well as the engineer's expectations, so that the latter elaborated this component further.

At the beginning of the following year at the latest, Isler worked out a method to produce skylights without gaps: strands of glass fiber fabric were arranged onto a substructure that consisted of a thin layer of sawdust on heaped-up sand; afterward, the fabric was laminated with polyester resin; ultimately, the skylight was flipped into the "correct" position in order to treat the surface of the cast polyester. These earliest large domed skylights were literally handmade. Only later were they produced on an industrial level by the Swiss company Eschmann in Thun, which became another important client of Isler in the following years.

CONCLUSION

The extent to which Pierre Lardy's work and way of thinking left an imprint on the advancement of Heinz Isler's professional career and his early built works is remarkable: all the guiding themes at Lardy's chair, from model testing to prestressed concrete, not only serve as the cornerstone for Isler's work in general, but ultimately amalgamate into his specific approach to shell design. The shallow pneumatic forms of Glas Trösch, for instance, are inconceivable without the extensive use of prestressed concrete at the edge beams in order

11 Aerial view of the company premises of Blaser in Rüegsau, showing the eight shells with provisional covers, ca. 1956

to take the horizontal thrust. After having taken a first step toward experimental form-finding with this design, Isler was out of necessity encouraged to experiment with another material in order to solve the specific problem of covering "holes of 5 m diameter" left in his Blaser buildings. Lardy's emphasis on material-appropriate structural design might have also opened the door into this field by at least a narrow slit.

Examining the early projects reveals insights into Isler's progress in terms of engineering as well as in architectural practice. The Glas Trösch factory building was, on the one hand, highly important for Isler's original form-finding methods—with these, he would finally be able to go beyond what he had experienced in Lardy's laboratory. On the other hand, the design variants for this project reveal Isler's architectural development: a drawback of the Glas Trösch shells is that he did not solve the lighting problem in a satisfactory manner. However, the clue for solving this problem already lies in this project, since Isler planned central skylights in one of the four variants. Although he rejected this for Glas Trösch, he would realize large skylights only shortly afterward in the pioneering project for Blaser, where he was even given the opportunity to gather firsthand experience with reinforced polyester as a building material. With the latter, he would be able to establish another important branch in his oeuvre over the following years.

1 Billington also points out Lardy's influence on Isler; see David P. Billington, "Heinz Isler as Structural Artist," in *Heinz Isler as Structural Artist,* exh. cat. (Princeton, 1980), 9–24, here 9–11.
2 See David P. Billington, "Pierre Lardy: From Mathematics to Aesthetics," in *The Art of Structural Design: A Swiss Legacy* (New Haven/London, 2003), 112–127.
3 See Max Ritter and Pierre Lardy, *Vorgespannter Beton: Theorie und Berechnung, Schweiz: Versuche und Ausführungen* (Zurich, 1946).
4 See Isler's respective transcripts in the gta Archives, ETH Zurich, bequest of Heinz Isler, 217-S-5: "Baustatik II" (Statics II), 1947; "Massivbau I" (Concrete Structures I), 1947/1948; "Massive Brücken" (Concrete Bridges), 1949; "Massivbau II" (Concrete Structures II), 1949/1950; and "Baustatik + Massivbau, ausgewählte Kapitel" (Statics + Concrete Structures, selected chapters), 1950. We thank Maria Garlock, Princeton University, for handing over these notebooks to the gta Archives.
5 See Billington, "Pierre Lardy," 123 (see note 2).
6 ETH Zurich University Archive, Pierre Lardy Papers, HS 829:4.
7 Ibid., HS 829:34.
8 Ibid., HS 829:35.
9 Ibid., HS 829:29.
10 See Fritz Stüssi, "† Pierre Lardy," *Schweizerische Bauzeitung* 76 (1958): 762–763, here 762.
11 ETH Zurich University Archive, Pierre Lardy Papers, HS 829:21.
12 See Billington, "Pierre Lardy," especially 116–117 (see note 2).
13 ETH Zurich University Archive, Pierre Lardy Papers, HS 829:63 and 829:64.
14 John Chilton, *Heinz Isler: The Engineer's Contribution to Contemporary Architecture* (London, 2000), 14.
15 Heinz Isler, quoted in ibid., 160.
16 See Heinz Isler, "Session IIIb: Discussion," in *Second Congress of the Fédération Internationale de la Précontrainte, Amsterdam* 1955 (no place [London], 1958), 736–743.
17 Heinz Isler, "Discussion," in A. Aas-Jakobsen et. al., ed. *Proceedings of the Second Symposium on Concrete Shell Roof Construction. 1–3 July 1957* (Oslo, 1958), 327–328, here 327.
18 Billington, "Heinz Isler as Structural Artist," 13 (see note 1).
19 Heinz Isler, "New Shapes for Shells," *Bulletin of the International Association for Shell Structures* 8 (1961): paper C-3, n.p., fig. 4.
20 Isler, "Discussion," 327 (see note 17).
21 Ibid., 328.
22 See for example, Chilton, *Heinz Isler,* 15 (see note 14).
23 Apart from the "membrane under pressure," Isler presented two other form-finding methods at the IASS conference: "the freely shaped hill" and "the hanging cloth reversed"; see Isler, "New Shapes for Shells" (see note 19).
24 Chilton, *Heinz Isler,* 16 (see note 14).
25 "[...] unter tatkräftiger Mithilfe der Belegschaft in den weiten Räumen der Firma [...]," quotation from "Eine interessante Neuerung im Baufach," *Emmenthaler-Blatt Langnau,* November 15/16, 1957: 23.

Heinz Isler's Experimental Approach to Form-Finding

GIULIA BOLLER AND JOHN CHILTON

Heinz Isler himself recounted at the IASS symposium in Copenhagen in September 1991: "My personal way is characterized by a constant use of physical models. On all stages of my numerous projects we worked with them: for developing, for presentation, for investigation of behavior, for checks."[1] The foundations of Isler's experimental approach were laid, soon after graduation, while working as an assistant to his teacher and mentor at ETH Zurich, Pierre Lardy (1903–1958). In the early 1950s, Lardy had returned from a visit to the Madrid laboratory of Eduardo Torroja (1899–1961) extremely enthusiastic about Torroja's use of physical models to explore the structural behavior of his designs.[2] In consequence, Lardy established a small laboratory in an attic at ETH in order to emulate Torroja's methods. Here Isler honed his skills in building physical models that properly represented the form and support conditions of the full-scale structures under investigation, and gained proficiency in the precise measurement of deformations and strains in the models when loaded.[3]

An important practice that Isler embraced during his time in Lardy's laboratory—one that he was to maintain throughout his whole career—was that of comparing behavior predicted through the models, in particular deformations, with that of the completed structure. For him the final full-scale model was the most significant, and he used feedback from completed projects to inform and influence design development. For example, this design development was seen in four tennis hall shells at the Sports Center, Heimberg (1978), where Isler modified the geometry of each successive shell following measurement of the previously constructed examples.[4]

HEINZ ISLER'S FORM-FINDING MODELS: A TOOL DESCRIPTION

Isler introduced his innovative experimental approach to form-finding of shells to an audience of eminent structural engineers and architects at the first congress of the International Association for Shell Structures, held in Madrid in 1959, where he presented his paper "New Shapes for Shells." In this paper he outlined three form-finding approaches—the freely shaped hill, the membrane under pressure, and the hanging cloth reversed—that departed from the conventional geometrically described surfaces being constructed at that time. The paper concluded with a matrix (ten rows by four columns) populated with 39 sketches by Isler of alternative shell forms. To highlight the infinite form-finding potential of his proposed techniques, the

1 Heinz Isler at the first symposium of the International Association for Shell Structures in Madrid, 1959

final square in the matrix contained the term "etc."[5] Due to the unconventional nature of the techniques he described and the challenge to the preconceptions of the expert audience he was addressing, discussion following his presentation of the paper was extensive.[6] More than 30 years later, in his presentation to the IASS symposium in Copenhagen, titled "Generating Shell Shapes by Physical Experiments," he gave an extensive description of his modeling and physical experiments. There he stressed the importance of precision—manual skill, technical craftsmanship, patience, and concentration—in all aspects of his experimental approach to form-finding. He also admitted (as he remarked "maybe for the first time") that it "has proved useful and necessary to superpose a slight mathematical function to most of my experimental shapes."[7] Physical modeling was clearly the most important tool in Isler's shell design, but not the only one.

Freely Shaped Hill

Although in "New Shapes for Shells" Isler described the freely shaped hill technique as "prehistoric" and "primitive," he suggested that it offers the greatest design freedom through direct modeling of space and form. However, he also cautioned that the designer requires a good understanding of statics and sufficient experience to determine the structural efficiency of the freely shaped form, adding that "[i]n case of doubt models may help."[8]

He first applied this technique in 1955 during his national service, modeling at full scale to develop a cheap reinforced concrete shelter to resist a nuclear bomb blast of 60 T/m^2.[9] Soil excavated from a roughly 4-meter diameter circular trench was mounded in the center and used as formwork for a 200-millimeter-thick reinforced concrete dome.[10] A more sophisticated deployment of this technique was a sand form for synclastically curved vaulted glass-reinforced polyester (GRP) shells with a span of 6 meters, which were used as roof components for a modular storage system (see the contribution by Elke Genzel and Pamela Voigt in the present volume, figs. 4 and 5). This technique can also be applied as an inverted form and was used by Isler in 1956 for a GRP swimming pool lining in Locarno.

Pneumatic Membrane

Inspiration for Isler's pneumatic membrane form-finding technique came from his contemplation of the pillow on his bed, while he was struggling with the design of a shell roof at the Hotel Kreuz, Langenthal, in 1954. It occurred to him that if he could make a technical pillow—that is, a flexible membrane inflated against a backing board while restricted within a border similar in shape to the projected roof plan—he would be able to generate a double-curved tension surface suitable for use as a thin compression shell if the applied load were to be reversed. Nevertheless, he recognized its key shortcoming: unlike in the reinforced concrete shell, where the predominant load is its own weight, which acts vertically, in the inflated membrane the internal pressure acts perpendicular to the curved surface. For instance, in the case of the full-scale pneumatic form-found shells, the corners are rounded to avoid the negative curvature that occurs in the inflated membrane with a square plan.

2 Heinz Isler's model laboratory with conceptual hanging models presented on a hat stand, 2011

3 Heinz Isler's model laboratory with measuring models and a set of models of the tennis hall series on the left, 2011

Hanging Membrane

Although the pneumatic form-finding method resulted in the greatest number of Isler's shells—the free span, corner-supported industrial "bubble" shells—the majority of his surviving form-finding models were generated using the hanging membrane method. This method, used for the more architecturally inventive shell forms, was prompted by Isler's noting the tension surfaces produced by wet burlap that he saw draped over steel reinforcement mesh on a construction site in 1955.[11]

The principle of this form-finding method seems simple: take a thin sheet of flexible material; cover it with a thin, uniform layer of liquid gypsum or similar material to represent the self-weight of the shell; hang it between supports disposed, to scale, like those in the proposed structure; let gravity form a double-curved tensile surface; wait for the gypsum to set; and invert and measure the model precisely to determine the scaled dimensions of the shell. However, the reality is not so simple, as will be shown in the form-finding of the Grob AG shell in Sargans. For instance, the flexible sheet needs to be isotropic—woven fabric will result in different forms depending on weave and weft orientation. The coating material needs to be of the correct consistency at the time of hanging the membrane to avoid its slipping off if too wet or cracking if too dry. The size, elasticity, and shape of the membrane sheet will also influence the resulting form—too small and stiff, and the form will be too flat; too large and flexible, and wrinkles will develop.

Precise measurement of the final selected shape is also critical. This precision was accomplished by Isler's using metal scales embedded in a timber box frame to locate points on an x–y grid, with the z coordinate being found using a counterbalanced fine point and dial gauge.[12] Imperfections in the cast surface and small discrepancies in location of the x–y grid will affect the accuracy of the z coordinates, which he measured multiple times. These he averaged, then plotted along grid lines, subsequently smoothing the curve if necessary. He was aware that this potential for inaccuracy was particularly relevant in the areas of steeper slope, for example near the supports, and for that reason he used a denser measurement grid in such locations.

Flow Form

The use of flow or growth forms as a method of form-finding was not mentioned in Isler's paper "New Shapes for Shells" and was only introduced later—the first application being for the Migros supermarket in Bellinzona in 1964 (see the contribution by Matthias Beckh: "From Foam to Form" in the present volume, figs. 6–10). In retrospect, Isler criticized the form, saying that it was "statically not good [...] because it is getting too steep here [at the supports]."[13]

The inspiration for this method came while Isler was observing a manufacturer's demonstration of the test they used to measure the rate and overall expansion of an expanding polyurethane foam constrained in a square tube.[14] He found himself more interested in the resulting shape of the hardened foam surface than the material itself, so he began to experiment with the foam to make similar shapes and, subsequently, once rationalized into a rotational symmetry, he adopted expansion forms for a number of projects, including the Kilcher factory, Recherswil (1965), and the Bürgi garden center, Camorino (1973).

Geometrical Shape

Heinz Isler's use of purely geometrically defined shells was quite limited and usually in order to comply with an architect's concept—for instance, the triangular spherical segment shells with sides up to 45 meters in length in Chamonix, in collaboration with Roger Taillibert.[15] However, he also designed a few shells based on hyperbolic paraboloid (hypar) geometry. To assist him in this, in his studio he had a square, hinged wooden frame strung with flexible cords with which he was able to quickly generate a variety of hypar surfaces.

As standard hypar shells can be analyzed mathematically, there was little need to make experimental models. However, for a few projects the basic hypar form was modified, as in the Villa Camoletti or the Villa Darier, both in collaboration with architect Pierre Camoletti, and also in the Heilig-Geist-Kirche (Church of the Holy Spirit) in Lommiswil, designed together with Roland Hanselmann. At the first building, two hypars intersect along a slightly curved common axis and share one of the three supports; at the Villa Darier, four connected hypar-based shells of three different plan forms rest on four bifurcated columns;[16] and at the Heilig-Geist-Kirche a free-form segment was cut from an inclined hypar surface and acts contiguously with the perimeter walls.[17] In these cases, Isler used physical models to determine structural behavior.

Others (Tensile Hanging Forms, "Stempelform")

Although mainly recognized for his reinforced concrete shells, Isler also experimented with tensile structures. His experiments with hanging nets and fabrics, which, by spraying water onto them, he transformed into spectacular ice sculptures at his home in Zuzwil, informed his understanding of both tensile and compressive double-curved surfaces.

It is sometimes overlooked that Isler was the engineer for architect Günter Behnisch's competition-winning design for the Olympic stadium in Munich, which included a spectacular tensile roof. However, the

4 Heinz Isler, initial model for the Olympic Stadium, Munich, ca. 1967

final roof configuration, further developed by Frei Otto in collaboration with Jörg Schlaich at the office of Leonhardt and Andrä to avoid large, relatively flat areas in the roof, was different from that proposed for the competition.[18] It is hardly coincidental that the stadium design was under development at around the same time (ca. 1967/1968) that Isler was experimenting with hanging membrane models for the design of some of his most iconic shells, such as Gips Union in Bex, the roof for the motorway service station Deitingen Süd, or the Sicli factory building in Geneva.

IT IS ALL IN THE SHAPING

Looking at the number of physical form-finding models that Heinz Isler produced during his career and their broad use in free-form shells, those based on the hanging membrane principle are the most numerous. In other typologies the form is quickly defined and the use of physical models is linked to later stages of design development. However, in free-form shells, Isler used form-finding models extensively.

By considering two contemporary examples that belong to his first explorations in more free-form shells, it is possible to have a closer look at Isler's design process. The first is a pure hanging membrane shell, whereas the second example, the Villa Camoletti, is a shell defined through geometry.

E. Grob AG in Sargans, 1968

The free-form shell for the architectural office Grob in Sargans, built in 1968, represents one of Isler's very first free-form shells defined through the form-finding method of the hanging membrane. It is part of a larger project that the engineer designed for the company Grob AG, consisting of four industrial shells 17 × 17 meters, developed with the pneumatic membrane method. The office of the architect (and client) Ernest Grob is centrally located with respect to the bubble shells and it originally stood as an iconic building that welcomed visitors. With a trapezoidal plan of 24 × 20 meters tapering to 12 meters and an average thickness of 11 centimeters, the unconventional shell sits on four feet: two at ground level and two on the roof of the adjacent single-story building behind.

The Sargans shell is contemporary with two other well-known Isler shells obtained with the hanging membrane method: that for the Gips Union in Bex, considered to be his very first free-form shell,[19] and Deitingen Süd, probably the most pure and elegant shell that Isler ever constructed.[20] What is interesting about the building in Sargans is that it integrates the characters of both shells, as well as the form-finding approach. This is evident from the annotations found on the documents produced during the design phase,[21] since Isler refers continuously to the two contemporary projects: as both shells have supports located at different heights, the mass calculations and basic assumptions for the load configuration are referred to those considered for the Deitingen shell, whereas the form-finding technique that was adopted looks very similar to that of the Bex project, having four supports and a symmetrical, tapering geometry.

In general, the form-finding phase represents the first active involvement in the design of the shell, since it helps to materialize the conceptual idea, bringing together structural principles, physical laws, and architectural understanding. The form is defined by

5 Erne5st Grob with Heinz Isler, Grob cement plant and architectural office, Sargans, 1968

the boundary conditions, the load cases, and the understanding of the stresses within the shell.[22] Through physical models, an experienced shell builder like Isler understands the problems related to the geometrical shape and to the structural behavior by working actively on them, handling them, and understanding the weak areas where buckling problems could occur.[23] The design is then modified with the use of further small-scale physical models.

In the case of the free-form shell of the Sargans project, looking at the documents recorded in the Isler archive,[24] the actual form-finding phase happened quite late in the design process and was not commenced until eight months after the first exchanges between Isler and the client: the first documents are dated September 1967, and only in May 1968 did Isler work on the gypsum models, form-found by the hanging membrane principle. The crucial question is: why did Isler, being famous for his experimental design approach, not start using physical models until so late? A potential answer lies in the cost and time needed for the making of a physical model. For economic reasons, the engineer might have waited until the agreement between the client, the contractor, and his own office was signed.

The overall architectural concept appears already in the initial plans developed by Ernest Grob, showing the arrangement of the different volumes in plan and elevation. Isler, not being mentioned on these initial drawings, was involved as an expert for shell design responsible for translating Grob's sketches into the actual free-form shape. Interestingly, all the calculations that Isler developed for the project are confined to the initial negotiation phase instead of to the actual design development. They mainly consist of basic estimation of the required concrete volume and simplified load calculations. The estimates are related to the definition of the foundations, which represent the biggest cost factor. From the archival materials, there appears to be no direct relation between these calculations and the form-finding phase that occurred some months later. It is as if this information would have been useful mainly for the bid submitted by the construction company Bösiger AG, Isler's most-trusted contractor—indeed, these documents date from the same time as exchanges with the very same company that later was responsible for the construction of the shell.

The form-finding phase itself began in May 1968. In his first free-form projects, of which this is one, Isler produced a lot of physical models in gypsum, based on the hanging membrane principle. His inexperience in that shell typology called for multiple explorations with different materials, as well as boundary conditions, in order to understand the limits of the proposed method and to annotate potential issues. Compared to any other project that Isler realized in his entire career, the Sargans shell produced the greatest number of gypsum models for form-finding: in one month, Isler and his collaborators Anton Friedli and Hans Glanzmann produced seven different gypsum models in order to define in an accurate way the correct shape for the free-form shell.

6 Heinz Isler, form-finding models developed for the Grob project, Sargans, 1968

Isler always took part in the production process and pictures of the different steps needed in the model development that were taken by him represent an important source for the understanding of his method, since they can be linked with his written annotations referring to the respective models.

The materials used were simple, but the form-finding tool was quite complex. The hanging membrane was made of a homogeneous material reinforced with a 1-centimeter-wide strip along the membrane edges. It was cut according to the plan, following the proportion of the designed shell, to scale, but bigger than the actual hole in the timber frame. Small horizontal timber elements put perpendicularly to the shell's feet attached the membrane onto the frame while keeping it flexible and able to hang freely when loaded by the gypsum. The cutout frame and membrane were placed on a flat board and a quantity of gypsum was poured and equally distributed over the surface with a constant thickness of 1 centimeter, in order to simulate the dead load of the actual shell. After some minutes, the gypsum started to harden and, simultaneously, the model was vibrated manually in order to remove any air bubbles. A water hose was always at hand during this phase to rework the gypsum layer if needed. The cutout timber board was then carefully lifted off the base board and onto the given supports to simulate the difference of height in the proposed project design, with the back feet sitting at a higher level than the front supports.

The first form-finding models were developed in just one day. The same device was used for multiple explorations, changing the amount of gypsum poured on it, the membrane type, and dimension. The very first model that was produced showed an unsymmetrical response in the hanging phase under the gypsum load; Isler considered this to be caused by the use of a membrane that was not fully under tension. From the second exploration onward, the membrane was, therefore, stretched while being fixed to the timber frame. In this way the response that resulted was much more symmetrical, which is visible in the images taken during the model-making process, where wrinkles can be seen at the corners of the model.[25]

For every gypsum model, Isler took precise notes for the evaluation of the material quantity, the geometrical properties such as symmetry, and position of the legs or curvature of the shell, as well as a first rough structural understanding of the form found. He then drew the curvatures of the different side views and compared them to improve his overall understanding of the building. Out of the three initial models, Isler chose one in order to conduct the premeasurement of the found form, studying closely the curvatures on the main axis and along the edges. On this basis, he detected which aspects—both geometrical and structural—needed to be improved. Therefore, the form-finding procedure was an iterative design process in which every step was carefully studied to define the weak elements.

7 Contact print sheet with a series of pictures documenting the form-finding procedure for one of the latest models for the Grob project, Sargans; in the lower half, a series of pictures documents the construction site of the Deitingen motorway station, 1968

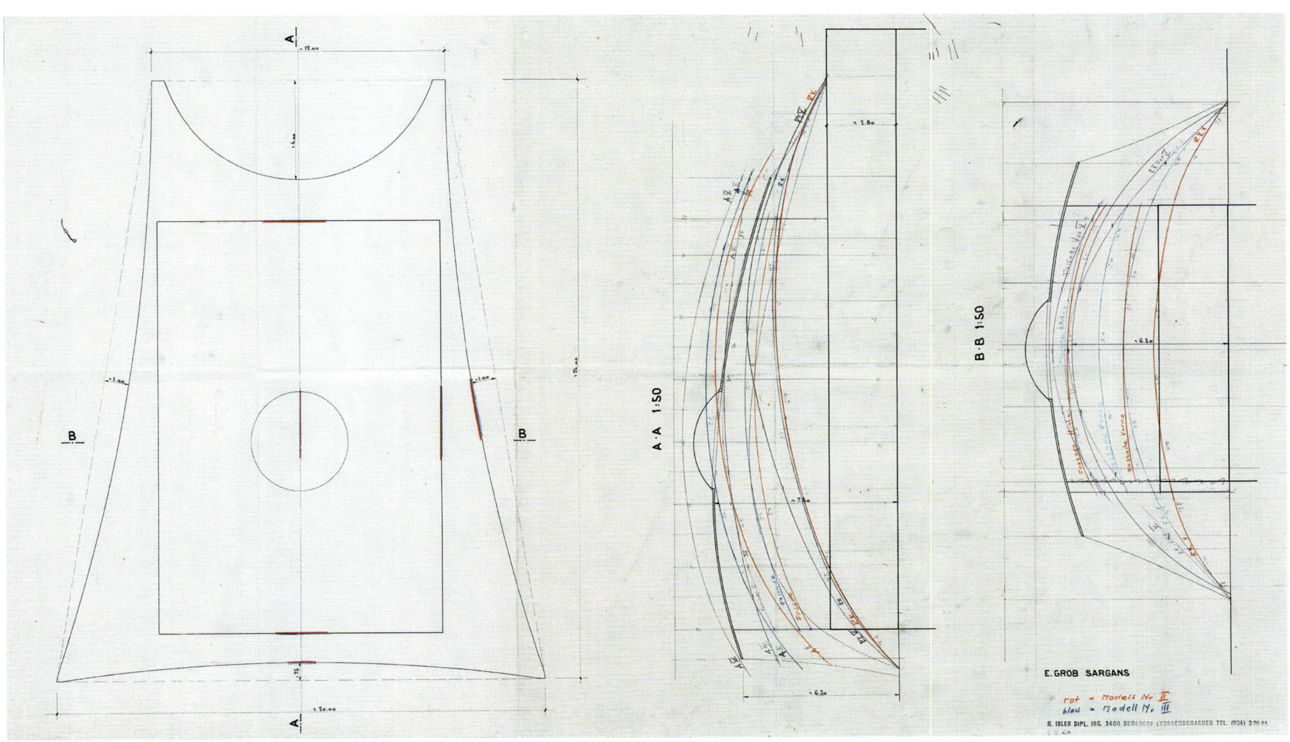

8 Heinz Isler, comparative study of the curvature of different plaster models for the Grob project, Sargans, 1968

9 Pierre Camoletti with Heinz Isler, Villa Camoletti, Geneva, 1970

Further gypsum models were made between June and July 1968, almost concurrent with the beginning of the construction on site. A form-finding model that accomplished the requirements of geometry, symmetry, structural behavior, and architectural appearance was finally chosen in July and reproduced as a more accurate fiber-reinforced polyester model to allow thorough structural testing at a small scale. On this basis, the free-form shell roof was built between September and November 1968.

Villa Camoletti in Collonge-Bellerive, 1970

The project of Villa Camoletti, conceived in 1970 as the private house of the architect Pierre Camoletti, represents one of the few residential projects that Isler realized in his career. The house is located on the outskirts of Geneva, close to the lake, and is placed in the middle of a gently sloping garden. Though the project has always been recorded as a geometrical shell based on the combination of two hyperbolic paraboloids, mathematically definable and produced by straight lines arranged in space,[26] it does not represent a common hypar, since the starting geometry was modified on the side length of the ruled surface and on the intersecting point. The two merged shells of Villa Camoletti are symmetrical along their intersection, with each having a long axis of 17 meters, a short axis of 13 meters, and a thickness of 8 to 12 centimeters.

Similar to the Grob project, the first documentation of Villa Camoletti is the architectural plans dating from September 1969. These were carried out by the architect and client Camoletti, who then asked Isler to assist him in the further development of the project. Unlike in Sargans, the architect conceived the overall design alone,[27] and Isler was involved only as a consultant engineer. The first active involvement is evident in April 1970, when Isler and his collaborators worked on the physical models for the characterization of the shape and the related structural measurements. Before that came a long negotiation phase, with basic mass calculations and bids for the construction. Again, it seems as if Isler started being fully active in the project only after contracts had been signed, so he could be sure to have his contractor Bösiger on board for the construction phase.

Between September and December 1969, Camoletti exchanged proposals for the shell design with Isler, working on its development with plan and elevations. The main revisions were developed in the drawings and controlled by accurate calculations of the geometrical properties of the shape so defined. In other words, in this project Isler did not work with form-finding physical models at the conceptual phase; rather he made annotations on paper. He postponed the physical exploration, carried out using small-scale models, until the later design phase.

10 Wooden model for Villa Camoletti, Geneva, developed as a mold for measuring models, 1970

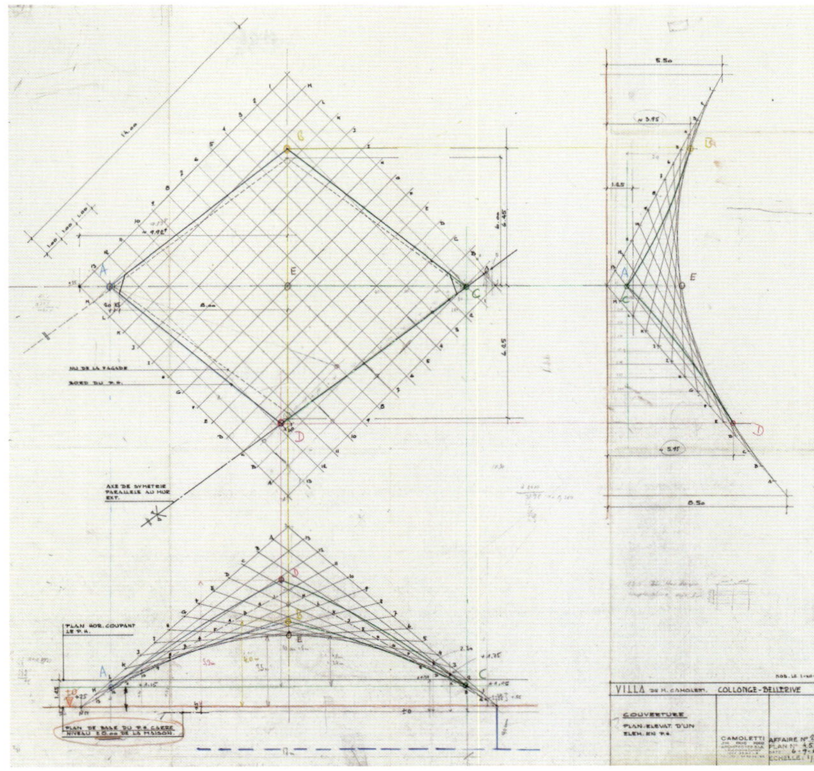

11 Initial studies about the geometry of the single shell for Villa Camoletti, Geneva, 1969

Among the archival documents,[28] there is one that has a special value in the overall understanding of Isler's experimental design: a document dated January 1970 (that is, during the negotiation phase) casts light on the details for the construction of a physical model, which refers to one of the models that Isler built for the control of the structural behavior of his shells at a scale of 1:50. Isler annotated carefully the different steps for its construction. First, the single shells are developed separately based on a wooden mold that defines the actual shape; then they are joined together and attached, and movable support conditions are defined; finally, a load application system is installed and electrical strain gauges are connected to the model. The cost of labor is considered, along with the necessary materials. According to Isler's calculations, the preparation of the small-scale model requires seven weeks of work, representing a total of 350 working hours and at a total price between 7,500 and 10,000 Swiss francs, depending on the support type chosen.[29] In addition, the time required and the cost for taking the measurements is disclosed. Three potential variations, which underline the experimental character of this typology of physical modeling, are indicated in the document: the first exploration requires two weeks of work, the second ten days, and the third just one week, for a total price of 3,400 Swiss francs.[30]

The information that relates to the construction of Isler's physical model shows both the difficulty and the high level of complexity of the project, in which time, cost, and expertise were the main factors involved. The considerable amount of time required and the related cost constitute obstacles to making a lot of different physical explorations. At this stage, Isler had to be convinced of the design and just using the physical model to test small variations of the form. In the project for Villa Camoletti, since it is a modified geometrical shape, the lack of form-finding models is probably justified by the time- and cost-consuming operation described above: in this case Isler modified the initial geometry mathematically and worked physically at a later stage, on the structural validation model and on the building. Additionally, he used models for the structural characterization of his shells, testing them in different configurations and changing the support conditions to define the potential problems that could occur in the built shell on site.

The consequent wooden model acted as a mold for the fiber-reinforced polyester model, which was then used for the measurements of the structural behavior of the shell. It was made on the basis of the geometrical definition of the project in plan and elevation. On the side of the model, some reference lines are visible, which define with regular distances the height of each point along the edges for the reliable reproduction of the shape. Furthermore, at the axis between the two hyperbolic paraboloids the line of intersection is curved, as a result of the geometrical modifications that

12 Construction site of Villa Camoletti, Geneva: fitting of the permanent formwork, 1970

occurred at the initial design phase. The slope toward the central support is steeper, so that the two initial shells are not juxtaposed but slightly intersected along the main axis of the building. Interestingly, the same detail is visible on the construction site, with the timber scaffolding elements cut shorter to achieve the needed curvature of the peak line.

It is obvious that during design and construction (June and July 1970), the phases of model measurements and shell construction overlapped, just as they did in the Sargans project. The high number of measurements on the built shell show the direct relationship between the small-scale physical model and the constructed building, the latter being conceived as a full-scale physical model.

Even though Isler did not use form-finding models in this project at the conceptual phase, the experimental approach is visible at all the different steps of the design, that is, in the definition of the actual shape by iterative procedures with very different tools: beginning with the drawings that led to the wooden mold and the structural validation model to the final result: the built shell. Thus, Isler's form-finding process did not end with the found shape to be tested on the more accurate physical models, but actually it continued until the very end of the construction process and beyond.

Looking at his other projects, Villa Camoletti represents the initial collaboration between Heinz Isler and Pierre Camoletti, which continued through their design for the Villa Darier, in Cologny, built in 1985. Consequently, the first residential house can be seen as the prototype for the development of the more architecturally and structurally ambitious second villa, which was also conceived as a combination of (now four) hyperbolic paraboloids with modifications in their geometry.

CONCLUSION

In his presentation at the IASS symposium in 1991, as reported later in the *Bulletin* of IASS,[31] Isler revealed some—but by no means all—of the secrets of his experimental approach to form-finding. However, due to his recording of his experiments in meticulous detail, his habit of keeping absolutely everything on file, and the availability of this information for the first time in the gta Archives, it is now possible to gain deeper insight into his methods. For instance, the sequence of photographs and his accompanying notes for the form-finding of the Grob shell using a hanging membrane confirm that the process is more sophisticated than it would initially appear. Additionally, the physical model, being a time-consuming and costly device, becomes a relevant actor in the actual development of the project. In particular, the form-finding model arises as the most important source to be investigated for the understanding of Isler's design process, together with the constructed shell. Its physicality, even if at a small scale, is comparable to the built shells as a proof of Isler's innovative intuition in shell design. The model gains importance because it gives answers to questions not yet responded to by other methods.[32]

In both of the shell designs considered in this chapter Isler started the form-finding explorations as soon as the project agreement was officially reached. The form-finding models refer to the first active involvement in the design, since they represent the shell definition in geometry and support conditions. Being based on physical principles, they become part of the engineering development of the project. At the same time, they are easily understood by people who are not experts in the field. For this reason, they became the main feature of his innovative shell design, and Isler used them for the communication of his experimental approach in multiple conferences, exhibitions, and workshops.

Heinz Isler's identification of the critical value of physical form-finding models can be seen in the discussion following the presentation of his paper "New Shapes for Shells" in 1959, where he stressed that the most important issue in the design of shells was their shaping.[33] Thus he was very supportive when the IASS Working Group 15: Structural Morphology was established, attending the initial meeting in a bar in Copenhagen in 1991 and actively participating in their seminars and colloquia. This included on-stage demonstrations of his form-finding by inflated and hanging membranes, respectively, at the second seminar, in Stuttgart in 1994. However, both in his accompanying paper and during the live performance he made it very clear that, although it is "interesting to see such models appearing by themselves"[34] produced by the forces of gravity and air pressure, such models can only be used as the basis for the design of full-scale shells if they are produced and tested with the utmost precision at all stages. This encapsulates Heinz Isler's experimental approach.

1 Heinz Isler, "Generating Shell Shapes by Physical Experiments," *Bulletin of the International Association for Shell and Spatial Structures* 34, no. 111 (1993): 53–63, here 54.
2 See John Chilton, *Heinz Isler: The Engineer's Contribution to Contemporary Architecture* (London, 2000), 21.
3 See ibid.
4 See Heinz Isler, "New Shapes for Shells—Twenty Years After," *Bulletin of the International Association for Shell and Spatial Structures* 20.3/21.1, no. 71/72 (1979): 10–19.
5 See Heinz Isler, "New Shapes for Shells," *Bulletin of the International Association for Shell Structures* 8 (1961): paper C-3, n.p.
6 Ibid., fig. 9. See also David P. Billington, *The Tower and the Bridge: The New Art of Structural Engineering* (Princeton, 1983), 224; and John Chilton, "39 etc...: Heinz Isler's Infinite Spectrum of New Shapes for Shells," in Alberto Domingo and Carlos Lázaro, ed., *Proceedings of the International Association for Shell and Spatial Structures (IASS) Symposium 2009, Valencia: Evolution and Trends in Design, Analysis and Construction of Shell and Spatial Structures* (Valencia, 2009), 51–62, here 55–59.
7 Isler, "Generating Shell Shapes," 61 (see note 1).
8 Isler, "New Shapes for Shells" (see note 5).
9 Heinz Isler in recorded conversation with John Chilton and Ekkehard Ramm, Lyssachschachen, August 18, 2003.
10 See Heinz Isler, "Feldmässiger Unterstand in Beton (Atom-Schutzbunker)," *Technische Mitteilungen für Sappeure, Pontoniere und Mineure* 21, no. 4 (1956): 158–179.
11 See Chilton, *Heinz Isler,* 35 (see note 2).
12 See ibid., 42–43.
13 Heinz Isler in recorded conversation with John Chilton, Lyssachschachen, August 18, 1999.
14 See ibid.
15 See Chilton, *Heinz Isler,* 86–89 (see note 2).
16 See ibid., 132–134.
17 See John Chilton, "Shells for Two Churches," *Journal of the International Association for Shell and Spatial Structures* 52.3, no. 169 (2011): 173–183.
18 See Irene Meissner and Eberhard Möller, "Roofing for the Main Sports Facilities in the Olympiapark in Munich," in Winfried Nerdinger, ed., *Frei Otto: Complete Works. Lightweight Construction: Natural Design* (Basel/Boston/Berlin, 2005), 260–269, here 267.
19 See John Chilton, "Heinz Isler and His Use of Physical Models," in Bill Addis, ed., *Physical Models in Civil and Building Engineering: Their History and Current Use* (Berlin, 2020 [in press]).
20 See Chilton, *Heinz Isler,* 92–96 (see note 2).
21 See gta Archives, ETH Zurich, bequest of Heinz Isler, 217-0134, box 2/3.
22 See Kai-Uwe Bletzinger and Ekkehard Ramm, "Computational Form Finding and Optimization," in Sigrid Adriaenssens, Philippe Block, Diederik Veenendaal, and Chris Williams, ed., *Shell Structures for Architecture: Form Finding and Optimization* (London/New York, 2014), 45–56, here 46.
23 See Ekkehard Ramm, "Heinz Isler Shells—The Priority of Form," *Journal of the International Association for Shell and Spatial Structures* 52.3, no. 169 (2011): 143–154, here 152.
24 See gta Archives, ETH Zurich, bequest of Heinz Isler, 217-0134, box 3/3.
25 See gta Archives, ETH Zurich, bequest of Heinz Isler, 217-FX-2-68.
26 See Isler, "New Shapes for Shells—Twenty Years After," 11 (see note 4).
27 Confirmed by a conversation between Heinz Bösiger, Hans Glanzmann, Matthias Beckh, Giulia Boller, and Rainer Schützeichel, Langenthal, September 24, 2019.
28 See gta Archives, ETH Zurich, bequest of Heinz Isler, 217-0207.
29 The price indicated corresponds today with an amount between 23,000 and 30,000 Swiss francs; the inflation is calculated on the basis of the Swiss annual index: http://www.portal-stat.admin.ch/lik_rechner/d/lik_rechner.htm (accessed October 20, 2019).
30 Today 10,300 Swiss francs; ibid.
31 Isler, "Generating Shell Shapes" (see note 1).
32 See "Die Natur ist millionenfach stärker als ich: Christoph Allenspach im Gespräch mit Heinz Isler," *Baudoc-Bulletin* 27, no. 12 (1999): 15–18, here 16.
33 Isler, "New Shapes for Shells," discussion (see note 5).
34 Heinz Isler, "Creating Models," in Ralf Höller, Jürgen Hennicke, and Frieder Klenk, ed., *Application of Structural Morphology to Architecture: Proceedings of the 2nd International Seminar on Structural Morphology* (Stuttgart, 1994), 221–230, here 222.

From Foam to Form
The Peculiar First Free-form Shells of Heinz Isler

MATTHIAS BECKH

Undoubtedly, Heinz Isler is among the most prolific creators of shell buildings in the twentieth century. Besides the multitude of realized projects, he is first of all known for his radically new approach to the design of concrete shells. With his relentless pursuit of using physical models and experiments for form-finding, he revolutionized this branch of structural engineering and introduced an abundance of unprecedented forms and shapes to the design of these structures.

After he had realized a variety of projects based on pneumatic form-finding models in the late 1950s, he started to experiment with another medium to explore new geometries for shells: polyurethane foam. The self-formation process that was triggered by a chemical reaction led to smooth and gently curved organic shapes that clearly fascinated him. While Isler explored new ways to design free-form shells in the early 1960s, the foam experiments provided him with valuable inspiration. This essay traces Isler's first steps when working with the so-called expansion or flow-form method up to the first projects based on this approach.

NEW SHAPES FOR SHELLS

Isler built his first reinforced concrete shells from 1954 onward. By the end of the 1950s, he had realized an impressive number of projects—mostly bubble shells for the Swiss manufacturing industry—based on pneumatic form-finding models (see the contribution by Matthias Beckh and Rainer Schützeichel in the present volume, fig. 10).[1] When Isler participated in the founding congress of the International Association for Shell Structures (IASS) in 1959 in Madrid, he had—although only 33 years old—already gained an astonishing wealth of experience in the construction of reinforced concrete shells. His seminal presentation "New Shapes for Shells" was certainly one of the most influential contributions to the congress and triggered a lively discussion among the eminent shell designers of the day who were present. In his talk, Isler championed the introduction of three new methods to define the shapes of shells: the freely shaped hill, the membrane under pressure, and the hanging cloth reversed. Concluding with 39 diagrams of "natural hills on different edge lines," he revealed endless untapped possibilities and an abundance of unfamiliar forms to shell design.[2] In order to understand the sensation that his presentation provoked, one has to recall the common practice of shell

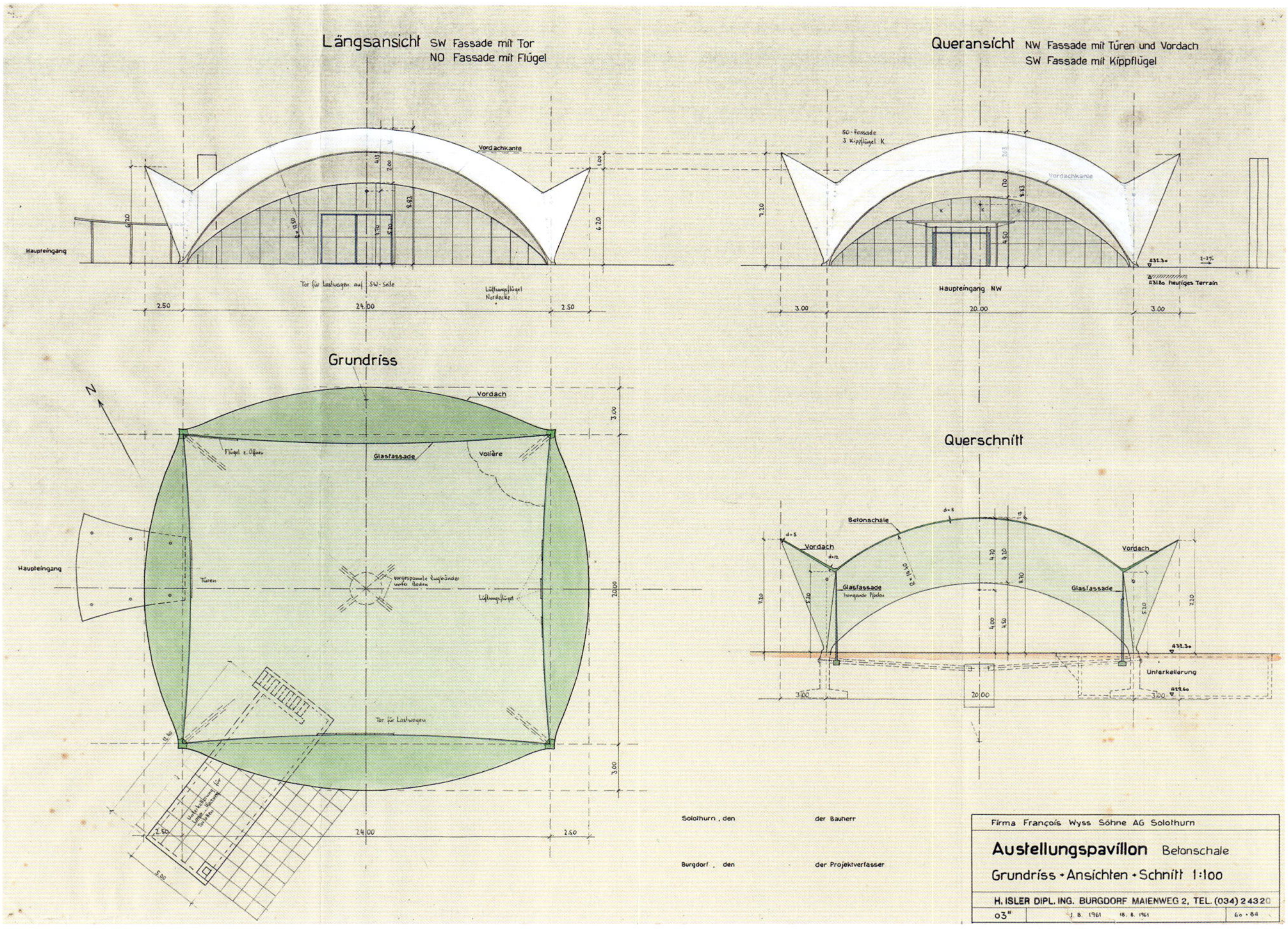

1 Heinz Isler, Wyss garden center, Zuchwil: floor plan, elevations, and cross-section, 1961

design in the postwar era: the vast majority of shells were based on mathematically defined geometries. Cylindrical shapes, spherical segments, and hyperbolic paraboloids were the prevailing configurations of reinforced concrete shells. In this context, Isler's proposed form-finding techniques were highly unorthodox.[3]

Despite his progressive presentation in Madrid and the anticipated profusion of forms, almost all of Isler's shells around 1960 were conceived with the "membrane under pressure" approach and looked quite similar. The great economic success of the bubble shell system in central Switzerland absorbed much of his attention at the time. According to Isler's own reference list, the first free-form was realized for the Wyss garden center in Zuchwil near Solothurn.[4] In 1961 Heinz Isler began work on the design of this expressive structure, which only rests on its four corners. With its wide cantilevering canopies and thin edges, this glaring white shell structure is quite unlike the hitherto built bubble shells and their modular and rational character.

If one takes a closer look at this first free-form structure, it turns out that the shell geometry was not developed by means of one of the form-finding procedures that he had famously championed at the IASS conference in Madrid. Instead, the shell surface of the garden center is based on a translation surface: a first generatrix, a spherical segment with a radius of 14.40 meters, was moved along a second spherical segment (r = 17.50 meters). The resulting translation surface geometry therefore belongs exactly to the group of mathematically defined shapes that he had denounced in Madrid.

Dubbed "form 29," the system was advertised in brochures for Isler's office. Isler had laid high hopes on reusing the wooden lattice girders for the formwork to replicate the layout of the garden center for similar applications. Unfortunately, the system would only be repeated once: in 1963 a "form 29" shell was built to house a modest Coop supermarket, with a covered area of 440 square meters, in the small village of Biasca in the Ticino Alps.[5] Most likely, the preset curvatures of the formwork system made of wooden lattice girders proved to be too inflexible to respond to more complex design briefs and spatial requirements.

THE FIRST FOAM EXPERIMENTS

About the same time as the Wyss garden center was built, Isler had started to experiment with polyurethane foam. Plenty of undated models and photographs in his bequest suggest that this material intrigued him. With

2 Advertisement for “form 29” with photographs of the Wyss garden center, Zuchwil: advertising brochure of Heinz Isler’s engineering office, undated (after 1962)

3 Heinz Isler, Coop supermarket, Biasca; photograph with collaged design sketch, ca. 1963

4 Polyurethane model, undated (early 1960s)

5 Sliced polyurethane specimen, undated (early 1960s)

his inquisitive mind, Isler must have been fascinated by the richness of unexpected and surprising shapes that appeared just after the chemical reaction had taken place. The self-formation process of the expanding foam led to seemingly natural shapes with even surfaces and smooth curvatures. Organic shapes of inorganic descent.

Apart from the surprising variety of forms and shapes that could be stimulated with this chemical process, the experiments with polyurethane foam had another advantage. As the surface of the foam hardens quickly, experiments with this method could be done quite swiftly—a significant benefit over models made of gypsum or other liquid materials that required a much longer time to set. The expansion process could be controlled by the mixture itself and the confinement in which the chemical process took place. The jottings on Isler's sketches suggest that he usually used mixtures that expanded with a ratio of 1:30 in volume. As the components react quickly after the two emulsions of the polyurethane have been mixed together, the experiments required a careful arrangement of the setup. The expansion typically starts 30 to 60 seconds after the mixture of the components and lasts for about another minute. After a few minutes, the polyurethane models have hardened. They can then be easily cut, carved, or sanded.

Many of the initial studies during this time were carried out in small wooden boxes of 10 × 10 × 10 centimeters. The friction along the wooden walls inhibited the expansion at the perimeter, particularly at the corners. The resulting shapes were, therefore, most of all a product of the size and geometry of the confining matrix. In the case of the small wooden boxes, the resulting form was gently curved at the apex with a more pronounced curvature toward its edges, particularly toward the corners. After the foam had hardened, Isler studied the found shapes by slicing the models and measuring their geometry and surface curvatures.[6]

MIGROS SUPERMARKET IN BELLINZONA (1964)

In 1964 the flow-form method was used for the first time to conceive the geometry of a shell structure: the domed Migros supermarket in the city center of Bellinzona. Similar to the Wyss shell, the design brief called for a shell structure over a square footprint with spans of approximately 31.30 meters between the supports in either direction. An initial sketch shows the spatial requirements, with strict constraints for the heights at the perimeter and at the apex. Early conceptual sketches by Isler show that he tried to find suitable geometries based on spherical segments or ellipsoids. But the geometric constraints could not be fulfilled with any of these approaches. Photographs from the archive, as well as his notes and sketches, show that he undertook a variety of experiments with the flow-form method, carefully altering mixtures and boundary conditions in order to find a form that would best suit the architectural brief—with a steep inclination at the support and a rather low curvature toward the apex of the shell.

The flow-form experiments were first carried out within wooden boxes of 10 × 10 × 10 centimeters, and later in boxes made at a scale of 1:100. After the best-fitting form to suit all spatial requirements was finally found, a replica at a scale of 1:50 was made, which was carved out of polyurethane cubes. A negative cast taken from this replica served then as the basis to produce representational models as well as structural models made of polyester and Plexiglas. In addition to the various models at 1:100 and 1:50, a larger 1:10 model made of cement mortar was built in the garden of Isler's office in Lyssachschachen. This model, with a shell of a mere 8-millimeter thickness, could be entered from below, allowing the designers to study the spatial qualities and the indoor light conditions of the structure.

6 Polyurethane model for the Migros supermarket, Bellinzona, in a wooden box measuring 10 × 10 × 10 centimeters, undated

7 Heinz Isler, Migros supermarket, Bellinzona: structural model of polyester with wires representing the prestressed elements, ca. 1964

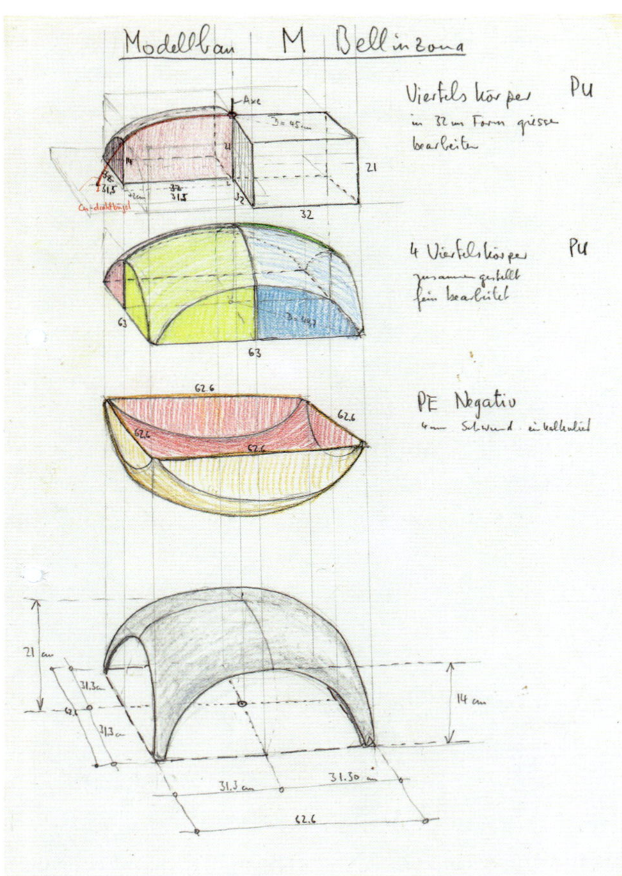

8 Heinz Isler, Migros supermarket, Bellinzona: sketch showing the making of the 1:50 model carved out of polyurethane, ca. 1964

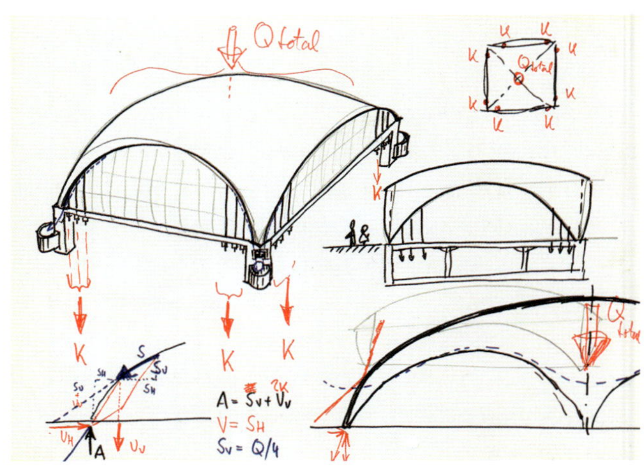

9 Heinz Isler, Migros supermarket, Bellinzona: sketch of the shell showing the function of the vertical tendons at the corners, ca. 1964

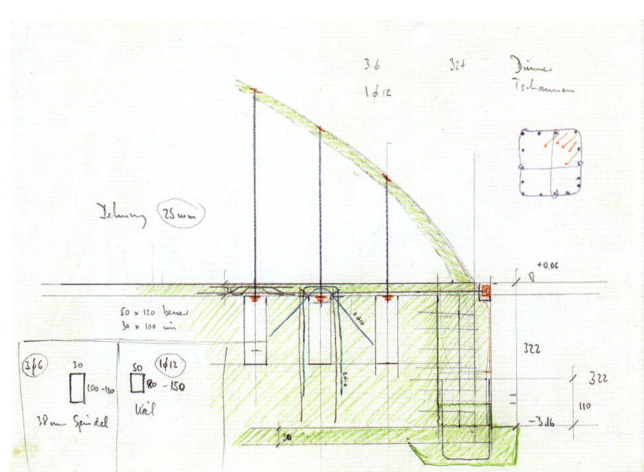

10 Heinz Isler, Migros supermarket, Bellinzona: sketch showing the arrangement of vertical tendons and rebars, before 1964

11 Heinz Isler, Kilcher headquarters, Recherswil: view of the construction site, 1965. The billboard "Schalenbau System Isler" in the foreground shows the shell variant with canopies.

The final design consisted of an 8-centimeter-thick concrete shell without an edge beam or any other stiffening element around the perimeter, such as the canopies used at the Wyss garden center. Isler was well aware that the developed shell geometry was far from ideal in terms of its structural behavior, as it differs significantly from a funicular form. The steep inclination at the corners of the shell was required to attain the necessary clear heights in the supermarket. But the geometry of the shell was obviously far off the thrust line of the internal forces. In order to improve the force flow above the supports, vertical tendons were introduced to divert the horizontal thrust from the upper part of the shell into the steep abutments. Three prestressed elements had to be integrated into the facade plane at each side of the corners to redirect the forces from the shell into the supports.

The construction of the shell started in the autumn of 1964 and was finished in early 1965. The formwork followed, in general, the example of the bubble shells that Isler had already built in large numbers with his longtime contractor, the firm of Willy Bösiger from Langenthal. It consisted of a radial arrangement of glulam beams supporting thinly laid-out battens and left-in-place cement-bound wood fiber boards as shuttering. The steep portions at the supports were made of dry mix shotcrete, whereas the concrete of the upper portions of the shell was poured conventionally.

Isler's notebooks unveil the painstaking monitoring process he undertook after removal of the formwork in February 1965. The movement of the surface of the shell was precisely recorded over the course of each day. This strict monitoring procedure, which had already been followed at his previous shells, seemed of particular importance in the case of Bellinzona. A series of cracks had appeared on the surface of the shell after the removal of the scaffolding, with notable cracks at the northeast corner of the structure. The crack propagation soon came to a halt, and the fissures at the corner could be attributed to a poorly executed construction joint at the transition between shotcrete and regular concrete; however, the incident concerned Isler and made him rethink the steep inclination of the abutments in Bellinzona.[7]

KILCHER HEADQUARTER IN RECHERSWIL (1965)

The second concrete shell based on the flow-form method was built shortly afterward in the town of Recherswil near Solothurn. The client, Kilcher, a progressive manufacturer of neoprene bearings and isolation systems for the construction industry, asked for a spacious, well-lit, and column-free exhibition space where the firm could showcase their products. Located in the vicinity of an important highway route, Kilcher also

12 Heinz Isler, Kilcher headquarters, Recherswil: model of the shell on archetypal form, ca. 1965

wished for a recognizable and innovative structure that would become part of the company's corporate identity.

In association with the architect Paul Wirz, Isler designed an extremely elegant and light-looking shell that seems to float above the ground. Built over a square floor plan and resting only at its four corners, 25.30 meters apart, the 8-centimeter-thick shell without edge stiffeners covers a floor area of 460 square meters. The geometry was again conceived with the help of a polyurethane model. This time, a circular polyurethane model served as the pattern for the shell. By means of a negative mold, the original was transferred to a primary form with a gypsum finish at a scale of 1:50. In the next step, the outline of the shell was drawn on the surface of the primary form. Unlike the Bellinzona shell, where the spatial requirements dictated very steep abutments at the corners, the resulting geometry of the Recherswil shell is shallower and its curvatures more even, resulting in a smoother transition between the apex of the shell and its supports, which are spread wide apart. Despite this better-suited shape, two vertical tendons had to be placed at each support to tie the shell downward in order to improve its buckling behavior.[8]

GARDEN CENTER FLORÉLITES CLAUSE IN PLAISIR (1966)

Attracted by the publicity of the Wyss garden center, the French company Société L. Clause approached Isler for the design of a garden center in the suburb of Plaisir, 30 kilometers west of Paris. The requested shell would serve as the main exhibition space on a larger compound. Based on a pentagonal layout with a span of 39 meters across the diagonal, the realized shell covers a floor area of 1,250 square meters. The construction of the shell was finished in 1966 with the same formwork system that had already been used for the shells in Bellinzona and Recherswil.[9]

It was by far the largest of Isler's free-form shells at the time. Its form owes something to both of its predecessors. From the Wyss garden center, it had inherited the canopies that stiffen the edges of the shell. From the Bellinzona shell, it had inherited a resemblance in curvature. Although Isler counted this shell as one of his flow forms, little can be found in the archives about the exact genesis of its form.[10] With very little time at hand, it seems likely that Isler conceived a structural concept that would fuse the geometries of his previous flow-form shells with the spatial requirements of the present case, omitting any new flow-form experiments. Isler himself wrote in a publication about the geometry that the inner part of the shell consisted of a rotation form with an arbitrarily chosen meridian curve, without giving any more information about the origin of this curve.[11] The shell itself became the first of a series of 17 shells that the Clause firm would commission in the following years as garden centers all across France.[12]

CONCLUSION

The foam experiments represent one of the most fascinating and curious chapters within Heinz Isler's mani-

13 Heinz Isler, Florélites Clause garden center, Plaisir, 1966

fold oeuvre. It may seem bewildering at first that Isler resorted to the self-formation processes of polyurethane foam to inform the shape of his first free-form shells. Compared to the two other form-finding techniques that Isler had propagated in 1959 in Madrid, namely the membrane under pressure and the hanging cloth reversed, both of which result in quasi-funicular or funicular forms, the structural deficiencies of the expansion method are obvious and the generated shapes must be interpreted carefully.

Despite this fact, however, the flow-form method had its own advantages: the quick-setting polyurethane foam allowed Isler to approach given architectural constraints quickly by altering the polyurethane mixture and its boundary conditions. The autonomous process of the expanding foam provided geometries that followed physical laws—albeit not structural ones—and provided even surfaces and smooth transitions. Moreover, the quickly hardened surface of the foam allowed Isler to immediately cast polyester models in order to test the structural qualities of the newly found shapes. For Heinz Isler, with his inquisitive character and his fondness for organic forms, the foam experiments were a welcome playground in which to explore uncharted territories in the world of forms. They also bear witness to his unconventional way of approaching architectural problems.

The flow-form method can be considered a branch of the third group of form-finding methods that Isler had referred to in Madrid: the freely shaped hill. And his words in Madrid do equally apply to working with foam: "The method [...] offers the greatest freedom for design. But it needs a good sense of statics and experience to distinguish the statically better form from the worse one. In case of doubt models may help."[13]

1 See Matthias Beckh and Rainer Schützeichel, "Paths to Form Finding: The Formative Years of Heinz Isler," in Annette Bögle and Manfred Grohmann, ed., *Proceedings of the IASS Annual Symposium 2017: "Interfaces: Architecture, Engineering, Science," September 25–28th, 2017, Hamburg, Germany* (Hamburg, 2017), 1–10.
2 Heinz Isler, "New Shapes for Shells," *Bulletin of the International Association for Shell Structures* 8 (1961): Paper C-3, n.p.
3 See Heinz Isler, "New Shapes for Shells—Twenty Years After," *Bulletin of the International Association for Shell and Spatial Structures* 20.3/21.1, no. 71/72 (1979): 10–19.
4 See Heinz Isler, Referenzliste In- und Ausland, B. Ausgeführte ISLER-Spannbetonschalen in freien Formen (1962–1999), undated, gta Archives, ETH Zurich, bequest of Heinz Isler.
5 See gta Archives, ETH Zurich, bequest of Heinz Isler, 217-09.
6 See gta Archives, ETH Zurich, bequest of Heinz Isler, 217-061.
7 Conversation between Heinz Bösiger, Hans Glanzmann, Matthias Beckh, Giulia Boller, and Rainer Schützeichel, Langenthal, September 24, 2019.
8 See gta Archives, ETH Zurich, bequest of Heinz Isler Archive, 217-082.
9 See John Chilton, *Heinz Isler: The Engineer's Contribution to Contemporary Architecture* (London, 2000), 84.
10 See gta Archives, ETH Zurich, bequest of Heinz Isler Archive, 217-083.
11 Heinz Isler, "Modellversuch für die Schalenkonstruktion Garten-Zentrum Clause, St. Appoline, Paris," *Bauen + Wohnen* 22 (1968): 197–203.
12 Conversation between Heinz Bösiger, Hans Glanzmann, Matthias Beckh, Giulia Boller, and Rainer Schützeichel, Langenthal, September 24, 2019.
13 Isler, "New Shapes for Shells" (see note 2).

More than Concrete
Heinz Isler's Projects in Glass Fiber Reinforced Plastics

ELKE GENZEL AND PAMELA VOIGT

When did we first notice that Heinz Isler is hardly known as a plastic shell designer? We became aware of it when we were reporting on his plastic structures. Obviously, we regarded Isler as a great concrete shell designer, and yet our approach to his work was from the very beginning characterized by treating his role as a plastic designer on equal footing. We met him in person in 2002 as members of the Forschergruppe Materialgerechtes Entwerfen und Konstruieren mit faserverstärkten Kunststoffen (FOMEK, Research Group Material-Compatible Design and Construction with Fiber-Reinforced Plastics) of Bauhaus-Universität Weimar. We visited him at his office in Burgdorf, and in a lecture, which can be described as our initial stimulus, he showed us his entire oeuvre of plastic structures.[1] Thus, we learned firsthand what kind of material GRP actually is, what it is capable of—and what the pioneers did with it. In this essay, we give an overview of Isler's plastic structures and explore the question of why Isler's outstanding achievements as a plastic designer have as of yet seen so little recognition compared to his other works.

HOW GLASS FIBER REINFORCED PLASTIC (GRP) WAS INTRODUCED INTO THE BUILDING SECTOR

In an industrial age like the twentieth century, the idea of finding industrially manufacturable materials as a substitute for naturally occurring ones held obvious appeal. Glass fiber reinforced plastic is one such material: a liquid resin that solidifies with the addition of a hardener at normal temperature. When (glass) fibers are incorporated, the mechanical resistance of the material increases many times over. The use of GRP reveals parallels to traditional building materials: its mechanical characteristics are of the same order of magnitude as timber, and just as in concrete construction, it can be laminated into any kind of formwork that can be produced.

At first, the synthetic resins found application in boat construction as an efficient and corrosion- and decay-resistant alternative to metal and wood. In 1944 the American Owens-Corning Fiberglass Corp. presented the first GRP boat hull—and what could be applied to boat construction would soon be used in the explosively expanding automotive industry.[2] But especially in the aircraft industry, GRP was the desperately

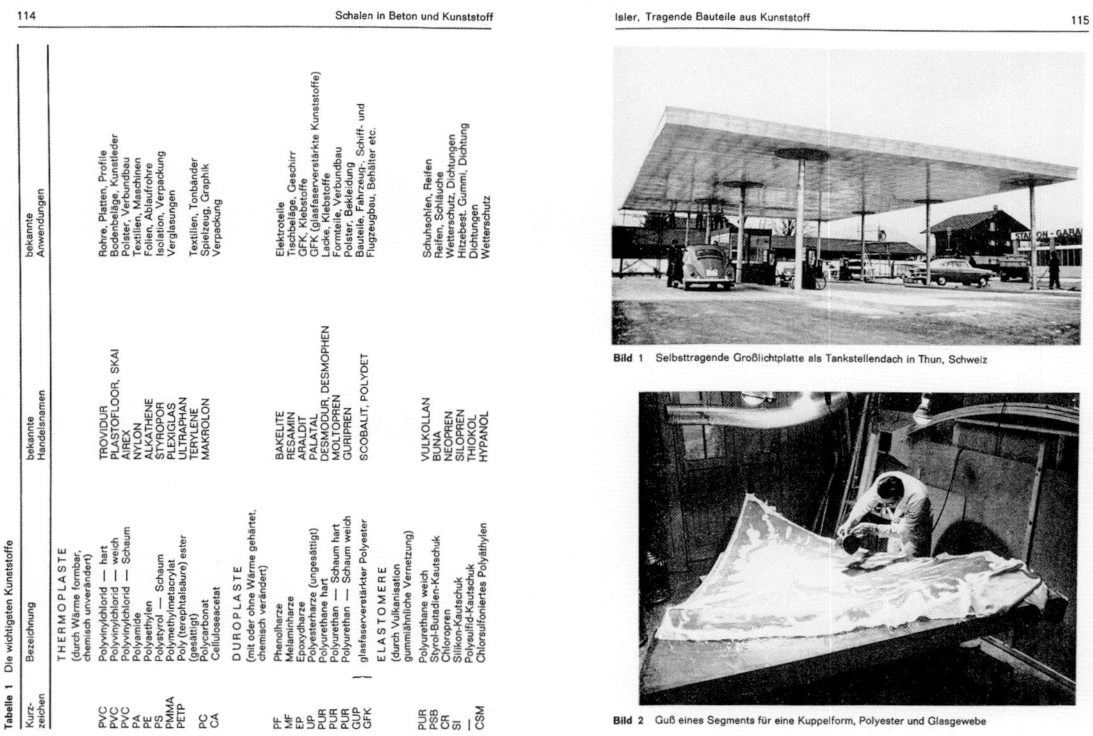

1 Canopy for a filling station, Thun, 1960 (top right). Saturating the glass fibers on the mold for the prototype of the large domed skylight for the Blaser factory, Rüegsau, 1956 (bottom right). Chart "The most important plastics" (left). Double page from Heinz Isler's contribution to the publication *Schalen in Beton und Kunststoff*, edited by Stefan Polónyi, 1970.

needed substitute for the ever scarcer steel during World War II.[3] After the war, almost all aircraft and boat builders—both engineers and manufacturers—were looking for new fields of work. The construction industry was one of the chosen areas of application, not only in the USA but also in Europe. The question arose, why should one not build a house like a boat or an airplane?

However, the beginning of building construction using GRP had military origins instead. In 1954 Richard Buckminster Fuller (1895–1983) designed a geodesic dome on Mount Washington on behalf of the US military. No other material would have been suitable to erect a metal-free radome like that. The domes were needed and produced en masse, and it was precisely this mass production that brought the material to a level of attention that spurred on other engineers and architects, since Buckminster Fuller's rotundas were the whole package: lightweight, translucent, extremely durable, and above all, aesthetically pleasing. Heinz Isler would highlight the radomes as a "pioneering achievement of the first order" in a lecture given in 1975 on "Plastics for Load-bearing Components" and recognized it as a hit product that contains everything, "which is essential in this area: shell construction, prefabrication, serial elements."[4]

THE IMPLEMENTATION OF THE MATERIAL IN THE WORKS OF HEINZ ISLER

The first component that Isler realized with GRP is related to the fact that he had to solve a lighting problem for his large pneumatic form shells. As early as 1955, while designing a warehouse for the company Glas Trösch in Thunstetten, Isler had already explored a version with central skylights that were then left uncovered (see the contribution by Matthias Beckh and Rainer Schützeichel in the present volume, figs. 6–9), as well as various shed versions, and a year later he managed to succeed in implementing his skylights of translucent plastic in the pneumatic-form shells for the company Blaser in Rüegsau. The commercially available skylights at the time were usually made of Plexiglas, an unreinforced resin, and consequently were not feasible for a diameter of 5 meters. Hence, Isler made the proposal to manufacture such a wide skylight himself, using glass fiber reinforced polyester to achieve the desired load-bearing capacity while maintaining the greatest possible translucency.[5]

He settled on the shape of a spherical cap and divided it into eight segments. The individual segments of the prototype were cast in of a plaster mold and

2 Blaser factory, Rüegsau: assembling of the first segments of the prototype, ca. 1956

3 Blaser factory, Rüegsau: installation of the large domed skylight on one of the warehouses, ca. 1956

combined to form a dome. "When this prototype skylight came out satisfactorily, we poured a second, continuous dome. The largest transparent piece ever at the time, with a surface of 20 m^2, also succeeded and eventually served as a mold for further shells" which had a material thickness of 3.5 millimeters.[6]

Isler himself did not specify a year for this pioneering act, but he began the narrative proceeding from his ice sculptures, which he started experimenting with in the mid-1950s. "In search of decent shell shapes [...] in 1954 [he conducted] experiments with suspended membranes. [...] Shortly afterward, [they] were in search of a skylight of 5-m-diameter for a shell construction."[7] On the other hand, he could convey with a narrative elegance the material polyester in search of a suitable liquid that "freezes but does not thaw."[8] It must be assumed, however, that Isler had encountered at least the material unreinforced polyester resin beforehand—to be more precise, during his assistantship at ETH Zurich.

Isler had studied there under Pierre Lardy and later, between 1950 and 1953, was an assistant to his professorship, where his colleague Hans Hauri had already established a modeling laboratory two years earlier.[9] "Using the simplest of means, he [Hauri] set up a real laboratory for model statics in the cramped rooms of the former institute. For various models he tested new materials, particularly plastics, of which their properties and behavior were still little known and which had to be painstakingly determined by him in multiple experiments."[10] It is likely that Isler had access to this lab. Furthermore, Lardy's lecture script "Experimental Methods"[11] should have been available to him, which contained, among other things, the material properties of Plexiglas,[12] so Isler should have been able to assess the load-bearing capacity of unreinforced Plexiglas.

But the skylights made for Blaser are made of resin and fibers. Since only unreinforced resin was used as a modeling material, Isler could not yet know much about this composite material. If we assume that the first skylight was constructed in 1956, then there were only six buildings in the USA using fiberglass-reinforced polyester in their load-bearing structures at the time, and not a single example in Europe.[13] But even knowledge of the American structures would not have enabled Isler to produce the skylights and attest to their load-bearing capacity. Since there were no mechanical characteristics for the durability of the material at the time, Isler had two possible ways to substantiate the capacity: the first being an experiment on 1:1 models or prototypes with varying loads, the second being mathematical evidence, for which he needed material samples to determine the resistance to various stresses. Isler used both methods for his skylights: during our visit to his office in 2002, he showed us a buckling test using a sandbag on a 1:1 model,[14] and in a lecture given in 1968 at Stefan Polónyi's symposium on shell structures as roofing, he noted that the polyester domes realized for Blaser were "mathematically optimized using the well-known buckling model tests and rotational body formulas."[15]

SWIMMING POOLS, CLIMATIC CHAMBERS, AND LARGE LIGHT PANELS

After the skylight domes for the pneumatic-form shells, Isler is likely to have made the swimming pool in Losone and the climate chamber shells for the Swiss military as the next GRP projects, both of which are free-form shells. The swimming pool was freely modeled as a basin out of sand, the mold then coated in mortar, covered with two layers of glass fiber mats and then polyester was poured onto it and rolled out.[16] That was a typical boat-building technique that Isler may have known at the time.

In the sand of Losone, Isler became acquainted with the new manufacturing technique which he described as a "freely shaped hill" in 1959 at the founding congress of the International Association for Shell Structures (IASS) in Madrid.[17] Later, he would also apply the same form-finding method to concrete shells, while continuing to use it in his GRP projects as well. He also applied this to the climate chamber shells.

However, Isler not only made shells out of GRP, but also large panel structures. According to his personal account, in 1959 a friend wanted a light, semitransparent, flat roof for a weekend home.[18] With a size of 4.50 × 9 meters, a single-shell polyester roof would have been extremely thick, hence also expensive and hardly translucent. Isler developed a simple yet ingenious support core design for this task: light, yet with a high load resistance and very translucent. The first top layer was directly laminated on-site in a tent, the prefabricated round support core elements were then set down on the still wet polyester before applying another top layer. For subsequent large panels using the same technique, both triangular and rectangular support core structures were implemented. The spans that Isler achieved with these panels were considerable: with square panels it was 12 meters, and with folded structures, such as in the courtyard canopy of the Realschule (secondary school) in Geislingen an der Steige (1969/1970), he even succeeded in achieving 20 meters.

ISLER'S FORM-FINDING FOR GRP SHELLS

All in all, it can be said that Isler made significantly more panel structures out of GRP than shells. Unlike with his concrete projects, Isler applied two different

4 Climate chamber shell for the Swiss military: preparation of a sand mold, ca. 1956

5 Climate chamber shell with a span of 6 meters: demonstration of the light weight of the structure, ca. 1956

6 Fabrication of a large light panel from two layers of GRP boxes with dimensions of 50 × 50 × 25 centimeters each, 1959

7 Heinz Isler, canopy of a filling station, Thun, 1960

8 Heinz Isler, courtyard canopy of the secondary school, Geislingen: view of the construction site, 1969

9 Franz Ulrich Dutler with Heinz Isler, prototype of a Röhrenhaus (tube house), 1969

philosophies side by side for his plastic shell structures: he used mathematically describable shapes as well as free-forms. On closer inspection, however, their use is by no means random. Projects commissioned by a client or architect are invariably describable shapes, where Isler does not alter a given geometry. In his independently initiated projects, however, the approach was a different one from the beginning, because he always sought the ideal shape—that is, a shell without bending stress—experimentally.

An example of the first category is the Röhrenhaus built in 1969 in cooperation with the architect Franz Ulrich Dutler: a cylindrical shell. It has all the advantages of a describable shape: it is statically calculable, and the client got a verifiable substantiation on paper, which was actually desired in this project. Even the mold is calculable due to this descriptiveness. The idea that this residential tube is really nothing but a horizontal silo—it was constructed in the same manner using a winding technique—probably appealed to Isler. However, what he probably did not like at all is how the shell was supported. It rests on a girder grid, which destroys the beautiful planar shell-bearing effect at the support.[19] Isler always aimed to optimize the load dissipation at the support of his projects by varying the radii of curvature in such a way that neither bending nor shear load would damage the shell, yet this project would not allow him to do so. He would have had to construct mushroom-like bearings or stand the cylinder upright. Therefore, it was obvious in this project that the girder support was needed to keep the shape of the cylindrical shell.

In his independent, free-form projects using GRP, the form emerged in an iterative process, just like his concrete shells. He designed a primary shell, tested it experimentally, determined where damaging stresses were generated, changed the shell, and rechecked it, until the shape came as close as possible to what could be considered ideal. He followed this procedure in the abovementioned climatic chamber shells. "A large polyester cast was made using a sand mold. The full-size test shell was put under load, which let us find its weakest points, in particular the base area. Simply by improving the geometric curvature proportions instead of thickening parts of the shell, the load-bearing capacity could be improved."[20] One can only speculate about the number of iteration steps it took to achieve the final shell.

Comparing the Röhrenhaus with the climatic chamber projects, the advantages and disadvantages of describable and natural—that is, geometrically nondescribable—forms are immediately apparent. The natural form has to be painstakingly developed; it costs time, countless attempts, and, consequently, money. But the result is an ideal structure, which is both extremely sturdy and cheap. The nondescribable forms are therefore perfectly suited for serial production. For a unique project like the Dutler house, on the other hand, a describable shape is a perfect fit.

10 Sewage treatment plant roofing with buckling shell elements, Rudolfstetten, 1983

TERRAIN VAGUE: GRP AND ITS STATIC CALCULATION

In the mid-1950s, there were no design rules for a supporting structure made out of GRP. These were only developed over the course of successive structures and thus were not yet available to Isler. Of course, as an engineer, he was able to calculate the stresses on a structure, be it concrete or GRP. The uncertainty was at the other end—the material resistance. Details like material properties could be found in specialist journals such as *Modern Plastics* or *Kunststoffe* by the late 1950s due to aircraft manufacturers providing them.[21] GRP, however, can be produced in an infinite variety of resin mixtures and glass fiber structures—and with every adjustment to the proportions, the mechanical properties vary significantly. So how was Isler supposed to know which of the published fiber-resin blends used in aircraft construction would also be suitable for supporting structures? Additionally complicating things was the fact that all the characteristic values provided were only based on short-term information. The significant factor about GRP is that it changes its mechanical properties over time. Due to continuous load, temperature, and UV radiation, its mechanical resistance can decrease by up to 70 percent. Fatigue strengths have not as much a relevance to an aircraft or boat manufacturer as for a building structure. It is the structural engineer who has to estimate how much load capacity the material will still be able to provide even after 50 years of use.

Short-term fatigue could be measured in an experiment; long-term fatigue, however, could not be accurately determined. It could only be estimated by interpolating the curve from a longer trial—for example, several weeks—to 50 years. Also, Isler could only provide validation of the correct estimation of these long-term values after years, by verifying the in situ stability of his buildings. However, this still does not state how much safety the structure provides during a state of failure.

In the course of our research, we have so far seen two static calculations: first, the statics for the roof of the Realschule in Geislingen, which we tested in the course of the replacement of the project we worked on, and second, the statics for the Dutler Röhrenhaus. In both projects, the very high short-term strengths estimated by Isler were conspicuous; according to some companies, these values do not conform with experience or the current German standard (DIN 18820) and are not achievable.[22] In the records of the Geislingen project, these values are purported requirements—hence desired but not actually documented test values. It is unclear how Isler came up with these high short-term values, since there are no test certificates in either the statics or the archive. The reduction factors that he applied to the long-term strength calculation also appear rather small and do not comply with current or previous recommendations. Ultimately, Isler attributed a resistance to the material that was twice as high compared to other engineers back then (and still today). This means that there is no extra margin for error concerning the stability of his GRP structures. Hence, the structures support exactly what they are expected to—without a safety net, so to speak.

CONCLUSION

Heinz Isler was one of the first pioneers in Europe to use GRP for shells and panel structures. The GRP shells designed by him are free-forms, which consistently exhibit a correction of the curvature at the shell base analogous to concrete shell construction. If the project was not his own, however, but initiated by an architect or artist, he stuck to the given, calculable geometry.

In contrast to all other plastic pioneers, he was extremely daring—one could even say reckless—in the estimate of material resistance. He designed inspired by his guide, nature, and trusted that if correctly shaped, there would be a redundancy in the load transfer through the curved surface itself. Since he did not take an overall safety coefficient into account, his experience from experimenting was as essential as it was helpful. In the estimates of long-term behavior of the material, however, he lacked such experience. Since it could only be confirmed at the earliest after 15 to 20 years, Isler proceeded cautiously when it came to publications on his plastic structures.

In the field of concrete shell construction, he wanted to be noticed as a free-form shell designer. This is demonstrated by his lectures, especially at large forums such as the IASS. A presentation of his plastic projects could have been as sensational as his presentation at the founding congress of the Association in 1959, in which of all his plastic projects he only revealed the swimming pool in Losone, which should rather be classified as spontaneous experiential construction.[23] The sensational, major article in which all his GRP structures were depicted in detail, was published by Isler in 1977 in *Schweizerische Bauzeitung*. By then, he "was working with plastics for over 20 years."[24] In this essay, he acknowledged that in retrospect, "a good deal of luck was involved, nevertheless all structures have actually held up pretty well so far."[25] Due to his obvious respect for GRP, he did not publish this remarkable contribution about his plastic constructions until late, and avoided doing it where shell makers generally exchanged opinions. Presumably for this exact reason, Heinz Isler is not widely known as a plastic shell designer.

1 Heinz Isler, "Tragende Bauteile aus Kunststoff," unpublished lecture for the members of the FOMEKK of Bauhaus-Universität Weimar, Burgdorf, 2002.
2 See www.toledoblade.com/Retail/2013/10/27/Owens-Corning-company-timeline.html (accessed June 8, 2019).
3 See Elke Genzel, "Zur Geschichte der Konstruktion und der Bemessung von Tragwerken des Hochbaus aus faserverstärkten Kunststoffen 1950 bis 1980" (diss., Bauhaus-Universität Weimar, 2006), 1.
4 Heinz Isler, "Kunststoffe für tragende Bauteile," lecture presented to SIA specialist group, Burgdorf, 1975, 2 (offprint from the conference proceedings, Heinz Isler's private archive).
5 See ibid., 3.
6 Ibid.
7 Heinz Isler, "Tragende Bauteile aus Kunststoff: Anwendungsbeispiele," *Schweizerische Bauzeitung* 95 (1977), 13–20, here 13.
8 Ibid.
9 See the contribution "The Formative Years of Heinz Isler" by Matthias Beckh and Rainer Schützeichel in the present volume.
10 Christian Menn, "Hans H. Hauri zum 60. Geburtstag," *Schweizer Ingenieur und Architekt* 102 (1984): 501–503, here 501.
11 ETH Zurich University Archive, Pierre Lardy Papers, HS 829:4.
12 See ibid., 13.
13 See Pamela Voigt, "Die Pionierphase des Bauens mit glasfaserverstärkten Kunststoffen (GFK) 1942 bis 1980" (diss., Bauhaus-Universität Weimar, 2006), 115.
14 See Isler, "Tragende Bauteile aus Kunststoff" (see note 1).
15 Heinz Isler, "Schalen für Repräsentativ- und Industriebauten," in Stefan Polónyi, ed., *Schalen in Beton und Kunststoff: Entwurf—Bemessung—Ausführung* (Wiesbaden/Berlin [West], 1970), 97–129, here 117.
16 See Isler, "Kunststoffe für tragende Bauteile," 4 (see note 4).
17 Heinz Isler, "New Shapes for Shells," *Bulletin of the International Association for Shell Structures* 8 (1961): Paper C-3, n.p.
18 See Isler, "Tragende Bauteile aus Kunststoff" (see note 1).
19 See Elke Genzel and Pamela Voigt, *Kunststoffbauten*, vol. 1, *Die Pioniere* (Weimar, 2005), 220.
20 Isler, "Kunststoffe für tragende Bauteile," 4 (see note 4).
21 See Genzel, "Zur Geschichte der Konstruktion," 105 (see note 3).
22 Here the company Fiber-Tech in Chemnitz and SKZ Das Kunststoff-Zentrum in Halle (Saale) were consulted.
23 Isler, "New Shapes for Shells," fig. 2 (see note 17).
24 Isler, "Tragende Bauteile aus Kunststoff," 13 (see note 7).
25 Ibid.

(Re)presenting Shells
Heinz Isler's Work on Display

RAINER SCHÜTZEICHEL

After Heinz Isler had designed and completed several projects between the mid-1950s and the late 1970s, his work became the subject of a public display. In 1979 he was, for the first time, given the opportunity to present a selection of his works to a broader audience in the relatively small space of a shop window in Basel. Only one year later, though, the prestigious Princeton University Art Museum hosted a show that was entirely dedicated to his designs: at the same venue, a second exhibition would, 23 years later, again feature some of Isler's projects, now interwoven in the narration of a Swiss legacy of structural engineering. The most intimate insight into his working methods, however, Isler granted in a little-known exhibition he had set up only a few years after the initial Basel show in a private art gallery in Berne.

It is remarkable that the three early exhibitions took place around a turning point of Isler's career, considering that in 1979, he had passed the peak of his success in terms of gaining commissions. Although it would be an overestimation to state that the Basel exhibition prepared his legacy, it at least added another branch of communication to his oeuvre that reached beyond the built work—since the subject of exhibitions is representations of built works that potentially reach a broad international public far more easily than actual buildings could—and that he would rely on more and more in the decades to come.

The essay addresses the (re)presentation of selected projects via photographs, models, and other means. It sheds light on the exhibits as a means of communication and reveals what was shown as well as what was excluded from the respective panoramas of Isler's work. Such exclusions are characteristic of exhibitions in general, and of architectural exhibitions in particular; as Margareth Otti has put it: "What remains is a filtered selection of supposedly 'identical' projects, a made-up coherent unity."[1] In the specific case at hand, such an understanding allows insights into the construction of Isler's original contribution to engineering in the second half of the twentieth century with the help of various media.

MODERNE SCHALENBAUTEN, FIDES, BASEL, JANUARY–FEBRUARY 1979

In 1979 Isler "on the occasion of Swissbau"[2] in Basel presented a handful of his projects in a shop window of the computer center FIDES. Although this exhibition was shown during a trade fair, there is no indication that

1 Heinz Isler, design sketch for the exhibition *Moderne Schalenbauten* in the FIDES computer center shop window, Basel, 1978

it was widely promoted; the only organ that might possibly have made announcements was the *RZ-News*,[3] a company-owned newsletter.

Since the exhibition space was very limited—the shop window was only 3.75 meters wide, no more than 1.55 meters high and 75 centimeters deep—the layout of the presentation had to be simple. The only surviving photograph shows a tripartite installation: a big measuring model of the shell for the Deitingen filling station dominated the window on the left, while the middle and right part were taken up by two wooden boards on which 14 black-and-white photographs were hung; in front of these, three smaller presentation models completed the exhibited projects.

The exhibition did not reveal Isler's experimental approach to form-finding, and a hint at the engineer's rational work behind such projects was only given by the single measuring model. The presentation rather concentrated on the built work, and with a model and two photographs of tennis center shells, it included Isler's latest designs. It is striking that Isler's earliest projects were not represented in the exhibition, nor did his industrial shells receive much attention at all. The only project used from this category was the warehouse for the firm Charles Jaccaz in Regensdorf near Zurich, which was erected in 1964, which with its 29 shells of 15.50 × 15.50 meters represents one of the largest individual projects. Nonetheless, it remained a single representative for a large total of "bread and butter"[4] buildings that make up the biggest part of Isler's oeuvre and that are in their seriality much more typical of his designs than other—for instance free-form—projects that provided the majority of exhibits in Basel.

The reason for that selection (and for the exclusion of industrial shells) is that the exhibition did not primarily address potential clients from industry. Even though the projects were rather coincidentally shown during Swissbau, the exhibition was not part of its program, and the venue was a good way from the trade fair. Isler obviously rather wanted to attract a broader public, so he promoted a wide variety of designs. He even hinted

2 Exhibition *Moderne Schalenbauten* at the FIDES computer center, Basel, 1979. The picture shows the tripartite structure of the exhibition.

3 Exhibition *Heinz Isler as Structural Artist* at Princeton University Art Museum, 1980

4 Cover of the catalogue of the Princeton University Art Museum exhibition *Heinz Isler as Structural Artist* with a photograph of the Heimberg tennis center shells, 1980

at the possibility of applying his shell designs to residential buildings, as a photograph of bubble house prototypes and a small-scale model of a house designed by the architect Michael Balz reveal.

HEINZ ISLER AS STRUCTURAL ARTIST, PRINCETON UNIVERSITY ART MUSEUM, APRIL–MAY 1980

A remarkably larger exhibition was held only one year later. The Princeton University Art Museum opened its doors for a first comprehensive show on Heinz Isler, curated by David P. Billington, who had previously organized exhibitions on Robert Maillart and Christian-Menn in 1976 and 1978 respectively. The Isler exhibition hence linked into a loosely connected series on Swiss engineers. Over the following years, Billington would cultivate this specific interest and, in 2003, he finally curated the survey exhibition *The Art of Structural Design: A Swiss Legacy*, described further below.

As Allen Rosenbaum, director of the museum, stated in his foreword to the 1980 catalogue, the exhibition resulted from "a week of lectures that Isler gave at Princeton's School of Engineering and School of Architecture in April 1979."[5] At the time, the engineer certainly still had the impression of the small Basel exhibition in mind, so it is feasible that the invitation to Princeton triggered the idea of exposing his work on a more prestigious stage.

The Princeton exhibition would indeed become influential. One of its most obvious effects is the consolidation of the term *structural artist* that Billington had originally coined in his earlier exhibition on

5 Exhibition *Heinz Isler as Structural Artist* at Princeton University Art Museum, 1980. The picture shows a presentation model of the Sicli factory building, Geneva, (foreground) and photographs documenting the production of a hanging-reversed-membrane model.

6 Exhibition *The Art of Structural Design: A Swiss Legacy* at Princeton University Art Museum, 2003. The picture shows the large table in the center of the exhibition space and the copied hanging-membrane model of Heinz Isler's design for a typified tennis center shell.

Maillart's bridges, in which he had recognized "not only remarkable achievements in engineering but also works of art—structural art."[6] By applying this term to Isler, he constructed a kind of Swiss tradition in which he saw him embedded—and by that prepared the thread of his 2003 exhibition.

The paperback cover of the catalogue *Heinz Isler as Structural Artist* shows the Heimberg tennis center. The motif was hardly chosen coincidentally: at that time, the recently finished project represented the state-of-the-art status of Isler's design and building practice, and since the brochure was the very first monograph on him, it became prominently significant in shaping a possibly lasting impression of his work. The scholarly part of the catalogue contains an introduction written by Billington, as well as a reprint of Isler's paper "New Shapes for Shells—Twenty Years Later," which had originally been delivered as keynote lecture at the anniversary IASS conference in Madrid in 1979. It is flanked by a documenting part that includes a checklist of the exhibition, in which the exhibits are listed along with a set of technical data, such as location, year of completion, form-finding principle, number of shells, and dimensions.

The cover picture provides a first link to the Basel exhibition: It was exactly this building type that Isler had addressed there as "new developments."[7] Besides the "flagship" of the tennis centers, the list of exhibits as well as a set of pictures taken in the exhibition prove that several projects that had been shown in the Basel shop window reappeared in Princeton. Both Chamonix sports center projects (1971 and 1974) can be found

7 Cover of the leaflet *Nautilus: Heinz Isler* advertising the exhibition at Ausstellungsgemeinschaft Postgasse (AGP) 46, Berne, 1982

among them, also the Sicli company building in Geneva (1969) and the Villa Camoletti (1970; see the contribution by Giulia Boller and John Chilton in the present volume, fig. 9), the emblematic Deitingen roofs (1968), as well as projects for the French retailer Florélites Clause (1975) or the Bürgi garden center in Camorino (1971).

A major distinction between the two exhibitions is a stronger emphasis on the experimental character of Isler's design methods in the more recent one. Various pictures on the walls and in the catalogue reveal this, among them an inflated membrane (no. 12)[8] and a hanging cloth (no. 8). What is most enlightening in this context is that even the process of making models was made visible in the exhibition, as a series of eight photographs (no. 30), some of them also printed in the catalogue, depicts the production of a hanging-reversed-membrane model in its single steps.[9] But even though this process was now made explicit, form-finding models as such were still only represented via photographs—unlike in the 1982 Berne exhibition, all models on display at Princeton in 1980 were exclusively presentation models.

A SWISS LEGACY, PRINCETON UNIVERSITY ART MUSEUM, MARCH–JUNE 2003

The same is true for the 2003 exhibition, that Billington dedicated to a group of Swiss engineers, in which he saw the embodiment of *A Swiss Legacy*: besides Robert Maillart, Christian Menn, and Heinz Isler, Othmar Ammann and their respective teachers Wilhelm Ritter and Pierre Lardy formed this exquisite group.

A prominent feature of this later exhibition was a large table placed in the center of the exhibition space, on which relatively large presentation models were placed. An exception from the models standing on that table is a single hanging-membrane model, which represents Isler's design for the Heimberg tennis center shell. This installation was framed by two walls, on one of which plans and large-format pictures of major projects of each of the engineers were shown—in the case of Isler, the Sicli company building—as well as small foldable boards on the opposite side.

In the accompanying catalogue, this time a veritable hardcover book, Billington, in the Isler chapter, used almost the same set of photographs that he had already relied on in 1980, and also a good portion of the text was based on the older essay, which had been proofread by Isler.[10] It is therefore no surprise that the latter demanded "only punctual" alterations in the manuscript.[11]

What Billington invested more effort into was the manufacturing of new models: unlike in 1980, it was not Isler himself who shipped his original models to the museum; instead, copies of the Naturtheater Grötzingen shell (1977) and the Heimberg tennis center were produced by the Princeton graduate student Maria Janaro.[12] With this, Isler fundamentally disagreed, and during the preparation of the exhibition he tried to intervene and prevent such copies from being made. In a quite agitated letter to the curator, he argued that "without an orderly built up course of education on my specific subject nobody is able to understand the essential problems in the domain of the new generation of shells which I had the opportunity to develop."[13] It was again the tennis center typology that Isler alluded to when speaking of a "new generation of shells."

The letter brings to the surface Isler's strict idea of authorship: Thanks to several decades of experimentation and experience, he claimed that only he himself was able to cope with the task of making these specific models. As a result, he implied that his shells could never be properly constructed by anyone else.

NAUTILUS, AUSSTELLUNGSGEMEINSCHAFT POSTGASSE (AGP) 46, BERNE, NOVEMBER 1982

A rare opportunity for immediate curatorial influence on the publicizing of his own work had been given to Isler more than 20 years before the second Princeton exhibition. In 1982 he was invited to equip AGP 46, a small art gallery in Berne, with documents, pictures, models, and other materials. He seized this opportunity and put his working methodology—that is, his playful and experimental approach to form-finding—on display. The exhibition addressed the general public rather than experts, and Isler most probably used it as a means of experimentation to test new methods of presenting his work.

In a draft manuscript, he wrote down his thoughts about naming the exhibition *Nautilus* and noted that he had a threefold interest in this eponymous squid: first, plain and simple, it had "a particularly light and elegant shell"; second, it was "a spiral form of magnificent beauty," with proportions of the curves that obeyed "strict mathematic principles"; and third, the most intriguing insight for him was that the nautilus had chambers which grew larger as the animal itself grew: "I would have liked to have such a house, in which every chapter of life would have been kept intact, with all the things that were so important back then."[14] These chambers can therefore be understood as some kind of time capsules in which things could be saved—in the case of Isler, they mark different stages of his career, which are materialized in buildings, presented in exhibitions, or preserved in books.

Nautilus was flanked by at least two workshops led by Isler himself. These events were part of the concept right from the beginning: as a note from July 1982 proves, Isler wanted to enrich the exhibition with them and thought of "experiments with wax under the arcades," that is, outside the gallery in the public space.[15] The demonstration of the very process of model making, that had in both Princeton exhibitions been entrusted to a series of photographs, in this way became not only three-dimensional (and therefore more graspable), but also vivid, thanks to the presence of the engineer. This surely enhanced the effect it had on visitors, who were even invited to take part in the experiments.[16]

Instead of a catalogue, a four-page leaflet provided visitors with some background information. In it, no more than a short text that fills roughly three-quarters of a page is dedicated to Isler. Superficially described as an "engineer [...] and an internationally recognized expert in the field of free-spanning shell design," it provides no unexpected insight.[17] But the text still reveals what had attracted the curators in the first place—namely the idea that "he is not 'only' an engineer, but in a certain sense also an inventor, a researcher, and an artist."[18] In these lines, one can hear an unadulterated echo of Billington's portrayal of Heinz Isler.[19]

Photographs of the exhibition document the importance of nature as a source of inspiration and experimental form-finding for its conception. From the perspective of natural inspiration, it is instructive that Isler turned directly to nature by including snail shells, leaves, and walnut shells in the exhibits. The intention was twofold: first, through the presentation of a nautilus shell, he revealed the inspiration for the title of the exhibition right away; and second, these realia demonstrated nature's ability to build robust structures with a minimum of material as an ideal for structural engineering. Apart from these exhibits, nature was incorporated on an abstract level as well, through a set of photographs of ice sculptures that Isler had experimented with in his garden.

With other technical objects, such as chain and hanging models or a pneumatic model, this rather inspirational reading of nature was flanked by the engineer's methodological investigation into natural laws. As he had stated on a manuscript sheet, with the exhibits he wanted to make visible the "shell principle and its laws," a headline under which he listed his basic form-finding principles: "pneumatic form [Blasform], hanging forms [Hängeformen], forms under tension [Spannformen]"; according to him, their qualities were that they were "harmonic, beautiful, correct, economical, variable, play[ful]."[20]

The aspect of play builds a bridge to the experimental character of Isler's designs. Not only did the engineer hold his public workshops as part of the exhibition program, but even when he was absent, he allowed visitors to get a firsthand impression of his models. To the pneumatic model on exhibit, for instance, a bicycle pump was attached, which made it possible to inflate the rubber membrane that was clamped between its wooden frames. Close to this device, the measuring model for Deitingen that had already been shown in the FIDES shop window was positioned, giving an impression of the more sophisticated, scientific aspects of shell design. Presentation models, such as—again—for tennis center shells, pneumatic-form shells with skylights, or bubble houses, completed the set of exhibits.

CONCLUSION

In a time span of only four years, from 1979 on, Isler put together no less than three exhibitions of his work, whereas he had previously never used that format as part of his strategy to publicly promote it. These three early exhibitions, in particular, represent exemplary case studies on the question of how his ideas, projects,

8 Exhibition *Nautilus* at Ausstellungsgemeinschaft Postgasse (AGP) 46, Berne, 1982. The picture shows photographs and a model representing Heinz Isler's ice sculpture experiments.

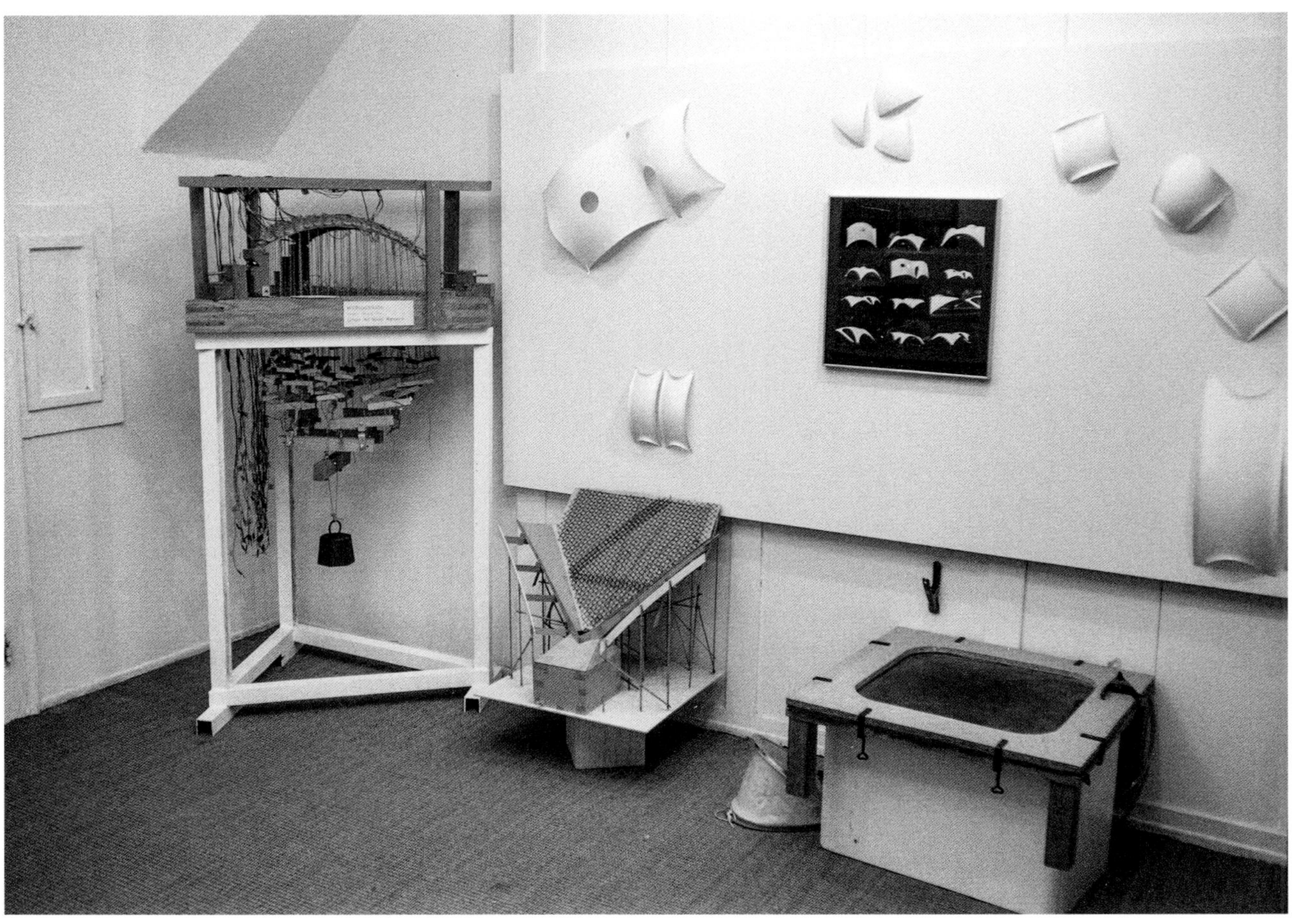

9 Exhibition *Nautilus* at Ausstellungsgemeinschaft Postgasse (AGP) 46, Berne, 1982. The picture shows the measuring model for the Deitingen filling station (left) and an interactive pneumatic model (bottom right).

and buildings were linked together in a dramaturgy in order to convey them to both specialists and lay people.

In 1979 the exhibition space that was available led to a comparatively simple presentation, excluding major aspects of Isler's work such as (and above all) his experimental form-finding methods. In comparison, the presentation of his designs in the spaces of the Princeton University Art Museum—although partly falling back upon projects that had already been shown in Basel—was much more elaborated and comprehensive. This exhibition certainly enhanced international interest in Isler's work, and it can be seen as a precursor of the influential 1986 traveling exhibition *Heinz Isler: Schalen*, curated by Ekkehard Ramm and Eberhard Schunck.[21] With regard to Isler's work, though, the 2003 Princeton exhibition was rather a continuation of the earlier exhibition at the same venue, distilled from older content, bottled into the larger Swiss context, and spiced with some newly made models.

The Berne exhibition instead, held two years after Isler's first Princeton appearance, was by far the most personal revelation of the engineer, because it revealed a remarkable tendency toward disclosing the experimental background of his work. Be it the informal framework of an art gallery, be it the orientation toward nature captured in the title *Nautilus*—in Berne, Isler drew the most vivid cross-section through his work and philosophy, and at the same time installed an almost intimate exhibition that rewarded its visitors with the deepest insights into the engineer's working practice.

1 Margareth Otti, "Der Elefant im Kühlschrank: Architektur und Institution," in Carsten Ruhl and Chris Dähne, ed., *Architektur ausstellen: Zur mobilen Anordnung des Immobilen* (Berlin, 2015), 28–41, here 30 (translation, as in the following, by the author).
2 Ekkehard Ramm and Eberhard Schunck, ed., *Heinz Isler: Schalen*, 3rd, enl. ed. (Zurich, 2002), 110. In the first edition of the book (Stuttgart, 1986, 102), the 1979 exhibition is not even mentioned.
3 See FIDES Rechenzentrum, terms and conditions for the use of the shop window at Elisabethenstrasse 15, Basel, undated [1975], n.p. [1], gta Archives, ETH Zurich, bequest of Heinz Isler.
4 Maria Garlock, "Heinz Isler and 'Natural' Forms for Shells," lecture outline, undated; http://www.curee.org/IUSE-4/Objects/Lecture%20Outline%20-%20Heinz%20Isler%20and%20'Natural'%20Forms%20for%20Shells.docx (accessed November 18, 2019).
5 Allen Rosenbaum, "Foreword," in *Heinz Isler as Structural Artist* (Princeton, 1980), 5–7, here 5.
6 Ibid.
7 Heinz Isler, design sketch for the FIDES exhibition, undated [1978], n.p. [1], gta Archives, ETH Zurich, bequest of Heinz Isler.
8 These numbers refer to the counting in the "Checklist of the Exhibition," in *Heinz Isler as Structural Artist*, 44–47 (see note 5).
9 See ibid., 46.
10 See David P. Billington, "Heinz Isler: Structural Art in Thin-Shell Concrete," in *The Art of Structural Design: A Swiss Legacy* (New Haven/London, 2003), 128–162.
11 See David P. Billington, "Heinz Isler: Structural Art in Thin Shell Concrete Structures," typescript, June 3, 2002; and letter from Heinz Isler to David P. Billington, June 25, 2002; both gta Archives, ETH Zurich, bequest of Heinz Isler.
12 See Maria Janaro, "Heinz Isler's Reinforced-Concrete Structures," in *A Symposium in Honor of David P. Billington at Seventy-Five and Forty-Five Years of Teaching at Princeton University* (Princeton, 2003), 115–117.
13 Letter from Heinz Isler to David P. Billington, July 9, 2002, gta Archives, ETH Zurich, bequest of Heinz Isler.
14 Heinz Isler, "Nautilus," manuscript, undated [1982], gta Archives, ETH Zurich, bequest of Heinz Isler.
15 Heinz Isler, note dated July 30, 1982, gta Archives, ETH Zurich, bequest of Heinz Isler.
16 See "Künstler-Ingenieur Heinz Isler zeigt, wie er seine Schalen 'entwirft,'" *Der Bund*, November 20, 1982, n.p. [42].
17 *Nautilus: Heinz Isler*. AGP 46 leaflet, [Berne], November 1982, n.p. [3].
18 Ibid.
19 The term *structural artist* was even translated into German rather awkwardly as "Strukturenkünstler" in a report on this exhibition; see Martin Sterchi, "Märchenlandschaft eines Bauingenieurs," *Berner Zeitung*, November 17, 1982, n.p. [part 2].
20 Heinz Isler, "Ausstellung AGP Bern," manuscript, November 6, 1982, n.p. [1], gta Archives, ETH Zurich, bequest of Heinz Isler.
21 See Ramm and Schunck, *Heinz Isler: Schalen* (see note 2).

"New Constructions"
The Beginnings of Shell Building in the German Democratic Republic

ANDREAS SCHÄTZKE

In 1968 the Teepott restaurant opened its doors in the Baltic seaside resort of Warnemünde, a district of the city of Rostock. To this day, it is one of the best-known shell constructions erected in the German Democratic Republic.[1] The main feature of its shape is the widely curved undulating roof with a diameter of 36 meters, a combination of three identical hyperbolic paraboloids made of reinforced concrete. A two-story cylindrical structure with a steel and glass facade was erected under the roof. The architects Erich Kaufmann, Carl-Heinz Pastor, and Hans Fleischhauer planned the building together with the civil engineer Ulrich Müther.[2]

With the beach restaurant located right next to a lighthouse from the late nineteenth century, Warnemünde not only received a new architectural landmark, but the building also became an important testimony to East German postwar modernism. It clearly shows the influence of international trends in the 1950s and 1960s, when the bold and elegant shell constructions by Eduardo Torroja in Spain, Félix Candela in Mexico, Pier Luigi Nervi in Italy, Eero Saarinen in the USA, René Sarger in France, or Heinz Isler in Switzerland also inspired engineers and architects in the GDR. The nightclub La Jacaranda, built by Candela with Juan Sordo Madaleno in Acapulco in 1957, is regarded as a model for the Teepott.

Shell construction in the GDR is closely and mainly linked with the name of Ulrich Müther. The buildings in whose planning Müther was involved owe a large part of their memorable appearance to his contribution. However, most of them could only be realized in close cooperation with architects who, in a Communist dictatorship like the GDR, were usually employees of state institutions. Müther's roof constructions, which were predominantly made using the shotcrete process, not only characterize the appearance of the Teepott, but also that of other individual buildings. The execution always dominated an enterprise led by him.

When Müther was commissioned to do the planning and construction of the restaurant in Rostock-Warnemünde at the end of 1966, he was already known in his profession beyond the coastal region in the north of the GDR. Shortly before that, he had erected an exhibition hall for the building and oil industries on the Rostock-Schutow fairgrounds, which he had designed together with Erich Kaufmann. They only needed five months for the planning and execution. The building consists of two halls of the same size, staggered and with square floor plans. They are spanned by two 20 × 20-meter concrete shell roofs in the form of hyperbolic paraboloids. The thickness of the shells is only 7 centimeters.[3] Such a project, which demonstrated the new

1 Erich Kaufmann, Carl-Heinz Pastor, Hans Fleischhauer, and Ulrich Müther, Teepott restaurant, Rostock-Warnemünde, 1968

2 Erich Kaufmann and Ulrich Müther, exhibition hall for the building and oil industries on the Ostseemesse fairgrounds, Rostock-Schutow, 1966

3 Visit by the First Secretary of the SED (Socialist Unity Party) Walter Ulbricht (center) to the exhibition hall for the building and oil industries, Rostock-Schutow, 1966. In the front row, among others, are his wife, Lotte Ulbricht; the Chairman of the Council of Ministers of the GDR, Willi Stoph; and the Head of the Office for Industry and Construction of the Central Committee of the SED, Günter Mittag. Ulrich Müther is in the background.

construction technique in a striking design language on a building dedicated to the representation of East German economic strength, attracted the attention of leading Party and state officials.

The exhibition hall was one of the first shell constructions made by Ulrich Müther. As early as 1965 he and Erich Kaufmann had developed a design for a building with a dance bar and café called Pinguin, which was not realized, but was later obviously incorporated into the plans for the Teepott. In both cases, a boldly curved roof of combined hyperbolic paraboloids spans a largely glazed structure. The Teepott, which contained a restaurant, a café with a dance floor, and two bars, became very popular with the general public. The building was also appreciated by the experts. The journal *Deutsche Architektur*, the central organ of the East German architectural press, awarded it a second prize in 1969 in a competition for "the best buildings completed in the GDR."[4] In 1970 PGH Bau Binz, the specialist building cooperative run by Ulrich Müther, was awarded the state order Banner der Arbeit (Banner of Labor). On this occasion, the sectional leadership team of the SED, the East German Communist Party, explicitly mentioned the exhibition hall in Schutow and the Teepott. They praised the technology used by Müther, which corresponded to the "current international standard" and was of particular importance in the GDR for the construction of community buildings (Gesellschaftsbauten).[5]

4 Ulrich Müther and Erich Kaufmann, Pinguin dance bar and café, unexecuted design; drawing by Erich Kaufmann, 1965

5 Construction of a kindergarten with prefabricated "HP shells," developed by Herbert Müller, in the residential complex I of Halle-Neustadt, 1968

6 Jörg Streitparth and Gerd Wessel, Kosmos milk bar, Cottbus, 1969

7 Cover of the book *Form und Bauweise der Schalen* by Manuel Sánchez Arcas, 1961

THE BEGINNINGS OF SHELL BUILDING IN THE GDR

In the GDR, the first shell structures were built around 1960, which is quite late in an international comparison. Various approaches were pursued.[6] From 1959 to 1961 the Deutsche Akademie der Wissenschaften (German Academy of Sciences) erected the spherical laboratories of its Institute of Physical Chemistry in Berlin-Adlershof, designed under the direction of Horst Welser, as a concrete shell construction. Wilhelm Bärwolf planned a filling station with a concrete roof in the form of an umbrella shell for the *1. Internationale Gartenbauausstellung der sozialistischen Länder* (1st International Horticultural Exhibition of the Socialist Countries) in Erfurt in 1961.[7] From 1962 onward, various public buildings in the city of Halle were covered with "HP shells," prefabricated hyperbolic concrete elements developed by engineer Herbert Müller. A few years later, in 1968, a related type of shell was used in the residential complex I of Halle-Neustadt for the construction of a kindergarten with a circular ground plan.[8]

However, concrete was not the only material used. In Cottbus, the Kosmos milk bar, which was built in 1968/1969 according to a design by Jörg Streitparth and Gerd Wessel, received a hypar shell roof similar to Ulrich Müther's constructions, but made of wood. The architects saw this as a viable alternative to the conventional choice of materials in shell construction: "Instead of the concrete shells frequently used in the GDR, a wooden construction was chosen for the first time, which, in addition to short assembly times and simple technology, offers the design advantage of a wooden ceiling."[9]

Undoubtedly, however, it was the heyday of concrete shell construction, although this technology was not new: it had been used successfully since the mid-1920s. In the GDR, too, international developments in this field were followed closely and exchanges with foreign colleagues were sought.[10] At the end of 1958 the East Berlin section of the Bund Deutscher Architekten (Association of German Architects) hosted René Sarger, who reported on "concrete shell constructions and their application in France."[11] One of the first events of the International Association for Shell Structures (IASS), founded in 1959, took place in the GDR: in March 1961 participants from 22 countries met for a symposium on precast shell structures in Dresden.[12] Not only in the GDR, but also elsewhere, efforts were being made to connect shell construction with the principles of prefabrication as a particularly economical way of planning and execution.[13]

In 1961 the Deutsche Bauakademie (German Building Academy), the central institution in the field of building in the GDR, published a book on the shape and construction of shells that offered an international overview of contemporary trends and was primarily aimed at architects.[14] It is not without significance that the author, the Spanish architect Manuel Sánchez Arcas, as a Communist, former fighter against Franco in the Spanish Civil War, and later emigrant in Moscow, Warsaw, and East Berlin, was also highly accepted ideologically.[15] Félix Candela, also from Spain, who had emigrated to Mexico in 1939 as a result of the Civil War in his country and had meanwhile achieved international fame in the field of concrete shell construction, visited the GDR in 1961. The young architect Ingo Schönrock reported in the specialized press on a lecture that Candela gave as a guest of the Association of German Architects in East Berlin.[16] His article on umbrella shell elements appeared in July 1962 in an issue of *Deutsche Architektur* that was devoted to the topic "spatial structures and cable net constructions." It was one of the earliest publications on Candela in the GDR, whereas in the Federal Republic of Germany his work had already been reported on for a decade.

When Ulrich Müther realized his first shell building in 1963/1964, Candela's works were also his inspiration. Ingo Schönrock had encouraged his friend from his student years to develop a construction based on Candela's model for the Haus der Stahlwerker, a holiday home for steelworkers in Binz on the island of Rügen, for which Müther planned the roofing of a dining room.

8 Ulrich Müther, addition to the Haus der Stahlwerker (Steelworkers' Home), Binz, 1964

Müther calculated this construction, added to the roof terrace of an existing building, as a construction of four combined concrete shells in the form of hyperbolic paraboloids.[17] A few years later he confidently adapted the silhouette of a Candela building, the San José Obrero church in Monterrey from 1959, for the logo of the PGH Bau Binz. Not only the elegance and boldness of this creation, but also the fact that the Mexican was equally successful as a constructor and entrepreneur may have moved Müther to this tribute.[18]

SPECIALIZATION IN SHELL CONSTRUCTION: ULRICH MÜTHER'S NICHE IN THE COMMUNIST PLANNED ECONOMY

In 1922 Willy Müther and his wife, Elisabeth, had opened a building enterprise in the small coastal town of Binz. Their son Ulrich Müther, born in 1934, initially took a similar path to his father and, after completing an apprenticeship as a carpenter in the family business, attended the Fachschule für Bauwesen in Neustrelitz, a building trades school, from 1951 to 1954. During this time, he got to know Erich Kaufmann and Ingo Schönrock, who later worked together with him several times as architects. After completing his education, Müther worked for four years in a state-owned industrial project planning company in Berlin and in 1956 also took up a correspondence course in civil engineering at the Technische Hochschule Dresden.[19]

The topic of his diploma thesis was directly related to a project in his hometown of Binz in 1963, when he planned the extension for the Haus der Stahlwerker, his first shell construction. In 1964 he was able to carry out the project himself.[20] His parents' company, whose technical management Ulrich Müther had taken over at the end of the 1950s after his return from Berlin, had been united with another company in 1960 to form a cooperative. It existed under Müther's chairmanship until 1972, when it was absorbed into a Volkseigener Betrieb (VEB, publicly owned enterprise), also managed by him, with the name Spezialbetonbau Binz (later Spezialbetonbau Rügen).

The fact that Ulrich Müther soon assumed a singular position in the GDR construction industry was not least due to his dual profession. As an engineer and as an entrepreneur—albeit in a centrally controlled economic order—he was both designer and executor. In addition, he developed an increasingly sought-after special field early on. Müther specialized more than anyone else in the GDR in the planning and execution of concrete shells. Above all, he realized several dozen striking buildings in the form of hyperbolic paraboloids, which were appreciated for their high load-bearing capacity, but also as spherical, humpback, and hanging shells. It was architecture that was able to give the appearance of high technology, but was produced with a considerable amount of craftsmanship based on extensive experience.

Starting in the mid-1960s, Ulrich Müther was in close contact with experts. Like other engineers from the GDR, above all Herrmann Rühle, he took part in IASS symposia. Müther was also allowed to travel to Western countries for some of the Association's meetings and on other occasions. In 1967 he was permitted to accept an invitation from Fritz Leonhardt to the Technische Hochschule Stuttgart and spend a study visit in the Federal Republic. In addition, he could inform himself about West German shotcrete technology, particularly the company Torkret in Essen. However, the GDR refused to allow him to participate in the IASS congress in Mexico City in the same year, which he tried very hard to attend.[21]

Ulrich Müther's success in the GDR, which began at the end of the 1960s, cannot be explained solely by his abilities as an engineer and by the skill and assertiveness he displayed as head of a state-owned company over a long period of time. Under the conditions of the Communist planned economy, it was considered advantageous that the construction of his shells required a great deal of manpower, yet was possible in a short time and with economical concrete consumption. Once calculated, such structures could also be erected at different locations in the same way or with slight adaptations, thus reducing the effort required for planning and execution. The contemporary discussion of the question of whether the construction of such buildings in large numbers in the GDR was possible and desirable, was held, inter alia, at a colloquium in 1967 of the Kammer der Technik (Chamber of Technology) on "new constructions for the building industry."[22]

UNDER THE SIGN OF THE INDUSTRIALIZATION OF CONSTRUCTION: MASS PRODUCTION AND INDIVIDUAL BUILDINGS

In the 1960s the GDR saw an increasing need for buildings that could fulfill functions for the infrastructure of their surroundings: places for recreation in holiday regions, but above all facilities for consumption, leisure, education, and upbringing in the large housing estates that were now being built in many places. Their formal language often differed markedly from that of the surrounding architecture. This was true not only but rather especially for Müther's shell buildings. They possessed an expressivity that was seldom achieved in GDR architecture and were suitable for making the postulated striving for technological and social progress widely visible. In retrospect, Müther summed up his activities quite aptly, even though he did not mention his clients or the urban planners and architects involved: "In order to set urbanistic accents and to roof large areas without supports in modern, light architecture, VEB Spezialbetonbau Rügen built a large number of shells. Thus, event halls, exhibition halls, restaurants, swimming pools, department stores, and churches were built."[23]

In terms of design, many of these buildings are among the most sophisticated examples of the third phase of architectural and urban development in the GDR. Immediately after World War II, there had been a short period during which, similar to the West, there had been relatively pluralistic discussions about how to build after the experience of twelve years of National Socialism. Many saw the modern movement of the 1920s and early 1930s as something to be picked up again and continued. Shortly after the founding of the GDR in 1949, however, a strong ideological constriction could be observed. Following the example of the Soviet Union, historicism under the dogma of "national tradition" became binding. In the late 1950s—again dictated by the Soviet Union—a profound change took place, with the forced industrialization of construction and the opening up to some principles and methods previously favored only in the West.[24] The image of the following phase is determined by the numerous residential areas built under ideological dictates and planned economic constraints using the means of standardization and mass production in so-called large panel construction. The quality of the results varied, but oversizing, monotony, and inhospitalableness are regarded as the signatures of the urban development and architecture of that time. At the same time, some of the most important distinctive buildings were built, often for educational and cultural purposes.[25]

Ulrich Müther and his staff also erected buildings with special functions and of memorable design for state clients.[26] Buildings for leisure and recreation form an early and important group. In a country such as the GDR, with a leisure culture standardized by the state, there was a need for restaurants that—like the Teepott in Rostock-Warnemünde—could accommodate a large number of guests. On the island of Rügen, Müther built the Inselparadies (Island Paradise) in Baabe (1965/1966), which the Handelsorganisation (HO), the state-run retail business, recommended as the "most modern HO restaurant," and the Ostseeperle (Pearl of the Baltic Sea) in Glowe (1967/1968). Müther's activities soon extended to other regions of the GDR. In the late 1960s and early 1970s, he provided shell roofs for restaurants in Halle, Templin, Eberswalde, at the Hohenfelden reservoir, in Döbeln, Schwerin, and a decade later the Seerose (Water Lily) café on the banks of the Havel in Potsdam.

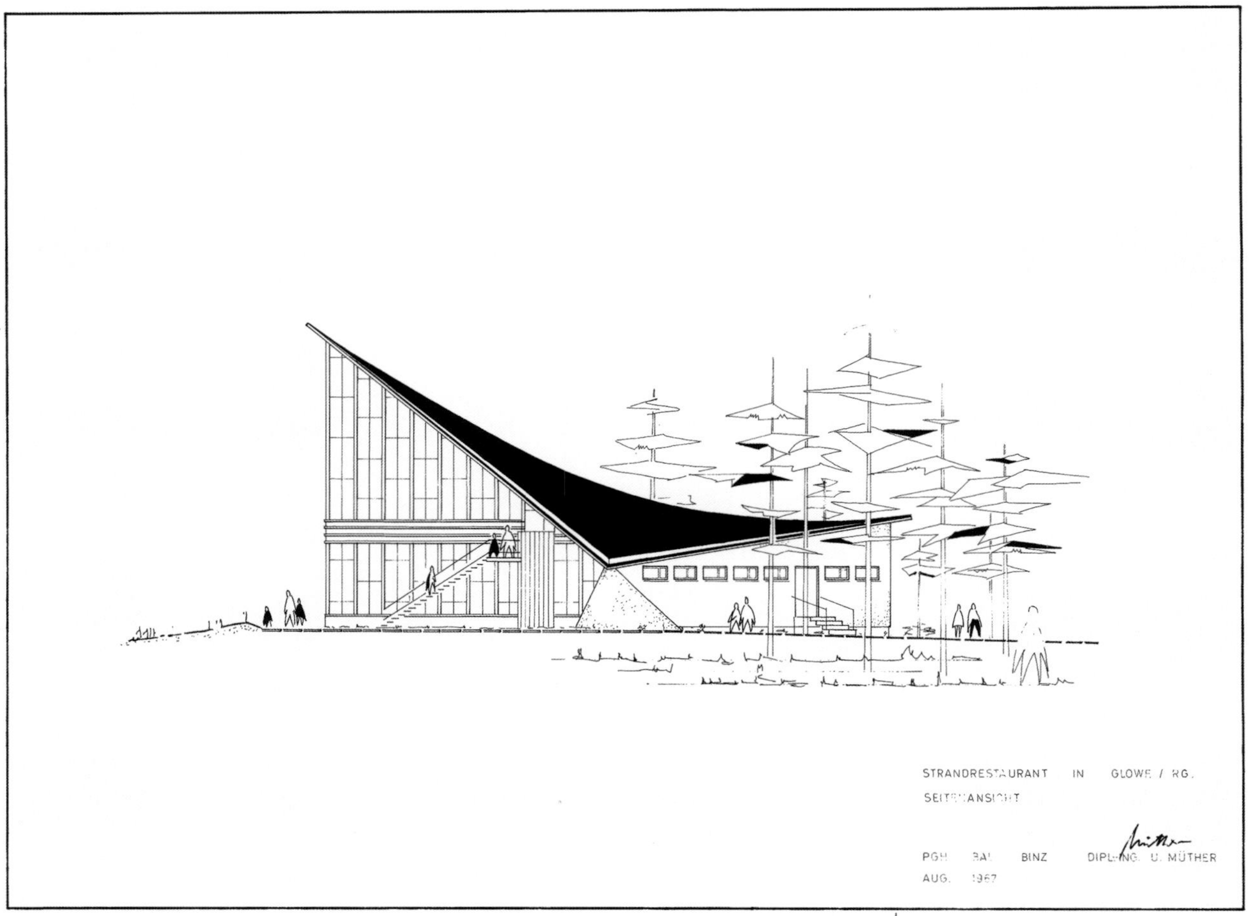

9 Ulrich Müther, Ostseeperle restaurant, Glowe; drawing by Ulrich Müther, 1967

10 Erich Kaufmann, Carl-Heinz Pastor, and Ulrich Müther, multipurpose building with a department store, restaurants, and event rooms, Rostock-Lütten Klein, 1968

11 Helmut Stingl, Gerhard Lehmann, Rüdiger Plaethe, and Ulrich Müther, Ahornblatt restaurant, Berlin, 1973

According to the participating architect Dieter Ahting, the model for the Seerose was Los Manantiales restaurant in Xochimilco, Mexico City, built in 1958 by Félix Candela.[27] The new café in Potsdam, opened in 1983, fulfilled tasks similar to those of many other buildings enclosed by shell constructions from the Binz company. A particularly large number have been built in Rostock since the end of the 1960s. There they were to accommodate community facilities in the new development areas and at the same time stand out as eye-catchers from their often quite uniform surroundings. Müther's first project of this kind in Rostock, a multipurpose building with a department store, restaurants, and event rooms in the Lütten Klein district (with Erich Kaufmann and Carl-Heinz Pastor, 1967/1968), was followed by further large restaurants. The Ahornblatt (Maple Leaf) had comparable functions as a canteen for the residential quarter Fischerinsel in East Berlin's Mitte district (with Helmut Stingl, Gerhard Lehmann, and Rüdiger Plaethe, 1969–1973). The halls in Neubrandenburg and Magdeburg were built in 1968/1969 as venues for events and exhibitions.

The Binz company was also involved in a wide range of other shell construction projects. These included sports facilities as well as sacred buildings. In cooperation with architects from the company VEB Carl Zeiss Jena, planetariums were built from the end of the 1970s, which were also successfully exported by the GDR and, as completely manufactured products, found their clients in Wolfsburg in West Germany as well as in the Libyan capital of Tripoli.

The period of shell building in the GDR, which began quite late, lasted little more than a decade. Most of Ulrich Müther's concrete shells were constructed during this time. Changing needs and habits, other focal points in urban planning, and new architectural fashions—not only in the GDR—were reasons for the declining demand. The shell constructions are, therefore, a significant characteristic of the East German version of late modernism in architecture and urban planning.

1 See most recently Bauhaus Kooperation Berlin Dessau Weimar, ed., *Bauhaus 100: Sites of Modernism: A Grand Tour* (Berlin, 2019), 40–41.
2 See Erich Kaufmann and Ulrich Müther, "'Teepott' Rostock-Warnemünde," *Deutsche Architektur* 18 (1969): 157–161.
3 See Erich Kaufmann and Ulrich Müther, "Messehalle in Rostock," *Deutsche Architektur* 15 (1966): 676–679.
4 "Architekturwettbewerb 1969: Schöpferische Leistungen im Wettbewerb der 'deutschen architektur' ausgezeichnet," *Deutsche Architektur* 18 (1969): 585–589.
5 Letter from the Rügen sectional leadership team of the SED to the board of the PGH Bau Binz, April 29, 1970, Müther Archive, Hochschule Wismar, 669.
6 See Günther Ackermann, "Der Bau von Schalen für Dachtragwerke aus Stahlbeton im Osten Deutschlands (1945–1985)," *Bautechnik* 78 (2001): 18–35; and Tanja Seeböck, *Schwünge in Beton: Die Schalenbauten von Ulrich Müther* (Schwerin, 2016), 130–143.
7 See M[anuel] Sanchez-Arcas, *Form und Bauweise der Schalen* (Berlin [East], 1961), 67–68.
8 See Herbert Müller, "Die HP-Schalenbauweise in ihrer bisherigen Anwendung," *Deutsche Architektur* 15 (1966): 83–92; idem, "Das Uni-HP-System," *Deutsche Architektur* 18 (1969): 631–633.
9 Jörg Streitparth and Gerd Wessel, "Milch-Mocca-Bar im Stadtzentrum Cottbus," *Deutsche Architektur* 18 (1969): 234–235, here 235.
10 See Andreas Baudisch, "'Was Besonderes': Der Schalenbau in der DDR zwischen 1963 und 1971," *kunsttexte.de/ostblick*, no. 3 (2013).
11 See Heinrichs, "Französische Ingenieure über Betonschalenkonstruktionen," *Deutsche Architektur* 8 (1959): 171.
12 See Reinhold Rabich and Günther Ackermann, "Bericht über das Internationale Schalenkolloquium in Dresden vom 14. bis 18. 3. 1961," *Wissenschaftliche Zeitschrift der Hochschule für Bauwesen Cottbus* 4 (1961): 311–325.
13 See Herrmann Rühle, "Wie wurden Schalen gebaut: Ein erlebter Rückblick," in *Zum Werk von Félix Candela: Die Kunst der leichten Schalen*, Arcus 18 (Cologne, 1992), 32–49, here 42–47.
14 See Sanchez-Arcas, *Form und Bauweise der Schalen* (see note 7). The following year, Jürgen Joedicke published a thematically similar but broader volume in the Federal Republic of Germany: *Schalenbau: Konstruktion und Gestaltung*, with contributions by Walter Bauersfeld and Herbert Kupfer (Stuttgart, 1962).
15 On Sánchez Arcas in this context see Henry Vicente Garrido, "De Europa y Asia: Elogio de la trashumancia," in Henry Vicente Garrido, ed., *Arquitecturas desplazadas: Arquitecturas del exilio español* (no place [Madrid], 2007), 37–50; see also the biographical information, 186–187.
16 I[ngo] Schönrock, "Pilzförmige Schalenelemente," *Deutsche Architektur* 11 (1962): 420.
17 See Seeböck, *Schwünge in Beton*, 77–78 (see note 6).
18 For the reception of Candela's buildings by Müther see Massimo Laffranchi, "Concrete Shell Structures: A Historical Perspective," in Rahel Lämmler and Michael Wagner, *Ulrich Müther: Shell Structures in Mecklenburg-Western Pomerania* (Sulgen, 2010), 16–29, here 24–26; and Seeböck, *Schwünge in Beton*, 175–184 (see note 6).
19 For the biography of Müther, also in the following, see Klaus Stiglat, *Bauingenieure und ihr Werk* (Berlin, 2004), 258–262; Lämmler and Wagner, *Ulrich Müther*, 30–35 (see note 18); Seeböck, *Schwünge in Beton* (see note 6); and Andreas Schätzke, "Der Ingenieur: Ulrich Müther und die Architekturmoderne in der DDR," in Bundesingenieurkammer, ed., *Der Teepott in Rostock-Warnemünde* (Berlin, 2018), 38–52.
20 See Lämmler and Wagner, *Ulrich Müther*, 40–41 (see note 18); and Seeböck, *Schwünge in Beton*, 312 (see note 6).
21 See Müther's correspondence with Fritz Leonhardt and Jörg Schlaich as well as with the Chairman of the Council of Ministers of the GDR, Willi Stoph, the Minister of Building Industry, Wolfgang Junker, and the Kammer der Technik (Chamber of Technology), 1966 and 1967, Müther Archive, Hochschule Wismar, 668.
22 See Otto Patzelt, "Kolloquium über neue Konstruktionen für das Bauwesen," *Deutsche Architektur* 16 (1967): 556–557.
23 Ulrich Müther, "Die praktische Anwendung des modernen Schalenbaues," in Manfred Specht, ed., *Spannweite der Gedanken: Zur 100. Wiederkehr des Geburtstages von Franz Dischinger* (Berlin [West]/Heidelberg/New York/London/Paris/Tokyo, 1987), 111–121, here 112.
24 See Andreas Schätzke, *Zwischen Bauhaus und Stalinallee: Architekturdiskussion im östlichen Deutschland 1945–1955*, 2nd, rev. ed. (Basel/Gütersloh/Berlin, 2017).
25 On architecture and urban planning in the GDR in the 1960s see Gerhard Krenz, *Architektur zwischen gestern und morgen: Ein Vierteljahrhundert Architekturentwicklung in der Deutschen Demokratischen Republik* (Berlin [East], 1974); Thomas Topfstedt, *Städtebau in der DDR 1955–1971* (Leipzig, 1988); Joachim Palutzki, *Architektur in der DDR* (Berlin, 2000), esp. 183–289; and Ralf Lange, *Architektur und Städtebau der sechziger Jahre: Planen und Bauen in der Bundesrepublik Deutschland und der DDR von 1960 bis 1975* (Bonn, 2003).
26 For the shell buildings developed with the participation of Ulrich Müther, see the catalogue raisonné in Seeböck, *Schwünge in Beton*, 311–389 (see note 6).
27 See Dieter Ahting, "Café 'Seerose' in Potsdam," *Architektur der DDR* 35 (1986): 552–553.

Safe at Last?
The Fate of Ulrich Müther's Magdeburg Hypar Shell in a Changing Society

TANJA SEEBÖCK

Ulrich Müther built almost all of his famous shell constructions during the time of the German Democratic Republic. Most were commissioned by the state as special projects for important locations and purposes. The public generally cherished the elegant buildings that were remarkable exceptions among the often monotonous output of contemporary local architecture.

After the demise of the Socialist state and German reunification in 1990, a lot of Müther's creations faced crucial problems: many lost their original functions, and the public mood toward the architectural heritage of the GDR was generally unfavorable. Therefore, a lot of Müther's buildings faced uncertain destinies, either for economic, technical, or functional reasons. Over the next few years, some were demolished or significantly altered; some were simply left empty and fell into disrepair. It took some time before Müther's work was newly appreciated and plans were drawn up to restore and repurpose some of his remaining buildings.

A remarkable example of the tough and drawn-out struggle for the conservation of Müther's work is the so-called Hyparschale (Hypar Shell) in Magdeburg. Its fate is a good example of the changing appreciation of most of Müther's shells.[1] The Hyparschale had always been a communal property and was used as a multipurpose hall. The building became a listed monument in 1998, but its fate remained uncertain for 21 years.[2] During that time, the city government made several failed attempts to find an investor who could come up with a financially viable development concept to preserve the building. Only after more than two decades of decay, did the city finally make a last-minute decision to redevelop the Hyparschale at its own cost to save the building from total destruction.

THE BUILDING, ITS HISTORY, AND ITS SURROUNDINGS

The Magdeburg Hyparschale was built in 1969, following plans by Ulrich Müther and the local architect Horst Freytag. It was used for trade fairs, exhibitions, sports, and other events. Covering 2,304 square meters, the Hyparschale is Müther's largest surviving building. In terms of space, it was surpassed only by the Ahornblatt restaurant in Berlin, which was erected a few months after the Magdeburg hall and demolished in 2000.

The building was located in the city's exhibition site, a communal park close to the older Stadthalle. This literally translates as "city hall," but in German, the term designates a city's main event location, not the seat of the city government. The park is situated on an island

1 Horst Freytag and Ulrich Müther, multipurpose hall (Hyparschale), Magdeburg, 1969: view from the southeast

in the river Elbe, just opposite Magdeburg's city center. Its landmark, the famous gothic cathedral, is in direct line of sight of the Hyparschale and the Stadthalle.

The 7th Party Conference of the ruling Socialist Unity Party of Germany decided that the cities of the GDR should "improve social living conditions of all workers."[3] They were meant to develop more cultural and recreational spaces for their citizens. Because of this, the city government of Magdeburg made plans to redevelop the existing 200-hectare municipal park as an attractive local recreational area and cultural space. The shell construction was part of these plans and would function as an event center. In Magdeburg, the first step was to enhance the former exhibition site, which had been built for the *Deutsche Theaterausstellung* (German Theater Exhibition) in 1927.[4] From that period, some imposing buildings in the early Modernist style have survived. The monumental brick structure of the Stadthalle and a tall observation tower still dominate the park.

The old Stadthalle was big enough for cultural events such as concerts and congresses but too small for exhibitions and trade fairs. Therefore, in 1967 a larger, modern exhibition center was planned for the park. The intention was "to show the economic face of the city, exemplified by objects and displays of achievements."[5] Müther's Hyparschale served as the impressive focal point of the complex, connected to four smaller exhibition halls. These have since been demolished. The Hyparschale was deliberately planned as a modern extension of the existing buildings. Therefore, it was placed in a direct axial relationship to the Stadthalle. It was not only meant to be a space for exhibitions, but also an exhibit of contemporary East German architecture in itself.

The construction consists of four smaller hypar shells, each covering a square area of 24 × 24 meters. The four segments are linked by light-bands. Together they span an area of 48 × 48 meters without interior supports. The roof construction is made from reinforced concrete with a thickness of just 7 centimeters.

The shell edges are carried by vertical steel supports, which were originally painted bright red, leading to a vibrantly articulated appearance. The steel-glass facades differ from most of Müther's other buildings, as the glazing is not clear but made of translucent Copilit glass[6] resulting in the industrial character of the whole building. As is typical for Müther's work, the shell segments are tilted: in Magdeburg their outer high points reach up to 15 meters, the inner high points to 12 meters. All four shells are stabilized by edge beams. Inclined supports carry resultant forces from the edge beam into

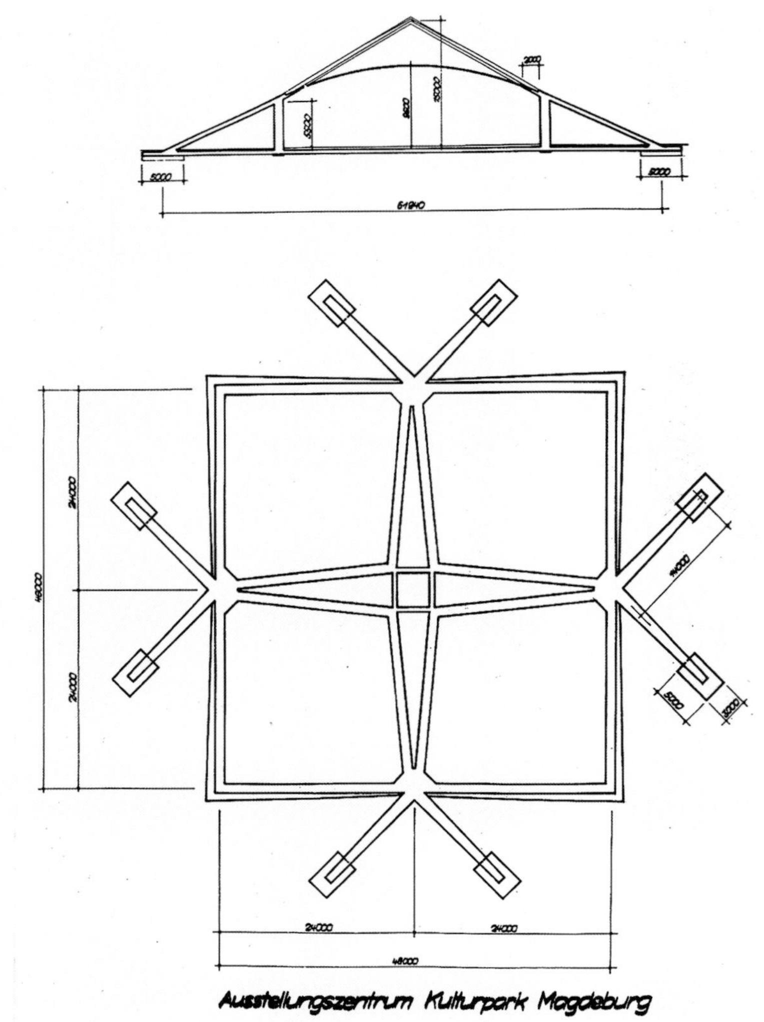

2 Horst Freytag and Ulrich Müther, multipurpose hall (Hyparschale), Magdeburg, 1969: section and top view

the foundations. The foundations are reinforced by tie rods linking opposing base points of the shell.

The building once had a particularly impressive interior atmosphere because of the room-high glazing on all sides made of semitransparent profiled glass, which screened out the outside world and created the impression of an almost floating roof construction. The star-shaped overhead light-bands made of glass bricks and concrete elements (glass prism concrete slabs) ensured effective lighting. However, the roof skylights, which leaked due to construction errors, had to be covered with welded sheets and closed just a few years after construction.

THE PLACE OF THE BUILDING IN MÜTHER'S WORK

The Magdeburg Hyparschale is one of the outstanding shell constructions in Ulrich Müther's work. One reason for this is its particular design history: although it is very similar to the multipurpose hall in Rostock-Lütten Klein, which was already under construction at the time, the Magdeburg project is not a reuse, but an individual new design.

At first, it was actually planned to reuse the plan of the Rostock multipurpose hall due to time constraints in order to open the Magdeburg hall as early as 1968. However, after a visit to the Rostock multipurpose hall and discussions with Müther's cooperative PGH Bau Binz, those involved in the planning process came to the conclusion that the floor plan dimensions and height of the Rostock hall did not fit the requirements at Magdeburg, as they limited the range of use. The planning committee also preferred a less austere shape than that which it found on the island of Rügen: Müther's hypar shell construction in Glowe, with its maximum height of 13 meters, which was just about to be stripped of its formwork at the time, served as a visual inspiration for the Magdeburg construction. This was a single, tilted shell above a square ground plan for the Ostseeperle beach restaurant. A new structural calculation was necessary for the Magdeburg project, which proved to be very complex and complicated and caused Müther great difficulties. He explained: "With its size and type, this roof construction is unique in the Republic and cannot be compared to the hypar shell constructions carried out so far."[7]

Müther erected three further buildings with ground plans similar to that of the Magdeburg Hyparschale. All

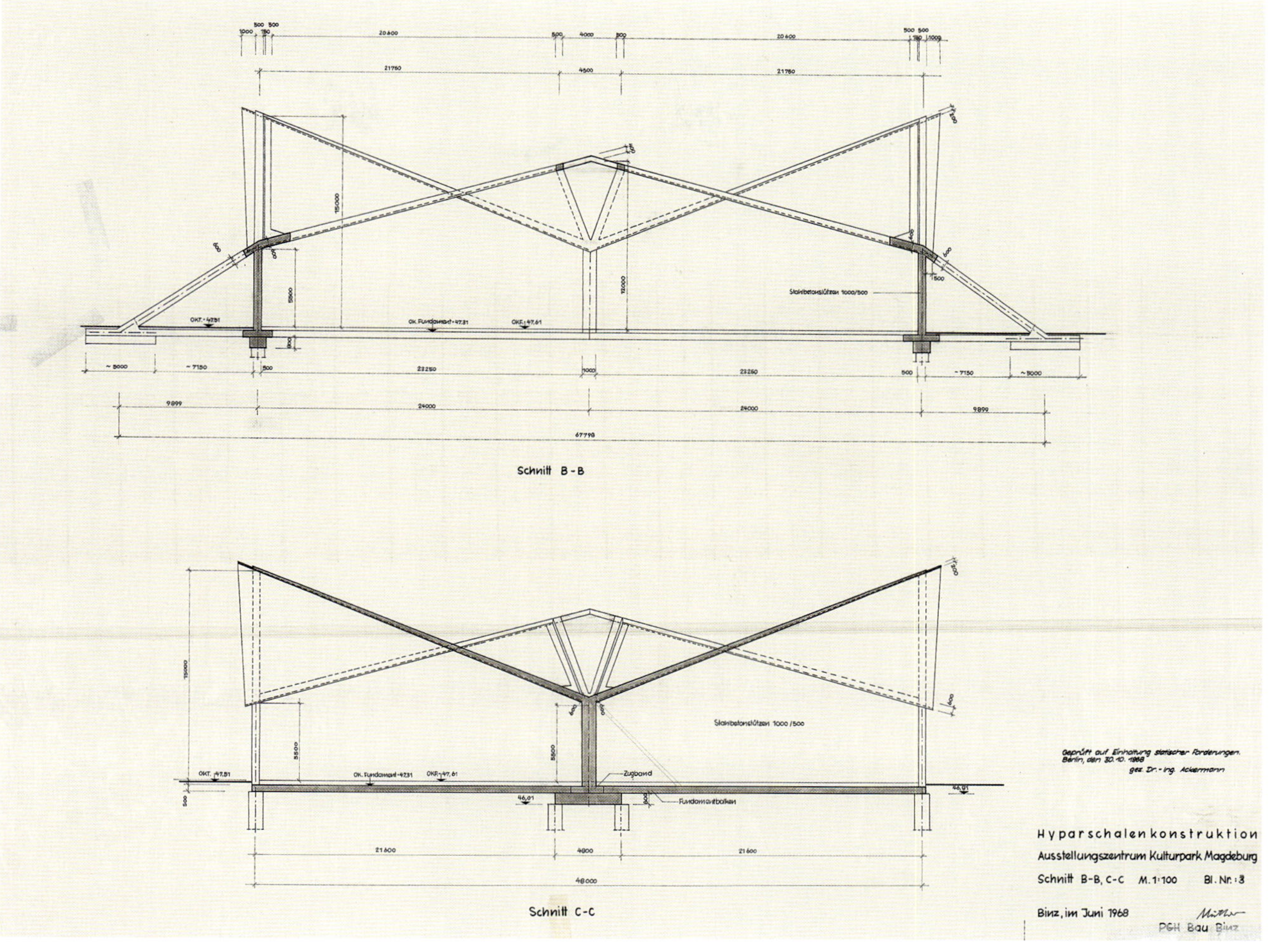

3 Sections; drawing by Ulrich Müther, 1968

of them were unique projects: the multi-purpose hall in Rostock-Lütten Klein and the Stadthalle in Neubrandenburg (both built in 1968), as well as the rowing center in Dresden (completed in 1972). All consisted of four combined hypar shells over a square ground plan, but they had different dimensions and roof pitches, which made it necessary to recalculate the structures each time. For the Rostock hall, for example, eight additional interior columns were needed to support the roof loads. None of the three buildings reached the dimensions of the Magdeburg construction.[8]

At the Magdeburg Hyparschale, Müther assembled the four shells for the first time with the shell surfaces tilted outward—in Neubrandenburg they are tilted inward, and in Dresden and Rostock they are not tilted, but arranged horizontally at a similar height. The new combination of the single shells, which is responsible for the star-shaped skylighting as well as the large dimensions in space and height, distinguishes the Magdeburg building from Müther's other shells and demonstrates the highest possible engineering capabilities of that time. The Magdeburg Hyparschale was individually designed as a prestigious building, executed with craftsmanship and acknowledged international architectural trends. It is an important building in Müther's work and a building of international standing. By European comparison, the Magdeburg Hyparschale belongs to the small group of large composite hypar shell structures.[9]

DECAY AND CONSERVATION EFFORTS

As early as the 1980s, concrete damage was discovered in individual columns, but the necessary renovation was not carried out. These two issues had already affected the overall architectural impression of the hall during the GDR era. Then the Hyparschale and Stadthalle area lost its traditional function as a trade fair location when a new, larger exhibition center was built in nearby Elbauenpark in 1999. The shell building had by then been closed in 1997 due to structural defects. At the time it was closed, most of the original fittings were still well preserved.

However, only one year later, the community applied for a demolition permit, as a study deemed the building decayed beyond repair. A second report, demanded by the conservation authorities, stated that a restoration of the building was possible. As a result, it was decided that

4 Interior view during the last construction period, 1969

5 Interior view, 1980s

6 Damage due to moisture on the roof and on the supports, 2010

the building would be preserved and a comprehensive restoration plan was worked out. The restoration costs for the shell construction were calculated at 1.5 million euros, with an estimated overall cost of 3 million euros.

As the city was unable to raise funds, even for emergency measures such as waterproofing the roof, the empty building decayed more and more. In the meantime, appreciation for the neglected landmark grew. Several citizens' initiatives were formed to demand the rescue of the Hyparschale. Students developed preservation concepts, and a conference of architects, art historians, and conservation professionals was held, where the salvation of the building was argued together with local politicians and inhabitants.[10] Nevertheless, for several years, all public initiatives came to nothing, as nobody would finance the necessary measures.

The consequences of this were severe. About ten years after its closure, the damage to the abandoned building had become much worse due to the ongoing neglect. The main problem was moisture damage to the roof and the supports. Moreover, cracks had appeared in other concrete structures, such as the oblique supports. For several years, the city government offered the premises with a long-term building lease under the condition that the building had to be restored. Several potential investors emerged with different concept proposals, but all came to nothing due to the high restoration costs.

As the city still could not afford even urgently needed basic repairs, the decay of the building advanced further. Finally, a support structure had to be erected two years ago to prevent the collapse of the shell.

Things only changed recently. The city government finally set up a plan for the redevelopment of the derelict landmark after 21 years of neglect. Under the new plan, the city will now fund the restoration at an estimated cost of about 17 million euros. The state capital itself has pledged to contribute 57 percent of that sum, that is, 9.7 million euros. The payment was finally cleared in August 2019. The rest of the amount will be covered by grants, including 5 million euros from the Federal Government of Germany.[11]

Under the new concept, the Hyparschale will be redeveloped into a multifunctional conference center with a capacity of up to 500 visitors, following plans by the Berlin office gmp · von Gerkan, Marg and Partners Architects. The focus of the project is the preservation of Müther's shell construction; other elements, such as the Copilit glazing or the remaining interior fixtures, will have to be sacrificed. The new interior concept represents a good compromise between necessary renewal and the conservation of the historical monument. By inserting a gallery level into the main hall, a second floor will provide additional space. This upper level is supported by four cubes containing meeting rooms and auxiliary rooms.[12] Despite the introduction of these new facilities, the shape of the Müther shell remains visible, thus maintaining its original spacious character.

The shell construction will be treated with an innovative procedure utilizing carbon-reinforced concrete, which was developed at Technische Universität Dresden. This new method offers considerable advantages, as carbon is much stronger and lighter than steel. As the material is also corrosion-resistant, the use of concrete can be cut to a minimum, because the concrete cover is only required for the composite effect and can be kept extremely thin. This reduces the total consumption of materials and the weight of the structure.[13] The shell construction will be strengthened with a 10-millimeter-thick carbon-reinforced concrete layer on the top and underside of the existing structure. According to a paper by the developers of the method, these measures will make the building fit for permanent use and increase the load-bearing capacity of the shell by 50 percent compared to the current state.[14]

The project is currently behind schedule due to lack of building permits. Construction was scheduled to start in spring 2019, but had to start later, beginning with the restoration of the roof. The reopening is scheduled for autumn 2022, one year later than planned.[15] The hall could possibly be operated by Magdeburg's communal fairs and events company as a conference and training center. This plan would preserve the original function of the remarkable hall, but it remains to be seen if the planned use will meet the economic and social needs of the present. Hopefully, the city of Magdeburg can develop a sensible event concept that sustainably secures the use of the Hyparschale. That is the most important condition to reestablish the monument as a vibrant location in Rotehorn communal park and a source of identity for the citizens.

7 Interior view with temporary supporting structure, 2018

8 Renovation and conversion by gmp · von Gerkan, Marg and Partners Architects: design visualization, 2018

1 For case studies of lost and surviving concrete shells by Ulrich Müther, see Tanja Seeböck, "Ulrich Müther's Concrete Shells between Rejection and Appreciation: An Architectural Survey and Practical Examples of Their Treatment," in Stephanie Herold and Biljana Stefanovska, ed., *45+: Post-War Modern Architecture in Europe*, ISR Graue Reihe 43 (Berlin, 2012), 141–150 (https://depositonce.tu-berlin.de/handle/11303/3655). See also Tanja Seeböck, "Die Betonschalen von Ulrich Müther zwischen Ablehnung und Wertschätzung: Imagewandel und Beispiele der gesellschaftlichen Rezeption," in Mark Escherich, ed., *Denkmal Ost-Moderne: Aneignung und Erhaltung des baulichen Erbes der Nachkriegsmoderne*, Stadtentwicklung und Denkmalpflege 16 (Berlin, 2012), 226–239; and Tanja Seeböck, *Schwünge in Beton: Die Schalenbauten von Ulrich Müther* (Schwerin, 2016), 197–272.

2 Information from the State Office for Monument Conservation Saxony-Anhalt, July 26, 2010, see Seeböck, *Schwünge in Beton*, 246 (see note 1).

3 Concept for the development of the cultural park, Council of the City of Magdeburg, July 20, 1967, in ibid., 242.

4 See ibid.

5 Ibid. See also "Die Ausstellungs- und Messehalle im Park Rotehorn," in *Ulrich Müther: Schalenbauten in Magdeburg*, Publikationen des Müther-Archivs 3 (Wismar, 2017), 14–39, here 14.

6 *Copilit* is a profiled glass brand.

7 Seeböck, *Schwünge in Beton*, 254 (see note 1).

8 The dimensions were as follows: The shell of the multipurpose hall in Rostock-Lütten Klein spans an area of 47×47 meters and its high points reach up to 12.40 meters; the rowing center in Dresden covers an area of 36×36 meters, and the Stadthalle in Neubrandenburg has an area of 42×42 meters.

9 For international buildings comparable to Müther's group of composite hypar shells over square ground plans, to which the Magdeburg Hyparschale belongs, see Seeböck, *Schwünge in Beton*, 184–189 (see note 1).

10 The colloquium was coorganized and attended by the author.

11 See Martin Rieß, "Rat gibt Geld für Rettung der Hyparschale frei: Letzter Schritt für Investition in die markante Halle an der Elbe ist getan," *Volksstimme*, August 23, 2019, 13.

12 The cruciform ground-floor space between them can be used as a large seated conference area, but it is also possible to close off the central space to create a smaller, more intimate location.

13 See Manuel Hentschel, Alexander Schumann, Heinz Ulrich, and Stefan Jentzsch, "Sanierung der Hyparschale Magdeburg," *Bautechnik* 96 (2019): 25–30, here 25.

14 See ibid., 29. See also Alexander Schumann, Manuel Hentschel, Robert Zobel, and Manfred Curbach, "Strengthening of the Hypar Shell in Magdeburg with Carbon Reinforced Concrete—Design and Calculations," in Carlos Lázaro, Kai-Uwe Bletzinger, and Eugenio Oñate, ed., *Form and Force: Proceedings of the IASS Annual Symposium 2019—Structural Membranes 2019* (Barcelona, 2019), 855–862, here 856–857. Moreover, the authors present the design and the calculation procedure for the strengthening with Carbon Reinforced Concrete (CRC), 857–861.

15 See Peter Ließmann, "Hyparschale Magdeburg: Termin unhaltbar," *Volksstimme*, May 16, 2019.

The Music Pavilion in Sassnitz
A Shell Structure by Ulrich Müther in Collaboration with Dietmar Kuntzsch and Otto Patzelt

SUSANNE BRORSON

The iconic concrete concert shell in Sassnitz on the Baltic island of Rügen is one of the smaller and lesser known projects by Ulrich Müther: at least it does not appear as a typical project of Müther's company VEB Spezialbetonbau. The music pavilion was developed in collaboration with the architect and professor Dietmar Kuntzsch and the structural engineer Otto Patzelt during the late 1980s, just before the fall of the Berlin Wall.

Ulrich Müther, as a structural engineer, had collaborated with various architects on several of his hyperbolic shells, but rather often the architect's contribution to the project remained in the background and in the end the building was branded a "Müther shell." This has led to a lot of discussion in the past but also research into the question how much of an architect Müther was, or how great his involvement with the design of the shell buildings was in relation to the work of the architect involved.[1] A good example is the conflict that arose around the Seerose café in Potsdam (1982/1983), composed of eight intersecting hypars. The architect Dieter Ahting claimed to be responsible for its design, and so did Müther. However, the Seerose resembles Félix Candela's restaurant in Xochimilco, Mexico City, to a very high degree. A number of Müther's buildings were inspired by those of other shell builders, mostly Candela, whose work he had studied extensively. Therefore, the copyright/authorship question with many Müther buildings becomes almost irrelevant.[2]

The fact that the architect's name often tended to be forgotten with other Müther projects was certainly also a consequence of the centralized government-run and state-controlled planning offices of the GDR, where architects were employed as part of large planning teams and were not allowed to practice independently under their own names. Müther, however, was able to continue running his building company in Binz on the island of Rügen, which he had taken over from his parents, even though it had been converted into a Volkseigener Betrieb (VEB, Publicly Owned Enterprise) in 1972, as it was slightly off the radar, being far away from Berlin.

The music pavilion in Sassnitz, completed in 1988, was one of the last concrete shells that Müther and his VEB Spezialbetonbau Rügen built, resulting in the fact that there is still a very good record of planning documents and correspondence in both the local archives in Sassnitz and the Müther Archive in Wismar. It proved very valuable that a number of people who were involved in the project could be interviewed in 2015, which makes it possible to retrace the design development in detail.[3] It became evident that, at least with the concert

1 Dietmar Kuntzsch, Otto Patzelt, and Ulrich Müther, music pavilion, Sassnitz, 1988

shell in Sassnitz, the architect Dietmar Kuntzsch and the structural engineer Otto Patzelt were mainly responsible for the design, and that Müther's role was more that of a consulting engineer, and later as general contractor.

Müther's success was rooted in his ability to offer both architectural and engineering services as well as building services in one package: his company numbered about 100 employees during the 1980s. While being director of a building company, he was also a shell building specialist who kept on researching and who had close contacts with other shell builders worldwide. To the Socialist party of the GDR Müther was of special interest, because he was able to realize large, symbolic buildings within just 150 days from planning to completion. His shell-building services were sold internationally, which was of economic importance to the government, which protected him in return.[4]

Dietmar Kuntzsch was one of the few renowned architects at the time based in East Berlin, where he was a young professor at the architecture department of the Kunsthochschule (Art School) in Weißensee. Before that, he had been project architect at the local planning authority for various schemes in the center of East Berlin. Otto Patzelt was a structural engineer who was teaching in Weißensee, too. He had been researching and working with the Bauakademie (Building Academy) in Berlin, where one focus of his work was with shell and tent structures, and he had been publishing extensively on nature as a role model for structural design.[5] Patzelt knew Müther from before. During a colloquium on shell structures in 1967, in Friedrichroda, Patzelt raised awareness of Müther's "beautiful concrete shells," and it was discussed whether his buildings should be "democratized." The question was raised whether the shells could be mass-produced due to their low building costs. Patzelt, however, called for the shells to remain exceptional architecture.[6]

2 View from above

The music pavilion in Sassnitz consists of three buildings; the actual concrete seashell, and two additional storage buildings, one on each side, which are simple blockwork constructions with a rounded in situ concrete roof. The pavilion marks the end of the seafront promenade in Sassnitz, which leads from the old fishing harbor toward the start of the white cliffs of Rügen. The concrete seashell is built right on the edge of the water with its back turned toward it, making it a landmark when approaching Rügen by ferry. As Dietmar Kuntzsch has pointed out, the pavilion simply provides a roof for the artists, while at the same time allowing views from the audience to the best possible backdrop: the sea. There had been a wooden orchestra pavilion at the same location that was destroyed in a storm.

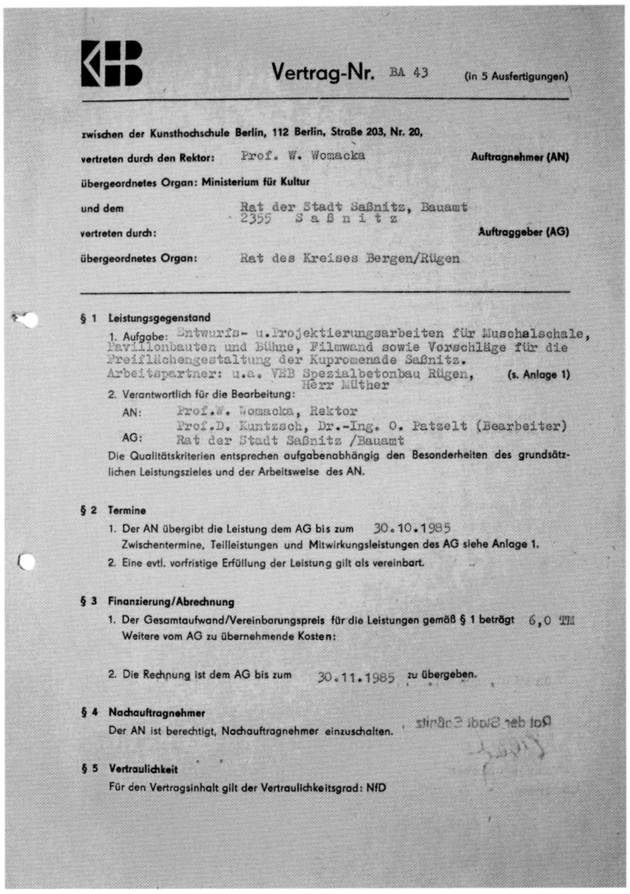

Vertrag-Nr. BA 43 (in 5 Ausfertigungen)

zwischen der Kunsthochschule Berlin, 112 Berlin, Straße 203, Nr. 20,
vertreten durch den Rektor: Prof. W. Womacka — Auftragnehmer (AN)
übergeordnetes Organ: Ministerium für Kultur
und dem Rat der Stadt Saßnitz, Bauamt
2355 Saßnitz
vertreten durch: — Auftraggeber (AG)
übergeordnetes Organ: Rat des Kreises Bergen/Rügen

§ 1 Leistungsgegenstand

1. Aufgabe: Entwurfs- u.Projektierungsarbeiten für Muschelschale, Pavillonbauten und Bühne, Filmwand sowie Vorschläge für die Freiflächengestaltung der Kupromenade Saßnitz.
Arbeitspartner: u.a. VEB Spezialbetonbau Rügen, Herr Müther (s. Anlage 1)
2. Verantwortlich für die Bearbeitung:
AN: Prof.W. Womacka, Rektor
Prof.D. Kuntzsch, Dr.-Ing. O. Patzelt (Bearbeiter)
AG: Rat der Stadt Saßnitz /Bauamt
Die Qualitätskriterien entsprechen aufgabenabhängig den Besonderheiten des grundsätzlichen Leistungszieles und der Arbeitsweise des AN.

§ 2 Termine

1. Der AN übergibt die Leistung dem AG bis zum 30.10.1985
Zwischentermine, Teilleistungen und Mitwirkungsleistungen des AG siehe Anlage 1.
2. Eine evtl. vorfristige Erfüllung der Leistung gilt als vereinbart.

§ 3 Finanzierung/Abrechnung

1. Der Gesamtaufwand/Vereinbarungspreis für die Leistungen gemäß § 1 beträgt 6,0 TM
Weitere vom AG zu übernehmende Kosten:
2. Die Rechnung ist dem AG bis zum 30.11.1985 zu übergeben.

§ 4 Nachauftragnehmer

Der AN ist berechtigt, Nachauftragnehmer einzuschalten.

§ 5 Vertraulichkeit

Für den Vertragsinhalt gilt der Vertraulichkeitsgrad: NfD

3 Contract between the Kunsthochschule (Art School) Berlin-Weißensee and the city of Sassnitz, 1985

The story of the development of the music pavilion in Sassnitz is quite unique: however, it illustrates how Ulrich Müther worked under often complicated political and economic circumstances in the GDR. Müther's shell structures can only be discussed taking into consideration that they have been built in this context.[7] The music pavilion was realized during the last years of the former East Germany, when the economic situation had already deteriorated. If anything was built, it was mostly of poor quality, as it was difficult to source building materials. Often, the quality of materials, for example concrete, was compromised by incorporating cheaper additives, such as gypsum or ashes.[8] Aiming for a new cultural building was therefore an ambitious idea, as this kind of project was mostly on hold. On the other hand, political structures were starting to soften up, which suddenly opened up the opportunity for initiating individual projects outside political agendas.

Dietmar Kuntzsch had visited the island of Rügen regularly for private reasons. During the 1980s, he had started to organize summer workshops with architecture students, which they had been invited to by the city of Sassnitz, mostly to come up with ideas for regeneration schemes within the old town. At the same time, a few kilometers away from Sassnitz, a new ferry terminal was to be built, and the city of Sassnitz received funding as a compensation measure to improve its seafront promenade. Although it was not sufficient funding for a building, the city took the initiative to call for ideas for a new music pavilion in 1984.

The mayor of Sassnitz and the head of planning were well aware of the building material shortages and financial limitations of the time, but managed to divert concrete from the ferry terminal building site for the music pavilion project. As they explained during an interview in 2015, the only possibility for realizing the new orchestra shell was to make use of the concrete.[9] As records show, Kuntzsch started to work on initial ideas for the pavilion with his students, but soon after, he and Patzelt were formally appointed for the design stage of the project. The Sassnitz municipal archive keeps a contract between the Kunsthochschule Berlin-Weißensee (KHB) and the city of Sassnitz. This shows that the music pavilion project was not drawn up by the government-run planning collectives, as would normally have been the case, but that two art school professors were appointed for the planning stage—a rather unusual move.

4 Plaster models, convex version and concave version

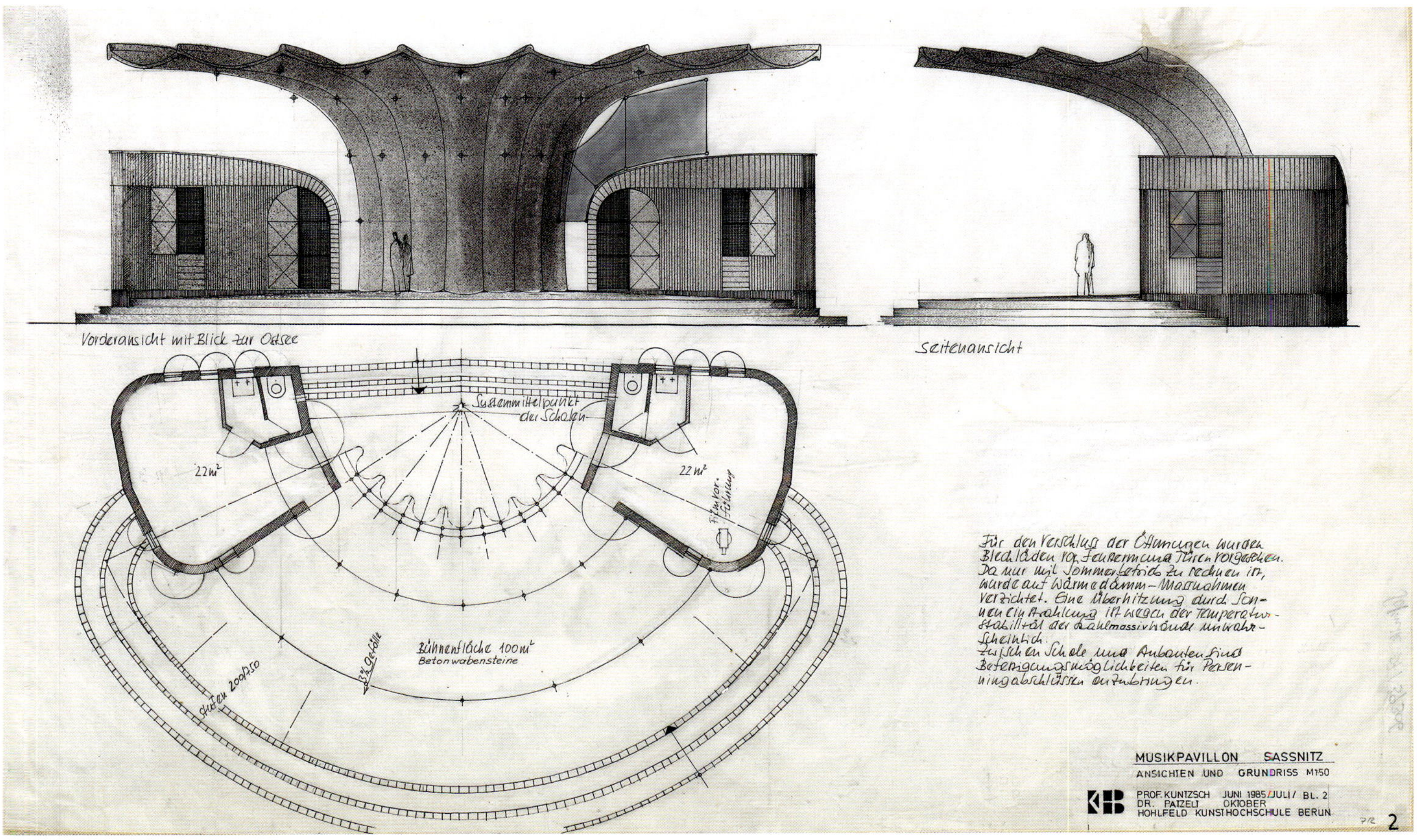

5 Front view, side view, and floor plan: design by Dietmar Kuntzsch, 1985

Ulrich Müther, the concrete shell specialist, was based not far away along the same bay in Binz, and was called up on to collaborate on the project. In the end, the difficult circumstance of concrete being the only available building material was turned into a big asset for the city of Sassnitz in getting their own prominent Müther building. Correspondence shows that at a very early stage of the design, Müther himself got in touch with Kuntzsch and Patzelt. Regular design meetings took place in Sassnitz, when Kuntzsch and Patzelt traveled by train to Rügen carrying large plaster models of the music shell with them.

The initial design and first model shows a voluminous seashell with several hypars pointing upward, which was later referred to by Patzelt as the "convex version." The design drawing below shows a radius of about 11 meters and a height of 7 meters. Interestingly, the design does not follow one of the main typological features of concert shells, namely that of being an enclosed space for acoustical reasons. On the contrary, Kuntzsch's design is essentially just a roof.

Müther was overseeing the design process and worked closely with Otto Patzelt on refining the structure of the shell. Müther's experience led to a crucial change in the design of the music pavilion, which also emphasizes his role during the design process as that of a consulting engineer. In order to avoid water ponding in the valleys in between the arches, which might have

6 Employees of VEB Spezialbetonbau Rügen during the concrete spraying work, 1987

led to damage, the structure was turned upside down into a "hanging" version. This version was referred to by the two structural engineers Müther and Patzelt as the "concave version," where single hypar shells were hanging between the ribs. Furthermore, Müther contributed critical technical knowledge with regard to the implementation process, and the capabilities of his building company in realizing the concrete shell could be taken into account during the early design stage. The engineer and teacher Patzelt remembered it as being "wonderfully exciting" to work together with Müther on a hypar shell project.[10]

During the design process, the city of Sassnitz expressed concerns about the steady wind from the sea that might disturb the musicians and affect the comfort of the audience. The overall acoustic qualities of the open shell structure were also questioned, and the design needed amending again. At first, Kuntzsch proposed textile sails to be put up around the music pavilion. As there were further practical requirements, such as the need for storage and toilets, Kuntzsch added two lower buildings, one on either side of the shell, to almost close off the area in front of it in order to protect it from wind and to improve acoustics.[11]

The concert seashell is not one hyperbolic paraboloid, but it consists of seven single hypar shells that are described by hyperbolas, which means it is not typical of the structures that Müther used to work with. Müther hardly experimented with new shapes: he saw himself as a pragmatic shell builder in creating beautiful shells that were precisely curved and properly constructed.[12] He furthermore called himself "the master builder from Rügen," referring to someone who can design, engineer, and build hypar shells. The expressive form of the music pavilion, therefore, clearly derives from the collaboration with Kuntzsch and Patzelt.

The seven hypar shells together form the roof, projecting out as a third of a circle with a radius of 11 meters. Toward the ground, the distance between the ribs decreases from 3.50 meters at the top to about half a meter at the bottom. The shell has an approximate thickness of 7 centimeters. Otto Patzelt designed and calculated the structure, first by hand, later using computers and the finite element method. In the 1980s the Kunsthochschule in Berlin-Weißensee had set up a computer room with machines bought from West Germany. However, computer programs were not very advanced at the time and Patzelt struggled to make sense of the computer calculations. As he explained in an interview in 2015, the computer was "just spitting out useless and enormous piles of paper." Patzelt, like most shell engineers, worked with models, as Müther did, too. In the end, Patzelt calculated the concert shell the old-fashioned way as a fixed T-beam.[13]

In preparing the planning documents to be handed in to the planning authorities for approval, Patzelt pro-

7 Opening of the music pavilion, 1988: from left to right: Dietmar Kuntzsch; Ulrich Müther; head of the municipal construction office, Günter Sauer; and mayor Hans-Joachim Lange

vided both the computer calculations using the finite element method and the fixed T-beam calculation. In the end, Müther handed in the structural scheme with his signature and company stamp because, as Patzelt stated "nobody would dare to question Müther's calculations." The second reason was that Kuntzsch and Patzelt, although officially appointed for the design stage, were not listed architects or engineers while teaching at the art school. Patzelt's structural scheme also states that the music pavilion was designed to match the technical capabilities of Müther's VEB Spezialbetonbau Rügen and the building material that the city of Sassnitz was able to find.[14]

After the design was approved, Müther and his company took over for implementation. At the time, Müther was busy with projects abroad and had no capacity to oversee the construction phase himself. The music pavilion was also a fairly small project compared to the large schemes Müther was working on in the late 1980s such as the planetarium in Vantaa (Finland) or the velodrome in Havana (Cuba). This led to yet another unconventional arrangement, in which Otto Patzelt—still teaching in Berlin—officially acted as the site supervisor in Sassnitz, pretending to be employed by Müther's company without any such contract or insurance in place.

Looking back, Müther remains an exceptional figure in the landscape of architects and engineers of the GDR. Müther was able to cleverly make use of the political system without being part of it: he was pragmatic and able to improvise.[15] As a businessman, he was able to put himself forward when it came to realizing hypar shell projects. In the GDR, where building material was difficult to obtain, thin concrete shells could be realized with limited resources. Labor was cheap, and the time-consuming and complex building process that had stopped concrete shells from being built in the West continued to a much later time in the East.

The development of the music pavilion in Sassnitz very much reflects the circumstances described above. As the city itself had no funds to pay for construction workers, it called for volunteers through the local newspaper. Various companies offered help in the shape of so-called Feierabendbrigaden who were essentially employees helping out after work for minimal pay (a very common model in the GDR). The local population was mobilized to take part in the music pavilion project and to realize it with a communal effort.[16] All other building materials apart from the concrete from the ferry terminal building site had to be organized, too. Müther had very good connections and was able to deliver the reinforcement steel. It was also common in the GDR to privately trade with goods, so the mayor of Sassnitz and his head of planning themselves exchanged salted herring from the local fish factory for timber boards; even wooden slats for fish boxes were used as shuttering. The city was also buying up leftover materials from private individuals such as small amounts of bricks or screws, as a number of invoices in the local archive in Sassnitz reveal.

The building material shortage also had an effect on the architectural appearance of the music pavilion and the two adjacent buildings. It proved difficult to purchase windows and doors, so they had to be sourced from a nearby shipyard, leading to round portholes being installed instead, a sudden twist to the design that the architect Dietmar Kuntzsch did not mind at all.[17] As the building site supervisor, Otto Patzelt was hence confronted with a high level of improvisation. In addition, the skilled and experienced workers of Müther's company shotcreting the shell were challenged by the special circumstances, especially by the concrete mixer truck going back and forth between the ferry terminal building site and the music pavilion. Martin Haase, a former employee of Müther's VEB Spezialbetonbau Rügen and his "first man on the shotcrete gun," explained that it was crucial to shotcrete in one continuous operation to ensure the quality of the concrete. Therefore, the arrival of the concrete mixer truck and the shotcreting process had to be carefully timed. Haase also stated that the actual delicate shape of a seashell was not easy to shotcrete and that the projecting structure of the reinforcement was slightly unstable. It was therefore propped up during the shotcreting process. The shell was shotcreted from the bottom up to the top for better stability: chicken wire mesh was added to the reinforcement to give a better base for the concrete. In the end, the concrete was made good and smooth-finished by hand.[18] In August 1988 the music pavilion was inaugurated with a weekend full of celebrations.

With the fall of the Wall, Dietmar Kuntzsch's design for a landscaping scheme around the music pavilion was abandoned. To many residents of the GDR, Ulrich Müther's buildings were politically charged and represented the former Socialist state, which used to exploit Müther's visionary buildings to demonstrate technological progress. The music pavilion was left unused and almost fell derelict—there were even voices calling for the concrete shell to be demolished.

In 2006, the music pavilion was partly refurbished to avoid further damage to the structure, and painted white all over. In 2015 the Wüstenrot Foundation started to explore the possibility of a full refurbishment and discovered that the concrete shell was in relatively good condition despite its constant exposure to seawater and driving rain. The pavilion received the status of a listed building and the Wüstenrot Foundation was subsequently able to secure funding for the refurbishment. In 2016 the Rügen-based architect Heike Nessler was appointed for the project and during building works it was discovered that the concrete shell only had to be refurbished up to a height of 3.50 meters because of its good condition: above that level only minor cracks had to be repaired. The original glass fiber–based sealant had to be removed by hand and a new sealant applied. The concrete shell was then painted in the original color gradient of ochre fading to white toward the edges, with the windows and doors of the two storage buildings being stained turquoise. After 2017 and the completion of the refurbishment of the "music shell," as the pavilion is called by the local population, it has become an even more popular destination for architecture tourists and Müther fans; most important, many music events have been taking place there again.

1 See Tanja Seeböck, *Schwünge in Beton: Die Schalenbauten von Ulrich Müther* (Schwerin, 2016), 166.
2 See ibid., 174.
3 See Matthias Ludwig and Susanne Brorson, *Der Musikpavillon in Sassnitz auf Rügen: Ein Schalenbau Ulrich Müthers in Zusammenarbeit mit Dietmar Kuntzsch und Otto Patzelt*, Publikationen des Müther-Archivs 2 (Wismar, 2015), 9.
4 See Seeböck, *Schwünge in Beton*, 166 (see note 1).
5 See Otto Patzelt, *Wachsen und Bauen: Konstruktionen in Natur und Technik* (Berlin [East], 1972).
6 See Seeböck, *Schwünge in Beton*, 139 (see note 1).
7 See ibid., 121.
8 See Joachim Palutzki, *Architektur in der DDR* (Berlin, 2000), 309.
9 See Ludwig and Brorson, *Der Musikpavillon in Sassnitz auf Rügen*, 41 (see note 3).
10 Ibid., 26–27.
11 Ibid., 16–19.
12 See Seeböck, *Schwünge in Beton*, 174 (see note 1).
13 See Ludwig and Brorson, *Der Musikpavillon in Sassnitz auf Rügen*, 26–27 (see note 3).
14 Ibid.
15 See Seeböck, *Schwünge in Beton*, 151 (see note 1).
16 See Ludwig and Brorson, *Der Musikpavillon in Sassnitz auf Rügen*, 40 (see note 3).
17 See ibid., 16–19.
18 See ibid., 36.

8 Dietmar Kuntzsch, Otto Patzelt, and Ulrich Müther, music pavilion, Sassnitz, 1988: view after the restoration, 2019

Ulrich Müther: Quantity or Quality?

GEORG GIEBELER

The first catalogue raisonné of Ulrich Müther's works not compiled by himself is by Wilfried Dechau and dates from 2000. His book, unfortunately out of print now, lists 79 shell constructions by Müther.[1] Since then, there have been, and continue to be, repeated attempts to compile a complete catalogue of his works, sometimes seriously, sometimes less seriously researched. This goes so far that some work catalogues attribute almost 200 buildings and projects to Müther. And even these wide-ranging attributions do not claim to be complete.

All list creators have been driven by the question: which buildings are by Müther and which are not? How many are there actually? And which attributions are wrong? Because again and again there have been attributions, by letter, e-mail, or telephone, along the lines of, "I think this roof is by Ulrich Müther." These came to me when I was the head of the Müther Archive.

The archive comprises the professional estate of Ulrich Müther. Gunnar Ceccotti arranged for the estate to be taken over by the Hochschule Wismar – University of Applied Sciences, Technology, Business and Design, in 2006. Through the voluntary, self-initiated efforts of a handful of architecture students, the estate was saved from destruction and moved from a damp attic in Prora on the island of Rügen to Wismar. The volume amounted to approximately 50 cubic meters of packing cases. Since the estate in Prora was completely abandoned and unsorted and the move had to be completed quickly, the archive material was not sorted there, but only packed and transported. These boxes were all opened in Wismar under my organization and searched for material on buildings. Any folders that were found were then stored and sorted on file shelves. No distinction was made between shell structures and other buildings. The examined, half-empty boxes remained in the archive rooms and were only reviewed again under the direction of Matthias Ludwig.

After my move to the Hochschule RheinMain – University of Applied Sciences in 2012, Matthias Ludwig took over the archive. I had handed it over to him with a still fragmentary catalogue raisonné that included uncertain assignments and without any claim to completeness. The reason for this was the lack of clarity of the work. Ulrich Müther designed, planned, calculated, and realized not only double-curved concrete shells but also domes and geometrically completely free concrete works. In addition, there are folding structures, monuments, sports facilities, and other things, because PGH Bau Binz, later VEB Spezialbetonbau Binz/VEB Spezialbetonbau Rügen, which was managed by Müther like a sole proprietorship, was regarded as a specialist in difficult shotcrete work that was known beyond the borders of the GDR. The company was, therefore, regularly commissioned as a subcontractor to work on multicurved concrete structures.

In addition to such commissioned work, Müther also initiated the realization of special structures on his own initiative. An example of this is one of his first works: a small, height-symmetrical hyperbolic paraboloid (HP) shell on a square ground plan. Conceived and planned as an experimental shell, he tried to realize it on the island of Rügen in 1963 as a lounge (Gesellschaftsraum) and in 1965 as an ice cream parlor (Eispavillon) without success, until he was allowed to build it in 1966, on a 7 × 7-meter floor plan, as a bus shelter in Binz.

Finally, a special feature of the GDR, the Wiederverwendungsprojekt (reuse project) leads to further confusion. Many of Müther's buildings were realized several times in identical form. An example of this is the Ostseeperle restaurant in Glowe on Rügen island, which, also as tourist restaurants, also stands in Dierhagen and Eberswalde with a completely identical roof shape.

With the bad conscience of having left Matthias Ludwig with a half-sorted chaos and having the chance to work on a concentrated scientific project during a research sabbatical of one semester, I started working on a commented and systematized catalogue raisonné in spring of 2016. My work was based exclusively on primary sources. I deliberately ignored lists that had been compiled up to that point, as they were partly based on earlier publications or other secondary sources and, thus, partly incorrect or misleading.

Therefore, the catalogue raisonné I have compiled is based on the documents of the Müther Archive. For this purpose, I examined completely about 20 linear meters of file material, as well as nearly 600 original plans, page by page. The data brought together in the catalogue raisonné is based on this research. They are supplemented for a few projects by correspondence with local building authorities and building archives in order to resolve ambiguities, especially regarding the realization. Even after this research, uncertainties remain regarding Ulrich Müther's participation in some of the works regularly mentioned in publications. The allocations in such cases were made according to the files. I have not included projects without any documents in the Müther Archive in my catalogue raisonné, but I have listed them as excluded projects in the appendix of the publication.[2]

The complexity of the estate in the Müther Archive, described above, combined with the uncertainty about whether all files and plans could be saved, results in some uncertainty in my catalogue raisonné. Nevertheless, it can be assumed that all relevant buildings and projects are recorded there. Ulrich Müther realized many projects as a structural engineer and/or building contractor during the GDR, and especially after 1990. Among them were many buildings with flat roof and ceiling structures. Apart from the abovementioned, undocumented special buildings, all non-shell constructions were excluded from the catalogue raisonné.

FAMILIES, SIBLINGS, AND TWINS

A major part of my research work consisted in classifying the works of Ulrich Müther. The works, arranged into groups and subgroups, are chronologically sorted within these categories in the catalogue raisonné. Compared to a possible sorting by place or time of origin, this sorting has the advantage that parallels of the works become clear and reuse projects can be easily recognized.

Buildings consisting of several shells were sorted according to the principal shell type that formed them: the Tripoli planetarium building, for example, is sorted in the buildings with HP shells on a trapezoidal ground plan, although it also contains a planetarium dome. I have not made a distinction between single shells and buildings composed of identical shells, since it is irrelevant for the scientific consideration of the relationships.

The sorting was done in the following groups:

- A. Roof-bearing structures: load-bearing reinforced concrete structures as the upper surface of a building
- A.1 HP shells: thin-membrane reinforced concrete structures of the geometry hyperbolic paraboloid
- A.1.1 HP shells on square ground plan: the top view of the shell is square
- A.1.1.1 HHHT: the shell is single mirror-symmetrical; it has three equal high points and one low point
- A.1.1.2 HHTT: the shell is double mirror-symmetrical; it has two identical high points and two identical low points
- A.1.1.3 HMTT: the shell is simply mirror-symmetrical; it has different high points and two identical low points
- A.1.2 HP trapezoidal shells: HMTT shells, but on a trapezoidal ground floor plan
- A.1.3 HP shells on a ground floor plan of two straight lines and an arc
- A.1.4 Composite HP shells on a central support (umbrella shells): shell composed of four HP shells (simultaneously concreted), each with three identical high points and one low point (HHHT) on a central support; all realized projects have a square top view composed of four squares
- A.2 Other multicurved roof structures
- A.2.1 Hump and hanging shells
- A.2.2 Free-forms and solids of revolution
- A.3 Load-bearing domes
- A.4 Folded structures

- B. Miscellaneous—sprayed concrete work
- B.1 Sports facilities
- B.2 Monuments

- C. Miscellaneous—projection domes
- C.1 Planetariums: non-load-bearing domes

- X. Excluded projects

RESEARCH RELEVANCE

The research relevance indicated in the book for each project is another key point of my work, because the catalogue raisonné is intended to be a stimulus and selection aid for future research. Although the research relevance assigned to the works is based on objective criteria according to the records, the results are not completely certain, due to the limitations of the source material mentioned above. Nevertheless, it can serve as an initial selection aid for future research projects, especially with the addition of the amount of archived material.

Research relevance is not the same as relevance of a building. Even a barely documented reuse project—that is, a project with little research relevance—can be of great importance for urban planning identification. A low research relevance is therefore by no means a reason for an insensitive handling of this heritage.

QUANTITY OR QUALITY

One hundred and fourteen works by Ulrich Müther have been safely assigned, sorted, and their research relevance assessed from the primary sources of the archive. However, this does not say anything about their relevance to the assessment of Müther's work. Is it only the sheer mass of his buildings and projects listed between 1963 and 1993, or was Müther a pioneer of building with concrete, underestimated for a long time? I think the latter.

I come to this conclusion precisely because I consider the majority of the works listed to be of little significance in terms of a cultural or technological assessment. If you subtract the large number of reuse projects, the shotcrete work carried out only as a contractor, the Félix Candela copies, the less complex planetariums and folding structures, and even the majority of the umbrella shells produced in bulk, I still have 20 buildings that justify Ulrich Müther's unique position in the ranks of concrete shell inventors. Hardly anyone (or even no one?) has realized such a wide range of different forms of multicurved shells supporting concrete structures: HP shells, hanging shells, hump shells, free-form surfaces. And in each of these categories there are examples of works that have been completely and independently worked from A to Z, that is, from conception to completion.

What remains of Ulrich Müther is not the multitude of buildings and projects, and it does not matter whether these are actually 114 or 200 or even more. A score of Müther's works remain for me after viewing his estate, but they are remarkable without reservation:

HHTT SHELLS

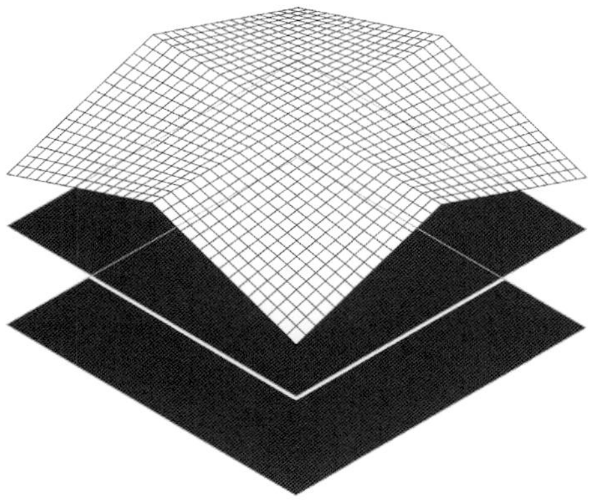

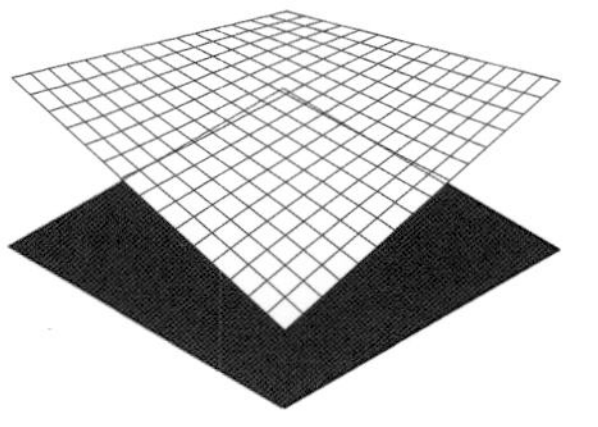

1963-1_Stahlwerker-Binz_ABR[3]

The Haus der Stahlwerker (Steelworkers' Home) was Ulrich Müther's diploma thesis. There were three variants: two with barrel roofs and one with the realized HP shells. The idea for the HP shells is supposed to have come from Ingo Schönrock.[4]

Participating planners: Possibly architect Rogge, Rügen district | ***Services:*** Statics and planning, other services not documented | Demolished in 2002 (date without source) | ***Research relevance:*** High

- \+ First building of this kind to be realized; in a similar form, this shell exists only in Borchtitz on Rügen island (project ID: 1965-1)
- ++ Ulrich Müther's diploma thesis
- ++ First, well-documented statics, partly based on model investigations
- – No correspondence in the Müther Archive

1966-1_Buswartehaus-Binz_EXIST

The bus shelter at the entrance to the municipality of Binz is the first HP shell by Ulrich Müther of this design. It also served Müther as a test shell for deflection measurements on the finished structure.

Participating planners: Inspecting structural engineer Günther Ackermann | ***Services:*** Planning, other services not documented | ***Research relevance:*** Average

- ++ First shell of this design
- \+ Statics and test statics available
- – No correspondence in the Müther Archive

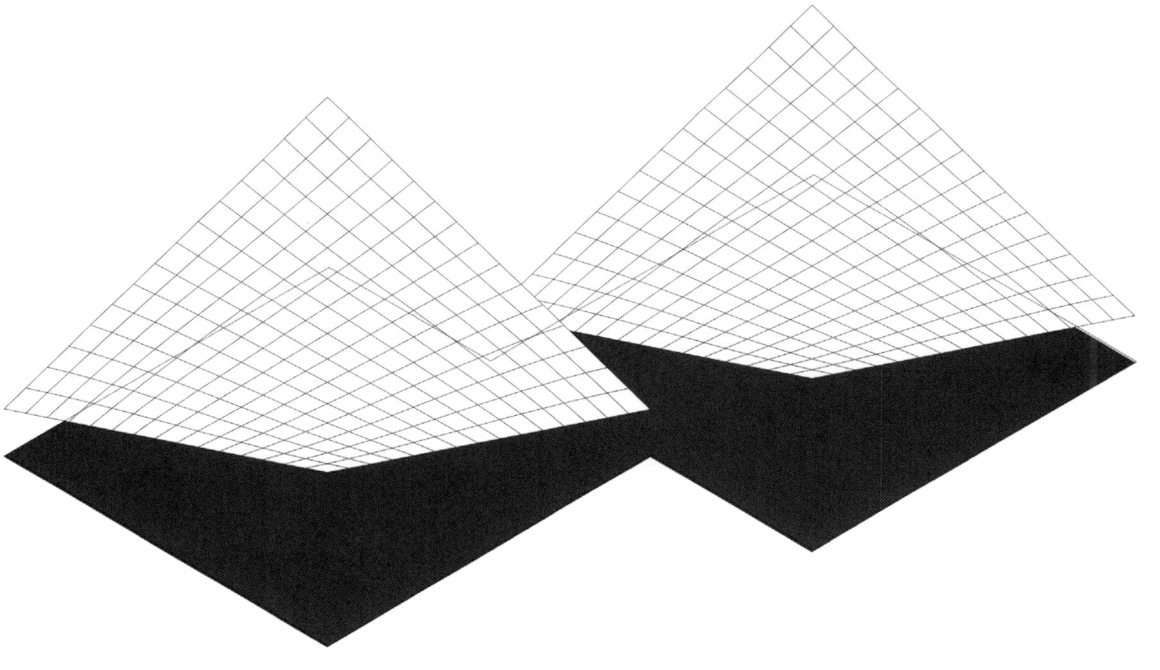

1966-2_Messehalle-Rostock_EXIST

The exhibition hall for the building and oil industries on the Rostock-Schutow fairgrounds has been used as a car dealership for quite some time.

Participating planners: Architect Erich Kaufmann, Rostock; structural engineer Günther Ackermann | ***Services:*** Statics and planning, construction | ***Research relevance:*** Very high

- \+ First shell with a large span
- \+ Unique, because the planned reuse project in Suhl (project ID: 1968-5) was not realized
- \+ Complete performance by Ulrich Müther
- \+ Regularly used by Ulrich Müther himself as an office reference
- ++ Very well documented

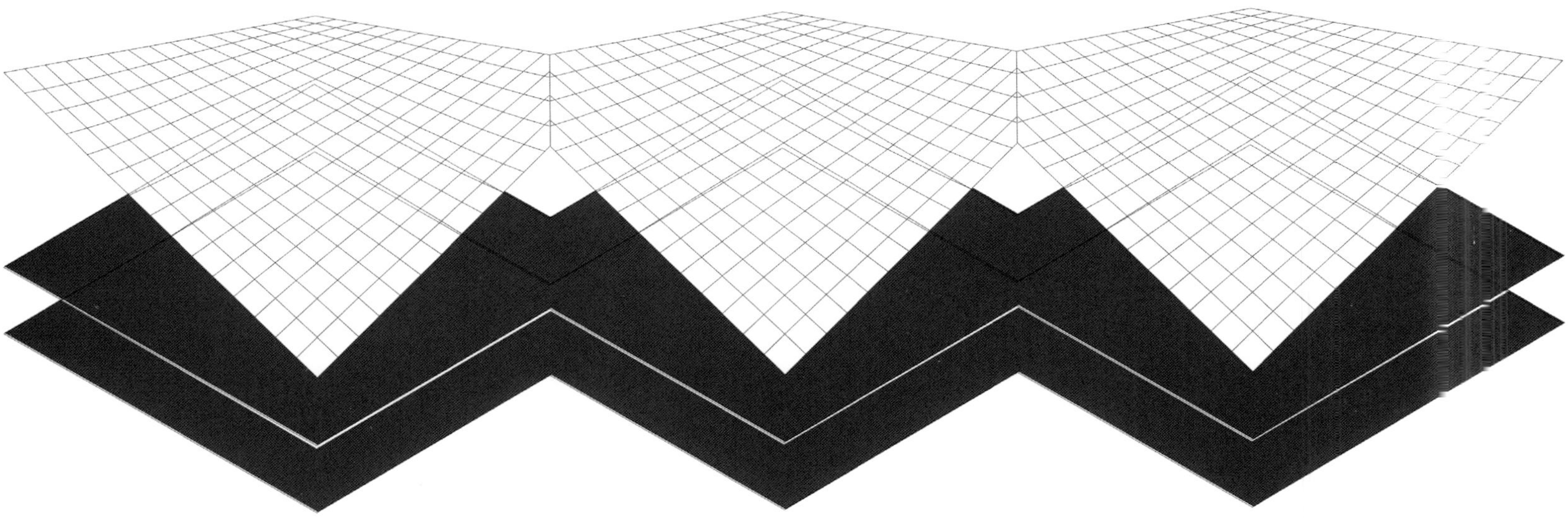

1968-2_Kosmos-Rostock_EXIST

The unmodified geometry of the triple shell roof structure for the Kosmos restaurant is identical to the Rostock exhibition hall (project ID: 1966-2) and other projects, but truncated in the overlap.

Participating planners: Unknown | *Services:* Planning, other services not documented | *Research relevance:* Low

+++ Unique specimen of a linearly connected shell construction

– Very little archive material

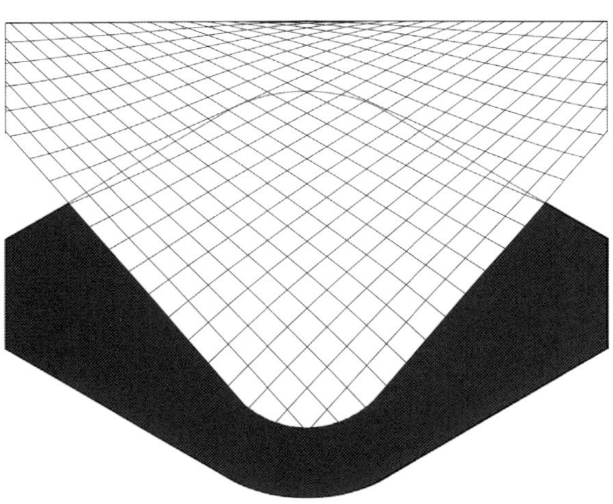

1970-2_Kirche-Rostock_EXIST[5]

The church in Rostock is the last realized building of the HHTT series.

Participating planners: Inspecting structural engineer A. Hampe | *Services:* Planning and construction | *Research relevance:* High

++ Unique specimen of one of HHTT shells with truncated high points

+ Extensive archive material

+ First church building by Ulrich Müther

HMTT SHELLS

1967-2_Halle-Rostock_EXIST[6]

The multipurpose hall in Rostock-Lütten Klein was Müther's first tilted HP shell; it has the largest span of this series with 22 meters and is also the first project realized with light bands running between the shells.

Participating planners: VEB Hochbauprojektierung Rostock | ***Services:*** Planning, other services unknown | ***Research relevance:*** Very high

+ First HMTT shell
++ Unique specimen
++ Very extensive archive material

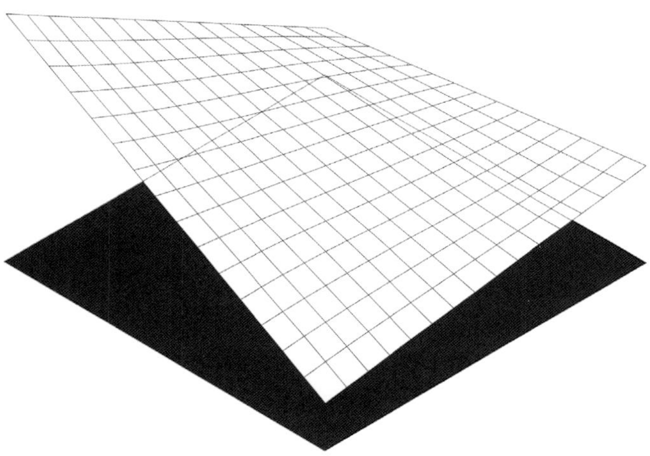

1967-3_Ostseeperle-Glowe_EXIST

The Ostseeperle restaurant in Glowe on Rügen island is the second realized HMTT shell. Compared to the multipurpose hall in Rostock (project ID: 1967-2), however, the difference between high and medium high point is much larger (8 meters, instead of 2.5 meters). This led on the one hand—due to the greater inclination—to a significantly more difficult construction and on the other hand to a more dramatic effect.

Participating planners: Inspecting structural engineer Günther Ackermann | ***Services:*** Planning and construction | ***Research relevance:*** High

+ First shell of a reuse projects series
+ First strongly inclined HMTT shell
+ Extensive collection of plans
+ Also construction
– Little correspondence

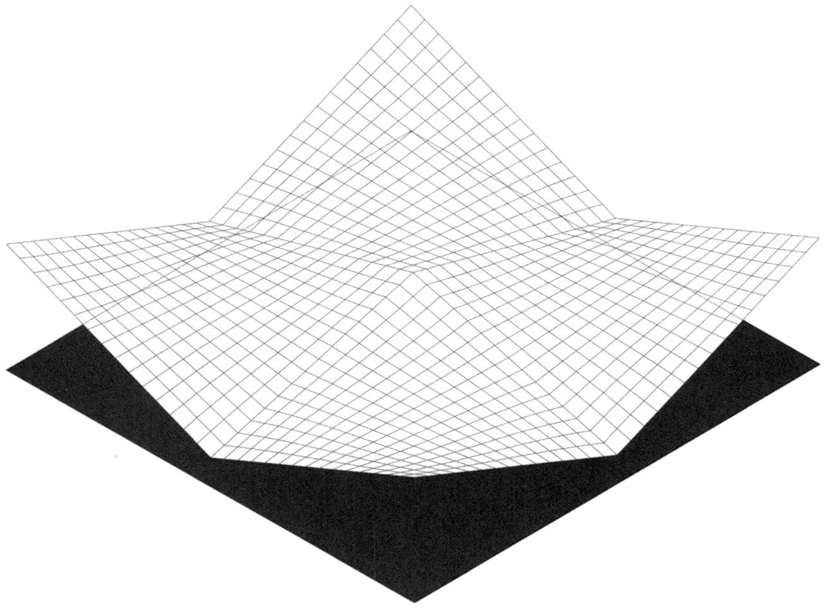

1970-6_Ruderzentrum-Dresden_EXIST

The rowing center in Dresden consists of very flat HMTT shells. The height difference between the high and middle point is 2.4 meters (in comparison: Ostseeperle restaurant in Glowe is 8 meters).

Participating planners: Unknown | ***Services:*** Planning and shotcrete works | ***Research relevance:*** High

++ Unique specimen

++ Extensive archive material, especially extensive correspondence

1968-1_Messehalle-Magdeburg_EXIST

The exhibition hall in Magdeburg is geometrically similar to the multipurpose hall in Rostock (project ID: 1967-2): similar spans, similar height geometry. However, the spatial impression in the unspoiled Magdeburg hall is much more spectacular.

Participating planners: Inspecting structural engineer Günther Ackermann | ***Services:*** Planning and shotcrete works | ***Research relevance:*** High

+ First HMTT shell on trapezoidal ground plan

++ Unique specimen

++ Spatial impression

– Little archive material

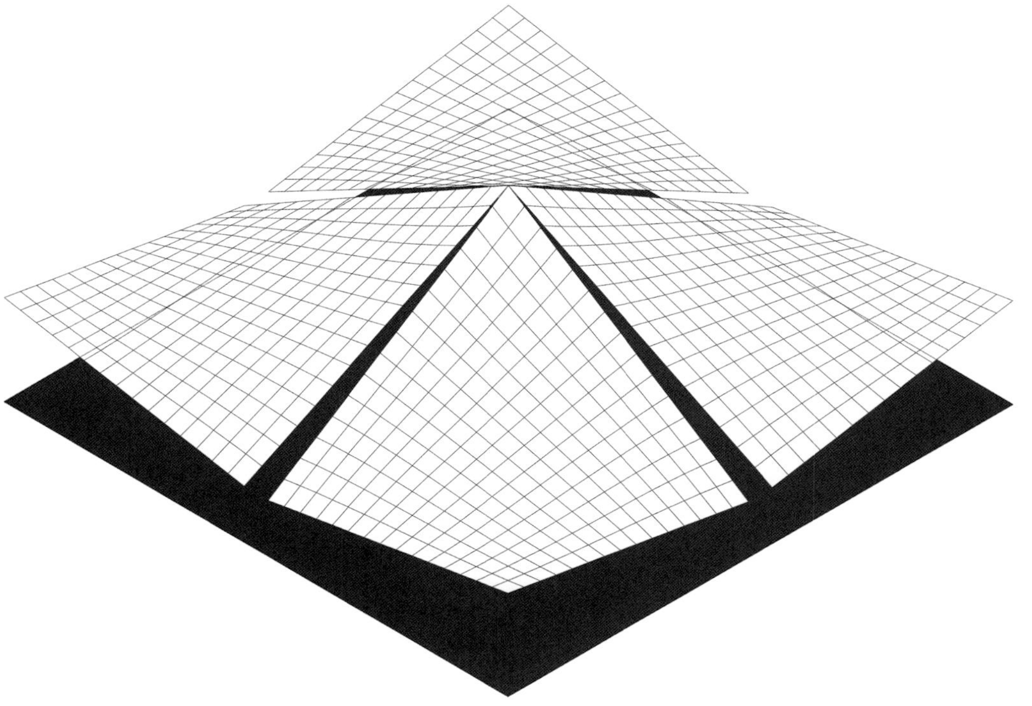

1968-7_Mehrzweckhalle-Neubrandenburg_EXIST

Although the overall dimensions of the multipurpose hall in Neubrandenburg are almost the same as those in Magdeburg (project ID: 1968-1), it follows a different geometry. The spatial impression is also unspoiled. The period between the building decision and the inauguration is only ten months.

Participating planners: Inspecting structural engineer Günther Ackermann | ***Services:*** Planning, other services not documented | ***Research relevance:*** High

+   Unique: high point in the center of the hall
++ Spatial impression
+   Extensive archive material

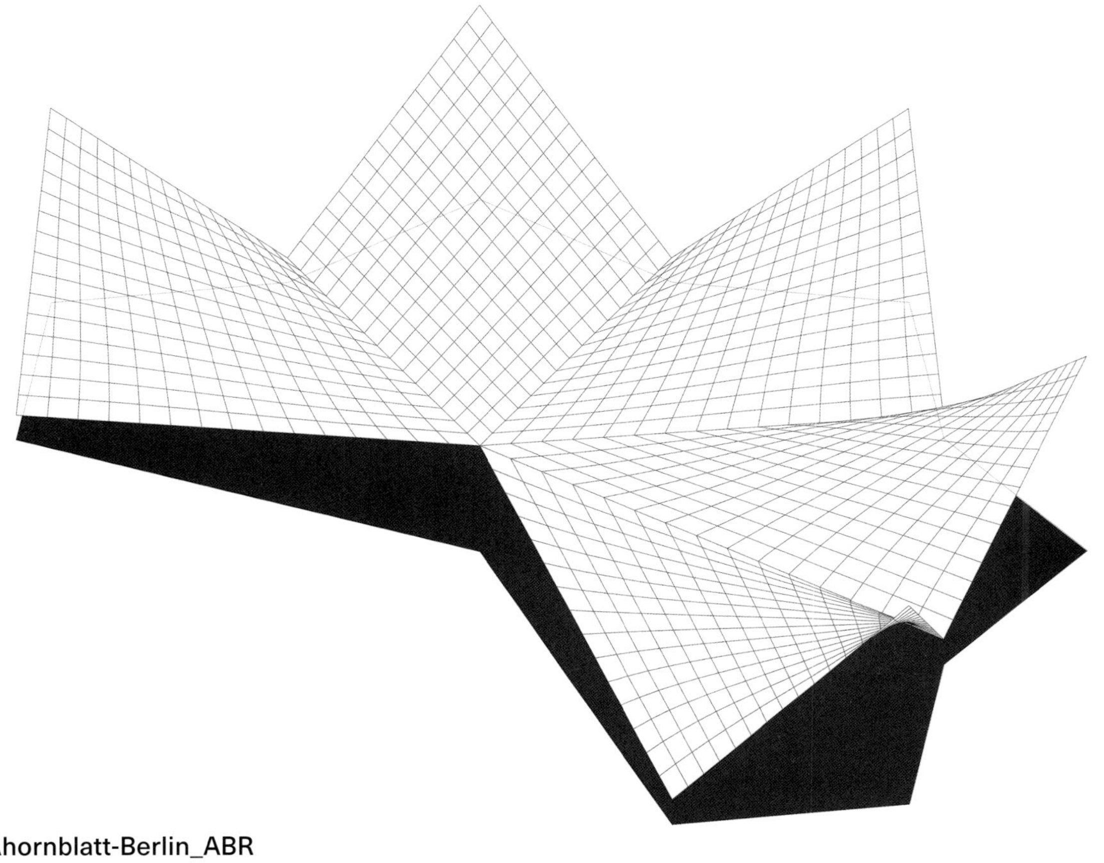

1969-8_Ahornblatt-Berlin_ABR

The Ahornblatt restaurant on the Fischerinsel in Berlin is one of Ulrich Müther's major works. After the Teepott restaurant (project ID: 1968-6), it is the second roof-bearing structure made of radially arranged HP shells, but here on a trapezoidal floor plan.

Participating planners: Inspecting structural engineer Günther Ackermann; architect Erich Kaufmann, Rostock | ***Services:*** Planning and construction | ***Demolition date:*** 2000 | ***Research relevance:*** Very high

+++ Main work
++   Very extensive archive material

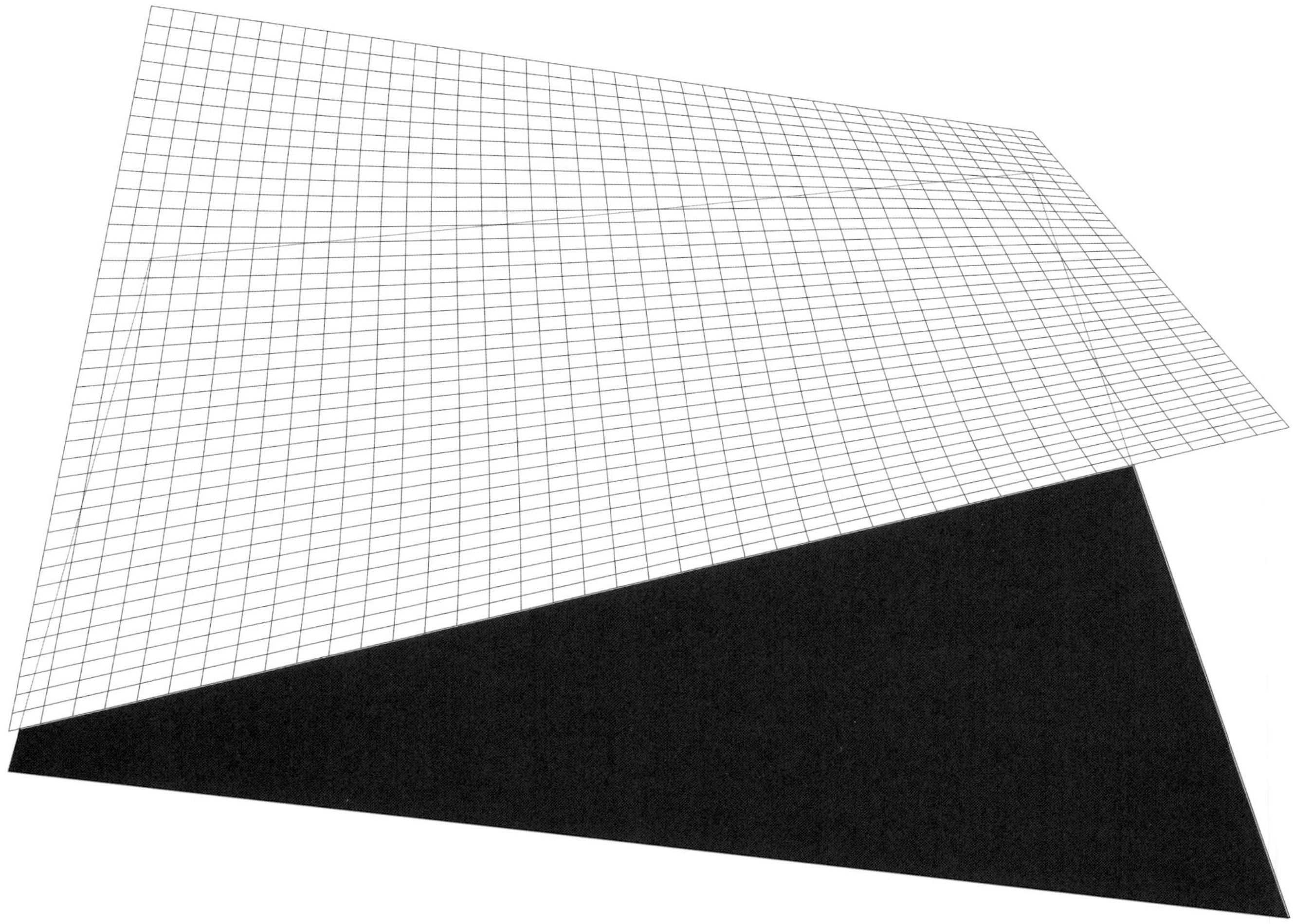

1970-7_Kongresshalle-Rostock-NR

The planned congress hall in Rostock would have been the largest building ever realized by Ulrich Müther. With a span of 100 meters between the low points and high points of 21 and 41 meters, it does not significantly exceed other projects composed of several shells in terms of floor space, but it does have a span five times the size of other buildings. This results in extensive static investigations, also on the model. As a result, the project was discarded, probably technically unfeasible or too expensive, and a conventional roof structure was realized. The hall is the chronologically penultimate HP shell by Müther before the special shell in Stralsund (project ID: 1975-2).

Participating planners: VEB Industriebaukombinat, Rostock; Büro für Stadtplanung, Rostock, Hochbauprojektierung Rostock | *Services:* Preliminary planning | *Research relevance:* Very high

+++ Unique specimen

++ Extensive archive material, especially on statics investigations

HP SHELLS, UMBRELLA-SHAPED

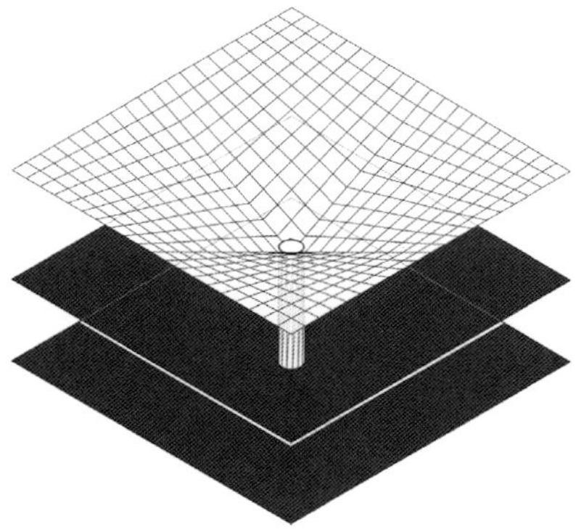

1965-3_Inselparadies-Baabe_EXIST[7]

The Inselparadies restaurant in Baabe on Rügen island is not only the first umbrella shell, but also one of the first shell constructions ever realized by Müther. Until then, there was only the not-very-conspicuous roofing of the Steelworkers' Home in Binz (project ID: 1963-1) and at the same time the construction of the rather hidden dining hall in Borchtitz (project ID: 1965-1). The ice cream parlor at the Inselparadies, on the other hand, was known to every holidaymaker on Rügen in the GDR. ***Participating planners:*** Inspecting structural engineer Günther Ackermann | ***Services:*** Planning and construction | ***Research relevance:*** Very high

+++ Main work
\+ First and largest umbrella shell
\+ Very early work
\+ Extensive archive material
\+ Historical photographs, also of the construction works, preserved

HP SHELLS, TWO STRAIGHT LINES AND AN ARC

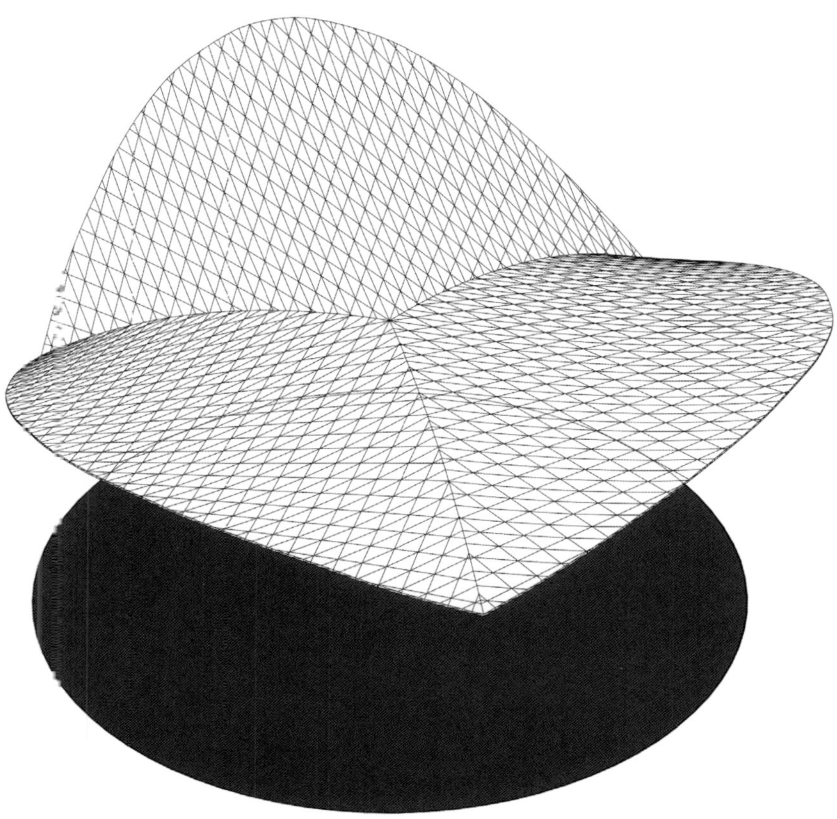

1968-6_Teepott-Warnemünde_EXIST[8]

The geometry of the Teepott restaurant in Rostock-Warnemünde is a "punching out" of a 120-degree segment, bounded by two straight edges and a curved edge from an HHTT shell. This cutout was then copied and rotated twice about the intersection of the straight edges. ***Participating planners:*** Architects Erich Kaufmann, Carl-Heinz Pastor, and Hans Fleischhauer; inspecting structural engineer Günther Ackermann[9] | ***Services:*** Planning and construction[10] | ***Research relevance:*** Very high

+++ Unique specimen
\+ Very extensive archive material

HUMP AND HANGING SHELLS

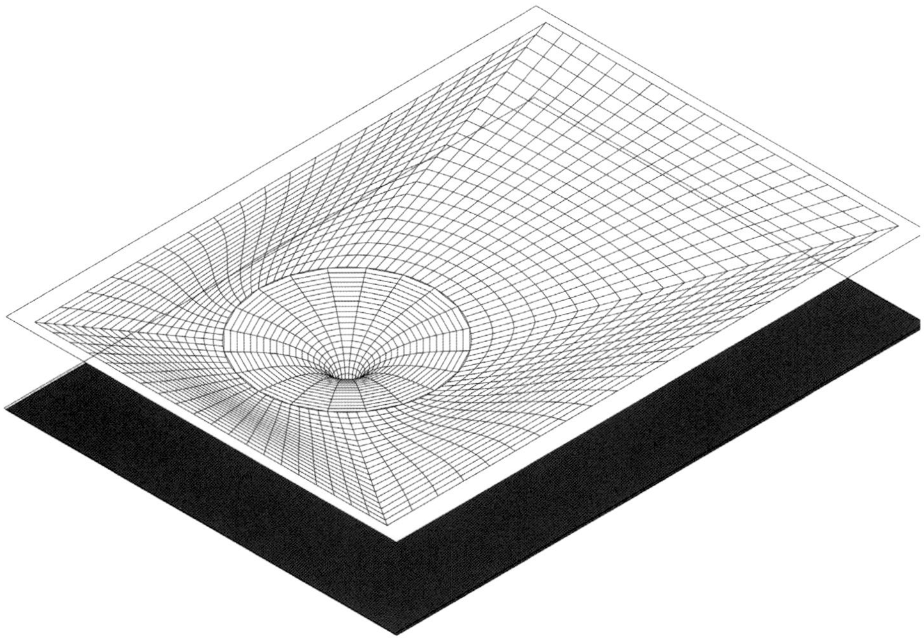

1976-1_Schwimmbad-Sellin_EXIST

The roof structure above the swimming pool in Sellin on Rügen island is the only hanging shell made by Ulrich Müther.

Participating planners: Model statics probably IS Rostock | *Services:* Probably work planning, in any case execution | *Research relevance:* Low

+++ Unique specimen
– Statics probably not by Ulrich Müther
+ Extensive archive material[11]

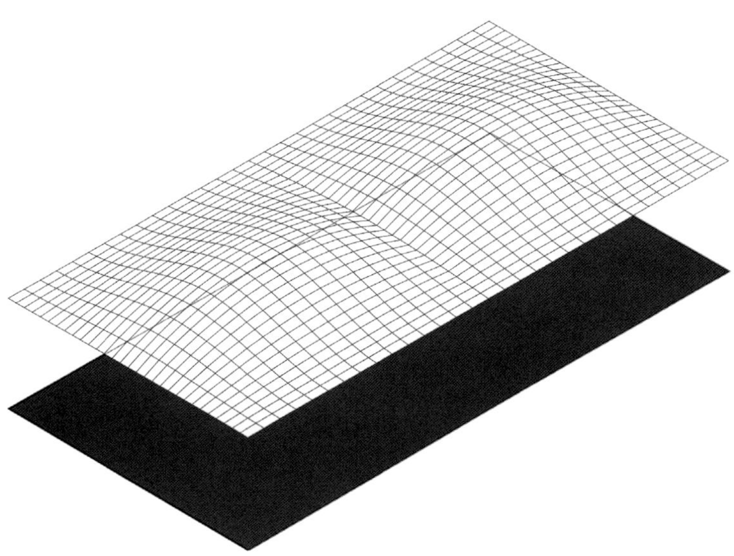

1984-2_Sporthalle-Gingst_EXIST

The gymnasium in Gingst on Rügen island has a stronger super elevation than the hump shell in Sassnitz (project ID: 1977-4).

Participating planners: Unclear | *Services:* Planning and construction | *Research relevance:* High

+ Unique specimen
++ Ulrich Müther was the general contractor for this building (turnkey)—probably the only time
+ Extensive archive material, but no statics

FREE FORMS AND SOLIDS OF REVOLUTION

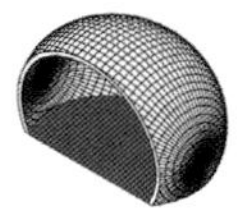

1973-2_Buswartehaus-Buschvitz_EXIST
Like the kiosk in Baabe (project ID: 1971-2), the rotation shell in Buschvitz on Rügen island was also shotcreted directly onto a wire mesh without any formwork. This bus shelter is the smallest shell by Ulrich Müther.
Participating planners: Unknown | ***Services:*** Planning and construction | ***Research relevance:*** Average
+++ Unique specimen
– Hardly any archive material

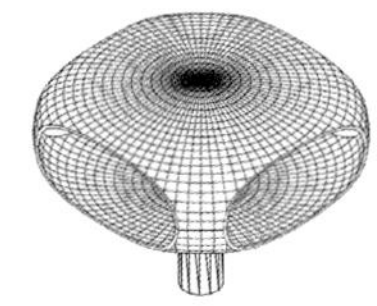

1975-5_Rettungsturm-1-Binz_ABR
The first of the two rescue towers in Binz differs from the still existing one (project ID: 1981-1) by the concrete platform attached to the central column.
Participating planner: Architect Dietrich Otto | ***Services:*** Planning and construction | ***Research relevance:*** Low
++ Unique specimen
– Little archive material

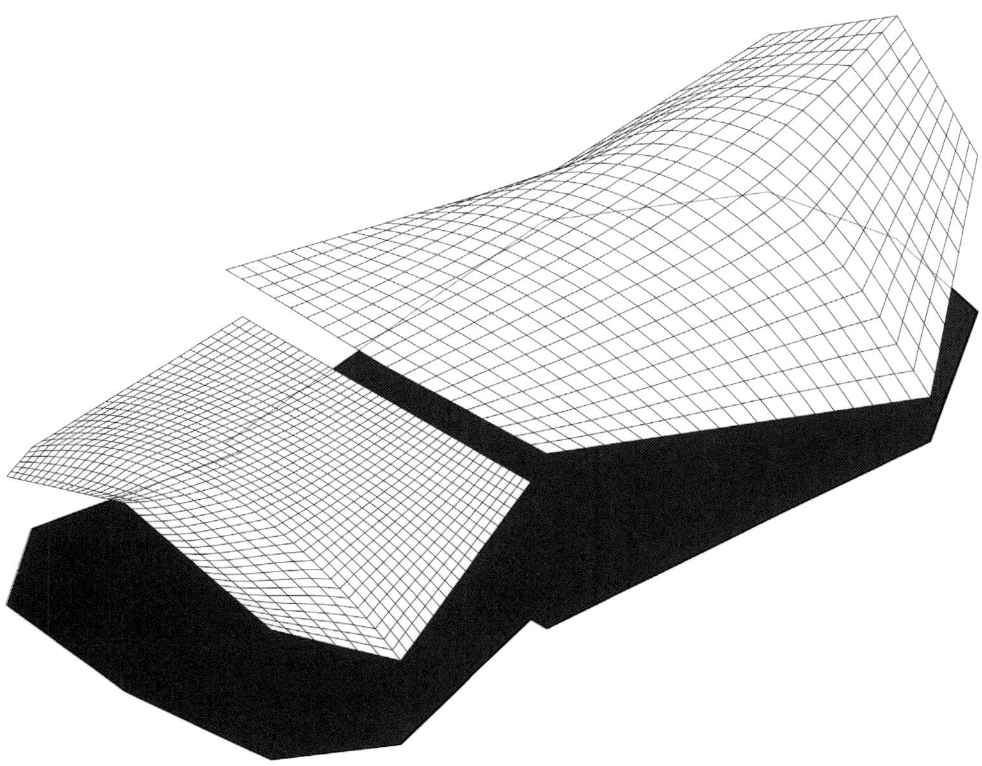

1978-4_Kirche-Neubrandenburg_EXIST
The shells above the church in Neubrandenburg develop along fourth-order ridge curves and straight eaves edges.

Participating planners: Inspecting structural engineering: council of the district of Rostock, district building authority; Henning Wolgast, Ingenieurhochschule für Bauwesen Neustrelitz | ***Services:*** Planning and shotcrete works | ***Research relevance:*** Very high
+++ Unique specimen
++ Very extensive archive material

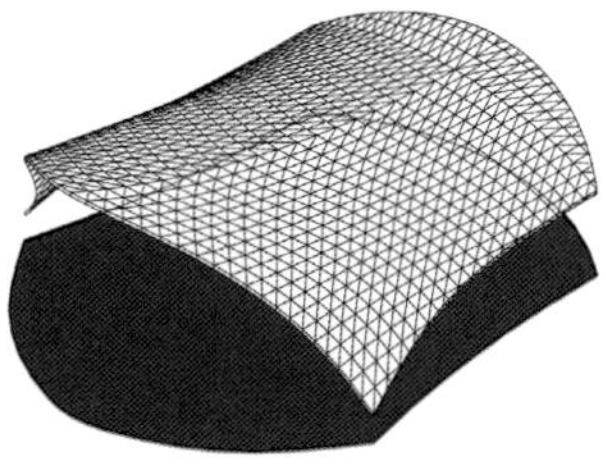

1980-1_Orchesterpavillon-Ralswiek_ABR

The music pavilion in Ralswiek on Rügen island was a double-curved wooden lattice shell made of two layers of 36/56 millimeters, connected with M8 bolts at the nodes. Roof surface made of 6-millimeter plywood with two layers of glass fiber fabric. The shell was demolished in 2012.[12]

Participating planners: Unknown | ***Services:*** Planning and construction | ***Research relevance:*** High

+++ Unique specimen

\+ Only wooden construction realized

– No correspondence

1 Wilfried Dechau, ed., *Kühne Solitäre: Ulrich Müther, Schalenbaumeister der DDR* (Stuttgart, 2000).

2 Georg Giebeler, *Müther-Archiv: Systematische und kommentierte Bestandsaufnahme des Nachlasses von Ulrich Müther* (Cologne, 2016, self-published).

3 The nomenclature begins with the year of construction and a consecutive numbering, followed by name and place, as well as ABR for demolished buildings, NR for unrealized buildings and EXIST for buildings still in existence today.

4 See Klaus Stiglat, *Bauingenieure und ihr Werk* (Berlin, 2004), 258.

5 The very extensive archive documents were only viewed on a random basis. The information provided may therefore be incomplete.

6 See note 5.

7 See note 5.

8 See note 5.

9 See Tanja Seeböck, *Schwünge in Beton: Die Schalenbauten von Ulrich Müther* (Schwerin, 2016); and Matthias Ludwig, Johannes Liess, Asko Fromm, Andreas Schätzke, and Antje Diebermann, *Der Teepott in Rostock-Warnemünde*, ed. Bundesingenieurkammer (Berlin, 2018).

10 See ibid.

11 In the meantime, extensive material has been found. Information from the Müther Archive, February 2020.

12 See Seeböck, *Schwünge in Beton*, 367 (see note 9).

Zusammenfassungen

Juan Gerardo Oliva Salinas

Drei Kulturen und Arten des Betonschalenbaus

Der Aufsatz beschreibt und vergleicht die unterschiedlichen Herangehensweisen an das Entwerfen und Bauen von Stahlbetonschalen bei Félix Candela, Heinz Isler und Ulrich Müther. Diese drei Konstrukteure zeichneten sich durch ihre meisterhafte Beherrschung von Geometrie und Technik aus. Sie gaben dem Entwurf und der Konstruktion von Schalen durch ihren Einfallsreichtum und ihre Beharrlichkeit starke Impulse, indem sie Betondächer schufen, die aufgrund ihrer Form in der Lage sind, nicht nur ihr eigenes Gewicht zu tragen, sondern auch allen anderen Einwirkungen von Lasten zu widerstehen, die durch Wind, Schnee, Hagel oder auch Erdbeben erzeugt werden. In der zweiten Hälfte des 20. Jahrhunderts realisierten sie eine große Anzahl von Stahlbetonschalen, hauptsächlich in Mexiko, der Schweiz und der DDR.

Von Candelas Geburt im Jahr 1910 bis zu Islers Tod im Jahr 2009 erstreckt sich ein Jahrhundert voller bedeutender technologischer Entwicklungen in Architektur und Ingenieurwesen. In diesem Kontext unternahmen alle drei Anstrengungen, um zu dem zu gelangen, was wir heute als „nachhaltig" bezeichnen: minimaler Aufwand an Material, um natürliche Ressourcen bestmöglich zu nutzen und zu schonen und die höchstmögliche statische Effizienz zu erreichen sowie Planungsaufwand, Kosten und Ausführungszeiten zu reduzieren.

Diskutiert werden die verschiedenen Arten, mit denen Candela, Isler und Müther – die zuweilen auch als „Baukünstler" (*structural artists*) bezeichnet werden – die Form ihrer Schalen bestimmten, geometrische Berechnungen durchführten und Lösungen fanden, um die Stabilität ihrer Konstruktionen zu garantieren, wie auch die verschiedenen von ihnen angewandten Konstruktionsverfahren. Der Einfluss, den Candela auf das Werk von Isler und Müther ausübte, wird ebenso behandelt wie die Frage, auf welche Weise diese drei Schalenbauer jeweils maßgeblichen Anteil an der Entwicklung des Betonschalenbaus im 20. Jahrhundert hatten.

Matthias Ludwig

Beziehungen zwischen Félix Candela, Heinz Isler und Ulrich Müther

Es gibt nur wenige Architekten und Ingenieure, die ihr Berufsleben fast ausschließlich dem Betonschalenbau gewidmet haben. Félix Candela, Heinz Isler und Ulrich Müther gehören zu diesem Kreis. Diese drei Protagonisten wirkten in sehr unterschiedlichen Kulturen und Regionen der Welt. Auf den ersten Blick möchte man annehmen, dass es keine Bezüge zwischen ihnen gegeben habe. Bei näherer Betrachtung ihres Werks und ihrer Lebensgeschichte ist jedoch festzustellen, dass es – bei allen Unterschieden – bestimmte Aspekte gibt, die das Werk von Candela, Isler und Müther verbinden.

Die drei unterhielten über verschiedene Netzwerke wie zum Beispiel die International Association for Shell Structures (IASS, heute: International Association for Shell and Spatial Structures) kollegiale, aber zum Teil auch freundschaftliche Beziehungen. Félix Candela, der älteste von ihnen, beeinflusste in den 1950er- und 1960er-Jahren eine große Anzahl von Architekten und Ingenieuren, während seine beiden 16 beziehungsweise 24 Jahre jüngeren Kollegen Heinz Isler und Ulrich Müther den Schalenbau in ihrem jeweiligen Umfeld – der Schweiz und der DDR – individuell prägten und voranbrachten. Müther ist dabei lange Zeit in der Öffentlichkeit wenig wahrgenommen worden, da er in Ostdeutschland hinter dem „Eisernen Vorhang“ wirkte.

Was erstens das Material betrifft, so verwendeten Candela, Isler und Müther in der Regel Stahlbeton, wobei es Ausnahmen gibt: Isler arbeitete auch mit glasfaserverstärktem Kunststoff (GFK) und errichtete temporäre „Bauten“ aus Eis; bei Müther gibt es mit dem Orchesterpavillon in Ralswiek auf Rügen (1980) eine einzelne Holzkonstruktion. Zweitens arbeiteten alle drei bei der Herstellung ihrer Betonschalen hauptsächlich mit Schalungen aus Holz. Anders als Candela verwendeten sowohl Isler als auch Müther Schalungen mit Pneus oder Erdhügel als Negative, ebenso realisierten sie schalungslos hergestellte Betonkonstruktionen. Drittens waren es vor allem geometrisch bestimmte Schalen (hyperbolische Paraboloide, Kugelschalen oder Tonnenschalen), die von Candela und Müther ausgeführt wurden, während Isler neben Buckelschalen für die Industrie eine Vielzahl von Freiformschalen schuf, was in geringem Umfang auch Müther unternahm. Viertens schließlich errichteten alle drei hauptsächlich Industriebauten, öffentliche Bauten und Plastiken – sämtlich Strukturen, die entweder viel freie Fläche benötigten oder Zeichen in ihrem Kontext setzen sollten.

Falls man zudem noch quantitative und geografische Aspekte ansetzen möchte: Müther realisierte mit 75 Schalenbauten – wobei hier Denkmäler, Faltwerke, Seilnetzkonstruktionen und weitere Projekte eingerechnet sind, bei denen er als Unternehmer lediglich die Betonarbeiten ausführte – die wenigsten Bauten, die regional allerdings eine bemerkenswerte Bandbreite aufweisen und in Europa, Nordafrika, Kuba und Kuwait entstanden. Candela schuf 900 Schalen, die er zumeist in Lateinamerika realisieren konnte. Isler erstellte mithilfe seiner standardisierten Konstruktionsweise („System Isler“) fast 1400 Schalenbauten, in der Schweiz, Deutschland, Frankreich, Österreich, Großbritannien und Saudi-Arabien.

Matthias Beckh

Räume für die Industrie
Ein Vergleich der modularen Schalensysteme von Félix Candela und Heinz Isler

Der Aufsatz analysiert und diskutiert die Industriebausysteme von Félix Candela und Heinz Isler. Nahezu gleichzeitig entwickelten beide in den frühen 1950er-Jahren modulare Schalentragwerke, die durch ihre sehr wirtschaftliche Herstellungsweise überaus erfolgreich wurden und jeweils den Großteil ihres gebauten Œuvres ausmachen. Beide konnten mit ihren Systemen im Zeitraum von 1955 bis 1970 mehrere hunderttausend Quadratmeter Hallenfläche überspannen. Im Fall von Candela sind dies aus vier hyperbolischen Paraboloiden (Hypars) zusammengesetzte Schirmstrukturen, die zu einer zentralen Stütze zusammenlaufen. Die einzelnen Module weisen einen rechteckigen oder quadratischen Grundriss auf und werden über ein Drainagerohr im Inneren der Stütze entwässert. Aufgrund von Durchbiegungen an den Rändern dieser dünnen, typischerweise 4 Zentimeter starken und weit auskragenden Dachkonstruktionen musste die Größe der Module auf circa 200 Quadratmeter beschränkt werden. Nach einigen Testbauten wurde 1954 mit dem Rio-Lagergebäude in Mexiko-Stadt das erste große Projekt nach dieser neuen Methode fertiggestellt.

Heinz Isler entwickelte auf der anderen Seite des Globus im Schweizer Mittelland ebenfalls ein neues System für den Industriebau, das erstmals 1955 für die Firma Glas Trösch realisiert wurde: die Buckelschale.

Deren Form wird durch eine unter Innendruck stehende Gummimembran aufgespannt, die in einen rechteckigen Holzrahmen eingelassen ist. Nachdem Isler bei einem Folgeprojekt eine 5 Meter weit gespannte Lichtkuppel aus Polyester am Scheitel der Buckelschale angebracht hatte, erreichte die neue Bauform ihre Serienreife.

Der Beitrag verfolgt die Entwicklung der beiden Bauweisen und erörtert architektonische, statische und funktionale Aspekte anhand realisierter Beispiele. Zu Beginn werden das prinzipielle Tragverhalten verschiedener Schalentragwerke und deren konstruktive Besonderheiten skizziert. Im Vordergrund stehen hier die von den Akteuren verwendeten Formen, die entweder mittels Formfindungsmethoden entwickelt wurden und somit statisch besonders optimiert oder aber wie Kugelausschnitte, Translationsflächen oder das hyperbolische Paraboloid mathematisch definiert sind.

Besonders eindrücklich ist Candelas große Virtuosität im Entwurf seiner Schirmstrukturen, deren Basisgeometrie und Anordnung er immer wieder auf raffinierte Weise variierte und kombinierte, um auf spezifische Anforderungen des Projekts – wie große Spannweiten oder besondere Lichtverhältnisse – zu reagieren. Die Größe der einzelnen Module hingegen blieb aufgrund der systemimmanenten Limitierung weitgehend unverändert. Im Gegensatz dazu ist bei Islers Buckelschalen mit ihrer hohen Materialeffizienz vor allem die enorme Bandbreite unterschiedlicher Modulgrößen bemerkenswert, die von einigen hundert bis zu 3200 Quadratmetern überdachter Fläche reicht.

Juan Ignacio del Cueto Ruiz-Funes

Félix Candelas Hypar-Kreuzgewölbe
Ein mexikanischer Beitrag zur Entwicklung von Betonschalen

Das weltweit erste Beispiel eines Kreuzgewölbes aus hyperbolischen Paraboloiden wurde in Mexiko-Stadt gebaut und entstand aus der fruchtbaren Zusammenarbeit zwischen den Büros von Enrique de la Mora y Palomar und Félix Candela, die Anfang der 1950er-Jahre begann und einige der herausragenden Werke der mexikanischen Architektur der zweiten Hälfte des 20. Jahrhunderts hervorbrachte. Der Aufsatz analysiert die historische Entwicklung der Hypar-Kreuzgewölbe, die ein besonderer Beitrag der mexikanischen Architektur zur Baugeschichte sind.

Im Jahr 1953 wandten sich de la Mora und sein junger Mitarbeiter Fernando López Carmona erstmals an Candelas Firma Cubiertas Ala, mit der dieser seine innovativen Bauten errichtete. Gemeinsam wollten sie die Konstruktion und die Ausführung der Betonschale angehen, die das Handelsparkett der Mexikanischen Wertpapierbörse überwölben sollte. Demselben Team gelang es drei Jahre später, beim Bau der Kirche San Antonio de las Huertas in Mexiko-Stadt die ersten Schalen mit freiem Rand (also ohne Verstärkungen an den Randbögen) zu realisieren. In der Folge nutzte Candela mehrere Varianten dieser Typologie und errichtete in Mexiko emblematische Bauwerke wie den Nachtklub La Jacaranda (Acapulco, 1957, mit Juan Sordo Madaleno), das Restaurant Los Manantiales (Xochimilco, Mexiko-Stadt, 1958, mit Joaquín Álvarez Ordóñez), das Restaurant des Hotels Casino de la Selva (Cuernavaca, 1960) und die Abfüllanlage für Bacardi (Tultitlán, 1960).

Elisa María Teresa Drago Quaglia

Schön gestaltete Formen
Die Schalen von Enrique de la Mora und Félix Candela

Die Sichtung der in den Archiven aufbewahrten Primärquellen ermöglicht es uns, die Lesarten der architektonischen Phänomene und Fakten, die unser historisches Erbe in Mexiko ausmachen, zu ergänzen. Im Mittelpunkt des Aufsatzes steht die Zusammenarbeit eines erfolgreichen Duos: die Kooperation zwischen dem Büro von Enrique de la Mora y Palomar und der Firma Cubiertas Ala unter der Leitung von Félix Candela. Zwar gibt es eine Dokumentation von mehr als 20 Projekten, bei denen diese beiden kooperierten, jedoch konzentriert sich der Aufsatz auf diejenigen, bei denen mit Schalen – Kreuzgewölben und hyperbolischen Paraboloiden – gearbeitet wurde.

Der Beitrag zeichnet die Entwicklung, die Suche nach architektonischen und strukturellen Lösungen sowie die Anpassungen, welche die beiden Architekten vornahmen, chronologisch nach. An 14 ausgewählten Beispielen wird gezeigt, wie die Integration von Wissen, Fertigkeiten und Fähigkeiten in Entwurf und Ausführung zu einigen der bemerkenswertesten Schalenbauten in Mexiko führte.

Die Bauten werden unter dem Gesichtspunkt untersucht, wie dank der Zusammenarbeit eines Architekten und einer spezialisierten Baufirma exemplarische Werke entstehen konnten. Ausgangspunkt ist der Entstehungsprozess der Entwürfe im Büro von de la Mora, den Schlusspunkt setzt deren strukturelle Überarbeitung und die Ausführung durch Cubiertas Ala. Es zeigt sich, dass die gemeinsame Arbeit es ermöglichte, einen positiven Wendepunkt in beiden Karrieren zu setzen – auf der einen Seite bedingt durch die Kreativität von de la Mora und dessen Versuche, in Form, Struktur und Material den Ausdruck der Architektur seiner Zeit zu finden, und auf der anderen Seite durch die Meisterschaft sowie das Wissen um die Handhabung und das strukturelle Verhalten von Beton und die Ausführungsqualität der Arbeiten von Candela.

María González Pendás

Die Ökonomie des Körpers im Betonschalenbau

Die Baustelle spielte eine besonders wichtige Rolle bei der Entwicklung dünner Betonschalen, die die mexikanische Baufirma Cubiertas Ala Mitte des 20. Jahrhunderts unter der Leitung von Félix Candela einführte. Ausgehend von Candelas eigener Beschreibung des Entwurfsprozesses ist oft erläutert worden, wie sein ingenieurwissenschaftliches Know-how in einem progressiven und vor allem empirischen Innovationsprozess Gestalt annahm, ähnlich einer handwerklichen Erkenntnistheorie, die sich stark auf die Baustelle, die Arbeiter und ihr Handwerk stützte. Candela selbst wies auf diesen Aspekt in seiner „humanistischen" Kritik an der Modernisierung hin, die sich in einer unerbittlichen Zelebrierung manueller Techniken äußerte. Am schwärmerischsten wurde dies in den Fotografien von Juan Guzmán und Armando Salas Portugal vermittelt, in denen mexikanische Arbeiter auf den im Bau befindlichen Schalen geradezu heldenhaft in Szene gesetzt sind.

In diesen eindrucksvollen Bildern, in Candelas Worten und in den Geschichten, in denen beides später aufgegriffen wurde, fehlten bislang jedoch Einzelheiten über die Körper, die so sehr im Mittelpunkt des Geschehens standen – Einzelheiten über die Arbeiter, ihre Arbeitsbedingungen und die sozialen und wirtschaftlichen Beziehungen, in denen sie sich befanden. Der Aufsatz deckt solche Beziehungen auf, indem er sich den Körpern widmet, die sich auf den Baustellen von Cubiertas Ala drängten: Körper, die im Prozess der Entwicklung der Schalentechnologie in den 1950er-Jahren einerseits das größte Risiko auf sich nahmen und die andererseits den Erfolg des Unternehmens entscheidend bestimmten, einschließlich der Tatsache, dass sie nach dem Konkurs von Cubiertas Ala in den 1970er-Jahren nicht mehr benötigt wurden. Als Ausgangspunkt wählt die Autorin einen Unfall, der sich 1966 auf einer der Baustellen der Firma ereignete: Ein Balken war auf das Handgelenk eines Arbeiters gefallen. Dieser an sich nicht schwerwiegende Unfall führt zu einem alternativen Archiv (der bürokratischen Papierspur von Cubiertas Ala, die an der Universidad Nacional Autónoma de México aufbewahrt wird) über die arbeitenden Körper und zu einem bestimmten Blick auf die Schalenbauten, die mit ihrer Hilfe errichtet wurden.

Dieser Ansatz erfordert eine analytische Verschiebung unserer historiografischen Methoden: weg von der ewigen Betonung technologischer Erfindungen und formaler Innovationen, hin zur Sozialgeschichte; weg von den gepflegten Archiven und den Stimmen der technischen Eliten, hin zu den verborgenen Spuren subalterner Subjekte, das heißt der anonymen Akteure, die die Geschichte der modernen Architektur auf ihren Schultern trugen – in diesem Fall buchstäblich die Arbeiter, die die Betoneimer beim Bau der Schalen hinauf und hinunter transportierten. Vor allem ruft dieser Ansatz dazu auf, unsere Berechnungsmodi der Schalentechnologie zu überdenken, uns also von den knappen bekannten Zahlen ihrer Geometrien und ihrer Materialökonomie abzuwenden und uns der maßlosen Zahl von Arbeitern und Eimern, dem Ausmaß von körperlichen Risiken und körperlicher Arbeit zu widmen. Diese anderen Zahlen untergraben radikal die „Effizienz" und den „Rationalismus", auf die Candela so stolz war, und enthüllen stattdessen die kostspielige Körperwirtschaft, die die mexikanischen Schalenbauten Mitte des 20. Jahrhunderts und ihre kurze Geschichte tatsächlich geformt hat.

Eduardo Alarcón Azuela

Die letzten Schalen von Félix Candela in Mexiko
Die Dachkonstruktionen für die U-Bahn-Stationen von Mexiko-Stadt

Im Jahr 1967 wurde mit dem ersten Bauabschnitt der U-Bahn von Mexiko-Stadt begonnen. Für das Projekt und seine Ausführung zeichnete die Firma Ingenieros Civiles Asociados (ICA) verantwortlich, deren Direktor der Ingenieur Bernardo Quintana war. Ursprünglich war vorgesehen, die Linie 1 der U-Bahn zu den Olympischen Spielen 1968 fertigzustellen, doch aufgrund technischer Schwierigkeiten beschloss man, sie erst im darauffolgenden Jahr zu eröffnen.

Der Architekt Ángel Borja Navarrete, ein Partner von Quintana, koordinierte eine Gruppe junger Architekten für den Entwurf der verschiedenen Stationen des U-Bahn-Netzes, war doch wegen der Dringlichkeit keines der großen Architekturbüros mit der Arbeit am Projekt von ICA beauftragt worden. Allerdings lud man Félix Candela ein, der bereits internationale Berühmtheit erlangt hatte, und beauftragte ihn damit, die Dächer der drei Stationen Merced, Candelaria und San Lázaro zu bauen, außerdem einen kleinen Schuppen für die U-Bahn von Balderas.

Der Aufsatz analysiert die Geschichte des U-Bahn-Projekts sowie die Geometrie und Struktur der von Candela entworfenen Stationen. Darüber hinaus wird der aktuelle Zustand dieser Bauten untersucht, die inzwischen starke Veränderungen erfahren haben. Der Aufsatz schließt mit einem Vorschlag zur Rettung des Bahnhofs San Lázaro, da dieser nach Meinung des Autors am stärksten zu seinem Nachteil verändert wurde.

Marisela Mendoza

Félix Candelas Erbe in Großbritannien

1959 reiste Candela auf Einladung des British Council und der Cement and Concrete Association nach Großbritannien, um Vorträge in verschiedenen Städten zu halten, unter anderem in London, Cardiff, Leeds, Edinburgh und Belfast. Schon vor seinem Besuch im Vereinigten Königreich war Candelas Arbeit auch außerhalb Mexikos bekannt, besonders durch die Veröffentlichungen des American Concrete Institute und dank verschiedener Vorträge, die Candela auf Konferenzen in den USA gehalten hatte. Während dieser Besuche entwickelte sich eine enge Freundschaft zwischen Candela und dem texanischen Architekten O'Neil Ford. Nachdem er mit Candela bereits 1958 beim Bau von umgekehrten Hyparschalen in Texas zusammengearbeitet hatte, erhielt Ford 1959 den Auftrag, eine Fabrik für Texas Instruments im englischen Bedford zu entwerfen und zu bauen – die erste Fabrik des Unternehmens außerhalb der USA.

Candelas umfangreiches Wissen und seine Erfahrung hinsichtlich des Potenzials von Stahlbetonschalenkonstruktionen für Industriegebäude wurden in Großbritannien durch seine Vorträge und deren Zusammenfassung in der Zeitschrift *Concrete Quarterly* bekannt gemacht. Der Artikel hob Candelas Zuversicht hervor, dass die Anwendung dieser innovativen Bedachungsmethode auch außerhalb Mexikos vielversprechend sei. Zweifellos inspirierten seine Vorträge britische Architekten und Ingenieure, die dadurch angespornt wurden, das Potenzial umgekehrter Hyparschalen weiter auszuloten. Candelas zweite Reise nach Großbritannien wurde für sein persönliches und berufliches Leben folgenreich: London wurde zu seiner Lieblingsstadt, hier traf er seinen Freund Ove Arup. Paradigmatisch waren Candelas Begegnungen mit dem Ingenieur Oliver Marcel und dem Architekten Francis Reginald Stevens Yorke, da aus ihnen 1963 – in Zusammenarbeit mit

Yorke, Rosenberg and Mardall (YRM), einem der bedeutendsten britischen Architekturbüros der Nachkriegszeit – Candelas erstes europäisches Projekt hervorging: die Lagerhalle für John Lewis in Stevenage, der ersten britischen *New Town*.

Darüber hinaus war die von Candelas Märkten in Mexiko und dem Lagerhaus in Stevenage inspirierte Hyparschale, mit der 1970 die Queensgate Market Hall in Huddersfield überdacht wurde, ein Meilenstein, war sie doch die letzte umgedrehte Hyparschale, die in Großbritannien errichtet wurde. Diese ikonischen Bauten zeugen von den städtebaulichen und regionalen Planungsentwicklungen sowie von den wirtschaftlichen, politischen und technologischen Faktoren, die die Industrie- und Handelsarchitektur in der Zeit nach der britischen Austerity-Politik förderten. Aufgrund ihrer architektonischen Bedeutung wurden sie von der staatlichen Denkmalpflegebehörde English Heritage (seit 2015 Historic England) in die Liste der schützenswerten Gebäude (Grade II) aufgenommen.

Matthias Beckh und Rainer Schützeichel

Heinz Islers prägende Jahre

In dem Aufsatz werden die frühen Jahre von Heinz Isler beleuchtet – von seinem Studienabschluss an der ETH Zürich im Jahr 1950 über die Assistenzzeit bei seinem früheren Professor Pierre Lardy bis zu seinen ersten Bauaufträgen, in denen sich sein Werk zu formen begann. Es wird gezeigt, dass der experimentelle, sich wesentlich auf Modelle stützende Entwurfsansatz, den Isler 1959 in seinem berühmten Vortrag „New Shapes for Shells" auf dem Gründungskongress der International Association for Shell Structures (IASS) in Madrid präsentierte, maßgeblich durch Lardy vorgeprägt worden war. Dieser stand nicht nur an vorderster Front bei der Entwicklung des Spannbetons in der Schweiz, sondern er baute zudem – inspiriert von Eduardo Torroja – gemeinsam mit seinem Assistenten Hans Hauri an seinem Lehrstuhl ein Modellprüflabor auf.

Bei der von Isler vorgelegten Diplomarbeit, in der er eine von Schalensheds überdachte Fabrikhalle projektierte, fungierte Lardy als Gutachter; kurz nach seinem Abschluss wurde Isler Assistent an dessen Lehrstuhl. Dort konnte er Erfahrungen in dessen Modelllabor sammeln, zudem boten sich ihm Einblicke in die Schwerpunktthemen von Lardys Lehre. Lardy verfolgte einen ganzheitlichen Ansatz und plädierte für eine Entwurfsmethodik, die das „globale" Verhalten einer Struktur und somit die positiven Effekte räumlichen Tragverhaltens berücksichtigt, statt Einzelkomponenten getrennt voneinander zu analysieren, wie es bis dahin üblich gewesen war. Überdies legte Lardy großen Wert auf materialgerechte Tragwerksplanung wie auch auf die Bedeutung der Ästhetik im Ingenieurbau. Kaum hoch genug einzuschätzen ist der Einfluss, den Lardys Kurse über Spannbeton – in denen er seine Schüler mit einer damals noch jungen Technologie vertraut machte – auf Isler hatten: Die Entwicklung seiner pneumatischen Schalen wäre ohne die Integration von Spanngliedern undenkbar gewesen.

Isler verließ Lardys Lehrstuhl 1953 und arbeitete für einige Jahre im Ingenieurbüro Weder & Prim in Burgdorf, wo er anschließend sein eigenes Büro gründete. Aus dieser frühen Zeit werden in dem Aufsatz drei realisierte Projekte betrachtet: die Überdachung eines Mehrzwecksaals im Hotel Kreuz in Langenthal (1954), drei Schalendächer für Glas Trösch in Thunstetten (1955) sowie Lager- und Produktionshallen für die Firma Blaser in Rüegsau (1956). Bei letzterem Projekt unternahm Isler auch erste Schritte im Bereich der experimentellen Kunststoffverarbeitung bei Bauteilen, da er ebenso für die Entwicklung weitspannender kuppelförmiger Oberlichter aus Polyester verantwortlich zeichnete, mit denen die zentralen Lichtöffnungen in den Hallendächern abgedeckt wurden.

Die Denkweise von Lardy hat Islers Methodik maßgeblich geprägt: angefangen bei seiner Arbeit mit Prüfmodellen über die Vermittlung wesentlicher Kenntnisse im Beton- und Spannbetonbau bis hin zu einem integralen, die Eigenschaften verschiedener Materialien berücksichtigenden Ansatz. Lardys Vorbild legte den Grundstein zu Islers Denken und wurde in dessen frühem Werk schließlich in einen eigenständigen Beitrag überführt.

Giulia Boller und John Chilton

Heinz Islers experimenteller Ansatz zur Formfindung

Der experimentelle Entwurfsansatz von Heinz Isler kann exemplarisch an Formfindungsmodellen herausgearbeitet werden, die der Ingenieur zur Konzeption, Entwicklung und Erläuterung seiner Bauten und Projekte verwendete. Auf der 1959 in Madrid abgehaltenen Gründungskonferenz der International Association for Shell Structures (IASS) präsentierte er erstmals drei Formfindungsmethoden für Schalentragwerke: den frei geformten Hügel, die pneumatische Membran sowie das hängende Tuch. Später modifizierte er zudem geometrische Formen, experimentierte mit Fließformen und erprobte weitere Formfindungsmethoden.

Im Entwurfsprozess kommen Formfindungsmodelle in der frühesten Phase zur Anwendung, da sie helfen, eine effiziente, den Stützbedingungen entsprechende Hüllengeometrie zu definieren. Die im Modell gefundenen Formen basieren auf physikalischen Gesetzmäßigkeiten, weshalb sie zugleich Teil der technischen Entwicklung eines Projekts werden. Solche Formfindungsmodelle waren für Isler ein zentrales Werkzeug im Entwurf von Tragwerken, wobei diese bei ihm vor allem in der Gestaltung von freigeformten Schalen Anwendung fanden. Die Erklärung hierfür liegt auf der Hand – war doch die Form bei anderen Typologien vergleichsweise schnell definiert, so dass dort eher Präsentations- als Formfindungsmodelle angefertigt wurden.

Der Aufsatz fokussiert auf zwei konkrete Beispiele: erstens eine Freiformschale für das Architekturbüro Grob in Sargans (1968) und zweitens eine als Wohnhaus für den Architekten Pierre Camoletti in der Nähe von Genf errichtete Villa (1970). Die Schale für das frühere Projekt, das zugleich das erste war, welches von Isler nach dem Prinzip der hängenden Membran konzipiert wurde, präsentiert sich als eine auf vier Stützenpunkten aufsitzende, schräg geneigte Freiform. Für dieses Projekt wurden insgesamt sieben verschiedene Formfindungsmodelle erstellt, mit deren Hilfe Schwachstellen analysiert und die Form optimiert wurden. Die expressive Dachform der Villa Camoletti dagegen wurde ausgehend von der Geometrie zweier hyperbolischer Paraboloide definiert, die auf den ersten Blick symmetrisch entlang einer Schnittachse liegen. Bei näherer Betrachtung ist jedoch zu erkennen, dass die Seitenlänge der Regelfläche sowie der Schnittpunkt der Segmente während des Entwurfsprozesses verändert wurden.

In ihrer Unterschiedlichkeit sind die beiden Beispiele repräsentative Fallstudien zur Arbeitsmethodik von Heinz Isler. Insbesondere die von ihm und seinen Mitarbeitern erstellten physischen Modelle, aber auch Notizen und weitere Dokumente helfen dabei, Entscheidungen herauszuarbeiten, die während der frühesten Entwurfsphase getroffen wurden. Damit erlaubt der Aufsatz einen Einblick in die ersten, maßgeblichen Schritte seiner Formfindungsprozesse.

Matthias Beckh

Vom Schaum zur Form
Die eigenartigen ersten Freiformschalen von Heinz Isler

Im Frühwerk von Heinz Isler nehmen seine Formfindungsversuche mit Polyurethanschaum eine Sonderrolle ein. Von den 1960er-Jahren an verwendete er diese Methode, um die Geometrie von Freiformschalen zu entwickeln. Durch das Mischen zweier Materialkomponenten wurde eine chemische Reaktion in Gang gesetzt, bei der sich das Polyurethan binnen einer Minute auf das 30-fache des Ausgangsvolumens vergrößerte. Die organischen Formen, die durch diesen Selbstbildungsprozess auf einfache und schnelle Weise generiert werden konnten, faszinierten Isler und bildeten die geometrische Grundlage für mehrere Projekte – auch wenn die so entstandenen Formen für Schalentragwerke statische Nachteile hatten.

Der Aufsatz verfolgt die Genese der ersten Freiformschalen von Isler, beginnend mit dem Gartencenter Wyss in Zuchwil bei Solothurn (1962), das auf einer geometrisch definierten Translationsfläche basiert. Zwei Jahre später realisierte Isler für den Migros-Supermarkt in Bellinzona die erste Schale, deren Form mit Polyurethanschaum experimentell entwickelt worden war. Um das Raumprogramm auf dem 31,30 Meter breiten, quadratischen Grundriss optimal ausnützen zu können, musste eine Form gefunden werden, die an den Auflagern möglichst steil war und am Scheitel nicht zu hoch wurde. Die Vorversuche wurden anfangs in kleinen kubischen Holzboxen von 10 Zentimetern Kantenlänge, später mit größeren Modellen im Maßstab 1:100 durchgeführt. Durch die Größe der Holzeinfassung und die resultierende Wandreibung während des Expansionsprozesses konnte die Geometrie der sogenannten „Schäumlinge" beeinflusst werden.

Zwei Jahre nach der Fertigstellung des Supermarkts in Bellinzona konnte Isler ein weiteres Mal die Expansionsmethode einsetzen: Bei der Firmenzentrale des Baustoffherstellers Kilcher in Recherswil wurde die Urform ebenfalls mittels Polyurethanschaum bestimmt. Allerdings konnte Isler die Schale hier zu den Auflagerpunkten deutlich flacher auslaufen lassen und damit die in Bellinzona aufgetretenen Probleme vermeiden. Mit dem etwa gleichzeitig geplanten Florélites-Gartencenter (1966) außerhalb von Paris erreichte die Expansionsmethode mit einer überdachten Fläche von 1250 Quadratmetern in punkto Größe zwar ihren Zenit, gleichzeitig aber auch ihren Abschluss. In den folgenden Jahren entwickelte Heinz Isler seine Freiformschalen mit Hängemodellen – eine Methode, die statisch deutlich günstigere Geometrien hervorbrachte.

Elke Genzel und Pamela Voigt

Mehr als Beton
Heinz Islers Projekte aus glasfaserverstärktem Kunststoff

Als einer der ersten in Europa verwendete Heinz Isler glasfaserverstärkten Kunststoff (GFK) für Schalen und Platten. Das Polyesterharz kannte er wahrscheinlich aus seiner Assistenzzeit bei Pierre Lardy, wohingegen er den Kompositwerkstoff Harz plus Fasern erst später für sich entdeckte, als er bei seinen Industrieschalen für die Firma Blaser (1956) durchscheinende Oberlichter einbauen wollte, die in der gewünschten Größe nicht erhältlich waren. Nachdem ihm die eigenständige Herstellung dieser Oberlichter aus GFK hervorragend gelungen war, stellte er weitere Schalen und Platten aus dem Werkstoff her. Die Formen der Schalen fand er entweder als Freiformen und, wie beim Betonschalenbau, stets mit einer Korrektur der Krümmungen an den Schalenfüßen, oder er übernahm – sofern das Projekt nicht sein eigenes, sondern durch einen Architekten initiiert war – eine vorgegebene Geometrie.

Dass Isler als Kunststoffschalenbauer weitgehend unbekannt ist, hat mit dem Material selbst zu tun: Es verändert seine mechanischen Eigenschaften über die Zeit, denn durch Dauerbelastung, Temperatur und UV-Strahlung nimmt seine Festigkeit um bis zu 70 Prozent ab. In den 1950er-Jahren konnten Tragwerksplaner nur schätzen, wie viel Tragfähigkeit ihnen das Material auch nach 50 Jahren Beanspruchung noch zur Verfügung stellen würde; selbst ein erfahrener Ingenieur wie Isler konnte diese Langzeitfestigkeit nicht exakt bestimmen. Im Bauwesen war das Material schlicht zu neu. Und so publizierte er seine Kunststoff-Projekte nur spärlich, nicht selten erst lange nach ihrer Fertigstellung. Als er sich 1977 erstmals umfassend in einem Aufsatz dazu äußerte, lag sein „Kunststoffanfang [...] über 20 Jahre zurück". Der Respekt, den Isler dem Material entgegenbrachte, war angemessen. Denn im Gegensatz zu allen anderen Pionieren war er beim Ansatz des Materialwiderstandes äußerst mutig, um nicht zu sagen: waghalsig. Dass alle seine Bauten aus GFK mittlerweile problemlos 50 Jahre überdauert haben, gibt seinem Wagemut jedoch Recht. In jedem Fall unterstreichen sie seine Leistung als Pionier auch auf dem Gebiet des Bauens mit Kunststoffen.

Rainer Schützeichel

Schalen (re)präsentieren
Heinz Islers Werk in Ausstellungen

Der Aufsatz fragt nach der (Re-)Präsentation des Werks von Heinz Isler in Ausstellungen. Die Exponate – Fotos, Modelle und anderen Medien – werden als Kommunikationsmittel verstanden, wobei schon allein aufschlussreich ist, was in welcher Form gezeigt wird und was andererseits aus dem jeweiligen Panorama von Islers Werk ausgeschlossen bleibt. In den nur vier Jahren von 1979 bis 1982 stellte Isler nicht weniger als drei Ausstellungen zusammen, während er zuvor noch nie auf dieses Format zurückgegriffen hatte, um Werbung für seine Arbeiten zu machen. Diese frühen Ausstellungen können exemplarisch darüber Aufschluss geben, wie Ideen, Projekte und Bauten von Isler in Narrativen miteinander verknüpft wurden, um sie sowohl an Fachleute als auch an Laien zu vermitteln.

1979 erhielt Isler eine erste Gelegenheit, eine Auswahl seiner Bauten öffentlich zu präsentieren. Der bescheidene Rahmen dieser ersten Ausstellung war ein Schaufenster in Basel. Nur ein Jahr später jedoch widmete das renommierte Kunstmuseum der Princeton University seinem Œuvre eine monografische Ausstellung; am selben Ort sollten 2003 wiederum einige von

Islers Projekten gezeigt werden, diesmal allerdings eingewoben in eine größere *Swiss Legacy*. Den intimsten Einblick in seine Arbeitsweise gewährte Isler in der kaum bekannten Ausstellung *Nautilus*, die er nur drei Jahre nach der ersten Basler Werkschau in der Kunstgalerie AGP 46 in Bern einrichtete.

Es ist bemerkenswert, dass die drei frühen Ausstellungen an einem Wendepunkt in Islers Karriere stattfanden – 1979 nämlich hatte er den Zenit seines Erfolgs bereits überschritten, nachdem er seit Mitte der 1950er-Jahre zahllose Bauten hatte realisieren können. Zwar wäre es überzogen zu behaupten, die Basler Ausstellung hätte bereits sein Erbe vorbereitet, doch eröffnete sie seinem Œuvre einen weiteren einflussreichen Kommunikationsweg, der über das gebaute Werk hinauswies und potenziell eine breitere (internationale) Öffentlichkeit erreichte, als es die Gebäude allein vermochten.

Die begrenzte Ausstellungsfläche hatte 1979 zu einer vergleichsweise einfachen Präsentation geführt, die wesentliche Aspekte von Islers Werk, insbesondere seine experimentellen Formfindungsmethoden, beiseiteließ. Im Vergleich dazu war die Präsentation seiner Entwürfe in den Räumen des Princeton University Art Museum im Jahr 1980 deutlich umfassender, auch wenn sie zum Teil auf Projekte zurückgriff, die schon in Basel gezeigt worden waren. Die zweite Ausstellung, die mehr als 20 Jahre später in Princeton gezeigt werden sollte, ist eher als eine Art Fortsetzung dieser früheren zu verstehen, da sie aus älteren Inhalten destilliert, in einen größeren Schweizer Kontext eingefügt und um einige neu gefertigte Modelle ergänzt worden war. Die Berner Ausstellung von 1982 hingegen offenbarte eine bemerkenswerte Tendenz hin zu einer persönlich gefärbten Offenlegung von Islers experimenteller Methodik. Hier zog er den lebendigsten Querschnitt durch sein Werk und seine Philosophie, und er installierte zugleich eine beinahe intim zu nennende Ausstellung, die die Besucher mit dem tiefsten Einblick in seine Arbeits- und Entwurfsweise belohnte.

Andreas Schätzke

„Neue Konstruktionen“ Die Anfänge des Schalenbaus in der Deutschen Demokratischen Republik

In der DDR entstanden die ersten Betonschalenbauten um 1960, im internationalen Vergleich also recht spät. Zu dieser Zeit sah man einen wachsenden Bedarf an Gebäuden, die Funktionen für die Infrastruktur ihrer Umgebung erfüllen konnten: Stätten der Erholung in Urlaubsregionen, vor allem aber Einrichtungen für Konsum, Freizeit, Bildung und Erziehung in den nun vielerorts im Zuge der forcierten Industrialisierung des Bauens entstehenden Großsiedlungen. Meist unterschieden sich diese Solitäre in ihrer Formensprache deutlich von ihrer oft recht gleichförmigen Umgebung und sollten als städtebauliche „Blickpunkte“ dienen.

Die Hochphase des Betonschalenbaus hatte weltweit Mitte des 20. Jahrhunderts begonnen. Auch im Osten Deutschlands verfolgte man die Entwicklungen auf diesem Gebiet aufmerksam und suchte den Austausch mit ausländischen Fachkollegen, besonders innerhalb der 1959 gegründeten International Association for Shell Structures (IASS). Nicht nur in der DDR, aber gerade auch dort bemühte man sich anfangs vor allem, den Schalenbau mit dem Prinzip der Vorfertigung zu verbinden, da man dies als einen besonders ökonomischen Weg der Planung und Ausführung ansah. So begann man in den frühen 1960er-Jahren zuerst in Halle, verschiedene öffentliche Gebäude mit „HP-Schalen“ zu überdachen. Bei ihnen handelte es sich um vorgefertigte hyperbolisch geformte Betonelemente, die der Ingenieur Herbert Müller entwickelt hatte.

Ein anderer Ansatz im Bereich des Schalenbaus verfolgte den Weg der individuell geplanten Konstruktion. Dieser Aspekt ist eng und hauptsächlich mit dem Namen des Bauingenieurs Ulrich Müther verknüpft. Dass Müther in der DDR seit den ausgehenden 1960er-Jahren eine singuläre Stellung einnahm, hing nicht zuletzt mit seiner zweifachen Profession zusammen. Als Ingenieur und als Unternehmer – wenn auch in einer zentral gelenkten Wirtschaftsordnung – war Müther Konstrukteur und Ausführender zugleich. Darüber hinaus erschloss er sich mit dem Schalenbau früh ein zunehmend gefragtes Spezialgebiet. Unter den Bedingungen der kommunistischen Planwirtschaft galt es als vorteilhaft, dass die Ausführung seiner Schalen zwar einen hohen Einsatz an Arbeitskraft erforderte, aber in kurzer Zeit und bei sparsamem Betonverbrauch möglich war. Einmal berechnet konnten solche Konstruktionen überdies an verschiedenen Orten baugleich oder mit leichten Anpassungen errichtet werden.

Die Gebäude, an deren Planung Müther beteiligt war, verdanken ihre einprägsame Gestalt zu einem großen Teil seiner Mitwirkung. Realisiert werden konnten die meisten von ihnen jedoch nur in enger

Kooperation mit Architekten, die in der DDR üblicherweise Angestellte staatlicher Institutionen waren. In Betonschalenbauweise errichtete Müther in den 1960er- und 1970er-Jahren mehrere Dutzend Restaurants, Kaufhäuser sowie Hallen für Messen, Ausstellungen und andere Veranstaltungen. Zum Aufgabenspektrum gehörten außerdem Sportstätten, Planetarien und Kirchen. Viele dieser Bauten besaßen eine Eleganz und Expressivität, die in der Architektur der DDR sonst nur selten erreicht wurde, und waren geeignet, dem postulierten Streben nach technologischem und gesellschaftlichem Fortschritt weithin sichtbar Ausdruck zu verleihen.

Tanja Seeböck

Endlich gerettet?
Das Schicksal von Ulrich Müthers Magdeburger Hyparschale im Wandel der Zeit

Ein bemerkenswertes Beispiel für das lange und zähe Ringen um die Erhaltung eines Schalenbaus von Ulrich Müther ist die sogenannte Hyparschale in Magdeburg, eine multifunktionale Veranstaltungshalle, die als Teil eines im Stadtpark gelegenen Messegeländes errichtet wurde. An ihrem Schicksal lässt sich die sich wandelnde Wertschätzung von Müthers Schalen im Laufe der Zeit nachvollziehen.

Das Ende der DDR im Herbst des Jahres 1990 bedeutete für zahlreiche Bauten Müthers eine einschneidende Zäsur: Viele von ihnen verloren im Zuge des politischen Systemwandels und der gesellschaftlichen wie wirtschaftlichen Veränderungen ihre ursprüngliche Funktion. Manche standen infolgedessen jahrzehntelang leer, wurden zur Zielscheibe von Vandalismus und verfielen aufgrund mangelnder Instandhaltungsmaßnahmen. Am Ende stand in einigen Fällen der Abbruch. Für andere Bauten fand sich eine neue Nutzung, und die Kommunen setzten sie behutsam instand oder sanierten sie durchgreifend, letzteres teilweise ohne Rücksicht auf das ursprüngliche Erscheinungsbild.

Die 1969 erbaute Magdeburger Multifunktionshalle ist das größte noch erhaltene Werk Müthers. Die aus vier Hyparschalen zusammengesetzte Konstruktion, die eine quadratische Grundfläche von insgesamt 2304 Quadratmetern stützenlos überspannt, wurde flächenmäßig nur noch von dem wenige Monate später erbauten Ahornblatt in Berlin übertroffen, einer Großgaststätte, die im Jahr 2000 abgerissen worden ist.

Der Magdeburger Schalenbau befand sich gut zwei Jahrzehnte lang in einem desolaten Zustand und war von der Zerstörung bedroht. Lange Zeit scheiterten alle Bemühungen der Stadt, einen Investor mit einem passenden Nutzungs- und Finanzierungskonzept zur Erhaltung des Gebäudes zu finden. 2019, nach 21 Jahren Leerstand, entschloss sich die Stadt Magdeburg quasi „in letzter Minute“, das Bauwerk auf eigene Kosten sanieren zu lassen, um es vor dem drohenden Totalverlust zu bewahren. Das Beispiel der Magdeburger Hyparschale verdeutlicht eindringlich die Schwierigkeit, passende Nutzungen sowie tragfähige Finanzierungsmodelle für die Sanierung solcher Großstrukturen zu finden, die aufgrund ihrer Dimensionen sehr teuer im Unterhalt sind.

Susanne Brorson

Der Musikpavillon in Sassnitz
Ein Schalenbau von Ulrich Müther in Zusammenarbeit mit Dietmar Kuntzsch und Otto Patzelt

Der Musikpavillon in Sassnitz auf Rügen ist eines der weniger bekannten Projekte Ulrich Müthers. Er entstand 1988, kurz vor dem Ende der DDR, in Zusammenarbeit mit dem Architekten Dietmar Kuntzsch und dem Tragwerksplaner Otto Patzelt. In den Archiven findet sich umfangreiches Material zur Planung, und einige der Projektbeteiligten konnten 2015 interviewt werden, so dass der Planungsprozess im Detail nachvollziehbar ist. Der Pavillon, der direkt am Ufer der Ostsee errichtet wurde, besteht aus einer Muschelschale und zwei seitlich angeordneten Nebengebäuden. Kuntzschs Absicht war es, eine offene Architektur zu schaffen, die den Wind und das Meer als Hintergrund hat.

Die Entstehungsgeschichte der „Konzertmuschel“ veranschaulicht, unter welchen politischen und wirtschaftlichen Bedingungen Ulrich Müther in der DDR arbeitete. Seine Schalen können nur beurteilt werden, wenn man sie in diesem Kontext betrachtet. In den 1980er-Jahren war die wirtschaftliche Situation in der DDR bereits sehr schwierig, trotzdem sollte in der Nähe von Sassnitz ein neues Fährterminal gebaut werden. Dem Bürgermeister gelang es, Beton von dieser Baustelle abzuzweigen, um den neuen Musikpavillon bauen zu lassen. Erste Ideen für die Konzertmuschel wurden während eines studentischen Workshops entwickelt, den Dietmar Kuntzsch als Professor an der Kunsthochschule in Berlin-Weißensee abhielt. Kurz darauf wurden Kuntzsch und Otto Patzelt, der dort ebenfalls lehrte, mit dem Entwurf beauftragt; Müther wurde hinzugezogen.

Die Konzertmuschel ist kein reines hyperbolisches Paraboloid, sie besteht aus sieben Einzelschalen, die Hyperbeln als Begrenzungskurven haben. Sie ist auch keine typische „Mütherschale", denn die expressive Form geht auf die Zusammenarbeit mit Kuntzsch und Patzelt zurück. Der erste Entwurf, eine „konvexe Variante", zeigt eine Muschel mit nach oben gewölbten Bögen. Müthers Expertise führte zu einer Änderung, bei der die Schalen andersherum gewölbt und so zu einer „konkaven Variante" umgearbeitet wurden.

Patzelt berechnete die Statik am Computer unter Zuhilfenahme der Finite-Elemente-Methode, jedoch wurde die Muschel zuletzt per Hand als eingespannter Plattenbalken kalkuliert, denn die Rechenprogramme waren noch nicht ausgereift. Müther reichte die Statik zur Baugenehmigung mit seiner Unterschrift und seinem Firmenstempel ein. Die von ihm geführte Firma VEB Spezialbetonbau Rügen übernahm die Realisierung. Müther war jedoch zu beschäftigt, so dass Patzelt als sein vorgeblicher Angestellter die Bauleitung übernahm, ohne dass es einen entsprechenden Arbeitsvertrag gab. Um den Pavillon fertigstellen zu können, war die Stadt Sassnitz auf die Hilfe Freiwilliger angewiesen. Baumaterial musste mühevoll organisiert werden. Der Materialmangel hatte auch Auswirkungen auf die Architektur, denn man setzte Bullaugen und Schiffstüren in den beiden Seitengebäuden ein. Nach dem Ende der DDR begann ein schleichender Verfall des Musikpavillons, der 2006 mit einer teilweisen Sanierung aufgefangen wurde. 2015 wurde mit Hilfe der Wüstenrot Stiftung eine denkmalgerechte Sanierung möglich, die 2017 abgeschlossen werden konnte.

Georg Giebeler

Ulrich Müther: Quantität oder Qualität?

Das erste nicht von Ulrich Müther selbst erstellte Verzeichnis seiner Werke stammt von Wilfried Dechau und listet 79 Schalenbauten auf. Seitdem gab es immer wieder ernsthafte und weniger ernsthafte Versuche, ein vollständiges Werkverzeichnis anzufertigen. Dies geht so weit, dass manche Werkverzeichnisse dem Ingenieur knapp 200 Bauten und Projekte zuschreiben.

2012 übergab der Verfasser, der bis dahin das Müther-Archiv an der Hochschule Wismar geleitet hatte, den sechs Jahre zuvor dorthin überführten Nachlass an seinen Nachfolger Matthias Ludwig – zu dieser Zeit immer noch mit einem fragmentarischen Werkverzeichnis. Der Grund hierfür war die Unübersichtlichkeit des Werks: Ulrich Müther entwarf, plante, berechnete und realisierte neben zweifach gekrümmten Betonschalen auch Kuppeln und geometrisch völlig freie Betonarbeiten. Dazu kommen Faltwerke, Denkmäler, Sportanlagen und anderes, denn das von ihm geleitete Unternehmen wurde regelmäßig als Subunternehmer mit Arbeiten an mehrfach gekrümmten Betonbauten beauftragt. Neben solchen Auftragsarbeiten initiierte Müther auch von sich aus die Realisierung von Sonderbauten, zum Beispiel ein Buswartehaus in Binz auf Rügen (1967). Schließlich führt eine Besonderheit im Bauwesen der DDR, das „Wiederverwendungsprojekt", zu weiteren Unklarheiten: Viele von Müthers Bauten wurden in identischer Form mehrfach realisiert. Als Beispiel hierfür sei die Gaststätte Ostseeperle in Glowe auf Rügen (1968) genannt, die – ebenfalls als Ausflugsrestaurant – mit identischer Dachform auch noch in Eberswalde (1968) und Dierhagen (1969) steht.

Im Jahr 2016 erstellte der Autor daher – nur auf Grundlage der Materialien des Müther-Archivs – das erste vollständig sichere Werkverzeichnis, das die Bauwerke zudem nach ihrer Geometrie sortiert. 114 realisierte und unrealisierte Projekte von Ulrich Müther konnten auf diese Weise sicher zugewiesen werden. Dies sagt aber noch nichts über die Relevanz der Werke aus: Ist es allein die schiere Masse seiner zwischen 1963 und 1993 ausgeführten Bauten und Projekte, oder war Müther ein lange Zeit unterschätzter Pionier des Bauens mit Beton? Wohl Letzteres.

Zu dieser Einschätzung kommt der Verfasser, obwohl er einen Großteil der gelisteten Werke im Sinne einer baukulturellen oder technologischen Beurteilung für wenig bedeutend hält. Zieht man die Vielzahl an Wiederverwendungsprojekten, namentlich die von Müther nur als Unternehmer ausgeführten Spritzbetonarbeiten, ebenso die Candela-Kopien, die wenig komplexen Planetarien und Faltwerke und sogar den Großteil seiner als Massenware ausgeführten Schirmschalen ab, bleiben noch immer 20 Bauten, welche die einzigartige Stellung Ulrich Müthers im Reigen der Betonschalenerfinder begründen. Kaum jemand sonst realisierte eine solch breite Auswahl unterschiedlicher Formen von mehrfach gekrümmten Schalentragwerken aus Beton: HP-Schalen, Hängeschalen, Buckel- und Freiformschalen.

Resúmenes

Juan Gerardo Oliva Salinas
Tres culturas y tres maneras de hacer cascarones de concreto armado

El objetivo de este trabajo es describir y comparar las diferentes maneras de diseñar y construir cascarones de concreto armado de Félix Candela, Heinz Isler y Ulrich Müther. Estos constructores se distinguieron por un manejo magistral de la geometría y de la mecánica, lo que les condujo a la realización de un gran número de cascarones, en su mayoría en México, Suiza y Alemania Oriental durante la segunda mitad del siglo XX. Desde el nacimiento de Candela en 1910 hasta la muerte de Isler en 2009, se cubre una centuria de importantes desarrollos tecnológicos para la arquitectura y la ingeniería. Estas tres figuras van a dar un fuerte impulso al diseño y la construcción de estructuras a través de su ingenio y perseverancia. Debido a su forma, las cubiertas de concreto generadas van a ser capaces de resistir su peso propio y todas las otras acciones de carga a las que serán sometidas: el viento, la nieve, el granizo y los sismos. En los tres casos se identifican objetivos comunes para lograr una arquitectura y una ingeniería que hoy identificamos como “sostenible”: utilizar un mínimo de material, conseguir la mayor eficiencia mecánica posible, aprovechar y cuidar de la mejor manera los recursos naturales, reducir los esfuerzos de planificación, los costos y los tiempos de ejecución.

Se discuten las tres maneras diferentes en que estos creadores determinan la forma de sus cascarones, realizan los cálculos geométricos y mecánicos que garantizan su estabilidad, así como los diferentes procedimientos constructivos que les permitieron, con razón, ser considerados verdaderos artistas estructurales. También se comenta la influencia que ejerció Candela en las obras de Isler y de Müther, así como la forma en que estos tres autores aportaron innovaciones y cómo, cada uno a su manera, desempeñó un papel decisivo en el desarrollo de la construcción de cascarones de concreto armado en el siglo XX.

Matthias Ludwig

Relaciones entre Félix Candela, Heinz Isler y Ulrich Müther

Hasta ahora, solo ha habido unos pocos arquitectos e ingenieros que se han dedicado casi exclusivamente a la construcción de cascarones de concreto. Félix Candela, Heinz Isler y Ulrich Müther pertenecen a este círculo. Estas tres figuras trabajaron en culturas y regiones del mundo muy diferentes. Por lo tanto, a primera vista se podría suponer que no existe conexión alguna entre ellos. Sin embargo, una mirada más cercana a su trabajo y sus historias de vida revela que hay ciertos aspectos que vinculan el trabajo de Candela, Isler y Müther, pero también algunos que los distinguen entre sí.

Los tres mantuvieron relaciones colegiadas pero también amistosas a través de varias redes como la International Association for Shell Structures (IASS, ahora: International Association for Shell and Spatial Structures). Félix Candela, el mayor de ellos, influyó en un gran número de arquitectos e ingenieros con las obras que construyó en México en las décadas de 1950 y 1960, mientras que sus dos colegas más jóvenes, Heinz Isler y Ulrich Müther (nacidos respectivamente 16 y 24 años más tarde), redefinieron y desarrollaron individualmente la construcción de armazones en sus respectivos entornos: Suiza y la RDA. Durante mucho tiempo, Müther fue poco notado por el público, ya que trabajó en Alemania Oriental, detrás de la "Cortina de Hierro".

Se pueden identificar algunas similitudes y diferencias esenciales. En primer lugar, en lo que respecta al material, Candela, Isler y Müther generalmente utilizaron concreto armado, aunque hay excepciones: Isler también trabajó con plástico reforzado con fibra de vidrio (PRFV) y construyó "edificios" temporales con hielo. El pabellón de orquesta ubicado en Ralswiek, en la isla de Rügen (1980), realizado por Müther, es su única construcción en madera. En segundo lugar, los tres trabajaron principalmente con encofrados de madera para la producción de sus cascarones de concreto. A diferencia de Candela, tanto Isler como Müther realizaron encofrados que utilizaban neumáticos o montículos de tierra como negativos y también ejecutaron construcciones de concreto sin cimbra. En tercer lugar, Candela y Müther ejecutaron principalmente cascarones determinados geométricamente (paraboloides hiperbólicos, conoides, cascarones esféricos o cascarones cilíndricos), mientras que Isler realizó un gran número de cascarones de forma libre además de conchas jorobadas para la industria, algo que Müther también hizo en menor medida. En cuarto y último lugar, los tres construyeron principalmente edificios industriales, edificios públicos y esculturas: todas estructuras que, o bien requerían mucho espacio abierto, o estaban destinadas a establecer señas de identidad en su contexto.

Se consideran también los aspectos cuantitativos y geográficos: Müther realizó 75 estructuras de cascarón – incluyendo monumentos, estructuras plegables, construcciones de redes de cuerda y otros proyectos en los cuales solo participó como empresario –, estructuras que muestran un rango regional notable y que fueron levantadas en Europa, África del Norte, Cuba y Kuwait. Candela llegó a materializar cerca de 900 proyectos, la mayoría de los cuales fueron realizados en América Latina. Isler creó, por mucho, la mayor cantidad de estructuras: gracias a su método de construcción estandarizado ("System Isler") construyó casi 1400 cascarones en Suiza, Alemania, Francia, Austria, Gran Bretaña y Arabia Saudita.

Matthias Beckh

Espacios para la industria
Una comparación de los sistemas modulares de cascarones realizados por Félix Candela y Heinz Isler

Este texto analiza y discute los sistemas de construcción industrial de Félix Candela y Heinz Isler. Casi simultáneamente, a principios de la década de 1950 ambos desarrollaron estructuras modulares de concreto armado que tuvieron un gran éxito debido a sus económicos métodos de producción. Asimismo, constituyen la mayor parte de sus respectivas obras construidas. Entre 1955 y 1970, ambos lograron cubrir varios cientos de miles de metros cuadrados de espacio con sus sistemas. En el caso de Candela, se trata de "paraguas", estructuras laminares compuestas por cuatro secciones de paraboloides hiperbólicos (*hypars*) que convergen en una columna central. Los módulos individuales tienen una planta rectangular o cuadrada y drenan a través de un tubo de bajada de aguas pluviales que corre por dentro de la columna. Debido a las deformaciones en los bordes de estas delgadas estructuras de cubierta, típicamente de 4 centímetros de espesor y con amplios voladizos, el tamaño de los módulos tuvo que limitarse a aproximadamente 200 metros cuadrados. Después de varios edificios de prueba, el almacén de Río en la Ciudad de México fue el primer gran proyecto que se completó, en 1954, con este nuevo método.

Al otro lado del globo, en la región central de Suiza, Heinz Isler también desarrolló un nuevo sistema para la construcción industrial que se realizó por primera vez en 1955 para la empresa Glas Trösch: el cascarón de burbuja (*bubble shell*). Su forma está definida por una membrana de goma bajo presión interna, que se incrusta en un marco rectangular de madera. En un proyecto subsiguiente, Isler instaló un domo de poliéster de 5 metros de diámetro en la cúspide del cascarón de burbuja, con lo que el nuevo diseño estuvo listo para la producción en serie.

Este artículo traza el desarrollo de ambos métodos de construcción y discute los aspectos arquitectónicos, estáticos y funcionales utilizando ejemplos de proyectos realizados. Al inicio, se esboza el comportamiento de carga básico de varias estructuras de caparazón y sus características especiales de diseño. En primer plano están las formas que utilizan los protagonistas: o bien se desarrollan mediante métodos de búsqueda de formas y, por tanto, están especialmente optimizadas a nivel estático, o bien se definen matemáticamente como secciones esféricas, superficies de traslación o de paraboloide hiperbólico.

El gran virtuosismo de Candela en el diseño de sus estructuras de paraguas es impactante. Variando repetidamente y con una sofisticada combinación de su geometría básica y disposición, respondía a los requerimientos específicos del proyecto, ya se tratase de grandes luces o de condiciones especiales de iluminación. El tamaño de los módulos individuales, por otra parte, permaneció en gran medida inalterado debido a las limitaciones inherentes al sistema. En contraste, la enorme gama de tamaños de los módulos, que va desde unos pocos cientos hasta los 3200 metros cuadrados de área techada, es particularmente notable en los cascarones de burbuja de Isler, gracias a su gran eficiencia material.

Juan Ignacio del Cueto Ruiz-Funes

Las bóvedas por arista de Félix Candela
Contribución mexicana al desarrollo de las estructuras laminares

El espíritu inquieto de Félix Candela le llevó a experimentar continuamente con las cubiertas que tuvo oportunidad de diseñar y construir a lo largo de su trayectoria profesional utilizando paraboloides hiperbólicos. No se conformaba con alcanzar una solución eficaz para sus propósitos: una vez que encontraba un tipo de estructura laminar que satisficiera las necesidades requeridas para cubrir cierto espacio, se volcaba en busca de mejoras que pudieran alcanzar resultados óptimos en proyectos subsiguientes. Así, como un compositor musical que encuentra una veta de inspiración, desarrolló "variaciones de un mismo tema" con algunos de los tipos de cubierta más eficientes que ofrecía por intermedio de su empresa constructora Cubiertas Ala, entre los que destacaron las que realizó utilizando bóvedas por arista. Este texto aborda la génesis y evolución de este tipo de estructuras resistentes por forma.

La primera bóveda por arista con paraboloides hiperbólicos (*hypars*) fue construida por Cubiertas Ala para techar la sala de remates de la Bolsa Mexicana de Valores (Ciudad de México, 1955), siguiendo el proyecto de los arquitectos mexicanos Enrique de la Mora y Fernando López Carmona. Con los mismos arquitectos, Candela pudo construir sus primeros cascarones de "borde libre" en la iglesia de San Antonio de las Huertas (Ciudad de México, 1956). Posteriormente, siguió haciendo "variaciones" para otros colegas, como el club nocturno La Jacaranda en Acapulco (1957, con Juan Sordo Madaleno), el restaurante Los Manantiales de Xochimilco, Ciudad de México (1958, con Joaquín Álvarez Ordóñez) – considerada por muchos como su obra maestra –, el restaurante del Hotel Casino de la Selva en Cuernavaca (1960, con Juan Antonio Tonda) y la sorprendente cubierta de la planta embotelladora Bacardí-México en Tultitlán (Estado de México, 1960), entre otras obras en las que queda patente la maestría de Candela en proponer soluciones adecuadas e ingeniosas para cubrir distintos tipos de edificios.

Elisa María Teresa Drago Quaglia

Bellas formas
Las cascarones de Enrique de la Mora y Félix Candela

La revisión de fuentes primarias documentales resguardadas en los archivos permite enriquecer y complementar las lecturas de los fenómenos y hechos arquitectónicos que constituyen nuestro legado histórico. Este trabajo se enfoca en mostrar las colaboraciones de la mancuerna exitosa entre el despacho de Enrique de la Mora y Palomar y la empresa Cubiertas Ala, con Félix Candela al frente. Si bien se tiene un registro con soporte documental de más de veinte proyectos que realizaron en colaboración, este capítulo se enfoca en mostrar aquellos que fueron resueltos con cascarones de paraboloide hiperbólico: bóvedas por arista y mantos de borde recto.

La primera parte del texto traza una línea temporal del desarrollo, las búsquedas y el logro de soluciones y propuestas arquitectónicas y estructurales de ambos arquitectos. Se revisan algunos antecedentes que permitieron fusionar conocimientos, capacidades y aptitudes que, combinando calidad de diseño y ejecución, dieron como resultado algunos de los ejemplos más notables de cascarones realizados en México. Estos ejemplos se presentan en la segunda parte.

Catorce edificios se estudian desde el punto de vista de la colaboración entre las oficinas de arquitectura e ingeniería para la creación de obras arquitectónicas. Se parte de los procesos de diseño acunados desde el despacho de Enrique de la Mora, hasta llegar a la revisión estructural y ejecución de obra a cargo de Cubiertas Ala. Se demuestra que, con el trabajo conjunto, se logra establecer un punto de quiebre positivo que se verá reflejado en las trayectorias individuales. Resulta un hecho afortunado que la capacidad creadora y la inquietud de Enrique de la Mora por encontrar la expresión de la arquitectura de su tiempo mediante la forma resultante de la estructura y del material se conjugara con la maestría y el conocimiento del comportamiento estructural y la calidad de ejecución de obra de Félix Candela.

María González Pendás

Las economías corporales de las tecnologías del concreto

La obra desempeñó un papel particularmente importante en el desarrollo del sistema de cascarones de concreto que la compañía constructora mexicana Cubiertas Ala promocionó a mediados del siglo XX bajo el comando ingenieril de Félix Candela. Haciendose eco de las descripciones que el mismo Candela proponia sobre su proceso de diseño descripciones que el mismo Candela proponía sobre de su proceso de diseño, muchos han explicado cómo su saber hacer tomó forma de manera progresiva y empírica, al modo de una epistemología artesanal que dependía en gran medida de la obra, de los trabajadores y de su oficio. Candela a menudo remarcó este argumento en su incansable crítica a la modernización tecnificada y en su propuesta por una alternativa “humanista” a través de los cascarones. Fue un argumento cuya representación visual más lírica ofrecieron las fotografías de Juan Guzmán y Armando Salas Portugal, y donde trabajadores mexicanos aparecen heroicos sobre los cascarones en construcción.

Sin embargo, ausente tanto de estas seductoras imágenes como de las palabras de Candela y las historias de los cascarones que las siguieron, queda todo detalle sobre tales protagonistas, toda información sobre los trabajadores, sus condiciones laborales y las relaciones sociales, económicas y raciales que estaban en juego en el proceso de construcción. En este capítulo apunto a dichas relaciones mediante un análisis de los cuerpos que abarrotaban las obras de Cubiertas Ala, cuerpos que incurrieron mayor riesgo en el proceso de invención de la tecnología de cascarones en la década de 1950 y que determinaron gran parte de su historia – incluyendo su obsolescencia después de que Cubiertas Ala se declarase en bancarrota en la década de 1970. Para ello, el capitulo comienza con un evento prosaico que tuvo lugar en 1966 en una de las obras de la empresa: la caída, durante el descimbrado, de una viga sobre la muñeca de uno de los peones. Este accidente, normal y a todas cuentas bastante intrascendente, nos dirige sin embargo a un archivo alternativo (documentos burocráticos que se mantienen en la Universidad Nacional Autónoma de México) y a una nueva forma de interpretar los cascarones a través de los cuerpos que la construyeron.

Así, el capítulo propone un giro analítico en nuestros métodos historiográficos: no un cansino énfasis en la invención tecnológica y la innovación formal, sino una historia social de la labor de construcción; no un eco de los archivos y voces de las élites técnicas, sino una reconstrucción del huidizo sujeto subalterno, el trabajador de la construcción, actor anónimo que ha llevado la historia de la arquitectura moderna sobre sus espaldas (literalmente en este caso, ya que el peón de obra acarreaba cubos de cemento liquido sobre sus hombros). Más concretamente, este enfoque exige nuevos modos de cálculo de los cascarones: no el cálculo de las dimensiones geométricas, de resistencia estructural o economía material, sino un cálculo de los números que revelan el exceso de trabajadores, de cubos, de riesgo y de trabajo corporal. Estas otras cifras socavan radicalmente la "eficiencia" y el "racionalismo" que Candela promovió con tanto orgullo, y revelan la costosa economía corporal que dio lugar a los cascarones de concreto a mediados del siglo XX.

Eduardo Alarcón Azuela

Los últimos cascarones de Félix Candela en México Cubiertas para las estaciones del metro de la Ciudad de México

La primera etapa del metro de la Ciudad de México empezó a construirse en 1967; el proyecto y su ejecución estuvieron a cargo de la empresa Ingenieros Civiles Asociados (ICA), cuyo director fue el ingeniero Bernardo Quintana. En un principio, se pensó que la Línea 1 del metro estuviese lista para la celebración de los Juegos Olímpicos de 1968. No obstante, por las propias dificultades técnicas que planteaba, se decidió que esta se inauguraría para el año siguiente.

El arquitecto Ángel Borja Navarrete, socio de Quintana, coordinó a un grupo de jóvenes arquitectos para diseñar las diferentes estaciones de la red del metro. Asimismo, debido a la premura, no se contrató a las grandes firmas de arquitectos para que trabajaran en el proyecto de ICA. Como caso excepcional se invitó a Félix Candela para la ejecución de las cubiertas de tres estaciones: Merced, Candelaria y San Lázaro, así como de un pequeño cobertizo para el metro Balderas.

En este texto se analiza la historia del proyecto del metro, así como el diseño geométrico y estructural de las estaciones creadas por Candela. Además, se presenta el estado actual de las estructuras, pues lamentablemente estos espacios han sufrido severas modificaciones con respecto a su estado original. El ensayo concluye con una propuesta de rescate de la estación San Lázaro, ya que a juicio del autor es la que se encuentra alterada en mayor medida, en detrimento del proyecto original.

Marisela Mendoza

El legado de Félix Candela en Gran Bretaña

En 1959, invitado por el British Council y la Cement and Concrete Association, Candela viajó a Gran Bretaña para dar una serie de conferencias en diferentes ciudades, entre ellas Londres, Cardiff, Leeds, Edimburgo y Belfast. Antes de su visita al Reino Unido en 1959, el trabajo de Candela era bien conocido fuera de México, particularmente a través de las publicaciones del American Concrete Institute, así como por las ponencias en diversas conferencias que había presentado en los Estados Unidos. Durante las visitas a ese país, Candela se convirtió en amigo cercano del arquitecto texano O'Neil Ford, quien tras colaborar con Candela en la construcción de los *hypars* en Texas en 1958, recibió el encargo de diseñar y construir los de la fábrica para Texas Instruments (TI) en Bedford (1959), la primera planta de TI fuera de los Estados Unidos.

El vasto conocimiento y la experiencia de Candela en relación al potencial de los cascarones de concreto armado para edificios industriales se tornó una voz fuerte durante sus conferencias en el Reino Unido y se resumió en un artículo publicado por la revista *Concrete Quarterly*. El artículo destacó la experiencia y la seguridad de Candela en el uso de este innovador método de techado fuera de México. Sin duda, las conferencias de Candela inspiraron e incitaron a los arquitectos e ingenieros británicos a explorar más a fondo el potencial de los *hypars* invertidos en el Reino Unido. La visita de Candela al Reino Unido en 1959 representó un momento notable en su vida personal y profesional. Londres se convirtió en su ciudad favorita, donde solía visitar a su querido y admirado amigo, Ove Arup. Asimismo, Stevenage, el primer *New Town* del Reino Unido, se convirtió en el anfitrión de su primer proyecto europeo. A las conferencias de Candela en 1959 en el Reino Unido asistieron notables arquitectos e ingenieros interesados en los innovadores métodos de construcción promovidos por aquel. Los encuentros de Candela con el ingeniero Oliver Marcel y el arquitecto Francis Reginald Stevens Yorke fueron fundamentales, ya que producirían en 1963 el primer proyecto europeo de Candela: el almacén de John Lewis en colaboración con una de las firmas de arquitectura de posguerra más representativas del Reino Unido: Yorke, Rosenberg and Mardall (YRM).

Además, en 1970, los *hypars* que cubren el Queensgate Market Hall en Huddersfield, inspirados en los mercados de Candela en México y en el John Lewis Warehouse en Stevenage, representan un hito y una memoria material de la larga historia del comercio en Huddersfield. Asimismo, el edificio fue el último que se cubrió con *hypars* en el Reino Unido. Estos icónicos cascarones de concreto armado dan testimonio de los desarrollos de planificación urbana y regional, así como de los factores económicos, políticos y tecnológicos que promovieron la arquitectura industrial y de mercados en el período posterior a la *Austerity* en Gran Bretaña. Por su mérito arquitectónico, a partir de 2015 estas estructuras han estado distinguidas con el grado II de arquitectura patrimonial (Historic England).

Matthias Beckh y Rainer Schützeichel

Los años de formación de Heinz Isler

El ensayo destaca los antecedentes educativos de Heinz Isler y los orígenes de su enfoque experimental del diseño, arrojando luz sobre los primeros años en la carrera del ingeniero desde su graduación en 1950 hasta su contribución fundamental, "New Shapes for Shells", presentada en el primer congreso de la International Association for Shell Structures (IASS) en Madrid en 1959. Revela hasta qué punto la forma de pensar del profesor de Isler, Pierre Lardy, fue la piedra angular y la fuente de las ideas rectoras del trabajo de su alumno. Lardy, que había sido nombrado profesor de la ETH de Zúrich en 1946 – un año después de que Isler iniciara sus estudios – estaba a la vanguardia del desarrollo del hormigón pretensado en Suiza y en otros países. Además, junto con su asistente Hans Hauri, construyó en su cátedra un laboratorio de pruebas de modelos inspirado en una instalación similar a la del eminente diseñador español de cascarones Eduardo Torroja.

Después de graduarse en la ETH de Zúrich en 1950, Isler se unió a la cátedra de su profesor. Lardy había estado supervisando la tesis de Isler – un diseño para un edificio de fábrica para una compañía textil – y la calificó como "excelente". En su cátedra, Isler obtuvo una visión de primera mano del taller de pruebas de modelos de Lardy, así como de sus temas clave en la enseñanza. Ambos campos influyeron decisivamente en el desarrollo profesional de la propia práctica de Isler. En los cursos que Lardy impartió en la ETH, siguió un enfoque holístico de la ingeniería e hizo hincapié tanto en el diseño estructural apropiado para los materiales, como en la importancia de la estética en la ingeniería estructural y civil. Defendía un concepto de diseño que consideraba el comportamiento "global" de la estructura, abarcando así el carácter monolítico de las estructuras de hormigón y el comportamiento resultante como un conjunto de todos los componentes. Esto se contraponía a la práctica hasta entonces comúnmente empleada de analizar solo los componentes individuales, que a menudo ignoraba los efectos positivos del comportamiento de carga espacial. Es precisamente esta nueva idea de integración estructural la que más tarde será empleada por Isler en la concepción de sus conchas. Lardy, además, dio cursos sobre hormigón pretensado, familiarizando así a sus estudiantes con una tecnología aún muy joven en ese momento. El desarrollo de los cascarones de forma neumática de Isler no es concebible sin la hábil integración de los tendones de pretensado y, por lo tanto, se basa una vez más en gran medida en el ejemplo de Lardy.

Isler dejó la cátedra de Lardy en 1953 y durante algunos años se unió a la empresa de ingeniería Weder & Prim en Burgdorf, donde poco después establecería su propia oficina. De este primer período, el ensayo examina tres proyectos: un cascarón para el Hotel Kreuz en Langenthal (1954), cascarones de burbujas (*bubble shells*) para Glas Trösch en Thunstetten (1955), y ocho almacenes para Blaser en Rüegsau (1956). En dichos proyectos, Isler dio los primeros pasos en el uso de poliéster reforzado en los componentes de la construcción, ya que también fue responsable del desarrollo de los grandes tragaluces con cúpulas de poliéster, necesarios para cubrir las aberturas centrales para la iluminación.

Es notable la medida en que la obra y la forma de pensar de Lardy dejaron una huella en el avance de la carrera profesional de Isler y sus primeras obras construidas: todos los temas rectores de la enseñanza y la investigación de Lardy no solo han servido de piedra angular para la obra de Isler en general, sino que en última instancia se amalgaman a su enfoque específico del diseño de cascarones.

Giulia Boller y John Chilton

El enfoque experimental de Heinz Isler en la búsqueda de formas

El enfoque de diseño experimental de Heinz Isler puede ejemplificarse con los modelos de búsqueda de formas que el ingeniero utilizó para diseñar, desarrollar y explicar sus edificios y proyectos. En el congreso inaugural de la International Association for Shell Structures (IASS) celebrado en Madrid en 1959, presentó por primera vez tres métodos de búsqueda de forma para estructuras de cascarones: el montículo de forma libre, la membrana neumática y la tela colgante. Más tarde, también modificó la geometría, experimentó con formas de flujo y probó otros métodos de generación de formas.

En las primeras etapas del proceso de diseño se utilizan modelos de búsqueda de formas, ya que ayudan a definir una geometría de envoltura eficiente que se corresponde con las condiciones de soporte. Las formas que se encuentran en el modelo se basan en leyes físicas, por lo que también son parte del desarrollo técnico de un proyecto. Para Isler, esos modelos eran un instrumento central en el diseño de estructuras. Por ello, se utilizaban principalmente en el diseño de cascarones de forma libre. La explicación para esto es obvia: la forma se define comparativamente rápido en otras tipologías, de modo que se produjeron modelos de presentación en lugar de búsqueda de formas.

La parte principal del ensayo se centra en dos ejemplos concretos: en primer lugar, una cáscara de forma libre para el estudio de arquitectura Grob en Sargans (1968) y en segundo lugar, una villa construida como residencia del arquitecto Pierre Camoletti cerca de Ginebra (1970). El armazón de aquel, el primero diseñado por Isler según el principio de la membrana colgante, se presenta como una forma libre inclinada diagonalmente que descansa sobre cuatro puntos de apoyo. Para este proyecto se crearon un total de siete modelos diferentes de búsqueda de formas, que se utilizaron para analizar los puntos débiles y optimizar el diseño. La expresiva forma del techo de la Villa Camoletti, por su parte, se definió sobre la base de la geometría de dos paraboloides hiperbólicos, que a primera vista parecen estar situados simétricamente a lo largo de un eje de intersección. Sin embargo, al examinarlos más de cerca, se puede observar que la longitud lateral de la superficie reglada, así como la intersección de los segmentos, se modificaron durante el proceso de diseño.

Con sus diferencias, los dos ejemplos son estudios de casos representativos de la metodología de trabajo de Heinz Isler. En particular, los modelos físicos creados por él y sus colegas, como también las notas y otros documentos, ayudan a resaltar las decisiones tomadas durante la primera fase de diseño. Por lo tanto, el ensayo permite una visión de los primeros y decisivos pasos de su proceso de búsqueda de formas.

Matthias Beckh

De la espuma a la forma
Los peculiares primeros cascarones de forma libre de Heinz Isler

En los primeros trabajos de Heinz Isler, sus experimentos de búsqueda de forma con espuma de poliuretano juegan un papel especial. A partir de los años 1960, utilizó este método para desarrollar la geometría de los cascarones de forma libre. Al mezclar dos componentes, se pone en marcha una reacción química en la que, en un minuto, el poliuretano aumenta hasta 30 veces su volumen inicial. Las formas orgánicas que podían generarse fácil y rápidamente mediante este proceso de autodesarrollo fascinaron a Isler y constituyeron la base geométrica de varios proyectos, aunque las formas resultantes de las estructuras de cascarón tenían importantes desventajas estáticas.

El ensayo traza la génesis de los primeros cascarones de forma libre de Isler, comenzando por el centro de jardinería Wyss en Zuchwil (1962), cerca de Soleura, Suiza, que se basa en una superficie de traslación geométricamente definida. Dos años más tarde, Isler realizó la primera cubierta para el supermercado Migros en Bellinzona, Suiza, cuya forma había sido desarrollada experimentalmente con espuma de poliuretano. Para poder aprovechar de manera óptima el espacio disponible en la planta cuadrada de 31,30 metros de ancho, había que encontrar una forma lo más empinada posible en los apoyos y que no fuera demasiado alta en el vértice. Las pruebas preliminares se llevaron a cabo inicialmente en pequeñas cajas de madera con una longitud de borde de 10 centímetros y luego con modelos más grandes a escala 1:100. El tamaño de la caja de madera y la fricción de la pared resultante del proceso de expansión pudieron influir en la geometría de las formas generadas.

Dos años después de la finalización del supermercado en Bellinzona, Isler pudo usar el método de expansión una vez más: en la sede del fabricante de materiales de construcción Kilcher en Recherswil, la forma original también se determinó utilizando espuma de poliuretano. Aquí, sin embargo, Isler fue capaz de dejar que el cascarón se extendiera a los puntos de apoyo de manera mucho más plana, evitando así los problemas que se produjeron en Bellinzona. Con el centro de jardinería Florélites (1966) en las afueras de París, que se planificó más o menos al mismo tiempo, el método de expansión con una superficie cubierta de 1250 metros cuadrados alcanzó su cenit en términos de tamaño, pero al mismo tiempo también su conclusión. En los años siguientes, Heinz Isler desarrolló sus cascarones de forma libre con modelos suspendidos, un método que produjo geometrías estáticamente más favorables.

Elke Genzel y Pamela Voigt

Más que concreto
Los proyectos de Heinz Isler en plásticos reforzados con fibra de vidrio

Heinz Isler utilizó poliéster reforzado con fibra de vidrio (PRFV) para realizar cascarones y losas, siendo uno de los primeros en utilizarlo en Europa. Probablemente conocía la resina de poliéster de su época como ayudante en la cátedra de Pierre Lardy, aunque no descubrió el material compuesto por resina y fibras hasta más tarde, cuando se planteó instalar tragaluces translúcidos en carcasas industriales para la empresa Blaser (1956), que no estaban disponibles en el tamaño deseado. Después de lograr producir estos tragaluces en PRFV por su cuenta, fabricó más carcasas y planchas a partir del material. Definiendo las formas de los cascarones como formas libres – así como en la construcción de los cascarones de concreto –, siempre corregía la curvatura a los pies del cascarón, o, si el proyecto no era suyo, sino iniciado por un arquitecto, adoptaba la geometría que le era dada.

El hecho de que Isler sea relativamente desconocido como constructor de cascarones de plástico tiene que ver con el material en sí mismo: este cambia sus propiedades mecánicas con el tiempo, ya que su resistencia disminuye hasta en un 70 por ciento debido a la tensión continua, la temperatura y la radiación UV. Para la década de 1950, los ingenieros estructurales solo podían estimar cuánta capacidad de carga les proporcionaba el material después de 50 años de uso. Pero incluso un ingeniero experimentado como Isler no podía determinar la resistencia a largo plazo con exactitud; en la industria de la construcción, el material era simplemente demasiado nuevo. De modo que sus proyectos plásticos fueron muy poco publicados y lo eran usualmente mucho después de su finalización. Cuando por primera vez, en un ensayo de 1977, realizó un comentario exhaustivo al respecto, apuntó que su “comienzo plástico [...] fue hace más de 20 años”. El respeto de Isler por el material era cuando menos adecuado. A diferencia de todos los demás pioneros, fue extremadamente valiente – por no decir atrevido – en su enfoque de la resistencia material. Sin embargo, el hecho de que todos sus edificios de PRFV hayan sobrevivido a los 50 años sin ningún problema grave demuestra que tuvo razón. En cualquier caso, destacan sus logros como pionero también en el campo de la construcción con plásticos.

Rainer Schützeichel

(Re)presentando los cascarones
La obra de Heinz Isler en exposición

El ensayo aborda la (re)presentación de ciertos proyectos de Heinz Isler en exposiciones con la ayuda de fotografías, maquetas y otros medios, arrojando luz sobre estas como medio de comunicación y revelando qué fue lo que se mostró y qué fue excluido de los respectivos panoramas de la obra de Isler. Entre 1979 y 1982, es decir, en un lapso de tiempo de solo cuatro años, Isler organizó no menos de tres exposiciones de su obra, siendo que nunca antes había utilizado ese formato como parte de su estrategia de promoción. Estas tres exposiciones representan estudios de casos ejemplares sobre cómo las ideas, los proyectos y los edificios de Isler se entramaron en una dramaturgia para comunicarlos tanto a los especialistas como a los profanos.

A Isler se le ofreció la primera oportunidad de promover públicamente una selección de su trabajo recién en 1979, después de haber diseñado y completado varios proyectos desde mediados de la década de 1950 en adelante. El lugar de celebración fue un pequeño espacio de un escaparate en Basilea. Sin embargo, solo un año después, el prestigioso Princeton University Art Museum acogió una exposición dedicada monográficamente a su obra; en el mismo lugar, una segunda exposición presentaría 23 años más tarde algunos de los proyectos de Isler, ahora entretejidos en la narración de un *Swiss Legacy* de ingeniería estructural. El conocimiento más íntimo de sus métodos de trabajo, sin embargo, Isler lo confirió en la poco conocida exposición *Nautilus* que montó apenas tres años después de la primera exposición de Basilea, en una galería de arte de Berna.

Lo que resulta especialmente interesante de las tres primeras exposiciones es que ocurrieron en un punto de inflexión en la carrera de Isler, quien en 1979 ya había superado la cúspide de su éxito en cuanto a la obtención de encargos. Aunque sería una sobreestimación afirmar que la exposición de Basilea sentó las bases para su legado, sí logró añadir otra rama de la comunicación a su obra para ir más allá de lo construido – ya que el tema de las exposiciones es su representación –, llegando potencialmente a un público internacional amplio mucho más fácilmente de lo que podían hacerlo los edificios por su cuenta.

En 1979, el espacio expositivo disponible dio lugar a una presentación comparativamente sencilla, que excluía aspectos importantes del trabajo de Isler, como por ejemplo (y especialmente) sus métodos experimentales de búsqueda de formas. Contrastando con ello, la presentación de sus diseños en los espacios del Princeton University Art Museum en 1980 – aunque recurriendo en parte a proyectos que ya se habían mostrado en Basilea – fue mucho más completa. La segunda exposición presentada en Princeton más de veinte años después fue más bien una continuación de la anterior, destilada de un contenido más antiguo, insertada en el contexto suizo más amplio y condimentada con algunos modelos de reciente creación. En cambio, la exposición de Berna de 1982 reveló una notable tendencia a descubrir los antecedentes experimentales de la obra de Isler, algo que fue promovido por el propio ingeniero. Aquí, Isler trazó la sección más completa a través de su trabajo y su filosofía, instalando al mismo tiempo una exposición casi íntima que dio a sus visitantes una visión profunda de su práctica laboral.

Andreas Schätzke

"Nuevas construcciones"
Los inicios de la edificación de estructuras laminares en la República Democrática Alemana

En la RDA, los primeros cascarones de concreto armado se construyeron alrededor de 1960, lo que es bastante tarde para los estándares internacionales. En aquella época, había una demanda creciente de edificios que pudieran cumplir funciones para la infraestructura de su entorno, por ejemplo, lugares de recreo en las regiones de vacaciones. Pero sobre todo se trataba de instalaciones para el consumo, el ocio, la educación y la formación en las grandes urbanizaciones que se estaban construyendo en muchos lugares que experimentaban una industrialización acelerada de la construcción. En la mayoría de los casos, el lenguaje formal de estos edificios solitarios difería significativamente de sus entornos – a menudo bastante uniformes – y estaban destinados a servir como "puntos focales" urbanos.

El apogeo en la construcción de los cascarones de concreto armado había comenzado en todo el mundo a mediados del siglo XX. También en la RDA se siguió de cerca la evolución de este campo y se buscó un intercambio con colegas extranjeros, especialmente por medio de la International Association for Shell Structures (IASS), fundada en 1959. No solo en Alemania Oriental, mas especialmente allí, se hicieron esfuerzos iniciales para combinar la construcción de cascarones con el principio de la prefabricación como una forma particularmente económica de planificación y ejecución. A principios de los años 1960, por ejemplo, varios edificios públicos en Halle comenzaron a ser techados con "cáscaras HP". Estos eran elementos prefabricados de concreto con forma hiperbólica desarrollados por el ingeniero Herbert Müller.

Otro enfoque en la construcción de cascarones siguió el camino de la construcción planificada individualmente. Este aspecto está íntimamente ligado al nombre del ingeniero civil Ulrich Müther. El hecho de que Müther ocupara una posición singular en la RDA desde finales de los años 1960 se debió, entre otras cosas, a su doble profesión. Como ingeniero y empresario, aunque en un orden económico controlado centralmente, Müther era tanto diseñador como contratista. Además, desde el inicio abrió un campo especial para la construcción de cascarones, cada vez más buscado. En las condiciones de la economía planificada comunista se consideraba ventajoso que la ejecución de sus proyectos requiriera un alto aporte de mano de obra, pero estos se concluían en poco tiempo y con un bajo consumo de concreto. Una vez calculadas, las estructuras podrían ser erigidas en diferentes lugares con una construcción idéntica o con ligeros ajustes.

Los edificios en cuya planificación Müther estuvo involucrado deben su memorable diseño, en gran medida, a su participación. Sin embargo, la mayor parte de ellos solo podía realizarse en estrecha colaboración con arquitectos que usualmente eran empleados de las instituciones estatales de la RDA. En los años 1960 y 1970, Müther construyó varias docenas de restaurantes, grandes almacenes y salas para ferias, exposiciones y otros eventos mediante la construcción de cascarones de concreto. La gama de tareas también incluye instalaciones deportivas, planetarios e iglesias. Muchos de estos edificios poseían una elegancia y una expresividad raramente logradas en la arquitectura de la RDA, y eran adecuados para dar expresión al postulado de la lucha por el progreso tecnológico y social.

Tanja Seeböck

¿Seguro al fin? El destino de la Hyparschale de Ulrich Müther en Magdeburgo en una sociedad cambiante

Un ejemplo notable de la larga y dura lucha de Ulrich Müther por preservar la construcción de cascarones es la llamada Hyparschale en Magdeburgo, un salón de eventos multifuncional que se construyó como parte de un recinto ferial situado en el parque de la ciudad. Su destino refleja la apreciación cambiante por las obras de Müther a lo largo del tiempo.

El fin de la RDA en el otoño de 1990 marcó una ruptura decisiva para muchos de los edificios de Müther: muchos de ellos perdieron su función original con el cambio de sistema político y las consiguientes transformaciones sociales y económicas. Como resultado, algunos de ellos permanecieron vacíos durante décadas, tornándose un blanco para el vandalismo, y cayeron en mal estado debido a la falta de medidas de mantenimiento. En algunos casos, la demolición fue el resultado final. Otros encontraron un nuevo uso y los municipios los repararon cuidadosamente o los renovaron a fondo, esto último a veces sin tener en cuenta el aspecto original.

La sala multifuncional de Magdeburgo, construida en 1969, es la mayor obra de Müther que ha sobrevivido. La construcción, que se compone de cuatro cascarones *hypar* y abarca una superficie de 2304 metros cuadrados sin soportes, solo se ve superada en cuanto a superficie por el Ahornblatt de Berlín, un gran restaurante construido unos meses más tarde y demolido en el año 2000.

La construcción del cascarón de Magdeburgo estuvo en estado de abandono durante dos décadas y sobrevolaba la amenaza de su destrucción. Durante mucho tiempo, todos los esfuerzos de la ciudad por encontrar un inversor con un concepto de utilización y financiación adecuado para la preservación del edificio fracasaron. En 2019, después de 21 años de abandono, la ciudad de Magdeburgo decidió, casi a último momento, renovar el edificio a su propio costo para salvarlo de la pérdida total. El ejemplo de la Hyparschale de Magdeburgo ilustra vívidamente la dificultad de encontrar usos adecuados y modelos de financiación viables para la renovación de estructuras de grandes dimensiones, que por ello son muy costosas de mantener.

Susanne Brorson

El pabellón de la música en Sassnitz Una estructura laminar de Ulrich Müther en colaboración con Dietmar Kuntzsch y Otto Patzelt

El pabellón de la música en Sassnitz en la isla de Rügen es uno de los proyectos menos conocidos de Ulrich Müther. Se construyó en 1988, poco antes del final de la RDA, en cooperación con el arquitecto Dietmar Kuntzsch y el ingeniero estructural Otto Patzelt. Los archivos contienen un amplio material de planificación y algunos de los participantes en el proyecto pudieron ser entrevistados en 2015, de modo que fue posible rastrear detalladamente el proceso de planificación. El pabellón, que se encuentra directamente a la orilla del Mar Báltico, consta del cascarón y dos dependencias dispuestas a los lados. La intención de Kuntzsch era crear una arquitectura abierta, con el viento y el mar como fondo.

La génesis de la "concha acústica" ilustra las condiciones políticas y económicas en las que Ulrich Müther trabajó en la RDA. Sus cascarones solo pueden ser juzgados si son vistos en este contexto. En la década de 1980, la situación económica de la RDA ya era muy difícil; no obstante, se iba a construir una nueva terminal de transbordadores cerca de Sassnitz. El alcalde logró desviar el concreto de esa obra para construir el nuevo pabellón de música. Las primeras ideas para la "concha acústica" se desarrollaron durante un taller estudiantil que Dietmar Kuntzsch llevó a cabo como profesor en la academia de arte de Berlín-Weißensee. Poco después, Kuntzsch y Otto Patzelt, que también enseñaba allí, fueron comisionados para diseñar la concha y Müther fue convocado. La "concha acústica" no es un paraboloide hiperbólico puro, sino que consta de siete conchas individuales que tienen hipérbolas como curvas limitantes. Tampoco es un típico "cascarón de Müther", porque la forma expresiva se remonta a la colaboración con Kuntzsch y Patzelt. El primer diseño, una "variante convexa", muestra una concha con arcos curvados hacia arriba. La experiencia de Müther condujo a un cambio en el que las conchas se curvaban al revés y así se reelaboraban en una "variante cóncava".

Patzelt calculó la estática en el ordenador con la ayuda del método de elementos finitos, pero la carcasa fue finalmente calculada a mano como una viga de placa sujeta, porque los programas de cálculo aún no estaban completamente desarrollados. Müther presentó la estática para el permiso de construcción con su firma y el sello de la empresa. La empresa VEB Spezialbetonbau Rügen, que él dirigía, se hizo cargo de la realización. Sin embargo, Müther estaba demasiado ocupado, por lo que Patzelt, como su presunto empleado, se hizo cargo de la dirección de la construcción sin el correspondiente contrato de trabajo. Para completar el pabellón, la ciudad de Sassnitz dependía de la ayuda de voluntarios y los materiales de construcción tuvieron que ser organizados laboriosamente. La falta de material también tuvo un impacto en la arquitectura: ojos de buey y puertas de barco fueron utilizados en los dos edificios laterales. Tras el fin de la RDA, comenzó un progresivo deterioro del pabellón de música, que se compensó en 2006 con una renovación parcial. En 2015, con la ayuda de la Fundación Wüstenrot, fue posible restaurar el pabellón de acuerdo con la orden de conservación, que se completó en 2017.

Georg Giebeler

Ulrich Müther: ¿Cantidad o calidad?

La primera lista de las obras de Ulrich Müther no fue compilada por él mismo sino por Wilfried Dechau y enumera 79 construcciones de cascarones. Desde entonces ha habido repetidos y menos serios intentos de generar un catálogo razonado completo; algunas publicaciones atribuyen casi 200 edificios y proyectos al ingeniero.

En 2012, el autor entregó el legado documental de Müther (Müther-Archiv), que había sido transferido a la Hochschule Wismar seis años antes, a Matthias Ludwig, en ese momento todavía con un fragmentario catálogo razonado. La razón de esto fue la complejidad del trabajo: Ulrich Müther diseñó, planificó, calculó y realizó no solo los cascarones de concreto de doble curvatura, sino también cúpulas y obras de concreto geométricamente libres. Además, hay estructuras plegables, monumentos, instalaciones deportivas y otros elementos, porque la empresa que dirigía se encargaba regularmente, como subcontratista, de trabajar en estructuras de concreto con múltiples curvas. Además de esos encargos, Müther también emprendió, por iniciativa propia, la realización de edificios especiales, por ejemplo, una marquesina de autobús en Binz, en la isla de Rügen (1967). Por último, una característica especial de la RDA, el "proyecto de reutilización", conduce a más ambigüedades: muchos de los edificios de Müther fueron realizados varias veces en forma idéntica. Un ejemplo de ello es el restaurante Ostseeperle en Glowe en Rügen (1968), que – también como restaurante de excursiones – sigue en pie en Eberswalde (1968) y Dierhagen (1969), con idéntica forma de techo.

Por lo tanto, en 2016, el autor creó – basándose solo en los materiales del Müther-Archiv – el primer catálogo razonado completamente inequívoco, que también clasifica los edificios según su geometría. 114 proyectos realizados y no realizados por Ulrich Müther podrían ser asignados de esta manera. Sin embargo, esto todavía no dice nada sobre la relevancia de las obras: ¿Se trata de la mera cantidad de sus edificios y proyectos listados entre 1963 y 1993, o fue Müther un pionero de la construcción con concreto que fue subestimado durante mucho tiempo? Probablemente lo último.

El autor llega a esta conclusión precisamente porque considera que la mayoría de las obras enumeradas son poco significativas en términos de valoración cultural o tecnológica. Si se resta el gran número de proyectos de reutilización, a saber, el trabajo de concreto proyectado que realizó solo como empresario, así como las copias de Candela, los planetarios y estructuras plegables menos complejas e incluso la mayoría de sus estructuras en forma de paraguas, que se produjeron a granel, todavía quedan 20 edificios que establecen la posición única de Ulrich Müther entre las filas de los inventores de cascarones de concreto. Casi nadie más ha realizado una gama tan amplia de formas diferentes de estructuras laminares de concreto de múltiple curvatura: cascarones de paraboloide hiperbólico, cascarones colgantes, conchas jorobadas y de forma libre.

Acknowledgments

The editors would like to express their gratitude for the funding, without which the cataloguing of the archives mentioned in the introduction to this volume, the establishment of our research network, and—last but not least—this book would not have been possible. From 2015 to 2017 and 2018 to 2020 respectively, two research projects (IN403915 and IN405218) were supported by the Dirección General de Asuntos del Personal Académico of the Universidad Nacional Autónoma de México (DGAPA-UNAM, Directorate General for Academic Staff Affairs of the National Autonomous University of Mexico) as part of the Programa de Apoyo a Proyectos de Investigación e Innovación Tecnológica (PAPIIT, Support Program for Research and Technological Innovation Projects) under the title "Cascarones de concreto armado en México y el mundo: pasado, presente, futuro" (Reinforced Concrete Shells in Mexico and the World: Past, Present, Future). Furthermore, the Faculty of Architecture at the UNAM gave its support for the realization of CIMIS 2018.

The still ongoing research project "Experimentelles Entwerfen in der Nachkriegszeit: Der Beitrag von Heinz Isler (1926–2009) aus ingenieur- und kulturhistorischer Perspektive" (Experimental Design in the Post-War Period: Heinz Isler's (1926–2009) Contribution in the Perspective of the History of Engineering and Culture) is generously funded by the Swiss National Science Foundation. Being able to study the extensive archive of Heinz Isler is only possible thanks to the fundamental groundwork of the gta Archives at the Swiss Federal Institute of Technology (ETH) Zurich, who are not only enabling our research by cataloguing the material, but first and foremost by providing us with every conceivable support.

The project "Müther-Archiv Wismar – DDR-Sonderbauten" (Müther Archive Wismar – GDR Special Buildings) at the Hochschule Wismar – University of Applied Sciences, Technology, Business and Design was funded by the German Federal Ministry of Education and Research as part of the program "Vernetzen – Erschließen – Forschen. Allianz für universitäre Sammlungen" (Networking – Developing – Researching. Alliance for University Collections). For the cataloguing of the Müther Archive and the organization of CIMIS 2019 in Berlin—an event which the Wüstenrot Foundation has made possible through generous funding—the support of our cooperation partner, the Architecture Archives of the Akademie der Künste (Academy of Arts), Berlin, was essential.

Debts of gratitude are owed to the staff of Birkhäuser Verlag for their professional support of the book publication, to Dirk Wagner of Wagner Rexin for his dedicated work in designing the book, and, in particular, to John Chilton who with his expertise—and, beyond that, with accuracy and patience—has ensured that all contributions can be published in presentable English. Wilfried Dechau has furthered the visual quality of the book by enriching it with his outstanding photographs of our three protagonists' buildings. Not least, we want to thank all the authors, as well as those who have contributed to our symposia and enriched them with their presentations and fruitful discussions.

Picture Credits

Eduardo Alarcón Azuela: 79, 80, 82 | Architecture Archives, Akademie der Künste, Berlin: 153 (fig. 5) | Archivo de Arquitectos Mexicanos, Facultad de Arquitectura, Universidad Nacional Autónoma de México: 9 (fig. 1), 10 (fig. 3), 14 (fig. 8), 25, 56–58, 60 (fig. 9), 63, 64, 66, 67, 69, 71, 73 (fig. 5), 74, 75 | Archivo Fotográfico, Fundación Televisa, Mexico City: 72 (fig. 2, photograph by Juan Guzmán) | Archivo Fotográfico Manuel Toussaint, Instituto de Investigaciones Estéticas, Universidad Nacional Autónoma de México: 10 (fig. 4, photograph by Juan Guzmán) | *Arquitectura México* (1952): 54 | Bacardi Mexico Archive: 29 (fig. 10), 60 (fig. 8) | Matthias Beckh: 28, 32, 33 | Susanne Brorson: 157 | Félix Candela Architectural Records and Papers, Avery Drawing & Archives Collections, Columbia University Libraries, New York: 60 (fig. 10), 72 (fig. 3), 73 (fig. 4) | Félix Candela Papers, Manuscripts Division, Princeton University Library: 84 | Félix and Dorothy Candela Archive, Princeton University: 77 | Esther Cheng, based on a plan by Seymour Harris Partnership: 88 (fig. 7) | *Concrete Quarterly* (1959): 85 (fig. 2) | Wilfried Dechau: 23, 35–53 | Jenny 8 del Corte Hirschfeld: 129 (fig. 6) | Juan Ignacio del Cueto: 29 (fig. 9), 61 | Marco Dziallas/ostmodern.org: 148 (fig. 7) | Moisés Escárcega Olivares, based on an illustration from Colin Faber, *Candela: The Shell Builder* (New York, 1963): 55 | ETH Zurich University Archive: 92 | Colin Faber, *Candela: The Shell Builder* (New York, 1963): 17 | Georg Giebeler: 161–170 | gmp · von Gerkan, Marg and Partners Architects: 148 (fig. 8) | gta Archives, ETH Zurich: 12, 21, 22 (fig. 10), 30, 91, 93 (fig. 3), 94–97, 99, 102–108, 111–117, 120, 122–124, 127, 128 (fig. 3), 129 (fig. 5), 130, 132 | Hannes Henz: 100 | *Heinz Isler as Structural Artist* (Princeton, 1980): 128 (fig. 4) | Gerhard Krenz, *Architektur zwischen gestern und morgen* (Berlin [East], 1974): 136 (fig. 6) | Dietmar Kuntzsch: 154 | John Lewis Partnership Archive Collection: 86, 87 (fig. 6) | Matthias Ludwig: 20 (fig. 5) | Marisela Mendoza: 85 (fig. 3), 88 (fig. 8) | Municipal archive, Sassnitz: 152, 153 (fig. 4), 155 | Municipal planning office, Magdeburg: 146 (fig. 5) | Müther Archive, Hochschule Wismar: 9 (fig. 2), 13, 14 (fig. 7, photograph by Wolfhard Eschenburg), 18 (photograph by Marilen Körwien), 19 (photograph by Annika Jahnke), 20 (figs. 4 and 6), 22 (fig. 9, photograph by Marilen Körwien), 135 (fig. 1, photograph by Wolfhard Eschenburg), 135 (figs. 2 and 3), 136 (fig. 4), 136 (fig. 5), 138, 140, 141, 143–145, 146 (fig. 4), 151 (fig. 1), 151 (fig. 2, photograph by Sylvia Krumm) | Stefan Polónyi, ed., *Schalen in Beton und Kunststoff* (Wiesbaden/Berlin [West], 1970): 119 | M[anuel] Sanchez-Arcas, *Form und Bauweise der Schalen* (Berlin [East], 1961): 137 | Joseph Schwartz, Chair of Structural Design, ETH Zurich, *Tragwerksentwurf*, I–IV: 26, 27 | *Second Congress of the Fédération Internationale de la Précontrainte, Amsterdam 1955* (no place [London], 1958): 93 (fig. 4) | Tanja Seeböck: 146 (fig. 6) | Verve Developments Ltd. Archive, Bedford: 87 (fig. 5)

Indices

Index of Names

Index of Places

SPONSORED BY THE

Federal Ministry
of Education
and Research

Copy editing
Keonaona Peterson (English), Kirsten Thietz (German), Carolina Gazzaneo (Spanish)

Project management
Freya Mohr, Alexander Felix

Production
Heike Strempel

Layout and typesetting
Wagner Rexin GbR, Stutensee

Cover and end papers design
Wagner Rexin GbR, Stutensee, using a drawing by Pia Mohring

Paper
Condat Matt Perigord 1.1, 150 g/m²

Printing
optimal media GmbH, Röbel/Müritz

Library of Congress Control Number: 2020944666

Bibliographic information published by the German National Library
The German National Library lists this publication in the Deutsche Nationalbibliografie; detailed bibliographic data are available on the Internet at http://dnb.dnb.de.

ISBN 978-3-0356-2096-2

e-ISBN (PDF) 978-3-0356-2098-6

P.O. Box 44, 4009 Basel, Switzerland
Part of Walter de Gruyter GmbH, Berlin/Boston

www.birkhauser.com
9 8 7 6 5 4 3 2 1